SCHAUM'S OUTLINE OF

THEORY AND PROBLEMS

OF

MACROECONOMIC THEORY

Second Edition

•

EUGENE DIULIO, Ph.D.
Associate Professor of Economics
Fordham University

•

SCHAUM'S OUTLINE SERIES

McGRAW-HILL PUBLISHING COMPANY

New York St. Louis San Francisco Auckland Bogotá Caracas Hamburg
Lisbon London Madrid Mexico Milan Montreal New Delhi Oklahoma City
Paris San Juan São Paulo Singapore Sydney Tokyo Toronto

Eugene A. Diulio, currently Associate Professor of Economics at Fordham University, received his Ph.D. from Columbia University. He is the author of *Schaum's Outline of Money and Banking* and the coauthor of *Schaum's Outline of Principles of Economics*. His research has been in the area of financial institutions and financial markets. He is an educational consultant to several money centers and super regional banks.

Schaum's Outline of Theory and Problems of
MACROECONOMIC THEORY

1 2 3 4 5 6 7 8 9 10 11 12 13 14 15 16 17 18 19 20 SHP SHP 9 3 2 1 0

ISBN 0-07-017051-7

Sponsoring Editor, John Aliano
Production Supervisor, Denise Puryear
Editing Supervisor, Meg Tobin

Library of Congress Cataloging-in-Publication Data

Diulio, Eugene A.
    Schaum's outline of theory and problems of macroeconomic theory / Eugene
Diulio. -- 2nd ed.
        p.   cm. -- (Schaum's outline series)
    Rev. ed. of: Schaum's outline of theory and problems of
macroeconomic theory. 1974.
    ISBN 0-07-017051-7
    1. Macroeconomics--Problems, exercises, etc.   I. Diulio, Eugene
A. Schaum's outline of theory and problems of macroeconomic theory.
II. Title
HB172.5.D58   1990
339.3'076--dc20
                                                                                        89-12909
                                                                                            CIP

Cover design by Amy E. Becker.

Preface

Macroeconomics is the study of employment, output and prices in a de-centralized, market economy. This book presents in a clear and systematic way the theoretical core of macroeconomics found in most intermediate macro-economics textbooks. The book is eclectic and embraces Keynesian, monetarist, and rational expectations approaches at various points. The book can be used by undergraduates or graduate business students as a supplement to current standard texts or by instructors as an independent text supplemented by empirical and/or policy readings. The book may also be useful to graduate economics students as a review of the analytical core of macroeconomic theory.

Each chapter begins with a concise presentation of concepts and theory with fully illustrated examples, followed by multiple-choice review questions and answers. Solved problems are presented with detailed, step-by-step solutions, which illustrate and amplify concepts and theories. Solved problems appear in a numerical, graphical and algebraic format and focus upon points about which students often feel uncertain. The learning-by-doing methodology involves the student in macroeconomic analysis and provides repetition of the analytical core which is imperative to the learning of economic theory.

The sequence for developing the macroeconomic model is traditional. Analy-sis progresses from simple Keynesian spending models, to a model of simulta-neous equilibrium in the money and goods markets, to a model of internal and external equilibrium, to aggregate supply-aggregate demand analysis of output and the price level, and to the dynamics of inflation. Chapters on the supply of and demand for money, consumption and investment appear at the end of the book but can be integrated at any point.

The content and methodology of this book have been tested in my macro-economic theory classes at Fordham University. I received helpful comments on portions of the book from Patrick O'Sullivan, Joseph Dziwura, and Anjana Varadhachary. I would like to express my sincere gratitude to the entire Schaum staff of McGraw-Hill for their patient assistance and to the continuous encourage-ment and support of my wife, Rosemary, and daughters, Karen, Anne-Marie, Jeanne and Mary Beth.

EUGENE A. DIULIO

Contents

CONTENTS

Chapter 1

Introduction to Macroeconomic Analysis

1.1 MACROECONOMICS

Macroeconomics is the study of the aggregate behavior of economic aggregates, such as level of output, price level and growth of output. Microeconomics, by contrast, analyzes household and firm behavior to understand the determinants of price and output in individual markets. Macroeconomics focuses upon economic stabilization—the use of monetary and/or fiscal policy to moderate the business cycle and foster real economic growth. Views on the effectiveness of these policies are diverse. Positions can be categorized as interventionist (Keynesian or nonmonetarist) and noninterventionist (monetarist). Although each school of thought supports different policies, theorists from both schools share elements of a common theoretical model.

EXAMPLE 1. Macroeconomic measures—real output (real GNP), price level (GNP deflator), inflation rate and growth of real output—are central to macroeconomic theory.

Current-dollar GNP (gross national product) measures the current market value of all final goods and services produced in an economy during a one-year period. When GNP is measured instead in constant dollars by holding the price level constant, *constant-dollar GNP* (real GNP) is a measure of real output. Real values are denoted by the use of small letters.

GNP deflator is a price index which measures the general price level. The GNP deflator is used to eliminate the effect of price changes upon nominal GNP, translating current-dollar market values to constant-dollar market values. Current-dollar (nominal) values are denoted by capital letters.

Inflation rate measures the rate of change in a price index by relating the change in the price level to the price level in the preceding year.

Growth of real output measures the rate of change in real GNP to the level of real GNP in the preceding year.

1.2 AGGREGATE SUPPLY AND AGGREGATE DEMAND

Aggregate output and the price level depend on the demand for and supply of goods and services. Aggregate demand can be conceptualized as a schedule of aggregate spending, consisting of the spending decisions of the household, business, government and international sectors. Aggregate supply depends on the state of technology and the supply cost of available human resources, capital resources and natural resources. The economy's actual output and price level are determined by the interaction of aggregate demand and aggregate supply.

EXAMPLE 2. Aggregate demand is the sum of consumption, investment, government and net export spending; aggregate supply is related to the availability and cost of economic resources and the state of technology. Aggregate output and the price level are determined jointly by aggregate demand and aggregate supply. See Fig. 1-1.

Aggregate supply and aggregate demand schedules S' and D' in Fig. 1-2 determine output y_0 and price level p_0. An increase in aggregate demand to D'' might result from an increase in the money supply (which increased consumption and investment spending), a decrease in taxes (which increased consumption and investment spending), and/or an increase in government expenditures. A supply shift from S' to S'' could result from technological advance, an increase in economic resources, and/or a reduction in the supply cost of economic resources. The effect on output and the price level from demand and supply shifts depends upon both the slope and the location of each schedule in space.

1

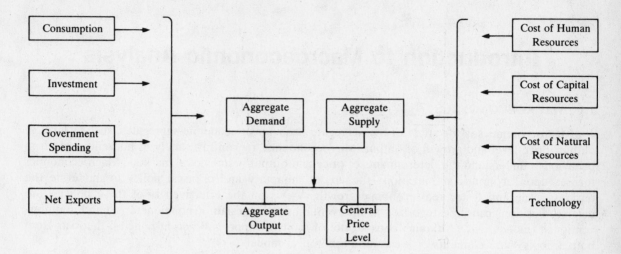

Fig. 1-1

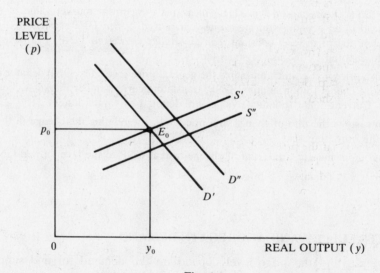

Fig. 1-2

EXAMPLE 3. Aggregate demand schedule D in Fig. 1-3 represents planned consumption, investment, government and net export spending, whereas aggregate supply schedule S represents the business sector's ability and willingness to supply goods and services. Suppose an increased money supply shifts the demand schedule from D to D'; with no change in the aggregate supply schedule, aggregate output increases from y_0 to y_1 and there is no change in the price level. A D to D'' rightward shift of aggregate demand, though, raises both output and the price level to y_2 and p_2, respectively.

1.3 FUNCTIONS, EQUATIONS AND GRAPHS

Economists explain economic behavior by linking the variable to be explained to a variable believed to be largely responsible for its behavior. For example, economists generally link household consumption to disposable income. Such behavior is specified by saying that consumption C is a function of disposable income Yd, or $C = f(Yd)$, meaning that consumption depends systematically upon household disposable income.

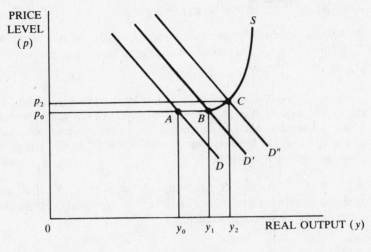

Fig. 1-3

Functional notation is both a concise and convenient way of presenting hypothesized economic behavior. Furthermore, it defines the economic relationship under study, i.e., it indicates which variable is dependent and which is independent. The expression $C = f(Yd)$ shows that aggregate consumption depends on the receipt of disposable income. Thus, consumption is the dependent variable and disposable income is the independent variable.

When the relationship between aggregate consumption and aggregate disposable income has been statistically established, it is possible to specify consumption behavior through an equation, graph or table.

EXAMPLE 4. Suppose that the measured relationship of consumption and disposable income is given by the equation $C = \$40 + 0.80Yd$. This measured relationship of aggregate consumption and aggregate disposable income is shown in Table 1-1 and Fig. 1-4.

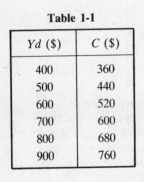

Table 1-1

Yd ($)	C ($)
400	360
500	440
600	520
700	600
800	680
900	760

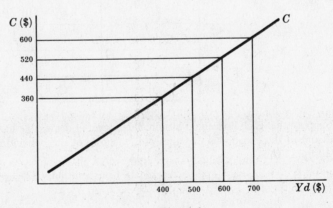

Fig. 1-4

In the absence of statistical measurement, it is possible to specify the form of the function (i.e., to specify the relationship between the dependent and independent variables). For instance, we could hypothesize that $C = \bar{C} + cYd$, where $\bar{C}$ and c have values greater than zero. Accordingly, aggregate consumption is a positive, linear function of aggregate disposable income. The behavioral coefficient for disposable income c measures the influence of disposable income upon the level of aggregate consumption. (c is in effect the slope of the consumption function.) The parameter $\bar{C}$ has a positive value and is independent of disposable income.

1.4 ENDOGENOUS AND EXOGENOUS VARIABLES

A variable is *endogenous* when its value is determined within the model and *exogenous* when its value is determined by forces outside the model. A change in an exogenous variable is classified as an *autonomous* change.

EXAMPLE 5. The consumption equation is specified by $C = \$40 + 0.80Yd$. In macroeconomics, the level of income is determined by the model, thereby making $0.80Yd$ an endogenous variable. The constant $40 represents exogenous forces since the effect of nonincome forces upon consumption is not specified. When outside forces change the consumption function from $C = \$40 + 0.80Yd$ to $C = \$50 + 0.80Yd$, there is a $10 increase in autonomous consumption spending.

Economists assume that parameters of equations are constant (i.e., that endogenous relationships are constant and exogenous forces do not change unless specified). This assumption is noted by *ceteris paribus*, meaning other things held constant.

1.5 AGGREGATE ECONOMIC BEHAVIOR

Aggregate economic behavior is the sum of individual behavior. Example 6 shows that aggregate consumption depends not only upon the behavior of individual units but upon the importance of each behavioral unit. To theorize about aggregate economic behavior, we assume that the behavior of individual units is stable and that the composition of the aggregate is constant or changing in some predictable way. In making the latter assumption, we assume that income changes are dispersed among and not concentrated within household units.

EXAMPLE 6. An economy is composed of five households. The spending behavior of each household is specified in Table 1-2.

Table 1-2

Household	Consumption Function
A	$C_A = 1.00Yd$
B	$C_B = \$10 + 0.90Yd$
C	$C_C = 10 + 0.80Yd$
D	$C_D = 5 + 0.85Yd$
E	$C_E = 0.95Yd$

Suppose that each household has the same level of disposable income. The aggregate consumption function is the sum of the exogenous variables plus the sum of the behavioral coefficients of the endogenous variable divided by 5. Thus,

$$\text{Aggregate Consumption} = \$25 + \frac{4.50Yd}{5}$$

$$= \$25 + 0.90Yd$$

Alternatively, if disposable income is not evenly distributed, weights are assigned to the behavioral coefficients according to the given distribution. The sum of these weights will be the denominator of the endogenous variable in the summing process. We shall assume that the disposable income of households B and C is twice that of A, D and E. A weight of one is attached to the behavioral coefficients of A, D and E and two to the behavioral coefficients of B and C. Thus,

$$\text{Aggregate Consumption} = \$25 + \frac{6.20Yd}{7}$$

$$= \$25 + 0.8857Yd$$

Review Questions

1.   Macroeconomics is concerned with

(a) The level of output of goods and services

(b) The general level of prices

(c) The growth of real output

(d) All the above

Answer: (d)

2.   Real GNP increases

(a) When there is an increase in the price level

(b) When there is an increase in the output of goods and services

(c) When there is an increase in the price level and/or the output of goods and services

(d) All the above

Answer: (b)

3.   An expansive monetary and fiscal policy shifts

(a) Aggregate demand to the right

(b) Aggregate demand to the left

(c) Aggregate supply to the right

(d) Aggregate supply to the left

Answer (a)

4.   A rightward shift of aggregate demand, with no change in the aggregate supply schedule, results in an increase in

(a) Real output and no change in the price level when aggregate supply is upward sloping

(b) Real output and no change in the price level when aggregate supply is horizontal

(c) The price level and no change in real output when aggregate supply is upward sloping

(d) The price level and no change in real output when aggregate supply is horizontal

Answer: (b)

5.   The equation $C = \$20 + 0.90\,Yd$ predicts that consumption is

(a) $90 when disposable income is $100

(b) $100 when disposable income is $90

(c) $110 when disposable income is $100

(d) $180 when disposable income is $200

Answer: (c)

6.   In the equation $C = \bar{C} + cYd$, the behavioral coefficient is (a) $\bar{C}$, (b) Yd, (c) c, or (d) all the above.

Answer: (c)

7.   In the equation $C = \bar{C} + cYd$, $\bar{C}$ is

(a) A parameter helping to determine the level of consumption

(b) A parameter whose value depends upon the level of disposable income

(c) A behavioral coefficient

(d) A dependent variable

Answer: (a)

8. *Ceteris paribus* means that

(a) Other factors are held constant.

(b) No other variable affects the dependent variable.

(c) No other model can explain the dependent variable.

(d) The model is logical.

Answer: (a)

9. Which of the following statements is correct?

(a) A variable is endogenous when its value is determined by forces outside the model.

(b) A change in an exogeneous variable is classified as an autonomous change.

(c) A variable is exogenous when its value is determined by forces within the model.

(d) A variable is autonomous when its value is determined by forces within the model.

Answer: (b)

10. In stating that $C = f(Yd, W)$

(a) It is hypothesized that Yd is a more important determinant of C than W.

(b) It is hypothesized that W is a more important determinant of C than Yd.

(c) W and Yd are dependent variables explaining C.

(d) Yd and W are independent variables explaining C.

Answer: (d)

Solved Problems

MACROECONOMICS

1.1 Explain and differentiate nominal GNP and real GNP.

Gross national product measures the total market value of all final goods and services produced in an economy during a 1-year period; quantitatively, it is the product of the quantity of goods and services produced times their respective prices. When current year prices are used in measuring output, nominal (current dollar) GNP includes the effect of price changes during the current year. To eliminate the effect of price changes, prices in a selected year can be used to measure output in preceding and proceding years; this provides a measure of real (constant dollar) GNP.

1.2 (a) What is a price index? (b) What does the GNP deflator measure?

(a) A price index measures the relationship between prices for a given year and prices for a selected (base) year. It is found by dividing the current year's prices by the base-year prices and multiplying by 100.

(b) The GNP deflator is a price index found by dividing nominal GNP by real GNP and then multiplying by 100. The GNP deflator is a measure of changes in prices for aggregate output relative to prices that existed in the base year used to calculate real GNP.

1.3   (a) What is the relationship between labor employment and real GNP? (b) What is the relationship between the rate of growth in real GNP and the rate of unemployment?

   (a)   Production occurs when economic resources—human, capital and natural—are employed. Hence, the greater the employment of labor the higher the level of real GNP.

   (b)   Because greater output is associated with higher levels of employment, we would expect less labor unemployed at higher output levels. It thereby follows that increases in the rate of economic growth would be associated with decreases in the rate of unemployment. Arthur Okun (Okun's law) found that an annual 2.5% increase in the rate of real growth above trend growth results in a 1% decrease in the rate of unemployment.

1.4   Explain the terms (a) *business cycle*, (b) *stabilization policy* and (c) *monetary and fiscal policy*.

   (a)   Business cycles are recurrent, but not periodic, fluctuations in economic activity that occur around the secular trend of GNP over a period of several years. The expansionary phase of the business cycle normally peaks at a point above trend growth, whereas the trough for the contractionary phase is normally below trend growth.

   (b)   A stabilization policy is an action taken by government to impact aggregate demand to moderate the expansion and contraction phases of the business cycle. During an expansion, the objective is moderation of the growth rate of spending; a reduction in the rate of decrease in aggregate spending is the objective during a recession (economic contraction).

   (c)   Monetary policy aims to stabilize economic activity by controlling the money supply or interest rate level while fiscal policy utilizes changes in tax rates and/or the level of government spending for the same objective.

AGGREGATE SUPPLY AND AGGREGATE DEMAND

1.5   (a) Do monetary and fiscal stabilization measures have a direct impact upon aggregate supply or aggregate demand? (b) Why must both aggregate supply and aggregate demand be considered in formulating monetary and fiscal policy?

   (a)   Monetary and fiscal policy directly impact consumption, investment, net export and/or government spending decisions; thus, they have a direct impact upon aggregate demand.

   (b)   Because there are output limitations due to a limited supply of economic resources, aggregate supply is integral to the successful implementation of monetary and fiscal policy. For example, excessive spending stimulation can result in demand exceeding production capabilities, causing prices to increase. Because economic policy is directed toward controlling employment and the price level, the study of the interaction of aggregate supply and aggregate demand is necessary in formulating monetary and fiscal policy.

1.6   Suppose aggregate supply and aggregate demand are initially at S and D in Fig. 1-5, determining output y_0 and price level p_0. Output y_0, we shall assume, is below trend growth; hence, there are unemployed economic resources. (a) What is the output and price level when an expansive monetary policy shifts aggregate demand from D to D'? (b) What is the output and price level when an expansive monetary and fiscal policy shifts aggregate demand from D to D''? (c) Why is there a difference in the price level change in the two demand shifts?

   (a)   Output increases from y_0 to y_1 in Fig. 1-5; there is no change in the price level due to the horizontal nature of the aggregate supply schedule between D and D'; the economy has the ability to supply additional output without an increase in the price of this additional output.

   (b)   The D to D'' shift increases output and the price level to y_2 and p_2, respectively.

   (c)   The absence of a price level increase in the D and D' shift in demand indicates excess capacity exists, and output can be increased without an increase in output prices. The D to D'' shift is

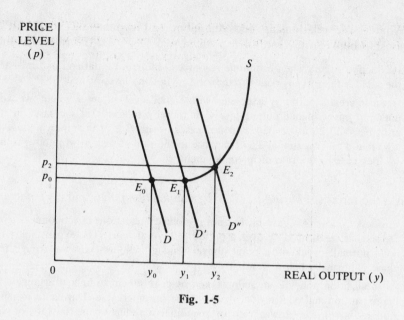

Fig. 1-5

accompanied by price increases; full capacity exists in some industries, and increased spending results in an increase in both price and output.

1.7 Aggregate supply S and aggregate demand D in Fig. 1-6 determine a y_0 output and p_0 price level. (*a*) What happens to aggregate output and the price level when the supply cost of natural resources increases causing aggregate supply to shift leftward to S'? (*b*) Is excess aggregate demand the sole cause of a higher price level?

(*a*) When the cost of economic resources (e.g., the cost of natural resources) increases with technology held constant, output is supplied at a higher price, and the aggregate supply schedule shifts leftward. With aggregate demand remaining at D in Fig. 1-6 and aggregate supply decreasing from S to S', the price level increases from p_0 to p_1, while real output falls from y_0 to y_1.

(*b*) Demand is obviously not the sole cause of changes in the price level. As seen in (*a*), continued availability of supply but at a higher price causes an increase in the price level.

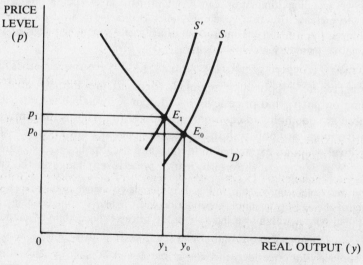

Fig. 1-6

1.8   Aggregate supply S and aggregate demand D in Fig. 1-7 determine output y_0 and price level p_0. (a) What happens to aggregate output and the price level when demand increases to D' and supply expands to S'? (b) To achieve price stability over time, at what rate should demand expand over time?

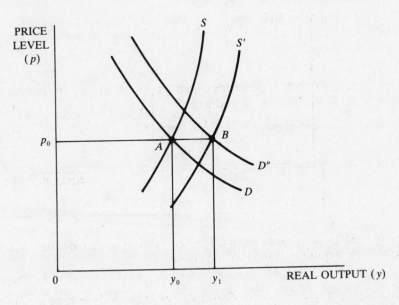

Fig. 1-7

(a)   Aggregate output increases from y_0 to y_1 in Fig. 1-7 with the price level remaining at p_0.

(b)   When price stability is an economic goal, policy makers should attempt to have spending increases (i.e., increases in aggregate demand) match expansion of productive capacity (i.e., increases in aggregate supply). The objective of price stability is to remain on trend growth over time.

FUNCTIONS, EQUATIONS AND GRAPHS

1.9   Explain the following functions and identify the dependent and independent variables for (a) $I = f(i)$ and (b) $I = f(Y_{t+1} - Y_t)$.

(a)   Investment I is a function of (depends upon) the rate of interest i. Investment is the dependent variable; the rate of interest is the independent variable.

(b)   Investment I is dependent upon the change in income Y between periods $t + 1$ and t. Investment is the dependent variable; the change in income is the independent variable.

1.10   (a) Explain the following statement: Aggregate consumption is explained by the receipt of disposable income, *ceteris paribus*. (b) What is the importance of the *ceteris paribus* assumption in economic theory?

(a)   Aggregate consumption is systematically related to (is a function of) disposable income. Other factors that influence consumption are held constant so that a precise statement can be made about the dependency of consumption upon disposable income.

(b)   *Ceteris paribus* allows the economist to make precise statements about the theoretical relationship between an independent and a dependent variable. For example, if consumption is assumed to be a function of disposable income, one is able to specify in the model how a change in aggregate disposable income affects aggregate consumption.

1.11   (*a*) Explain the components of the equation $C = \bar{C} + cYd$. (*b*) Explain the components of the equation $C = \$20 + 0.90Yd$.

(*a*) $\bar{C}$ represents other factors that are assumed constant. The behavioral coefficient c measures the relationship between disposable income and consumption. Since c is positive, consumption moves in the same direction as disposable income.

(*b*)   There is $20 of consumption regardless of the level of disposable income. Consumption changes by $0.90 for every $1 change in disposable income. Consumption changes in the same direction as disposable income.

1.12   Using the equation $C = \$20 + 0.90Yd$, construct a schedule for consumption when disposable income is $200, $250, $300, $350 and $400.

The schedule for consumption is shown in Table 1-3.

Table 1-3

Yd ($)	200	250	300	350	400
C ($)	200	245	290	335	380

1.13   Construct an equation from the straight-line consumption function in Fig. 1-8.

Consumption is $30 when disposable income is zero. Consumption increases $80 for each $100 increase in disposable income. Thus the behavioral coefficient c of the equation is 0.80. The linear consumption function is

$$C = \$30 + 0.80Yd$$

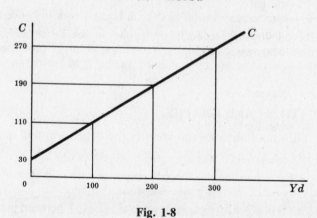

Fig. 1-8

1.14   Is there a difference between a graph, a schedule and an equation?

Graphs, schedules and equations are alternate ways of presenting relationships between variables. When only two variables are being related, each method has individual merits. Graphs and schedules become cumbersome when more than two variables are related.

ENDOGENOUS AND EXOGENOUS VARIABLES

1.15   Table 1-4 gives the consumption functions for five households. Identify the households in which there have been changes in autonomous consumption demand between periods t and $t + 1$.

Table 1-4

Household	Period t	Period $t+1$
A	$C_A = \$10 + 0.90\,Yd$	$C_A = \$20 + 0.90\,Yd$
B	$C_B = 5 + 0.95\,Yd$	$C_B = 5 + 0.95\,Yd$
C	$C_C = 30 + 0.80\,Yd$	$C_C = 30 + 0.80\,Yd$
D	$C_D = 15 + 0.85\,Yd$	$C_D = 10 + 0.85\,Yd$
E	$C_E = 10 + 0.80\,Yd$	$C_E = 10 + 0.80\,Yd$

Household A had a \$10 increase in autonomous consumption demand. Household D had a \$5 decrease in autonomous consumption demand.

1.16 Identify the exogenous and endogenous variables in the investment demand equation $I = \bar{I} + aY - bi$.

The value of an exogenous variable is determined by forces outside the model while the value of an endogenous variable is determined within the model. $\bar{I}$ is obviously an exogenous variable. In the model of income determination Y is an endogenous variable. The variable i is an endogenous variable if the level of interest rates is determined in the model of income determination and exogenous if not.

AGGREGATE ECONOMIC BEHAVIOR

1.17. Given the data in Table 1-5, construct aggregate consumption functions assuming (*a*) that there is equal distribution of disposable income, (*b*) that households A and C have three times the level of disposable income of B and D respectively and (*c*) that household A has four times the disposable income of B and D while C has twice the disposable income of B and D.

(*a*) Aggregate consumption $= \$84 + \dfrac{3.50\,Yd}{4} = \$84 + 0.875\,Yd$.

(*b*) Aggregate consumption $= \$84 + \dfrac{6.80\,Yd}{8} = \$84 + 0.85\,Yd$.

(*c*) Aggregate consumption $= \$84 + \dfrac{6.75\,Yd}{8} = \$84 + 0.84375\,Yd$.

Table 1-5

Household	Consumption Function
A	$C_A = \$50 + 0.80\,Yd$
B	$C_B = 5 + 0.90\,Yd$
C	$C_C = 25 + 0.85\,Yd$
D	$C_D = 4 + 0.95\,Yd$

Chapter 2

Measuring Aggregate Output

This chapter presents the framework for measuring real output; this framework is used in subsequent chapters to develop a theory of aggregate output. Aggregate measures discussed include gross national product (GNP), net national product (NNP), national income (NI), household disposable income Yd and measures of the price level.

2.1 MEASURING OUTPUT IN A PRIVATE, TWO-SECTOR MODEL

A private, two-sector model consists of a business sector and a household sector. We shall assume that the business sector is the organizer of economic resources and the producer of all goods and services. We also assume that all economic resources are owned by households. Thus, production occurs when business employs economic resources owned by households for which households receive wage, interest, rent and profit income and use this income to purchase output. This behavior is presented in Fig. 2-1 as a circular flow. The upper portion of this circular flow traces the flow of services from households to the business sector; the return flow consists of compensation (wages, interest, rent and profit) for these services. The lower portion shows households spending their income on goods and services with the return flow being the receipt of goods and services.

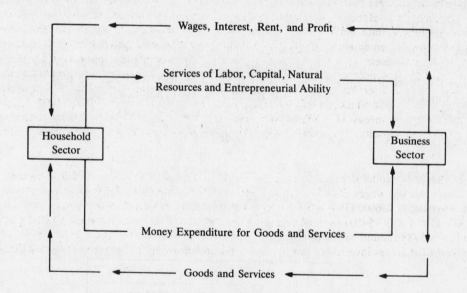

Fig. 2-1

EXAMPLE 1. Suppose households recieve the following compensation from the business sector: wages $3900; interest $400; rent $150; profit $550. One thousand items are produced and sold to the household sector at an average price per unit of $5. The market value of final output is $5000, which is the sum of total spending on output and the income to economic resources.

The circular flow in Fig. 2-2 differs from the one in Fig. 2-1 in that households save a portion of their income, which the business sector borrows in the capital markets to finance asset acquisitions. In Fig. 2-2, saving is a leakage from the circular flow which is returned by an injecton of investment spending. Thus, in a private sector model with household saving, income Y paid to economic resources has a return expenditure E flow

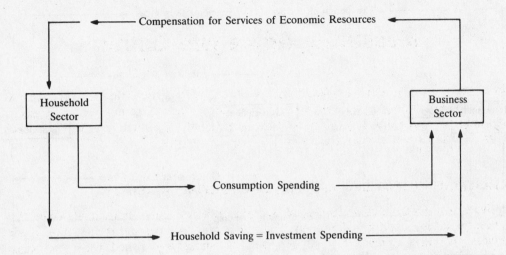

Fig. 2-2

through consumption C and invesment I spending, i.e., $Y = E$, where $E = C + I$. In this simplified model, the terms *national income* and *aggregate output* are interchangeable.

Gross investment includes business and residential construction, expenditures on buildings and equipment and additions to inventory. Because plant and equipment expenditures include additions as well as replacements, economists differentiate net investment from replacement investment. Net investment In consists of additions to inventory, incremental construction and plant and equipment expenditures which increase productive capacity; gross investment Ig includes net investment In and replacement investment D, also noted as depreciation. It is therefore necessary to differentiate GNP from NNP. Gross national product is the market value of all final goods and services produced in an economy during a one-year period. Net national product excludes that part of output which consists of replacement investment. Hence, NNP = GNP − depreciation. Macroeconomic theory, a theory of NNP, focuses upon the flow of output for household consumption and additions to productive capacity. The term *aggregate output* Y in macroeconomic theory thereby refers to the level of NNP.

EXAMPLE 2. Suppose capital depreciation is currently $350; households receive the following compensation from the business sector: wages $5000, interest $500, rent $50, and profit $450; gross investment is $750; consumption spending is $5600. GNP is $6350, found by summing depreciation and household compensation ($350 + $5000 + $500 + $50 + $450) or by adding gross investment to consumption spending ($750 + $5600). Net national product is $6000, found by summing the compensation of households ($5000 + $500 + $50 + $450) or by adding net investment (gross investment less depreciation) and consumption spending ($400 + $5600).

2.2 MEASURING OUTPUT IN A THREE- AND FOUR-SECTOR MODEL

Figure 2-3 presents the circular flow for a model inclusive of a private sector and a government sector. This model has three spending sectors: household consumption C, investment I (which we shall use to denote net investment) and government expenditures G. Income from the production of goods and services is paid to households or received by government as direct or indirect taxes. The household sector pays direct taxes to the government sector. Indirect taxes are imposed at the production level upon goods produced. Thus, the upper portion of the flow in Fig. 2-3 shows the business sector paying households for the services of economic resources and indirect taxes to the government. Household income is allocated to (direct) taxes, consumption spending and saving. When the federal budget is balanced, tax revenue equals government purchases of goods and services.

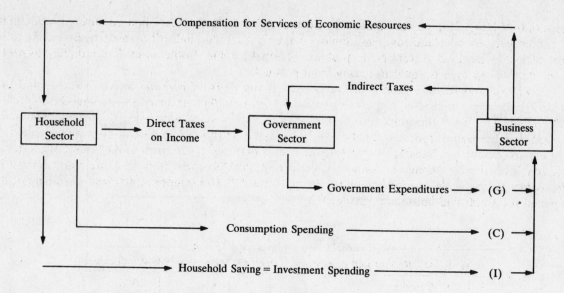

Fig. 2-3

EXAMPLE 3. Suppose indirect taxes are $35; household disposable income (gross income less direct taxes) is $5100; government net taxes revenue from households is $900; consumption spending is $4600; investment spending is $500; and government spending is $935. Aggregate output is $6035, found by summing indirect taxes, household disposable income and direct taxes ($35 + $5100 + $900) or by summing consumption, investment and government spending ($4600 + $500 + $935).

A four-sector model adds international transactions to the three-sector model above. Goods and services available for U.S. purchase Yg include domestic production Y and gross imports Mg; thus $Yg = Y + Mg$. Expenditures on U.S.-made goods include domestic consumption C, net investment I, government spending G, and gross exports Xg. Thus, $Y + Mg = C + I + G + Xg$. Subtracting Mg from both sides of the equation and substituting Xn for $Xg - Mg$, we have $Y = C + I + G + Xn$, an expression for domestic aggregate output for a four-sector model.

2.3 NATIONAL INCOME ACCOUNTS

Table 2-1 presents figures for 1988 aggregate measures GNP, NNP, and NI. GNP is the market value of all final goods and services produced in an economy during a one-year period. NNP is found by reducing GNP by capital consumption allowance (depreciation)—output which consists of replacement investment. National income measures the compensation of economic resources, i.e.,

Table 2-1   Measures of Aggregate Output for 1988 ($ billions)

Gross national product	4880.6
Minus capital consumption allowances	513.6
Net national product	4367.1
Minus indirect business taxes	394.5
National income	3972.6

Source: *Survey of Current Business, Sept. 1989.*

the sum of wages, rent, interest and profit. Because NNP includes taxes imposed during production or at final sale as well as the compensation of economic resources, indirect business taxes (excise and sales taxes) are subtracted from NNP to obtain national income. In the absence of indirect business taxes, national income is equal to net national product.

The household sector's receipt and allocation of its share of national income is presented in Table 2-2. Personal income is the share of national income actually received by the household sector (households plus unincorporated businesses). Note that in calculating personal income national income is reduced by corporate retained earnings (corporate profits less dividend payments made to households) and by net transfer payments made by business and government to the household sector. Disposable personal income is found by deducting income taxes from personal income; with disposable personal income allocated to personal outlays (consumption, interest payments and personal transfers) and household saving.

Table 2-2 Receipt and Allocation of Personal Income in 1988 ($ billions)

National income		3972.6
Minus:		
Corporate profits	328.6	
Net interest	392.9	
Social security contributions	444.6	(1166.1)
Plus:		
Government and business transfers	584.7	
Personal interest income	571.1	
Dividend income	102.2	1258.0
Personal income		4064.5
Less personal tax and nontax payments		586.6
Disposable personal income		3477.8
Minus personal outlays:		
Personal consumption expenditures	3235.1	
Interest paid by consumers to business	96.1	
Net personal transfers to foreigners	1.9	(3333.1)
Personal saving		144.7

Source: *Survey of Current Business, Sept. 1989.*

2.4 PRICE INDEXES

Price indexes are used to convert nominal values, where measurement is in current year prices, to real values by keeping prices at a selected, base year level. (See Problem 2.13.) The GNP deflator, consumer price index (CPI) and producers price index (PPI) are the best known of these price indexes. The implicit GNP deflator is the ratio of nominal GNP to real GNP. Nominal GNP is the market value of all final goods and services measured in current year prices, and real GNP is the market value of all final goods and services measured in the prices of a base year. Hence, real GNP measures real output at unchanged prices. The CPI is designed to measure price changes in the expenditures of urban consumers and is used as a measure of their cost of living. (See Problem 2.15.) The PPI measures the prices that businesses pay in the large-volume, wholesale markets. Components of the PPI selectively measure the prices of finished goods, intermediate goods, and crude materials. (See Problem 2.17.) Because each index measures a different basket of goods, each index does not change at the same rate over time; however, their movement is similar (Table 2-3).

Table 2-3   Comparison of Price Indexes

Year	GNP Deflator	CPI	PPI
1972	100.0	125.3	117.2
1977	140.1	181.5	180.6
1982	207.4	289.1	280.7
1985	231.7	322.2	293.7
Comparison of price changes over time			
1977/1972	1.40	1.45	1.54
1982/1972	2.07	2.31	2.40
1985/1972	2.32	2.57	2.51

Review Questions

1. The circular flow of income for a private sector model shows

   (a) The flow of income between the household and business sectors
   (b) The flow of income between the government and business sectors
   (c) The flow of income between the household, business and government sectors
   (d) The flow of income to the household and government sectors

   Answer: (a)

2. In a private sector model,

   (a) Household saving is a leakage from the circular flow.
   (b) Investment is a spending injection.
   (c) Saving leakages equal investment injections.
   (d) All of the above.
   (e) None of the above.

   Answer: (d)

3. In a model in which there is no government, net investment, capital replacement or international trade, the market value of final output equals

   (a) Aggregate consumption
   (b) The sum of the receipts of economic resources
   (c) The sum of wages, rent, interest and profit
   (d) All of the above
   (e) None of the above

   Answer: (d)

4. Which of the following is not included in gross investment?

   (a) Business and residential construction
   (b) Expenditures on consumer goods
   (c) Additions to business inventory

(d) Expenditures on machinery

Answer: (b)

5.   In a model in which there is a household, business, government and foreign sector, GNP is the sum of

(a) Consumption, gross investment, government spending for goods and services, and net exports

(b) Consumption, net investment, government spending for goods and services, and net exports

(c) Consumption, gross investment, government spending for goods and services, and gross exports

(d) Wages, rent, interest, profit and depreciation

Answer: (a)

6.   In a three-sector model,

(a) Household saving always equals net investment.

(b) Household saving always equals gross investment.

(c) Household saving plus depreciation always equals gross investment plus government spending.

(d) Household saving plus taxes equals net investment plus government spending.

Answer: (d)

7.   Which of the following is not correct?

(a) NNP – direct taxes equals national income.

(b) NNP + capital consumption allowances equals GNP.

(c) Gross investment equals net investment plus depreciation.

(d) Personal income equals disposable personal income plus direct taxes.

Answer: (a)

8.   If personal income equals $570 while personal income taxes equal $90, consumption is $430, interest payments total $10 and personal saving is $40, disposable income equals

(a) $500

(b) $480

(c) $470

(d) $400

Answer: (b)

9.   When nominal GNP is $1100 and real GNP is $1000, the GNP deflator is

(a) 9.09

(b) 90.91

(c) 1.11

(d) 110

Answer: (d)

10. Suppose nominal GNP is $500 in year 1, the base year. If the GNP deflator doubles by year 6 while real output has increased 40%, nominal output in year 6 equals

(a) $2000

(b) $1400

(c) $1000

(d) $750

Answer (b)

Solved Problems

MEASURING OUTPUT IN A PRIVATE, TWO-SECTOR MODEL

2.1   In a two-sector (household and business) model, suppose households receive the following compensation from business: wages $520, interest $30, rent $10, profits $80; consumption spending is $550 and business investment is $90. Find (*a*) the market value of output and household saving. (*b*) What is the relationship of saving and investment?

   (*a*)   The market value of final output is $640, found by summing household compensation (wages of $520 + interest of $30 + rent of $10 + profits of $80), or by summing consumption and investment ($550 + $90). Household saving is $90, found by subtracting consumption spending of $550 from the $640 received by households.

   (*b*)   Both saving and investment equal $90. This relationship always holds true in a two-sector model, since saving leakages must always equal spending injections.

2.2   (*a*) What is a saving leakage from the circular flow? (*b*) Why is investment spending viewed as a spending injection into the circular flow?

   (*a*)   A saving leakage occurs when income received from production is not spent by its recipient; for example, when households are the sole recipient of income from production, their decision to save and not spend is a leakage from the flow of income and spending.

   (*b*)   Investment represents an injection of spending into the circular flow. Those wishing to invest obtain dollar flows through the capital markets from those who have saved.

2.3   (*a*) What are the components of gross investment? (*b*) Why are additions to inventory a component of net investment? (*c*) Can inventory additions be negative?

   (*a*)   Gross investment consists of the current year's business and residential construction, purchases of machinery, equipment and tools and changes in inventory levels.

   (*b*)   Businesses hold materials as well as semifinished and finished goods as inventory to facilitate the production and sale of goods. These inventory holdings are similar in purpose to a firm's acquisition of machinery, equipment and tools—assets which are necessary in the production and sale of goods. Thus, additions to a firm's holding of inventory represents net investment as does the acquisition of additional machinery, equipment and tools.

   (*c*)   When expected sales do not materialize, firms hold undesired levels of materials, finished and semifinished goods inventory. Reducing such inventory levels, *ceteris paribus*, will result in a negative value for additions to inventory, that is, the change in inventory investment is negative.

2.4   Explain the following terms: (*a*) net investment and replacement investment, (*b*) gross national product and net national product.

   (*a*)   Net investment consists of additions to an economy's holding of inventory and its stock of capital (business and residential structures, machinery, equipment and tools); replacement investment consists of capital purchased to replace what was used up (depreciated) in producing the current year's output.

   (*b*)   GNP and NNP are gross and net measures respectively of the total market value of final goods and services produced in an economy during a one-year period. GNP includes the market value of all final output, whereas NNP excludes output which represents capital replacement. Thus, GNP − Depreciation = NNP.

2.5   (*a*) Find GNP and NNP for a private sector model from the following data: consumption, $850; gross investment, $100; depreciation, $40; household compensation (wages + rent + interest + profit), $910. (*b*) Prove that for a private sector model depreciation D plus household saving S equals gross investment Ig; (2) household saving equals net investment In.

(a) GNP is $950 for this private sector model, found by summing household compensation ($910) and depreciation ($40) or by summing consumption ($850) and gross investment ($100). NNP is $910, the sum of household compensation or the sum of consumption ($850) and net investment ($60).

(b) In a private sector model, $GNP = C + Ig$, $GNP = C + S + D$, and $Ig = In + D$. Thus, $Ig = GNP - C$ and $S = GNP - C - D$ or $S + D = GNP - C$. Because $GNP - C$ equals Ig as well as $S + D$, $Ig = S + D$. Subtracting D from both sides of $Ig = S + D$ gives us $Ig - D = S$ and $In = S$ since by definition $Ig - D = In$.

MEASURING OUTPUT IN A THREE- AND FOUR-SECTOR MODEL

2.6 In a three-sector (household, business and government) model, suppose household compensation is $760; taxes on household income is $100; government spending is $560; gross investment is $110; depreciation is $40; and government spending is $130. (a) Find GNP, NNP and household saving. (b) What leakage and spending injections are there for this three-sector model? What is the relationship of these leakages and spending injections?

(a) GNP is $800, the sum of consumption ($560), gross investment ($110) and government spending ($130). NNP is $760—GNP ($800) less depreciation ($40); NNP is also found by summing consumption ($560), net investment ($70) and government spending ($130). Household saving is $100, household compensation ($760) less taxes ($100) and consumption ($560).

(b) Household saving, taxes on household income and depreciation are leakages from the circular flow, whereas gross investment and government spending are spending injections. The $240 in leakages (saving of $100 plus taxes of $100 and depreciation of $40) equals the $240 sum of spending injections (gross investment of $110 and government spending of $130). Note that household saving does not have to equal net investment when there is a government sector.

2.7 What are direct and indirect taxes?

Direct taxes are taxes levied upon earned income. Examples of direct taxes include federal, state and/or local taxes imposed upon household and/or business income. Indirect taxes are taxes levied on goods and services at the production level or at final sale and are thereby passed on to the final buyer through higher prices. Examples of indirect taxes include excise taxes, sales taxes, business property taxes, import duties and licence fees.

2.8 (a) Find the sum of payment and expenditure flows in Fig. 2-4. (b) Find GNP, NNP and household saving. (c) What are the leakages and spending injections in Fig. 2-4?

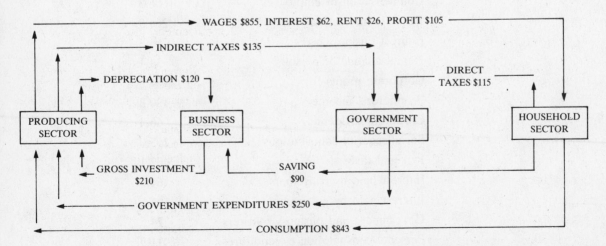

Fig. 2-4

(a) Household compensation is $1048 (wages $855 + interest $62 + rent $26 + profit $105); government receives $135 from indirect taxes; and capital consumption allowances (depreciation) are $120. The sum of payment flows is $1303. Spending flows consist of personal consumption $843, gross investment $210 and government expenditures $250. The sum of expenditure flows is $1303.

(b) GNP is $1303, the sum of payment flows (to households $1048, business $120 and government $135) or expenditure flows (personal consumption $843, gross investment $210 and government expenditures $210). NNP is $1183, which is GNP ($1303) minus depreciation ($120). Household saving is $90, found by deducting consumption ($843) and income taxes ($115) from household compensation ($1048).

(c) Leakages consist of household saving, indirect taxes, income taxes on household income and depreciation. Spending injections consist of government spending and gross investment. Leakages ($90 + $135 + $115 + $120) equal spending injections ($250 + $210).

2.9 (a) From the following data for the U.S., establish the amount of domestic output available for U.S. purchase and the total amount of goods and services available for U.S. purchase: GNP is $1000; gross exports equal $100 while gross imports are $150. (b) Does U.S. GNP always equal U.S. purchases of goods and services when there are international transactions? (c) What happens to U.S. GNP when U.S. imports increase *ceteris paribus*?

(a) The amount of domestic output available for U.S. purchase is $900—the $1000 U.S. GNP less the $100 of U.S. output which is exported. The total amount of goods and services available for U.S. purchase is $1050—the $900 from domestic production plus the $150 of imported goods and services.

(b) Purchases of goods and services can be equal to, less than, or greater than domestic output depending upon the relation of gross exports and gross imports. When gross imports (Mg) exceed gross exports (Xg) and there is a negative net export (Xn) balance, U.S. purchases of goods and services exceed U.S. output [the situation depicted by the data for part (a)]. However, when there is a positive net export balance (gross exports exceed gross imports), U.S. output is greater than U.S. purchases of goods and services.

(c) GNP in the United States falls since there are increased purchases of foreign-made goods and decreased purchases of U.S.-made goods.

NATIONAL INCOME ACCOUNTS

2.10 From the following data, find (a) national income, (b) NNP, (c) GNP, (d) personal income, (e) personal disposable income and (f) personal saving.

Capital consumption allowance	$ 356.4
Compensation of employees	1866.3
Business interest payments	264.9
Indirect business taxes	266.3
Rental income of persons	34.1
Corporate profits	164.8
Proprietors' income	120.3
Corporate dividends	66.4
Social security contributions	253.0
Personal taxes	402.1
Interest paid by consumers	64.4
Interest paid by government	105.1
Government and business transfers	374.5
Personal consumption expenditures	1991.9

(a) National income = compensation of employees + business interest payments + rental income of persons + corporate profits + proprietors' income. National income = $1866.3 + $264.9 + $34.1 + $164.8 + $120.3 = $2450.4.

(b) NNP = national income + indirect taxes = $2450.4 + $266.3 = $2716.7.

(c) GNP = NNP + capital consumption allowance = $2716.7 + $356.4 = $3073.1.

(d) Personal income:

National income		$2450.4
Minus: Corporate profits	$164.8	
Social security contributions	253.0	(417.8)
Plus: Government & business transfers	374.5	
Interest paid by government	105.1	
Corporate dividends	66.4	546.0
Personal income		$2578.6

(e) Personal disposable income = Personal income − personal taxes = $2578.6 − $402.1 = $2176.5.

(f) Personal saving = Personal disposable income − (personal consumption expenditures + interest paid by consumers)
Personal saving = $2176.5 − ($1991.9 + $64.4) = $120.2.

2.11 (a) GNP is the market value of final output. What is the difference between a final good and an intermediate good? (b) Why would inclusion of intermediate goods in measuring GNP involve double counting?

(a) A final good does not require further processing and is purchased for final use (e.g., clothing by a consumer or a machine by a manufacturer). An intermediate good (1) requires further processing during the year before it is ready for final use, (2) is being purchased for modification before final use, or (3) will be resold during the year for a profit.

(b) Intermediate goods are components of final goods. If the value of both intermediate and final goods is included in the measurement of final output, there would be a double counting of value and therefore an overstatement of GNP.

2.12 What is the difference between personal income and national income?

Personal income is the aggregate income received by households during a given year. National income is the sum of payments made to economic resources. In a free enterprise economy, economic resources are owned by households, but government and the corporate form of business organization divert some of the income flow from households when corporations earn profits and government mandates that households make contributions to social security. Some of these diverted funds, however, are returned to households as corporate dividends, government and business transfers and interest on the public debt. Thus, personal income can be less than, equal to, or greater than national income depending upon the net diversion of funds from households by government and corporations.

PRICE INDEXES

2.13 Table 2-4 presents the price of and units of aggregate output for 199x and 199y. (a) Present in Table 2-5, nominal GNP for 199x and 199y. (b) Also calculate in Table 2-5 real output for 199y by measuring 199y output in 199x prices. What is the purpose of such a calculation? (c) What is the GNP deflator in 199y?

Table 2-4 Aggregate Output in a Five-Good Economy

Good	199x Units Produced	199x Price	199y Units Produced	199y Price
A	25	$1.50	30	$1.60
B	50	7.50	60	8.00
C	40	6.00	50	7.00
D	30	5.00	35	5.50
E	60	2.00	70	2.50

Table 2-5 Nominal and Real GNP for 199x and 199y

Good	Value of 199x Output 199x prices	Value of 199y Output 199y prices	Value of 199y Output 199x prices
A	$ 37.50	$ 48.00	$ 45.00
B	375.00	480.00	450.00
C	240.00	350.00	300.00
D	150.00	192.50	175.00
E	120.00	175.00	140.00
GNP	$922.50	$1245.50	$1110.00

(a) Nominal GNP for 199x and 199y is found by multiplying the units produced each year times the respective price of each unit for that year and then summing the calculated values. Thus, as presented in Table 2-5, the value of good A in 199x is $37.50; nominal GNP (value of output for goods A through E for 199x) is $922.50 in 199x; it is $1245.50 in 198y.

(b) Measuring 199y output in 199x prices gives a measure of real output for 199y. The right column measures the value of 199y output for goods A through E in 199x prices; real GNP for 199y is $1110. A comparison of the first and last column (both measured at 199x prices) reveals the change in output, whereas a comparison of the first and second columns reveals a combined change in both output and prices.

(c) The GNP deflator for 199y is 112.2, found by dividing 199y nominal GNP (199y output measured in 199y prices) by 199y real GNP (199y output measured in 199x prices) and multiplying by 100: ($1245.50/$1110)100 = 112.2.

2.14   What is the GNP deflator?

The GNP deflator is an index of price changes for goods and services included in GNP. Thus, the deflator reflects changes in the price of goods and services purchased by consumers, businesses and government. The GNP deflator is found by dividing current-dollar GNP by constant-dollar GNP, with the spending components (C, I, G) of constant-dollar GNP derived separately.

2.15   (a) What is the CPI? (b) Do increases in the CPI always indicate an increase in the consumer's cost of living?

(a) The CPI is a measure of the prices paid by the typical urban working-class family. Statisticians have sampled these "typical" consumers to establish a relevant basket of goods which is purchased and the appropriate relative importance (weight) of each good. The basket consists of goods and services divided into the following categories: food and beverages, housing, apparel, transportation, medical care, entertainment, and other.

(b) Although the CPI is the most reliable measure of the cost of living, it may overstate price increases over time. Because it is a fixed-weight index, it does not allow for substitution effects, where consumers may "shop" for goods whose price is rising and/or select a substitute good whose price has experienced a smaller relative increase. The quality of goods also changes so that a price increase may reflect improved quality rather than inflation. For these reasons, the CPI may overstate price increases and therefore not truly reflect consumers' cost of living.

2.16 Suppose households purchase the categories of goods listed in Column 1 of Table 2-6; the relative importance of each category is given by the weight assigned in column 2. The price index for each category during year 1 and year 2 is found in columns 3 and 4, respectively. (a) From these data, calculate the CPI for year 1 and year 2. (b) What is the rate of inflation between year 1 and year 2 as measured by the change in the CPI?

Table 2-6

Category	Weight	Price Index for Each Category Year 1	Year 2
Food and beverages	0.175	270	270
Housing	0.460	300	330
Apparel	0.046	180	180
Transportation	0.193	280	308
Medical care	0.049	300	330
Entertainment	0.036	230	241
Other	0.041	250	250
	1.000		

(a) In Table 2-7 the price index for each spending category is multiplied by its respective weight and then summed. The CPI for year 1 is 280.80 and 301.87 for year 2.

(b) The rate of inflation is calculated by taking the change in the CPI between year 1 and year 2 and dividing by year 1 CPI. The rate of inflation indicated by the CPI is $(301.87 - 280.80)/280.80 = 0.75$, or 7.50%.

Table 2-7

Category	Year 1	Year 2
Food and beverages	0.175(270) = 47.25	0.175(270) = 47.25
Housing	0.460(300) = 138.00	0.460(330) = 151.80
Apparel	0.046(180) = 8.28	0.046(180) = 8.28
Transportation	0.193(280) = 54.04	0.193(308) = 59.44
Medical care	0.049(300) = 14.70	0.049(330) = 16.17
Entertainment	0.036(230) = 8.28	0.036(241) = 8.68
Other	0.041(250) = 10.25	0.041(250) = 10.25
CPI	280.80	301.87

2.17   What is the producers price index?

The PPI is an index of the prices charged by businesses for crude, intermediate and finished goods. Because these prices represent the stages of production, some goods enter the PPI as many as three times: as a crude good (e.g., wheat sold by the farmer), as an intermediate good (flour sold by the mill), and as a finished good (bread sold by the baker to a food retailer). A PPI is also published for crude goods, intermediate goods and finished goods to avoid the double counting that exists in the PPI for goods at all stages of production. Prices in the PPI are weighted as they are in the CPI, with weights based on the net selling value of commodities in 1972. Movements in the PPI can be used to forecast the CPI; however, because the PPI does not include services, such forecasts are subject to error when the principal cause of inflation is service prices.

Chapter 3

Private Sector Spending Model

In this chapter, we develop a private sector (two-sector) model of aggregate output (income) in which aggregate spending determines the level of aggregate output.

3.1 AGGREGATE OUTPUT IN A PRIVATE SECTOR MODEL

A private sector model consists of a household sector and a business sector. We shall assume that the business sector will supply output such that its revenue from sales is equal to its disbursement of money income. Aggregate output, therefore, depends upon the spending level of the household and business sector. In developing this model the following economic behavior is assumed: (1) regardless of the level of output Y, the business sector has a constant level of planned investment I; (2) household spending (aggregate consumption C) is a positive linear function of the level of disposable income Yd. Because household saving equals disposable income less consumption ($S = Yd - C$), aggregate saving is also a positive, linear function of aggregate disposable income. Household disposable income equals the business sector's cost of producing output ($Y = Yd$) when there is no government sector.

EXAMPLE 1. The assumed behavior of consumption, investment and saving is presented in Fig. 3-1. In Fig. 3-1(a), aggregate consumption is \$450 when disposable income is \$500 and \$530 when disposable income is \$600. Aggregate saving S equals $Yd - C$. Thus, aggregate saving, read from either Fig. 3-1(a) or 3-1(b), is \$50 when disposable income is \$500 and \$70 when disposable income is \$600. Intended investment in Fig. 3-1(c) is \$50 regardless of the level of income.

For the assumed economic behavior for the household and business sector, there exists only one output level—specified the equilibrium level of income—where the value of output equals revenues from sales. An equilibrium level of income occurs when planned aggregate spending ($C + I$) equals the value of output (Y) or equivalently where the household sector's intended saving (S) equals intended investment (I).

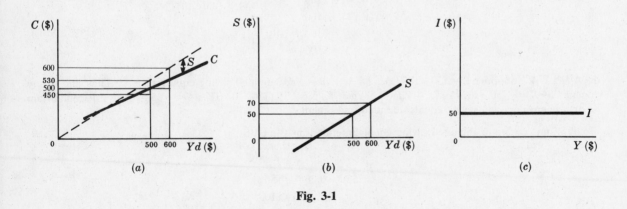

Fig. 3-1

EXAMPLE 2. In Fig. 3-2(a), equilibrium exists at a \$500 level of income where planned aggregate spending (C of \$450 plus I of \$50) equals the \$500 value of output. In Fig. 3-2(b) intended investment equals intended saving at this \$500 value of output.

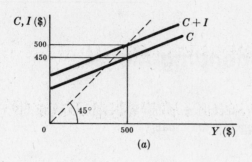
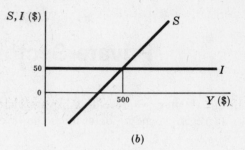

Fig. 3-2

3.2   AN ALGEBRAIC SOLUTION TO THE EQUILIBRIUM LEVEL OF INCOME

We have assumed that consumption is a positive, linear function of disposable income. For example, the consumption function in Fig. 3-1 can be presented in a numerical equation as $C = \$50 + 0.80Yd$. Given a constant level of intended investment, we can determine the equilibrium level of income by equating planned aggregate spending and the value of output (Example 3) or by equating intended saving and intended investment (Example 4). Using alphabetical symbols, planned investment is presented as $I = \bar{I}$ (planned investment is autonomous), and consumption is presented as $C = \bar{C} + cYd$, where $\bar{C}$ represents autonomous consumption (consumption which is independent of disposable income), and c is a behavioral coefficient relating consumption to disposable income. Equilibrium income is presented in Example 5 as $Y = (\bar{C} + \bar{I})/(1 - c)$.

EXAMPLE 3.   Suppose the household sector's planned consumption is $C = \$50 + 0.80Yd$, and intended investment is $50. In the absence of a government sector and taxes, the value of output equals the household sector's disposable income so that $Yd = Y$. Given the specified spending plans, *equilibrium income* is $500 where the value of output equals planned aggregate spending.

Equilibrium condition: Value of output equals planned aggregate spending:

$$Y = C + I$$
$$Y = (\$50 + 0.80Y) + \$50$$
$$Y - 0.80Y = \$100$$
$$Y(1 - 0.80) = \$100$$
$$Y(0.20) = \$100$$
$$Y = \$100/0.20$$
$$Y = \$500$$

EXAMPLE 4.   Suppose $C = \$50 + 0.80Yd$; $I = \$50$; $Y = Yd$. Intended saving equals $Yd - C$. Thus, the saving function is $S = -\$50 + 0.20Y$. [$S = Yd - C$; $Yd = Y$; $S = Y - (\$50 + 0.80Y)$; $S = -\$50 + 0.20Y$.] Equilibrium occurs where intended saving equals intended investment.

Equilibrium condition: Intended saving equals intended investment:

$$S = I$$
$$-\$50 + 0.20Y = \$50$$
$$0.20Y = \$100$$
$$Y = \frac{\$100}{0.20}$$
$$Y = \$500$$

EXAMPLE 5.   Suppose $C = \bar{C} + cYd$; $Yd = Y$; $I = \bar{I}$; $S = -\bar{C} + (1 - c)Yd$; [$S = Yd - C$; $S = Yd - (\bar{C} + cYd)$; $S = Y - \bar{C} - cYD$; $S = -\bar{C} + (1 - c)Yd$]. Equilibrium income is $Y = (\bar{C} + \bar{I})/(1 - c)$, found by equating $Y = C + I$ and $S = I$.

Equilibrium condition: Value of output equals planned aggregate spending:

$$Y = C + I$$
$$Y = \bar{C} + cY + \bar{I}$$
$$Y - cY = \bar{C} + \bar{I}$$
$$Y(1 - c) = \bar{C} + \bar{I}$$
$$Y = \frac{\bar{C} + \bar{I}}{1 - c}$$

Equilibrium condition: Intended saving equals intended investment:

$$S = I$$
$$-\bar{C} + (1 - c)Y = \bar{I}$$
$$Y = \frac{\bar{C} + \bar{I}}{1 - c}$$

3.3 THE MARGINAL PROPENSITY TO CONSUME

The marginal propensity to consume (MPC) measures the change in consumption resulting from a change in disposable income ($\Delta C / \Delta Yd$). As presented in Fig. 3-3, the change in consumption is less than the change in disposable income, with the MPC taking a value greater than 0 but less than 1. In the consumption equation, $C = \bar{C} + cYd$, the MPC is the behavioral coefficient c, the slope of the consumption function. Since households use their income to consume or save, the marginal propensity to save (MPS) equals $1 - $ MPC, or MPC + MPS = 1.

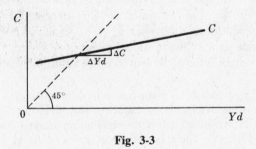

Fig. 3-3

EXAMPLE 6. Suppose the value of c is 0.80 for consumption equation $C = \bar{C} + cYd$. The MPC is 0.80, indicating that there is an $8 change in consumption for every $10 change in disposable income.

3.4 THE MULTIPLIED EFFECT OF CHANGES IN AUTONOMOUS AGGREGATE SPENDING

Changes in autonomous aggregate spending cause parallel shifts of the consumption function. [In the equilibrium condition $Y = (\bar{C} + \bar{I})/(1 - c)$, autonomous changes result from changing the value of $\bar{C}$ and/or $\bar{I}$.] Changes in autonomous spending alter output (the level of income) and induce changes in consumption spending because of the dependency of consumption upon disposable income. Thus, an increase in autonomous investment ($\Delta \bar{I}$) causes income to change by more than the autonomous change [$\Delta Y > \Delta \bar{I}$] due to the increased consumption caused by the dependency of consumption on disposable income.

EXAMPLE 7. Equilibrium income is $500 for the $C + I'$ schedule in Fig. 3-4; aggregate consumption is $450, and planned investment is $50. A $10 increase in planned investment shifts the aggregate spending schedule from $C + I'$ to $C + I''$ with the equilibrium level of income increasing from $500 to $550. At the higher income level, investment is $60 and consumption is $490. The $10 increase in autonomous investment spending induces $40 in additional consumption spending for a $50 change in income.

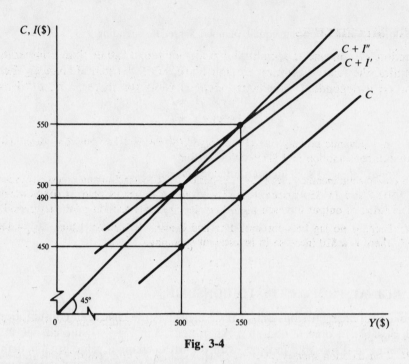

Fig. 3-4

3.5   THE EXPENDITURE MULTIPLIER

The expenditure multiplier measures the multiplied effect changes in autonomous spending have upon equilibrium income. In Example 7, a \$10 increase in planned investment increases equilibrium income \$50, i.e., the change in income is 5 times the \$10 increase in autonomous spending. Thus, $\Delta Y/\Delta \bar{I}$ equals 5, and the expenditure multiplier k_e is 5. Example 8 shows that the value of the expenditure multiplier depends upon c, the marginal propensity to consume. A larger MPC increases the value of k_e, and lower values reduce the expenditure multiplier.

EXAMPLE 8. Suppose $C = \bar{C} + cY$ and $I = \bar{I}$. Equilibrium income is $Y = (\bar{C} + \bar{I})/(1 - c)$ which is derived in Example 5. An increase in autonomous planned investment, with no change in $\bar{C}$ or c, increases equilibrium income by $\Delta Y = \Delta \bar{I}/(1 - c)$. The multiplied effect on equilibrium income from the change in autonomous planned investment $(\Delta Y/\Delta \bar{I})$ is $1/(1 - c)$. The expenditure multiplier k_e is $1/(1 - c)$; the value of the k_e depends upon c, the marginal propensity to consume:

$$Y = \frac{C + I}{1 - c}$$

Letting $\Delta \bar{I} > 0$, *ceteris paribus* (i.e., $\Delta \bar{C} = 0$ and there is no change in c)

$$\Delta Y = \frac{\Delta \bar{I}}{1 - c}$$

Thus,

$$\frac{\Delta Y}{\Delta \bar{I}} = \frac{1}{1 - c}$$

Letting $k_e = \Delta Y/\Delta \bar{I}$,

$$k_e = \frac{1}{1 - c}$$

EXAMPLE 9. The multiplier provides a short-cut method for determining the equilibrium level of income.

Equilibrium occurs where

$$Y = \frac{\bar{C} + \bar{I}}{1 - c}$$

or where

$$Y = (\bar{C} + \bar{I})\left[\frac{1}{1 - c}\right]$$

Letting $k_e = 1/(1 - c)$, then

$$Y = k_e(\bar{C} + \bar{I})$$

3.6 DYNAMIC MULTIPLIERS

In this section we analyze the multiplier under dynamic rather than comparative static conditions. In dynamics, the focus is on time and therefore on the process of change. There must be a lag structure between a dependent and independent variable for there to be a "dynamic process of change."

EXAMPLE 10. In a dynamic process, there is a *lagged* (Situation II) rather than simultaneous (Situation I) relationship between consumption and disposable income.

Given: An equilibrium income level of \$450 in period t. Consumption and investment spending are given as $C = \$40 + 0.80\,Yd$ and $I = \$50$ respectively. The value of output is paid to the household sector so that $Yd = Y$. The value of output for each period equals aggregate spending for that period.

Situation I: There is no lag between spending and disposable income. Thus, $C_{t+1} = \$40 + 0.80\,Yd_{t+1}$. In period $t + 1$, there is a \$10 increase in investment spending.

Period $t + 1$:
$$Y_{t+1} = C_{t+1} + I_{t+1}$$
$$Y_{t+1} = \$40 + 0.80\,Y_{t+1} + \$60$$
$$Y_{t+1} = \$500$$

Assuming no other changes, the level of income reaches a new equilibrium position in the same period that investment increased.

Situation II: Consumption spending lags disposable income by one period. Thus, $C_{t+1} = \$40 + 0.80\,Yd_t$. In period $t + 1$ there is a \$10 increase in investment spending.

Period $t + 1$:
$$Y_{t+1} = C_{t+1} + I_{t+1}$$
$$Y_{t+1} = \$40 + 0.80\,Y_t + \$60$$

Since $Y_t = \$450$,
$$Y_{t+1} = \$460$$

Period $t + 2$:
$$Y_{t+2} = C_{t+2} + I_{t+2}$$
$$Y_{t+2} = \$40 + 0.80\,Y_{t+1} + \$60$$

Since $Y_{t+1} = \$460$,
$$Y_{t+2} = \$468$$

Period $t + 3$:
$$Y_{t+3} = C_{t+3} + I_{t+3}$$
$$Y_{t+3} = \$40 + 0.80\,Y_{t+2} + \$60$$

Since $Y_{t+2} = \$468$,
$$Y_{t+3} = \$474.40$$

In each succeeding period, the income level moves closer to the equilibrium \$500 level of income.

Figure 3-5 presents graphically the multiplier process described in Example 10.

The dynamic multiplier process of Fig. 3-5(b) can be presented as a decreasing geometric series where the change in income after n periods is

$$\Delta Y = \Delta I(1 + c + c^2 + \cdots + c^n) \tag{3.1}$$

Using the change in investment and the MPC from Example 10, the change in income after three periods is

$$\Delta Y = \$10(1 + 0.80 + 0.80^2)$$
$$\Delta Y = \$24.40$$

Given the dynamic multiplier process in (*3.1*), it follows that the dynamic expenditure multiplier k_{de} after n periods is

$$\frac{\Delta Y}{\Delta I} = k_{de} = (1 + c + c^2 + \cdots + c^n) \tag{3.2}$$

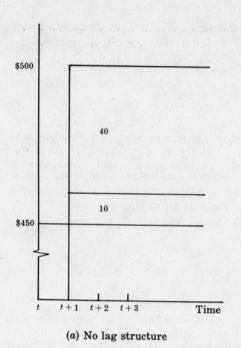

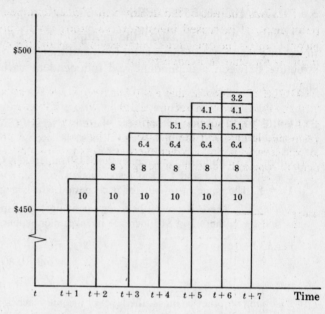

(a) No lag structure

(b) Consumption lags disposable income by one period

Fig. 3-5

EXAMPLE 11. If we compare the dynamic and static multipliers, we find that a major portion of the multiplier effect is realized in fewer periods when there is a smaller marginal propensity to consume.

Situation I: The MPC equals 0.90.

$$k_e = \frac{1}{1-c} = \frac{1}{1-0.90} = 10$$

$$k_{de} \text{ for 3 periods} = (1+c+c^2) = (1+0.9+0.81) = 2.71$$

$$\frac{k_{de} \text{ for 3 periods}}{k_e} = \frac{2.71}{10} = 0.271$$

After three periods, 27.1% of the multiplier effect is realized.

Situation II: The MPC equals 0.80.

$$k_e = \frac{1}{1-c} = \frac{1}{1-0.80} = 5$$

$$k_{de} \text{ for 3 periods} = (1+c+c^2) = (1+0.8+0.64) = 2.44$$

$$\frac{k_{de} \text{ for 3 periods}}{k_e} = \frac{2.44}{5} = 0.488$$

After three periods, 48.8% of the multiplier effect is realized.

Situation III: The MPC equals 0.50.

$$k_e = \frac{1}{1-c} = \frac{1}{1-0.50} = 2$$

$$k_{de} \text{ for 3 periods} = (1+c+c^2) = (1+0.5+0.25) = 1.75$$

$$\frac{k_{de} \text{ for 3 periods}}{k_e} = \frac{1.75}{2} = 0.875$$

After three periods, 87.5% of the multiplier effect is realized.

Previous analysis of the dynamic multiplier assumed that the increase in investment spending was permanent. If increased investment spending occurs only in the initial time period, the increase in income equals the one-period increase in investment spending, falling slowly back to the income level prior to the change in investment.

EXAMPLE 12. Suppose that a $10 increase in investment occurs only during period $t + 1$. If the MPC equals 0.80 and there is no lag structure, a $10 increase in investment spending in Fig. 3-6(a) increases income in period $t + 1$ by $50 with income in period $t + 2$ returning to its previous level. In Fig. 3-6(b), consumption lags disposable income and the income level increases $10 in period $t + 1$, declining in successive periods to the income level in period t. When there is a lag in consumption spending, induced consumption is dispersed over numerous periods rather than being concentrated in one period.

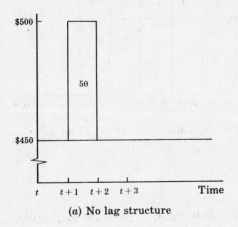

(a) No lag structure

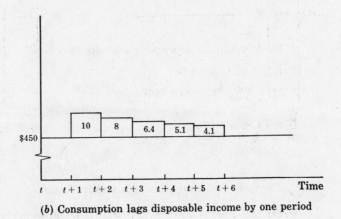

(b) Consumption lags disposable income by one period

Fig. 3-6

Review Questions

1. Equilibrium occurs in a two-sector model when

    (a) Saving equals investment.

    (b) Consumption plus investment equals the value of output.

    (c) Planned saving equals planned investment.

    (d) Aggregate spending equals the revenues of the business sector.

    Answer: (c)

2. When planned saving is greater than planned investment,

    (a) Output should increase.

    (b) Output should decrease.

    (c) Output should not change.

    Answer: (b)

3. When the value of output exceeds planned spending,

    (a) There is unsold output, and the level of income will fall.

(b) There is unsold output, and the level of income will rise.

(c) There is no unsold output, and the level of income does not change.

Answer: (a)

4. When planned consumption equals $40 + 0.90Yd$ and planned investment is \$50, the equilibrium level of income is (a) \$90, (b) \$400, (c) \$500 or (d) \$900.

Answer: (d)

5. When planned saving equals $-\$40 + 0.20Yd$ and planned investment is \$60, the equilibrium level of income is (a) \$100, (b) \$400, (c) \$500 or (d) \$1000.

Answer: (c)

6. By definition, the marginal propensity to consume

(a) Equals $\Delta C/\Delta Yd$

(b) Is the behavioral coefficient c in the equation $C = \bar{C} + cYd$

(c) Is the slope of the consumption function

(d) All of the above

Answer: (d)

7. The value of the expenditure multiplier relates

(a) The change in income to the change in autonomous spending

(b) The change in autonomous spending to the change in income

(c) The change in consumption to the change in income

(d) The change in income to the change in consumption

Answer: (a)

8. When the marginal propensity to consume is 0.75, the multiplier has a value of (a) 5, (b) 4, (c) 3 or (d) 2.

Answer: (b)

9. A change in autonomous spending is represented by

(a) A movement along a spending line

(b) A shift of a spending line

(c) A change in a behavioral coefficient

Answer: (b)

10. When $C_t = f(Yd_{t-1})$

(a) There is an imperfect relationship between consumption and disposable income.

(b) There is no relationship between consumption and disposable income.

(c) Consumption spending lags the receipt of disposable income by one period.

(d) The receipt of disposable income lags consumption spending by one period.

Answer: (c)

11. Dynamic multipliers occur when

   (a) The assumption of *ceteris paribus* is dropped.

   (b) The economy is not in equilibrium.

   (c) Consumption is unrelated to disposable income.

   (d) There is a lagged response between consumption and disposable income.

   Answer: (d)

12. When consumption spending lags the receipt of disposable income by one period, there is

   (a) No change in the income level when there is a one-period change in investment

   (b) Only a relatively small change in the income level when there is a one-period change in investment

   (c) A relatively small change in the income level when there is a permanent change in investment

   (d) No change in the income level when there is a permanent change in investment

   Answer: (b)

Solved Problems

AGGREGATE OUTPUT IN A PRIVATE SECTOR MODEL

3.1 From Fig. 3-7, determine consumption and saving at disposable income levels OYd_1, OYd_2 and OYd_3.

   For OYd_1, consumption is OA and saving is zero. Consumption is OB and saving is BD for disposable income level OYd_2; consumption is OC, and saving is CE when disposable income is OYd_3.

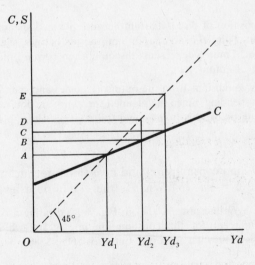

Fig. 3-7

3.2 (a) What is meant by an equilibrium level of output (income)? (b) Suppose the business sector produces goods and services valued at $500 for household consumption and $60 for business investment. Does saving equal investment when households plan to save $70 of their $560

disposable income and planned investment is $60? (*c*) Is the $560 output level in situation (*b*) an equilibrium level of income?

(*a*)   Equilibrium means an absence of forces for change. When the business sector sells output at prices they expect and buyers achieve their desired level of spending, there are no forces present for changing the output level.

(*b*)   Households consume $490 of the $500 produced for household consumption; the business sector retains $10 in output as unsold inventory. Planned investment plus unplanned inventory investment equals $70, which is the sum of household saving. Thus, when planned saving and planned investment are not equal, the saving-investment equality is reached through the involuntary holding of inventory by the business sector.

(*c*)   There is disequilibrium at the $500 output level because of unplanned inventory investment. Equilibrium exists only when the plans and expectations of all sectors are fulfilled.

3.3   (*a*) From Fig. 3-8, define the relationship between planned spending ($C + I$) and the value of output at points *A*, *B* and *C*. Do these points represent equilibrium or disequilibrium? (*b*) Why does equilibrium occur when planned consumption plus planned investment intersect the 45° line?

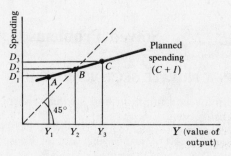

Fig. 3-8

(*a*)   Point *A* is a position of disequilibrium because planned spending of OD_1 is greater than the OY_1 value of output. Point *B* is an equilibrium position because planned spending OD_2 equals the OY_2 value of output. Point *C* represents disequilibrium because planned spending of OD_3 is less than the OY_3 value of output.

(*b*)   The 45° line is equidistant from the output (income) and spending axes. Anywhere on the 45° line income equals spending. Since the planned spending function is upward-sloping, it intersects the 45° line at only one point, this point being the position where planned spending equals the value of output.

3.4   (*a*) From Fig. 3-9, find consumption and investment for income levels (1) $600, (2) $650, and (3) $700. Assume $Y = Yd$. (*b*) What is the equilibrium level of income for this economy?

(*a*)   The *C* and ($C + I$) lines are parallel in Fig. 3-9 indicating a constant level of investment. $I = \$70$ since the *y* intercept for the consumption line is $60 while it is $130 for the ($C + I$) line. Consumption is $540 when aggregate output is $600, $580 when aggregate output is $650 and $620 when it is $700.

(*b*)   The equilibrium level of income is $650. Aggregate spending of $650 (*C* of $580 plus *I* of $70) equals the $650 level of output.

3.5   (*a*) What is meant by a saving leakage? (*b*) Will the income level expand or contract when (1) planned saving is greater than planned investment? (2) planned spending is greater than output?

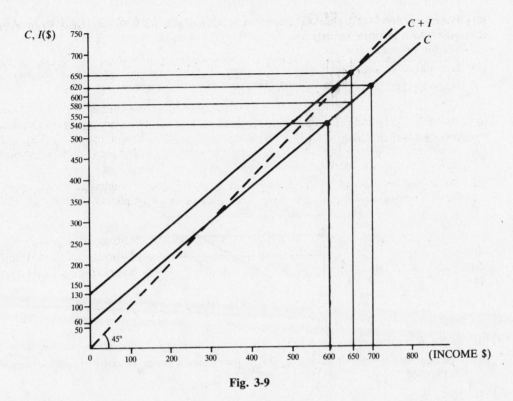

Fig. 3-9

(a) When the household sector does not consume its entire income, it is not purchasing the entire output it helped create. That is, there is a saving leakage. Investment must fill the void created by saving if the level of income is to be maintained.

(b) (1) The income level contracts since saving leakages are not replaced by an equal amount of planned investment spending. (2) The income level expands since planned spending exceeds output.

3.6 From Fig. 3-10, determine planned saving and planned investment for income levels OY_1, OY_2 and OY_3. (b) Find the equilibrium level of income by equating (1) planned spending with output and (2) planned saving and planned investment.

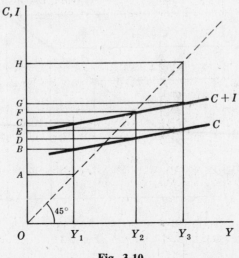

Fig. 3-10

(a)   For income level OY_1, planned investment is BC, and planned dissaving is AB. Planned investment is DF, as is planned saving when income is OY_2; planned investent is EG, and planned saving is EH for income level OY_3.

(b)   Equilibrium occurs at income level OY_2 where (1) planned spending OF equals the value of output OY_2 and (2) where planned saving DF equals planned investment DF.

3.7   (a) From Fig. 3-11, find planned saving for income levels OY_1, OY_2 and OY_3. (b) What is the equilibrium level of income?

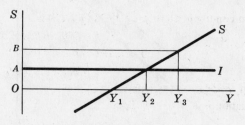

Fig. 3-11

(a)   Saving is zero when income is OY_1, OA when income is OY_2 and OB when income is OY_3.

(b)   The equilibrium level of income is OY_2 where planned saving equals planned investment.

AN ALGEBRAIC SOLUTION TO THE EQUILIBRIUM LEVEL OF INCOME

3.8   Suppose planned consumption is given by the equation $C = \$40 + 0.75Yd$. (a) Find planned consumption when disposable income is \$300, \$400 and \$500. (b) Plot this consumption function in Fig. 3-12.

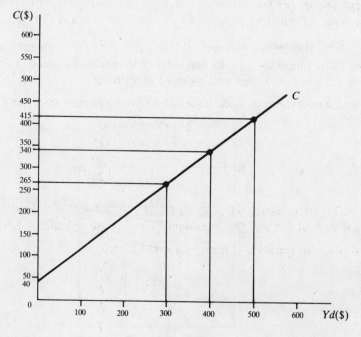

Fig. 3-12

(a) Substituting a \$300 disposable income into the consumption equation, we have $C = \$40 + 0.75(\$300)$; $C = \$40 + \$225 = \$265$. Consumption is \$340 when Yd is \$400 and \$415 when Yd is \$500.

(b) See Fig. 3-12.

3.9 Suppose planned consumption equals $\$40 + 0.75Y$, and planned investment is \$60. (a) Find the equilibrium level of income, the level of consumption and saving at equilibrium. (b) Show that at equilibrium planned spending equals the value of output and planned saving equals planned investment.

(a) The equilibrium condition is given by $Y = C + I$. Thus,

$$Y = \$40 + 0.75Y + \$60$$
$$Y - 0.75Y = \$100$$
$$Y = \$400 \text{ the equilibrium level of income}$$

When $Y = \$400$, $C = \$40 + 0.75(\$400) = \$340$.
The saving equation is $S = Y - C$. Thus,

$$S = Y - (\$40 + 0.75Y)$$
$$S = -\$40 + 0.25Y$$

When $Y = \$400$, $S = -\$40 + 0.25(\$400) = \$60$.

(b) Planned spending equals the value of output.

$$C + I = Y$$
$$\$340 + \$60 = \$400$$

Planned saving equals planned investment

$$S = I$$
$$\$60 = \$60$$

3.10 Suppose planned consumption equals $\$50 + 0.80Yd$; $I = \$80$; and $Yd = Y$ since there is no government sector. (a) Derive an equation for the saving function. (b) Find the equilibrium level of income by equating planned saving and planned investment.

(a) Planned saving equals $Yd - C$; and since $C = \$50 + 0.80Yd$,

$$S = Yd - (\$50 + 0.80Yd)$$
$$S = -\$50 + 0.20Yd$$

(b) The equilibrium condition is determined by equating planned saving and planned I; thus

$$-\$50 + 0.20Y = \$80$$
$$0.20Y = \$130$$
$$Y = \frac{\$130}{0.20} = \$650$$

3.11 Suppose planned consumption is $\bar{C} + cYd$; $I = \bar{I}$; $Yd = Y$. (a) Find an expression for the equilibrium level of income. (b) Find equilibrium income when $\bar{C} = \$50$; $c = 0.80$ and $\bar{I} = \$90$.

(a) The equilibrium condition is given by $Y = C + I$; thus,

$$Y = \bar{C} + cY + \bar{I}$$
$$Y - cY = \bar{C} + \bar{I}$$
$$Y(1 - c) = \bar{C} + \bar{I}$$
$$Y = \frac{\bar{C} + \bar{I}}{1 - c}$$

(*b*)   Substituting, we have $Y = (\$50 + \$90)/(1 - 0.80)$; $Y = \$140/0.20 = \$700$, the equilibrium level of income.

THE MARGINAL PROPENSITY TO CONSUME

3.12   (*a*) What does the marginal propensity to consume measure? (*b*) What is the relationship between the marginal propensity to consume and the marginal propensity to save?

(*a*)   The marginal propensity to consume measures households' willingness to change consumption spending as a result of a change in disposable income. It is generally assumed that households consume part of, but not the entire, change in disposable income. That is, $\Delta C < \Delta Yd$.

(*b*)   Disposable income that is not consumed is saved. Thus, MPC + MPS = 1.

3.13   (*a*) What is the MPC when (1) $C = \$40 + 0.75Yd$; (2) $C = \$60 + 0.80Yd$; and (3) $C = \$20 + 0.90Yd$? (*b*) What is the relationship of the MPC to the slope of the consumption function?

(*a*)   The MPC is the behavioral coefficient c in the consumption equation $C = \bar{C} + cY$. Thus, the MPC is (1) 0.75; (2) 0.80; and (3) 0.90.

(*b*)   The marginal propensity to consume measures the change in consumption due to a change in disposable income $(\Delta C/\Delta Yd)$, which by definition is the slope of the consumption line.

THE MULTIPLIED EFFECT OF CHANGES IN AUTONOMOUS AGGREGATE SPENDING

3.14   Suppose $I = \$70$; $C = \$60 + 0.80Yd$; $Yd = Y$. (*a*) Find the equilibrium level of income. (*b*) Find the equilibrium level of income when there is a \$10 increase in autonomous planned investment (planned investment increases from \$70 to \$80). (*c*) Establish the multiplier effect of the \$10 increase in autonomous spending.

(*a*)
$$Y = C + I$$
$$Y = \$60 + 0.80Y + \$70$$
$$Y - 0.80Y = \$130$$
$$Y = \frac{\$130}{0.20} = \$650$$

(*b*)
$$Y = C + I$$
$$Y = \$60 + 0.80Y = \$80$$
$$Y = \frac{\$140}{0.20} = \$700$$

(*c*)   The equilibrium level of income increases \$50 (from \$650 to \$700) as a result of a \$10 increase in investment. There is a multiplier effect of 5 (that is, $\Delta Y/\Delta \bar{I} = \$50/\$10 = 5$) as a result of the increase in autonomous investment.

3.15   Explain in terms of the saving-investment equality why the increase in the equilibrium level of income is greater than the increase in planned investment.

In a two-sector model, equilibrium income exists where planned saving equals planned investment. When investment increases, there is a shortage of planned saving at the initial income level. Income must increase until planned saving equals planned investment. Because only a portion of any increase in income is saved, income must increase by a multiple of the increase in investment to equate planned saving and planned investment.

3.16   Suppose the equilibrium condition is given by $Y = (\bar{C} + \bar{I})/(1 - c)$. (*a*) Letting $\bar{A}$ represent autonomous spending $(\bar{A} = \bar{C} + \bar{I})$, find an expression that relates income changes to changes in autonomous spending. (b) What is the change in the equilibrium level of income when $\Delta\bar{C} = -\$10$, $\Delta\bar{I} = +\$30$, and $c = 0.80$.

(a) Equilibrium income equals $\bar{A}/(1-c)$, where $\bar{A} = \bar{C} + \bar{I}$. It therefore follows that $\Delta Y = \Delta\bar{A}/(1-c)$.

(b) $\Delta\bar{A} = (-\$10 + \$30) = +\$20$. $\Delta Y = \$20/(1-0.80)$; $\Delta Y = \$100$.

THE MULTIPLIER

3.17 (a) Derive the multiplier when the MPC is 0.90, 0.80, 0.75 and 0.50. (b) What is the relationship between the marginal propensity to consume and the value of the multiplier? (c) Use the multiplier values found in (a) to establish what effect a $20 decrease in autonomous spending has upon equilibrium income.

(a) The multiplier k_e equals $1/(1-c)$; thus, k_e is 10 when the MPC is 0.90; 5 when MPC is 0.80; 4 when MPC is 0.75; and 2 when MPC is 0.50.

(b) There is a multiplier effect because consumption spending is related to the level of disposable income. Any change in income induces a change in aggregate consumption, with the magnitude of the change dependent on the value of the marginal propensity to consume. Thus, the value of the multiplier is directly related to the value of the marginal propensity to consume.

(c) The decline in income equals $\Delta\bar{I}(k_e)$. The decrease in equilibrium income is $200, $100, $80 and $40 for the four values of MPC, respectively.

3.18 Two spending functions are given in Fig. 3-13. In which one would the larger change in equilibrium income occur as a result of an change in autonomous spending?

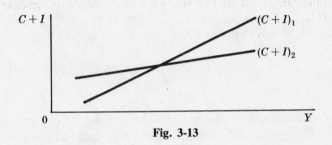

Fig. 3-13

$(C+I)_1$, since it is more steeply sloped and therefore has the larger marginal propensity to consume.

3.19 If investment falls $20 and the marginal propensity to consume is 0.60, what are (a) the change in the equilibrium level of income, (b) the change in autonomous spending and (c) the induced change in consumption spending?

(a) The change in the equilibrium level of income equals $k_e \Delta\bar{I}$. Since $k_e = 2.5$, $\Delta Y = -\$50$.

(b) The $20 decline in investment is the change in autonomous spending.

(c) The induced change in spending is the difference between the change in the level of income and the change in autonomous spending. That is $\Delta Y - \Delta\bar{I} = \Delta C$. Induced spending falls $30.

DYNAMIC MULTIPLIERS

3.20 (a) Explain the function $C_t = f(Yd_{t-1})$. (b) Differentiate between the static and dynamic multipliers.

40 PRIVATE SECTOR SPENDING MODEL [CHAP. 3

(a) The function $C_t = f(Yd_{t-1})$ indicates that consumption spending is a function of disposable income lagged by one period. That is, consumption is a function of disposable income, but disposable income received in period $t-1$ is not consumed until period t.

(b) The static multiplier establishes the change in the level of income from a change in autonomous spending, given no lag in induced spending. The dynamic multiplier establishes the change in the level of income for a specified number of periods, given a lag in induced spending.

3.21 The MPC c is equal to 0.90. Consumption is a function of disposable income lagged by one period. In period $t + 1$, there is a permanent $20 fall in investment. For periods $t + 1$ to $t + 3$, calculate (a) the decrease in the level of income and (b) the expenditure multiplier.

(a) For a one-period lag structure, the change in the level of income for each period is

$$\Delta Y_{t+1} = \Delta \bar{I}(1)$$
$$\Delta Y_{t+2} = \Delta \bar{I}(1 + c)$$
$$\Delta Y_{t+3} = \Delta \bar{I}(1 + c + c^2)$$
$$\Delta Y_{t+n} = \Delta \bar{I}(1 + c + c^2 + \cdots + c^{n-1})$$

Thus, the declines in income for periods $t + 1$ to $t + 3$ are

$$\Delta Y_{t+1} = -\$20$$
$$\Delta Y_{t+2} = -\$38$$
$$\Delta Y_{t+3} = -\$54.20$$

(b) The expenditure multiplier equals $\Delta Y / \Delta \bar{I}$. Thus,

for period $t + 1$, $\dfrac{\Delta Y}{\Delta \bar{I}} = -\$20/(-\$20) = 1$

for period $t + 2$, $\dfrac{\Delta Y}{\Delta \bar{I}} = -\$38/(-\$20) = 1.9 = 1 + c$

for perid $t + 3$, $\dfrac{\Delta Y}{\Delta \bar{I}} = -\$54.20/(-\$20) = 2.71 = 1 + c + c^2$

3.22 If consumption is a function of disposable income lagged by one period, derive the dynamic multiplier for four periods when the marginal propensity to consume is (a) 0.50, (b) 0.80 and (c) 0.90.

For four periods, k_{de} equals $1 + c + c^2 + c^3$. Thus,

(a) $k_{de} = 1 + 0.50 + 0.25 + 0.125 = 1.875$

(b) $k_{de} = 1 + 0.80 + 0.64 + 0.512 = 2.952$

(c) $k_{de} = 1 + 0.90 + 0.81 + 0.729 = 3.439$

3.23 Assume that consumption is a function of disposable income lagged by one period and that there is a permanent increase in investment. How many periods will it take to realize 50% of the eventual change in the level of income if the marginal propensity to consume is (a) 0.50? (b) 0.90?

(a) Since we want to determine 50% of the eventual change in the level of income, k_{de}/k_e must equal 0.5. $k_e = 1/(1 - \text{MPC}) = 2$. Since k_{de}/k_e must equal 0.5, k_{de} must have a value of 1. Time: one period.

(b) $k_e = 1/(1 - \text{MPC}) = 10$. Since k_{de}/k_e must equal 0.5, k_{de} must have a value of 5. Time: during the seventh period.

3.24 Suppose that the marginal propensity to consume c is 0.90 and investment increases \$10 in period $t+1$ and then returns to its previous level in $t+2$. Calculate the increase in the levels of income for periods $t+1$, $t+2$ and $t+3$.

Given a one-period lag structure, the changes in the level of income for a one period change in investment are

$$\Delta Y_{t+1} = \Delta \bar{I}(1) = \$10(1) = \$10.00$$
$$\Delta Y_{t+2} = \Delta \bar{I}(c) = \$10(0.90) = \$9.00$$
$$\Delta Y_{t+3} = \Delta \bar{I}(c^2) = \$10(0.81) = \$8.10$$

3.25 Assume that (1) the equilibrium level of income is currently \$500, (2) the marginal propensity to consume is 0.80 and (3) consumption is a function of disposable income lagged by one period (one period equals three months). (*a*) What permanent increase in investment is needed to bring the income level to \$559 within one year? (*b*) What is the eventual change in the equilibrium level of income?

(*a*) The dynamic multiplier for four periods is 2.95.

$$2.95 \, \Delta \bar{I} = \$59$$
$$\Delta \bar{I} = \$20$$

(*b*) The eventual change in the equilibrium level of income is \$100.

Chapter 4

A Four-Sector Spending Model

A government (federal, state and local) and an international sector are now added to the private sector model developed in Chapter 3. In addition to $(C + I)$ spending, aggregate output is now also affected by government sector spending, taxes and transfers and the import and export of goods and services.

4.1 GOVERNMENT EXPENDITURES, TRANSFERS AND TAXES

Government spending consists of the government sector's purchase of goods and services. Examples include payments to government employees and the military for their personal services and goods purchased to run government and the military. Transfers consist of government payments which involve no direct service by the recipient, such as unemployment insurance payments, interest on the public debt and welfare payments. Taxes are imposed upon property, goods (sales and excise taxes) and income to pay for expenditures and transfers.

4.2 GOVERNMENT SPENDING, TAXES, TRANSFERS AND AGGREGATE OUTPUT

Aggregate output rises when there are increases in government spending G and/or decreases in the government sector's net tax revenues Tn, *ceteris paribus*. (Net tax revenues equal gross tax revenues Tx less government transfers Tr.) Fiscal policy consists of changes in taxes, transfers and/or government spending to effect the level of aggregate output. In the following three-sector model, equilibrium occurs where $Y = C + I + G$ in the aggregate spending approach and $Tn + S = I + G$ in the saving/investment approach to aggregate output.

EXAMPLE 1. Aggregate output is Y_0 in the two-sector $(C + \bar{I})$ spending model in Fig. 4-1(a); the addition of a $\bar{G}$ level of government spending shifts the aggregate spending schedule from $(C + \bar{I})$ upward to $(C + \bar{I} + \bar{G})$ with equilibrium income increasing from Y_0 to Y_1. The saving/investment approach in Fig. 4-1(b) reaches the Y_1 output level when $\bar{G}$ government spending shifts the investment injection schedule $\bar{I}$ upward to $\bar{I} + \bar{G}$. Note that, in the absence of taxes to finance government spending, government spending of $\bar{G}$ is financed by private sector saving of $S_0 S_1$.

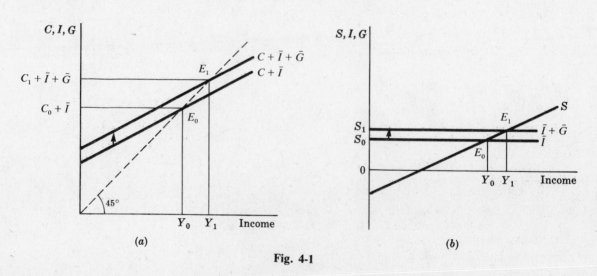

Fig. 4-1

42

EXAMPLE 2. Suppose autonomous tax revenues of $\bar{T}n$ are imposed to finance $\bar{G}$ government spending in Example 1. In Fig. 4-2(a) $\bar{T}n$ tax revenues shift the aggregate spending schedule downward to $C + \bar{I} + \bar{G} - c\bar{T}n$. Autonomous taxes reduce household disposable income which lowers consumption spending and therefore equilibrium income. But the reduction in equilibrium income from Y_1 to Y_2 leaves output above the initial equilibrium of Y_0 in the two-sector model. In Fig. 4-2(b) $\bar{T}n$ taxes appear as an increased leakage from the spending flow, which shift the leakage schedule upward from S to $(S + c\bar{T}n)$, reducing aggregate output from Y_1 to Y_2.

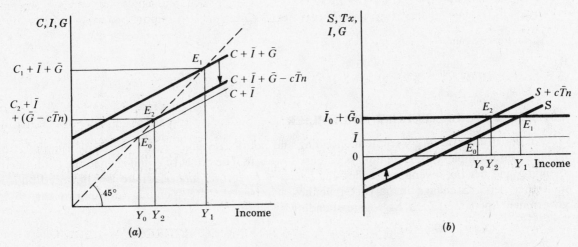

Fig. 4-2

EXAMPLE 3. Equilibrium income is $500 when $C = \$40 + 0.80Yd$ and $I = \$60$ in a two-sector model.

Situation I: Government spending of $10 is added to the model. There is no other parameter change.

The Spending Equation	The Saving/Investment Equation
$Y = C + I + G$	$S = I + G$
$Y = \$40 + 0.80Y + \$60 + 10$	$0.20Y - \$40 = \$60 + \$10$
$Y = 0.80Y + \$110$	$0.20Y = \$110$
$Y = \$550$	$Y = \$550$

The multiplier effect upon income from government spending is of the same magnitude as the effect from changes in autonomous investment.

Situation II: To equate government receipts and spending, $10 in taxes is added to the model. With taxes, $Yd = Y - Tx$.

The Spending Equation	The Saving/Investment Equation
$Y = C + I + G$	$S + Tx = I + G$
$Y = \$40 + 0.80(Y - 10) + \$60 + \$10$	$Y - \$10 - \$40 - 0.80(Y - \$10) + \$10 = \$60 + \$10$
$Y - 0.80Y = \$110 - \$8$	$Y - \$10 - \$40 - 0.80Y + \$8 + \$10 = \$60 + \$10$
$Y = \$510$	$0.20Y - \$32 = \$70$
	$Y = \$510$

A $10 increase in taxes lowers income by $40. Note that income falls by $40 when taxes are raised $10 while income increases $50 when government spending is increased $10.

EXAMPLE 4. An $X increase in transfers Tr or an $X decrease in taxes lowers net tax revenues $X, causing a similar effect upon the equilibrium level of income. The equilibrium level of income is $510 when $C = \$40 + 0.80Yd$, $I = \$60$, $G = \$10$, $Tr = 0$ and $Tx = \$10$, with $Yd = Y - Tx + Tr$. A $5 increase in transfers (Situation I) or a $5 decrease in taxes (Situation II) raises equilibrium output from $510 to $530.

Situation I: If the government increases transfers by $5, disposable income now equals $Y - Tx + Tr$ and

$$Y = C + I + G$$
$$Y = \$40 + 0.80(Y - \$10 + \$5) + \$60 + \$10$$
$$Y = \$530$$

Situation II: Now assume instead that taxes are reduced $5.

$$Y = C + I + G$$
$$Y = \$40 + 0.80(Y - \$5) + \$60 + \$10$$

so that once again

$$Y = \$530$$

4.3 THE BALANCED BUDGET MULTIPLIER

An equal increase in government spending and net tax revenues raises the equilibrium level of income (see Example 3), and an equal decrease lowers it. The effect of equal changes in government spending and net tax revenues is called *the balanced budget multiplier*. There is a balanced budget multiplier, since a change in net tax revenues affects aggregate spending less than a change in government spending affects aggregate spending.

4.4 GOVERNMENT SECTOR MULTIPLIERS

Once a government sector is added to the model, there are net tax revenue and balanced budget multipliers as well as an expenditure multiplier. These multipliers are presented in Example 5.

EXAMPLE 5. Given: $C = \bar{C} + cYd$, $Yd = Y - Tn$, $Tn = \bar{Tx} + \bar{Tr}$, $I = \bar{I}$, $G = \bar{G}$. For equilibrium

$$Y = C + I + G$$
$$Y = \bar{C} + c(Y - \bar{Tn}) + \bar{I} + \bar{G}$$
$$Y - cY = \bar{C} - c\bar{Tn} + \bar{I} + \bar{G}$$
$$Y = \frac{\bar{C} + \bar{I} + \bar{G} - c\bar{Tn}}{1 - c} \tag{4.1}$$

The Expenditure Multiplier. Assume a change in autonomous government spending of $\Delta\bar{G}$, *ceteris paribus*. The corresponding change in the equilibrium level of income is given by equation (*4.1*) as

$$\Delta Y = \frac{\Delta\bar{G}}{1 - c}$$

The expenditure multiplier k_e is then

$$k_e = \frac{\Delta Y}{\Delta\bar{G}} = \frac{1}{1 - c}$$

The Net Tax Revenue Multiplier. The change in the equilibrium level of income in equation (*4.1*) for a change in autonomous net tax revenues of $\Delta\bar{Tn}$ is

$$\Delta Y = \frac{-c\,\Delta\bar{Tn}}{1 - c}$$

The net tax revenue multiplier k_t is then

$$k_t = \frac{\Delta Y}{\Delta\bar{Tn}} = \frac{-c}{1 - c}$$

The Balanced Budget Multiplier.   Assuming equal changes in $\bar{G}$ and $\bar{Tn}$ (i.e., $\Delta\bar{G}=\Delta\bar{Tn}$), the change in the equilibrium level of income is

$$\Delta Y = \frac{\Delta\bar{G} - c\,\Delta\bar{Tn}}{1-c}$$

In assuming a balanced budget where $\Delta\bar{G}=\Delta\bar{Tn}$,

$$\Delta Y = \frac{\Delta\bar{G} - c\,\Delta\bar{G}}{1-c}$$

$$\Delta Y = \frac{\Delta\bar{G}(1-c)}{1-c}$$

$$\Delta Y = \Delta\bar{G}$$

Hence, the multiplier for equal changes in $\bar{G}$ and $\bar{Tn}$ is

$$k_b = \frac{\Delta Y}{\Delta\bar{G}} = 1$$

4.5   TAXES RELATED TO INCOME

Transfers, for the most part, are a fixed sum ($\bar{Tr}$) and thereby exogenous; the majority of U.S. tax revenue, however, is income related. Modeled, taxes equal $\bar{Tx} + tY$, where $\bar{Tx}$ represents an administered tax (such as property taxes) and t is a tax tied to earned income. It is customary to assume that t is unaffected by the income level; t therefore represents a proportional income tax. (When the tax structure is progressive, the value of t increases with Y.) The inclusion of an income tax in the model reduces the value of the expenditure and net tax revenue multipliers.

EXAMPLE 6.   When $C = \$40 + 0.80Yd$, $I = \$60$, $G = \$40$, $Yd = Y - Tn$, $Tn = \bar{Tx} + tY - \bar{Tr}$, $\bar{Tr} = 0$, $\bar{Tx} = 0$ and $t = 0.10$, the equilibrium level of income is \$500, and net tax revenues equal \$50. A \$20 increase in autonomous investment spending causes a multiplied effect upon income, raising the income level from \$500 to \$571.43; and net tax revenues increase from \$50 to \$57.14.

$$Y = C + I + G$$
$$Y = \$40 + 0.80(Y - 0.10Y) + \$80 + \$40$$
$$Y = \$571.43$$

When net tax revenues are unrelated to income and remain at \$50 ($t = 0$ and $\bar{Tn} = \$50$), a \$20 increase in autonomous investment raises equilibrium income from \$500 to \$600.

$$Y = C + I + G$$
$$Y = \$40 + 0.80(Y - \$50) + \$80 + \$40$$
$$Y = \$600$$

An income tax reduces the value of the multiplier. The \$20 increase in autonomous investment increases equilibrium income \$71.43 when there is an income tax rather than \$100 when taxes are autonomous.

4.6   MULTIPLIERS WHEN TAXES ARE RELATED TO INCOME

When tax revenues are linked to the income level, leakages from the spending flow are tied to the income level; the multiplier effect of changes in autonomous spending and net tax revenues upon equilibrium income is therefore smaller.

EXAMPLE 7.   Suppose $C = \bar{C} + cYd$, $Yd = Y - Tn$, $Tn = Tx - Tr$, $Tx = \bar{Tx} + tY$, $Tr = \bar{Tr}$, $I = \bar{I}$, $G = \bar{G}$. Equilibrium income is then

$$Y = C + I + G$$
$$Y = \bar{C} + c(Y - \bar{T}x - tY + \bar{T}r) + \bar{I} + \bar{G}$$
$$Y = \frac{\bar{C} + \bar{I} + \bar{G} - c\bar{T}x + c\bar{T}r}{1 - c + ct} \qquad (4.2)$$

The Expenditure Multiplier. Assume an change in autonomous $\bar{G}$. The change in the equilibrium level of income from equation (4.2) is

$$\Delta Y = \frac{\Delta \bar{G}}{1 - c + ct}$$

$$k_e = \frac{\Delta Y}{\Delta \bar{G}} = \frac{1}{1 - c + ct}$$

The Net Tax Revenue Multiplier. Assume an change in autonomous $\bar{T}n$ (which is the result of an autonomous change in $\bar{T}x$ or $\bar{T}r$). From equation (4.2), the change in the equilibrium level of income is

$$\Delta Y = \frac{-c \, \Delta \bar{T}n}{1 - c + ct}$$

$$k_t = \frac{\Delta Y}{\Delta \bar{T}n} = \frac{-c}{1 - c + ct}$$

The value of c and of t determine the size of the multiplier. In Fig. 4-3, a reduction in the income tax rate pivots the leakage schedule from $(S + Tn)'$ to $(S + Tn)''$ and reduces the slope of the saving leakage schedule. A decrease in induced saving, whether due to a reduction in the marginal propensity to save or to a reduction in income tax rates, results in an increase in the multiplier effect of autonomous spending. Thus, when government reduces income tax rates, there is a greater increase in the equilibrium level of income than there would be had autonomous net tax revenues been decreased by an equal amount. (See Example 8.)

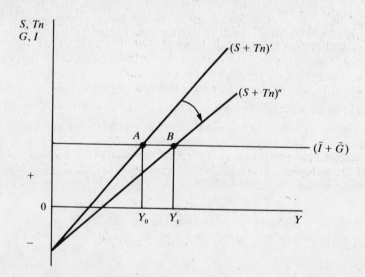

Fig. 4-3

EXAMPLE 8. When $C = \$40 + 0.80Yd$, $I = \$60$, $G = \$40$, $Yd = Y - \bar{T}x - tY + \bar{T}r$ with $\bar{T}x = \$50$, $\bar{T}r = \$50$ and $t = 0.10$, the equilibrium income level is \$500, and net tax revenues are \$50. A reduction in the income tax rate to 0.08 increases equilibrium income from \$500 to \$530.30; net tax revenues decline from \$50 [0.10(\$500)] to \$42.42

$$Y = C + I + G$$
$$Y = \$40 + 0.80(Y - \$50 + \$50 - 0.08Y) + \$60 + \$40$$
$$Y = \$530.30$$

A \$7.58 reduction in autonomous net tax revenues (a decrease in $\bar{T}x$ from \$50 to \$42.42 or an increase in $\bar{T}r$ from \$50 to \$57.58), increases equilibrium income from \$500 to \$521.66

$$Y = C + I + G$$
$$Y = \$40 + 0.80(Y - \$42.42 + \$50 - 0.1Y) + \$60 + \$40$$
$$Y = \$521.66$$

A decrease in the income tax rate increases the value of the expenditure multiplier; the lowered income tax rate has a greater stimulative effect upon equilibrium income than does an equal decrease in autonomous net tax revenue.

4.7 FISCAL POLICY AND *CETERIS PARIBUS*

So far, the results of various fiscal measures have been analyzed under the assumption of *ceteris paribus*. As we shall see in Chapter 6, other factors might change as a result of a fiscal action so that the fiscal measure is partially or totally offset by other parameter changes. It is important, therefore, to keep in mind the methodological observations of Section 1.4. Simple models allow us to analyze *with precision* the result of a single parameter change. Whether we can approximate reality with this model depends on the importance of and possible change in other factors.

4.8 NET EXPORTS AND AGGREGATE OUTPUT

A country exports domestic goods and services and imports foreign-made goods and services; its net export balance is the sum of gross exports minus gross imports. Gross exports are exogenous, largely determined by the level of income in foreign countries. Imports are autonomous or tied to the level of income. A country's net export balance X can be presented as $X = \bar{X} - xY$, where $\bar{X}$ represents autonomous net exports (autonomous exports less autonomous imports) and x is the domestic economy's marginal propensity to import. Variable x represents a leakage from the domestic spending flow; its inclusion in the model has the same effect upon the value of the multipliers and the leakage schedule's location in space as does an income tax. (See Examples 7 and 10.)

EXAMPLE 9. The marginal propensity to import x represents a leakage from the domestic spending flow which reduces the value of the multipliers. Suppose $C = \bar{C} + cYd$, $I = \bar{I}$, $G = \bar{G}$, $X = \bar{X} - xY$, $Yd = Y - (\bar{T}x + tY - \bar{T}r)$. Equilibrium income is then

$$Y = \frac{\bar{C} + \bar{I} + \bar{G} + \bar{X} - c\bar{T}x + c\bar{T}r}{1 - c + ct + x}$$

For autonomous changes in $\bar{C}$, $\bar{I}$, $\bar{G}$, and $\bar{X}$, the expenditure multiplier is

$$k_e = \frac{1}{1 - c + ct + x}$$

For autonomous changes in $\bar{T}r$ and $\bar{T}x$, the net tax revenue multiplier is

$$k_t = \frac{-c}{1 - c + ct + x}$$

The income tax t and marginal propensity to import x appear in the denominator with a positive sign; behavioral coefficients which appear in the denominator of the multiplier equations with a positive sign reduce the value of the multipliers.

EXAMPLE 10. The expenditure multiplier from Example 9 is $k_e = 1/(1 - c + ct + x)$. When $c = 0.75$, $t = 0.20$ and $x = 0$, the value for the expenditure multiplier is 2.5. The value for the expenditure multiplier is 2 when $c = 0.75$, $t = 0.20$ and $x = 0.10$. Thus, an increase in the marginal propensity to import reduces the multiplied effect that changes in autonomous variables have upon equilibrium income.

Review Questions

1. Which of the following will not result in an increase in the level of income?

    (a) An increase in autonomous spending

    (b) A decrease in autonomous taxes

    (c) An increase in autonomous transfers

    (d) An increase in net tax revenues

    Answer: (d)

2. An increase in autonomous net tax revenues, *ceteris paribus*, causes the

    (a) Aggregate spending schedule to shift upward by $c\Delta \bar{T}n$.

    (b) Aggregate spending schedule to shift downward by $c\Delta \bar{T}n$.

    (c) Leakage schedule to shift downward by $c\Delta \bar{T}n$.

    (d) Leakage schedule to shift downward by $\Delta \bar{T}n$.

    Answer: (b)

3. When there is an increase in autonomous taxes and government spending, *ceteris paribus*, then

    (a) The $(S + Tn)$ schedule shifts upward, and $(\bar{I} + \bar{G})$ schedule shifts upward.

    (b) The $(S + Tn)$ schedule shifts downward, and the $(\bar{I} + \bar{G})$ schedule shifts downward.

    (c) The $(S + Tn)$ schedule shifts downward, and the $(\bar{I} + \bar{G})$ schedule shifts upward.

    (d) The $(S + Tn)$ schedule shifts upward, and the $(\bar{I} + \bar{G})$ schedule shifts downward.

    Answer: (a)

4. Where there is an equal increase in net tax revenues and government spending, *ceteris paribus*,

    (a) $(C + I + G)$ is shifting upward.

    (b) $(C + I + G)$ is shifting downward.

    (c) $(C + I + G)$ does not shift.

    Answer: (a)

5. Which of the following statements is incorrect? (Assume all spending but consumption is exogenous.)

    (a) k_e is 4 when the MPC is 0.75.

    (b) k_t is -3 when the MPC is 0.75.

    (c) k_t is 2 when the MPC is 0.50.

    (d) k_b is 1 when the MPC is 0.50.

    Answer: (c)

6. When an increase in government spending is matched by an equal decrease in government transfers, the income level will

(a) Stay the same

(b) Increase

(c) Decrease

Answer: (b)

7.   *Ceteris paribus*, an income tax

(a) Increases the value of the expenditure and net tax revenue multiplier

(b) Increases the value of the expenditure multiplier and decreases the value of the net tax revenue multiplier

(c) Decreases the value of the expenditure and net tax revenue multiplier

(d) Decreases the value of the expenditure multiplier and increases the value of the net tax revenue multiplier

Answer: (c)

8.   Given a proportional income tax and a government budget that is currently in balance, an increase in autonomous investment, *ceteris paribus*, increases equilibrium income, and the budget

(a) Remains in balance

(b) Has a surplus

(c) Has a deficit

Answer: (b)

9.   Suppose the net export function is $X = \bar{X} - xY$ and the net export balance is zero. An increase in autonomous investment spending will

(a) Increase the net export balance and the income level

(b) Increase the income level but make the net export balance negative

(c) Increase the income level and have no effect upon the net export balance

(d) Have no effect upon the income level but cause the net export balance to become negative

Answer: (b)

10. An increase in the marginal propensity to import

(a) Has the same effect upon the multipliers as an increase in the MPC

(b) Has no effect upon the multipliers

(c) Increases the value of the multipliers

(d) Decreases the value of the multipliers

Answer: (d)

Solved Problems

GOVERNMENT SPENDING, TAXES, TRANSFERS AND AGGREGATE OUTPUT

4.1   Find the magnitude of the shift of the aggregate spending schedule D_0 in Fig. 4-4 as a result of the following events (assume that the MPC is 0.80): (a) There is a $10 decrease in autonomous government spending. (b) There is a $10 increase in autonomous taxes. (c) There is a $10 increase in autonomous government transfers.

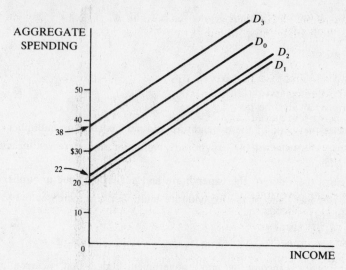

Fig. 4-4

(a) The aggregate spending schedule shifts downward $10 to D_1.

(b) In the consumption equation $C = \bar{C} + c(Y - \bar{T}x + \bar{T}r)$, the impact of tax and transfer changes upon autonomous spending is modified by c, the marginal propensity to consume. For a $10 increase in autonomous taxes there is an $8 [0.8($10)] downward shift of the aggregate demand schedule to D_2.

(c) The aggregate spending schedule shifts upward $8 to D_3.

4.2 Given $C = \$20 + 0.80Yd$, $I = \$50$, $G = \$20$, $Yd = Y - Tn$, $Tn = \bar{T}x - \bar{T}r$, $\bar{T}r = 0$ and $\bar{T}x = \$10$. (a) Find equilibrium income. (b) Find consumption and saving at the equilibrium level of income. (c) Show the equality of leakages and injections from the spending flow at equilibrium. (d) How is the $20 government expenditure financed?

(a)
$$Y = \$20 + 0.80(Y - \$10) + \$50 + \$20$$
$$Y = \$410$$

(b) When $Y = \$410$, $C = \$20 + 0.80(\$410 - \$10)$; $C = \$340$. $S = Y - C - Tn$. $S = \$410 - \$340 - \$10 = \$60$.

(c) Leakages consist of $(Tn + S)$ while investment injections equal $(I + G)$. Thus, $Tn + S = I + G$; $\$10 + \$60 = \$50 + \$20$.

(d) The $20 government expenditure is financed by $10 from tax revenues and $10 borrowed from household saving.

4.3 Recalculate equilibrium income for Problem 4.2 when (a) net tax revenues are increased $10 or (b) government spending is reduced $10 to balance the federal budget. (c) Does a change in autonomous net tax revenues or in autonomous government spending have a similar effect upon aggregate output?

(a) When autonomous net tax revenues increase $10,
$$Y = \$20 + 0.80(Y - \$20) + \$50 + \$20$$
$$Y = \$370$$

(b) When autonomous government spending is reduced $10,
$$Y = \$20 + 0.80(Y - \$10) + \$50 + \$10$$
$$Y = \$360$$

(c)　In bringing the federal budget into balance, the $10 decrease in government spending has a larger impact upon equilibrium income than the $10 increase in net tax revenues.

4.4　Why does a $10 increase in autonomous taxes have the same effect on equilibrium income as does a $10 decrease in autonomous transfers?

A $10 increase in autonomous taxes, *ceteris paribus*, increases net tax revenues $10 ($Tn = \bar{T}x - \bar{T}r$) as does a $10 decrease in autonomous transfers. Since each of the measures has the same effect upon net tax revenues, each measure must have the same effect upon equilibrium income.

4.5　Suppose a local government unit increases expenditures $50, funding these expenditures by a bond issue. Households in this locality, knowing that they eventually must repay the amount borrowed by the local government unit, increase saving $50. (*a*) Has the MPC or autonomous consumption changed? (*b*) What impact does the addition of $50 in local government spending have on equilibrium income? Assume a 0.90 marginal propensity to consume.

(*a*)　A change in saving indicates a shift of the aggregate saving function; there has been a change in autonomous consumption (the constant of the consumption equation has changed).

(*b*)　The $50 decrease in autonomous consumption is equal to the $50 increase in G so that there is no change in the level of income.

THE BALANCED BUDGET MULTIPLIER

4.6　Equilibrium income is $430 when $C = \$20 + 0.80(Y - Tn)$, $I = \$60$, $Tn = Tx - Tr$, $Tx = \$40$, $Tr = \$10$, and $G = \$30$. (*a*) Find equilibrium income when G increases from $30 to $40, *ceteris paribus*. (*b*) Find equilibrium income when Tx increases from $40 to $50, *ceteris paribus*. (*c*) Find equilibrium income when G increases from $30 to $40 and Tx increases from $40 to $50, *ceteris paribus*. (*d*) Compare the change in equilibrium income calculated in (*a*), (*b*) and (*c*).

(*a*)　　　　　　　　　　$Y = \$20 + 0.80(Y - \$40 + \$10) + \$60 + \$40$
　　　　　　　　　　　　$Y = \$480$

(*b*)　　　　　　　　　　$Y = \$20 + 0.80(Y - \$50 + \$10) + \$60 + \$30$
　　　　　　　　　　　　$Y = \$390$

(*c*)　　　　　　　　　　$Y = \$20 + 0.80(Y - \$50 + \$10) + \$60 + \$40$
　　　　　　　　　　　　$Y = \$440$

(*d*)　Equilibrium income is initially $430. The $10 increase in government spending (*a*) raises equilibrium income $50 to $480; the $10 increase in taxes in (*b*) lowers equilibrium income $40 to $390; whereas the $10 increase in both G and Tx in (*c*) raises equilibrium income $10 to $440.

4.7　Why does an equal increase in $\bar{G}$ and $\bar{T}x$ raise equilibrium income by the increase in the level of government spending and net tax revenues?

In the consumption equation $C = \bar{C} + c(Y - \bar{T}n)$, a change in taxes affects disposable income by the change in taxes but consumption spending by $c(\Delta Yd)$. Hence, a $10 increase in taxes reduces disposable income $10 but causes an initial reduction in consumption of $c(\$10)$, making the increase in autonomous taxes equal to a decrease in autonomous spending of less than $10. A change in autonomous government spending has a full, direct effect on spending. Therefore, an equal increase in $\bar{G}$ and $\bar{T}x$ means that the effect on equilibrium income of increased $\bar{G}$ is greater than the effect of increased $\bar{T}x$.

GOVERNMENT SECTOR MULTIPLIERS

4.8   Given $C = \bar{C} + cYd$, $Yd = Y - Tn$, $Tn = \bar{T}x - \bar{T}r$, $I = \bar{I}$, and $G = \bar{G}$. (a) Find the equilibrium level of income. (b) Find an expression for ΔY that results from changes in the autonomous variables. (c) Find ΔY when $\Delta \bar{G} > 0$, *ceteris paribus*. (d) Find an expression for the multiple effect of $\Delta \bar{G}$ upon ΔY ($\Delta Y/\Delta \bar{G}$) and label the equation k_e. (e) Find ΔY when $\Delta \bar{C} > 0$ or $\Delta \bar{I} > 0$. What is the multiplying effect of changes in autonomous spending variables $\bar{C}$, $\bar{I}$ and $\bar{G}$ upon equilibrium income?

(a)
$$Y = \bar{C} + c(Y - \bar{T}n) + \bar{I} + \bar{G}$$
$$Y - cY = \bar{C} - c\bar{T}n + \bar{I} + \bar{G}$$
$$Y = \frac{\bar{C} + \bar{I} + \bar{G} - c\bar{T}n}{1 - c}$$

(b)   The autonomous variables are $\bar{C}$, $\bar{I}$, $\bar{T}n$ and $\bar{G}$. Thus,
$$\Delta Y = \frac{\Delta \bar{C} + \Delta \bar{I} + \Delta \bar{G} - c\,\Delta \bar{T}n}{1 - c}$$

(c)   Assuming $\bar{C}$, $\bar{I}$ and $\bar{T}n$ are constant and $\Delta \bar{G} > 0$, we have
$$\Delta Y = \frac{\Delta \bar{G}}{1 - c}$$

(d)   Given $\Delta Y = \Delta \bar{G}/(1 - c)$, dividing both sides of the equation by $\Delta \bar{G}$ we obtain $\Delta Y/\Delta \bar{G} = 1/(1 - c)$—an expression for the change in income due to a change in government spending. Hence,
$$\frac{\Delta Y}{\Delta \bar{G}} = \frac{1}{1 - c} \qquad k_e = \frac{1}{1 - c}$$

(e)   When $\Delta \bar{C} > 0$, $\Delta Y = \Delta \bar{C}/(1 - c)$. $\Delta Y = \Delta \bar{I}/(1 - c)$ when $\Delta \bar{I} > 0$. Hence, changes in autonomous spending variables $\bar{C}$, $\bar{I}$ and $\bar{G}$ have the same k_e multiplier effect on equilibrium income.

4.9   (a) Using the equation $\Delta Y = (\Delta \bar{C} + \Delta \bar{I} + \Delta \bar{G} - c\,\Delta \bar{T}n)/(1 - c)$, derived in Problem 4.8(b), find an expression for ΔY when $\Delta \bar{T}n > 0$, *ceteris paribus*. (b) Find an expression for the multiplier effect of a change in net tax revenues upon equilibrium income and label the equation k_t. (c) Why is the net tax revenue multiplier negative? (d) Do increases in $\bar{T}r$ and $\bar{T}x$ have a negative or positive effect upon $\bar{T}n$? Therefore what effect should increases in $\bar{T}r$ and $\bar{T}x$ have upon equilibrium income?

(a)
$$\Delta Y = \frac{-c\,\Delta \bar{T}n}{1 - c}$$

(b)   Dividing both sides of the equation in part (a) by $\Delta \bar{T}n$, we have
$$\frac{\Delta Y}{\Delta \bar{T}n} = \frac{-c}{1 - c} \qquad k_t = \frac{-c}{1 - c}$$

(c)   An increase in autonomous net tax revenues reduces household sector disposable income, which lowers consumption spending and therefore output. Thus, an increase in autonomous net tax revenues, *ceteris paribus*, has a negative effect upon equilibrium income.

(d)   Since $\bar{T}n = \bar{T}x - \bar{T}r$, increases in $\bar{T}r$ reduces $\bar{T}n$ while increases in $\bar{T}x$ raises $\bar{T}n$. Thus, an increase in autonomous transfers has a positive effect on equilibrium income, and an increase in autonomous taxes has a negative effect.

4.10   (a) Using the equation $\Delta Y = (\Delta \bar{C} + \Delta \bar{I} + \Delta \bar{G} - c\,\Delta \bar{T}n)/(1 - c)$ derived in Problem 4.8(a), find ΔY when $\Delta \bar{G}$ equals $\Delta \bar{T}n$. (b) Find the multiplier for equal changes in $\bar{G}$ and $\bar{T}n$?

(a)
$$\Delta Y = \frac{\Delta \bar{G} - c\,\Delta \bar{T}n}{1 - c}$$

Since $\Delta \bar{G} = \Delta \bar{T}n$, substituting we have

$$Y = \frac{\Delta \bar{G} - c \Delta \bar{G}}{1 - c} \qquad \text{or} \qquad \Delta Y = \frac{\Delta \bar{G}(1 - c)}{1 - c}$$

and with $(1 - c)/(1 - c) = 1$, $\Delta Y = \Delta \bar{G}$.

(b) Since $\Delta Y / \Delta \bar{G} = 1$, equal changes in $\bar{G}$ and $\bar{T}n$ impact equilibrium income by $\Delta \bar{G}$, i.e., the balanced budget multiplier k_b is 1.

4.11 (a) Find k_e, k_t and k_b when c (the marginal propensity to consume) is 0.80. (b) Find ΔY for the following changes in autonomous variables and then rank each proposal (largest to smallest) in terms of effect upon equilibrium income: net tax receipts decrease $10; government spending increases $10; government spending and net tax revenues increase $10.

(a) The expenditure multiplier k_e is 5, that is, $k_e = 1/(1 - c)$; $k_e = 1/(1 - 0.80) = 5$. The net tax revenue multiplier k_t is -4, that is, $k_t = -c/(1 - c)$; $k_t = -0.80/(1 - 0.80) = -4$. The balanced budget multiplier k_b is 1.

(b) When net tax revenues are reduced $10, $\Delta Y = k_t \Delta \bar{T}n$ or $\Delta Y = -4(-\$10) = \$40$. When government spending increases $10, $\Delta Y = k_e \Delta \bar{G}$ or $\Delta Y = 5(\$10) = \$50$. And when government spending and net tax revenues increase $10, $\Delta Y = \$10$. The $10 increase in government spending has the larger effect upon equilibrium income followed by the $10 decrease in net tax revenues; the $10 increase in government spending and taxes has the smallest effect.

4.12 Suppose full employment occurs at a $600 level of income, equilibrium income is currently $500, and the MPC is 0.80. What is the necessary change in (a) government spending, (b) net tax revenues, and (c) net tax revenues and government spending when the government is committed to a balanced budget to bring the economy to full employment?

(a) The necessary change in Y is $+\$100$. With $k_e = 5$, government spending must increase $20: $\Delta Y = k_e \Delta \bar{G}$; $\$100 = 5 \Delta \bar{G}$; $\Delta \bar{G} = \$20$.

(b) $k_t = -4$. The necessary decrease in net tax revenues is $25: $\Delta Y = k_t \Delta \bar{T}n$; $\$100 = -4(\Delta \bar{T}n)$; $\Delta \bar{T}n = -\$25$.

(c) $k_b = 1$. The necessary increase in net tax revenues and government spending is $100.

4.13 Government plans to increase expenditures $15 in a full employment economy. Equilibrium income is currently $500, the marginal propensity to consume is 0.75 and net tax revenues are autonomous. What tax increase is needed to avoid excessive aggregate spending and thereby maintain price stability?

To remain at the $500 level of income ($\Delta Y = 0$), the stimulative effect of increased government spending must be completely offset by increased tax revenues. Thus, $k_e \Delta \bar{G} - k_t \Delta \bar{T}n = 0$. Since $k_e = 4$ and $k_t = -3$, $\Delta \bar{G} = \$15$ and $\Delta \bar{T}n = \$20$, that is, $4(\$15) - (-3)\$20 = 0$. Tax revenues must increase $20.

4.14 The economy is currently at full employment. If the government decreases its level of spending but does not want this policy to be deflationary, what reduction in autonomous net tax revenues is necessary for the economy to remain at full employment?

The equilibrium condition is given by

$$Y = \frac{\bar{C} + \bar{I} + \bar{G} - c\bar{T}n}{1 - c}$$

Assuming an equal reduction in $\bar{G}$ and $\bar{T}n$, ceteris paribus (i.e., $\Delta \bar{C}$ and $\Delta \bar{I} = 0$), we have

$$0 = \frac{\Delta \bar{G} - c \, \Delta \bar{T}n}{1 - c}$$

$$\Delta \bar{G} = c \, \Delta \bar{T}n$$

$$\frac{\Delta G}{c} = \Delta \bar{T}n = \text{the necessary decrease in taxes}$$

TAXES RELATED TO INCOME

4.15 In Fig. 4-5 equilibrium income exists at Y_0, the intersection of the leakage schedule $(S + Tn)$ and the injection schedule $(\bar{I} + \bar{G})$. Use Fig. 4-5 to show and explain the effect that a decrease in autonomous net tax revenues and a decrease in income tax rates have upon the leakage schedule and the equilibrium level of income. (b) What is the change in leakages at the initial equilibrium income level Y_0 as a result of the decrease in autonomous net tax revenues and the reduction in income taxes? (c) What is the new equilibrium level of income as a result of the decrease in autonomous net tax revenues and the reduction in income taxes?

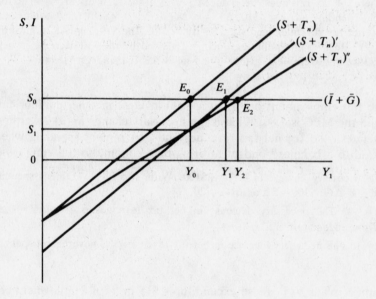

Fig. 4-5

(a) A decrease in autonomous net tax revenues shifts the leakage schedule rightward, for example, to $(S + Tn)'$. (Recall that a change in an autonomous variable causes a parallel shift in a schedule.) A reduction in income taxes reduces the slope of the leakage schedule and pivots it rightward to $(S + Tn)''$; there are smaller leakages associated with an income tax reduction for income levels above Y_0.

(b) There is a decrease in leakages of $S_0 S_1$ at income level Y_0 when the leakage schedule shifts rightward from $(S + Tn)$ to $(S + Tn)'$ or to $(S + Tn)''$.

(c) The new equilibrium resulting from the $(S + Tn)'$ shift is Y_1. It is Y_2 for the $(S + Tn)''$ shift. The $S_0 S_1$ reduction in income taxes at income level Y_0 has a larger stimulative effect upon equilibrium income than does the $S_0 S_1$ decrease in autonomous taxes.

4.16 Suppose $C = \$35 + 0.80 Yd$, $I = \$70$, $G = \$65$, $Tn = 0.10Y$. (a) Find the equilibrium level of income. (b) What are net tax revenues at equilibrium income? Does the government have a balanced budget? (c) Find equilibrium income when investment increases from $70 to $90. (d) What has happened to the relationship of government spending and tax revenues? Why?

(a)
$$Y = \$35 + 0.80(Y - 0.10Y) + \$70 + \$65$$
$$Y = \$607.14$$

(b) Tax revenues are $0.10(\$607.14) = \$60.71$. Government expenditures of $65 exceed the $60.71 in net tax revenues; there is a $4.29 deficit.

(c)
$$Y = \$35 + 0.80(Y - 0.10Y) + \$90 + \$65$$
$$Y = \$678.57$$

(d) Tax revenues have increased to $67.86. There is now a budget surplus of $2.86, which has resulted from higher tax revenues generated by a higher income level.

MULTIPLIERS WHEN TAXES ARE RELATED TO INCOME

4.17 When $C = \bar{C} + cYd$, $Yd = Y - Tn$, $Tn = \bar{Tx} - \bar{Tr}$, $I = \bar{I}$, and $G = \bar{G}$, equilibrium income is given by the equation $Y = (\bar{C} + \bar{I} + \bar{G} - c\bar{Tn}/(1 - c))$. The expenditure multiplier k_e equals $1/(1 - c)$, and the net tax revenue multiplier k_t is $-c/(1 - c)$. (a) Find the equation for equilibrium income when $Tn = \bar{Tx} + tY - \bar{Tr}$ rather than $Tn = \bar{Tx} + \bar{Tr}$. (b) Derive k_e and k_t for changes in autonomous spending and autonomous net tax revenues for the equilibrium condition found in part (a).

(a)
$$Y = \bar{C} + c(Y - \bar{Tx} - tY + \bar{Tr}) + \bar{I} + \bar{G}$$
$$Y - cY + ctY = \bar{C} - c\bar{Tx} - c\bar{Tr} + \bar{I} + \bar{G}$$
$$Y = \frac{\bar{C} + \bar{I} + \bar{G} - c\bar{Tx} + c\bar{Tr}}{1 - c + ct}$$

(b) For a change in $\bar{C}$ ($\bar{I}$ or $\bar{G}$), the change in income is specified as
$$\Delta Y = \frac{\Delta\bar{C}}{1 - c + ct}$$

and the expenditure multiplier is
$$\frac{\Delta Y}{\Delta\bar{C}} = \frac{1}{1 - c + ct}$$
$$k_e = \frac{1}{1 - c + ct}$$

For changes in autonomous taxes or autonomous transfers, the change in income is
$$Y = \frac{-c\,\Delta\bar{Tn}}{1 - c + ct}$$

and the net tax revenue multiplier is
$$k_t = \frac{-c}{1 - c + ct}$$

4.18 (a) Suppose the maringal propensity to consume is 0.75 and net tax revenues are unrelated to income. Find the change in the equilibrium level of income for the following autonomous changes: government spending increases $10, taxes increase $15 and transfers decrease $10. (b) Suppose the marginal propensity to consume is 0.75 and there is a 20% proportional income tax. Find the change in the equilibrium level of income for the following autonomous changes: government spending increases $10, taxes increase $15 and transfers decrease $10.

(a) The expenditure multiplier is 4 or $k_e = 1/(1 - 0.75)$, whereas the net tax revenue multiplier is -3 or $k_t = -0.75/(1 - 0.75)$. The change in income is found by solving the equation $\Delta Y = k_e\,\Delta\bar{G}$ for changes in autonomous government spending and $\Delta Y = k_t \Delta \bar{T}n$ for changes in autonomous net tax revenues. Equilibrium income increases \$40 for the \$10 increase in autonomous government spending; equilibrium income decreases \$45 for the \$15 increase in autonomous taxes and increases \$30 for the \$10 increase in autonomous transfers.

(b) The expenditure multiplier is $k_e = 1/[1 - 0.75 + (0.20)0.75] = 2.5$, whereas the net tax revenue multiplier is $k_t = -0.75/[1 - 0.75 + (0.20)0.75] = -1.875$. Equilibrium income increases \$25 for a \$10 increase in government spending, decreases \$28.125 for the \$15 increase in autonomous taxes and increases \$18.75 for the \$10 increase in transfers.

4.19 (a) Why do income taxes reduce the value of the multipliers? (b) Why is an income tax considered a "built-in" stabilizer?

(a) The multiplier derives its value from induced expenditures (i.e., induced consumption). When taxes depend on income, there is less induced consumption for each income level change, since the change in disposable income no longer equals the change in output.

(b) An income tax is an automatic or built-in stabilizer, since tax revenues change with the level of income. Thus, as the economy expands, more taxes are collected, dampening the expansion; as the economy contracts, tax receipts automatically fall, slowing the contraction.

NET EXPORTS AND AGGREGATE OUTPUT

4.20 Schedule $(S + Tn)$ in Fig. 4-6 represents leakages due to household saving, government net tax revenues and induced imports (x, the marginal propensity to import), whereas $I + G + X$ represents injections due to investment spending, government spending and autonomous net exports. What happens to the leakage and injection schedules and the equilibrium level of income when (a) induced imports increase, *ceteris paribus*, (b) autonomous net exports increase, *ceteris paribus*?

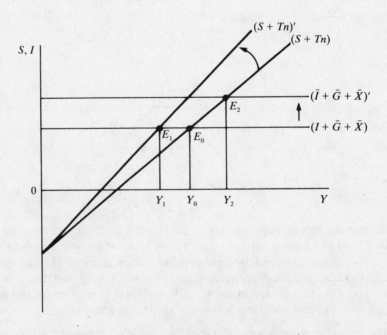

Fig. 4-6

(a) An increase in induced imports (the marginal propensity to import) means that for a given income level, a country is importing more goods and services and buying less from domestic producers. This increased leakage shifts the leakage schedule upward to $(S + Tn)'$, which reduces the equilibrium level of income from the initial Y_0 level to Y_1.

(b) An increase in autonomous net exports means that domestic producers have increased foreign sales and/or autonomous imports have decreased. Increased demand for U.S.-made goods shifts the injections schedule upward to $(I + G + X)'$ which raises the equilibrium level of income from the initial Y_0 position to Y_2.

4.21 Suppose $C = \$30 + 0.80Yd$, $Tn = \$50$, $I = \$60$, $G = \$50$ and $X = \$50 - 0.05Y$. (a) Find the equilibrium level of income. (b) Find the net export balance at the equilibrium level of income. (c) What happens to equilibrium income and the net export balance when investment increases from \$60 to \$70? (d) What happens to equilibrium income and the net export balance when the net export function changes from $\$50 - 0.05Y$ to $\$40 - 0.05Y$? (e) Which has the greater effect upon an economy's net export balance: a change in autonomous domestic spending or a change in autonomous net exports?

(a)
$$Y = \$30 + 0.80(Y - \$50) + \$60 + \$50 + \$50 - 0.05Y$$
$$Y = \$600$$

(b) At equilibrium, the net export balance is $X = \$50 - 0.05(\$600) = \$20$.

(c) Equilibrium income increases from \$600 [part (a)] to \$640 with the net export balance decreasing from \$20 to \$18.

(d) Equilibrium income decreases from its initial \$600 level [part (a)] to \$560; the net export balance decreases from \$20 to \$12.

(e) A \$10 change in autonomous investment or in autonomous net exports has a \$40 effect on equilibrium income; however, the change in autonomous net exports has the larger effect on the net export balance.

4.22 Given $C = \bar{C} + cYd$, $Tn = \bar{T}x + tY - \bar{T}r$, $I = \bar{I}$, $G = \bar{G}$, $X = \bar{X} - xY$. (a) Find an equation for equilibrium income. (b) Find the expenditure multiplier and the net tax revenue multiplier. (c) What effect does an import function and an income tax have on the expenditure and net tax revenue multipliers?

(a)
$$Y = \bar{C} + c(Y - \bar{T}x - tY + \bar{T}r) + \bar{I} + \bar{G} + \bar{X} - xY$$

$$Y = \frac{\bar{C} + \bar{I} + \bar{G} + \bar{X} - c\bar{T}x + c\bar{T}r}{1 - c + ct + x}$$

(b) Solving for $\Delta\bar{C}$ (or $\Delta\bar{I}$, or $\Delta\bar{G}$, or $\Delta\bar{X}$), *ceteris paribus*, we have

$$\Delta Y = \frac{\Delta\bar{C}}{1 - c + ct + x}$$

and the expenditure multiplier is

$$k_e = \frac{1}{1 - c + ct + x}$$

Solving for $\Delta\bar{T}x$ we have

$$\Delta\bar{Y} = \frac{-c\,\Delta\bar{T}x}{1 - c + ct + x}$$

and the net tax revenue multiplier is

$$k_t = \frac{-c}{1 - c + ct + x}$$

(c) The import function and an income tax are induced leakages which reduce the value of the multipliers.

Chapter 5

The *IS-LM* Framework

5.1 INTRODUCTION

This chapter develops schedules for equilibrium in the goods (*IS*) and money (*LM*) markets, an *IS-LM* framework which is the core of macroeconomic demand theory. An *IS* schedule is derived from the spending equilibrium models developed in Chapters 3 and 4 but differs in that investment spending is related to the rate of interest. The dependency of investment upon the rate of interest results in a distinct equilibrium income for each rate of interest so that there exists a schedule of equilibrium income for the goods market—an *IS* schedule. Money and the rate of interest necessitate a modeling of portfolio choice. Monetary equilibrium exists when the demand for money equals the supply of money. When the demand for money is related to the rate of interest, there exists a schedule of equilibrium in the money market—an *LM* schedule. The rate of interest and equilibrium income are jointly determined by the goods *IS* and money *LM* markets.

5.2 INVESTMENT AND THE RATE OF INTEREST

Firms invest in plant and equipment as long as they increase profits; thus, firms acquire real capital as long as the rate of return R on capital additions or replacements exceeds the cost of funds i, the rate of interest. An aggregate investment demand schedule is presented in Fig. 5-1 with investment proposals ranked in descending order of rate of return and variables other than the rate of interest held constant. From Fig. 5-1, we find that investment is \$40 when the rate of interest is 10%, \$52 when the rate of interest is 8%, \$64 when it is 6%, and \$76 when it is 4%. When investment has a negative, linear relationship to the rate of interest, investment spending can be presented as $I = \bar{I} - bi$, where $\bar{I}$ represents autonomous investment and b is a behavioral coefficient measuring the sensitivity of investment spending to the rate of interest.

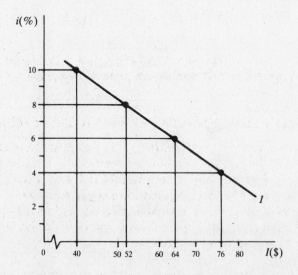

Fig. 5-1

EXAMPLE 1. Suppose planned investment is specified by the equation $I = \bar{I} - bi$. $I = \$100 - 5i$ when $\bar{I} = \$100$ and b is 5. Planned investment is $50 when the rate of interest is 10% [$I = \$100 - 5(10)$], $60 when the rate of interest is 8% and $70 when it is 6%. This relationship of investment and the rate of interest is plotted in Fig. 5-2 with the resulting schedule labeled I. The investment equation is $\$120 - 5i$ when autonomous investment increases from $100 to $120. Now a 10%, 8% and 6% rate of interest is associated with investment levels of $70, $80, and $90; these data are plotted in Fig. 5-2 and the schedule is labeled I'.

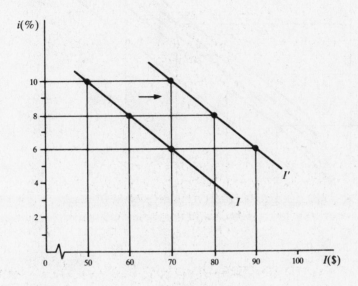

Fig. 5-2

5.3 THE *IS* SCHEDULE FOR A TWO-SECTOR MODEL

In the two-sector model of Chapter 3, equilibrium income occurs where planned saving equals planned investment or, equivalently, where the value of output equals planned spending. Thus, when $C = \bar{C} + cY$ and $I = \bar{I}$, equilibrium income occurs where

$$Y = \frac{\bar{C} + \bar{I}}{1 - c}$$

In the preceding model, investment spending is exogenous (i.e., determined by forces outside the model). When we specify investment spending as $I = \bar{I} - bi$, $\bar{I}$ represents the effect of outside forces upon investment spending, and b relates investment spending to the rate of interest. Equilibrium income then occurs where

$$Y = \frac{\bar{C} + \bar{I} - bi}{1 - c}$$

When investment spending is negatively related to the rate of interest, such as in Fig. 5-1, equilibrium income varies inversely with the rate of interest (Example 2). Equilibrium income consistent with selected rates of interest is presented in Fig. 5-3(a) and then plotted in Fig. 5-3(b) with the schedule labeled *IS*. The *IS* schedule in Fig. 5-3(b) shows the combinations of Y and i at which there is equality between planned investment and planned saving. When the saving (or consumption) function and the investment function are specified, we can derive an equation for the *IS* schedule and establish the equilibrium level of income which is consistent with different rates of interest (Example 3).

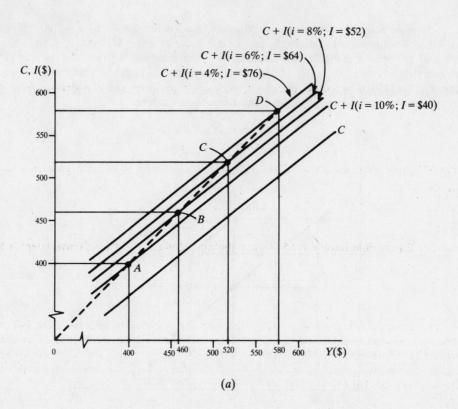

(a)

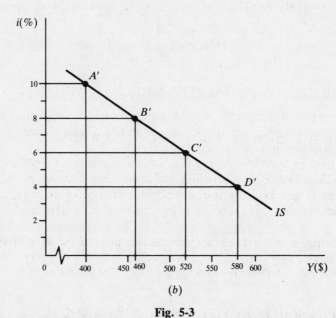

(b)

Fig. 5-3

EXAMPLE 2. Suppose planned saving is $S = -\$40 + 0.20Y$, and planned investment at selected interest rates is found in Fig. 5-1. Equilibrium income consistent with a 10%, 8%, 6% and 4% rate of interest is calculated below.

  Situation I: Investment is $40 when the rate of interest is 10%. Equilibrium income is $400, found by equating planned saving and planned investment.

$$S = I$$
$$-\$40 + 0.20Y = \$40$$
$$Y = \$400$$

Situation II: Equilibrium income is \$460 when the rate of interest is 8% and investment is \$52.

$$S = I$$
$$-\$40 + 0.20Y = \$52$$
$$Y = \$460$$

Situation III: Equilibrium income is \$520 when the rate of interest is 6% and investment is \$64.

$$S = I$$
$$-\$40 + 0.20Y = \$64$$
$$Y = \$520$$

Situation IV: Equilibrium income is \$580 when the rate of interest is 4% and investment is \$76.

$$S = I$$
$$-\$40 + 0.20Y = \$76$$
$$Y = \$580$$

As the rate of interest falls from 10% to 8%, the volume of investment increases from \$40 to \$52, raising equilibrium income through the multiplier effect from \$400 to \$460. Thus, a 10% rate of interest is consistent with a \$400 equilibrium income, and an 8% rate is consistent with a \$460 equilibrium income. The equilibrium income consistent with a 10%, 8%, 6% and 4% rate of interest is plotted in Fig. 5-3(b) with the schedule labeled *IS*.

EXAMPLE 3. Suppose $I = \$100 - 6i$ and $S = -\$40 + 0.20Y$. Equilibrium income occurs where

$$S = I$$
$$-\$40 + 0.20Y = \$100 - 6i$$
$$0.20Y = \$140 - 6i$$
$$Y = \$700 - 30i$$

When the rate of interest is 6%, $Y = \$700 - 30(6) = \$520$, as established in Example 2.

5.4 SHIFTS OF THE *IS* SCHEDULE FOR A TWO-SECTOR MODEL

Autonomous changes in spending (changes in constants $\bar{I}$ and $\bar{C}$) cause parallel shifts of the *IS* schedule. Since the *IS* schedule is a schedule of equilibrium income in the goods market, the magnitude of the shift is governed by the autonomous change is spending and the value of the expenditure multiplier.

EXAMPLE 4. In Fig. 5-4(a), a $\Delta\bar{I}$ increase in autonomous investment shifts the investment schedule rightward by $\Delta\bar{I}$. Holding interest rates constant at i_0, the *IS* schedule in Fig. 5-4(b) shifts rightward by $k_e \Delta\bar{I}$ since $\Delta Y = k_e \Delta\bar{I}$. A $\Delta\bar{C}$ increase in autonomous consumption would shift *IS* rightward by $k_e \Delta\bar{C}$.

5.5 SLOPE OF THE *IS* SCHEDULE FOR A TWO-SECTOR MODEL

The equation for the *IS* schedule can be presented as $Y = k_e(\bar{A} - bi)$ or when solving for the rate of interest $i = \bar{A}/b - (1/k_e b)Y$. $\bar{A}$ represents the sum of autonomous spending ($\bar{C} + \bar{I}$ in this model), k_e is the expenditure multiplier and b is a behavioral coefficient linking investment spending to the rate of interest. In Example 5, the slope for *IS* is presented as $1/(k_e b)$; the slope for *IS* increases when b and/or k_e have lower values. Although both the interest sensitivity of investment spending and the marginal propensity to consume determine the slope of *IS*, a necessary condition for a negatively sloped *IS* schedule is a value for $b > 0$ (Example 7).

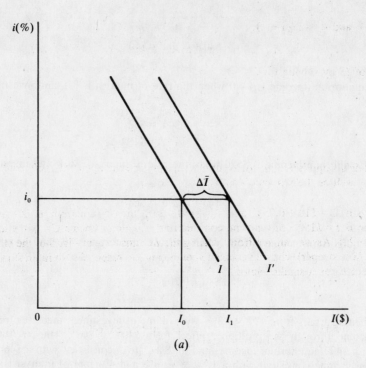

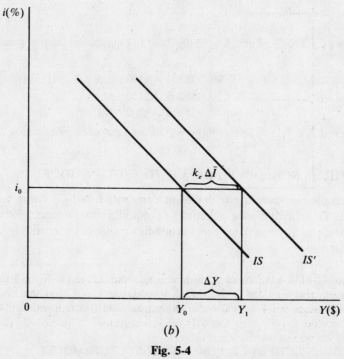

Fig. 5-4

EXAMPLE 5. Suppose $C = \bar{C} + cY$ and $I = \bar{I} - bi$. Equilibrium income occurs where

$$Y = \frac{\bar{C} + \bar{I} - bi}{1 - c}$$

or

$$Y = \frac{\bar{C} + \bar{I}}{1 - c} - \frac{bi}{1 - c}$$

Letting $\bar{A} = (\bar{C} + \bar{I})$, and $k_e = 1/(1 - c)$,

$$Y = k_e\bar{A} - k_ebi$$

We find the slope of *IS* by solving for i

$$i = \frac{\bar{A}}{b} - \frac{Y}{k_eb}$$

or

$$i = \bar{A}\left(\frac{1}{b}\right) - \left(\frac{1}{k_eb}\right)Y$$

Thus, the *IS* schedule's slope is $1/k_eb$; its location in space depends upon the multiplied effect of autonomous spending $(\bar{C} + \bar{I})$ as well as the schedule's slope.

EXAMPLE 6. When $C = \$10 + 0.75Y$ and $I = \$150 - 10i$, the *IS* equation is $Y = \$640 - 40i$. When the investment equation is $I = \$150 - 5i$, and the consumption equation remains $C = \$10 + 0.75Y$, the *IS* equation becomes $Y = \$640 - 20i$. As we can see from plotting the *IS* equations in Fig. 5-5, the slope of the *IS* schedule $(1/k_eb)$ is greater (*IS* is steeper) when investment spending is less responsive to interest rate changes, i.e., when behavioral coefficient b has a smaller value.

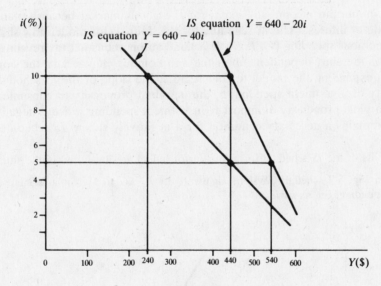

Fig. 5-5

EXAMPLE 7. When $C = \$10 + 0.75Y$ and $I = \$150 - 10i$, the *IS* equation is $Y = \$640 - 40i$. When the investment equation remains $I = \$150 - 10i$, and a smaller MPC changes the consumption equation to $C = \$10 + 0.60Y$, the *IS* equation is $Y = \$400 - 25i$. Plotting these *IS* equations in Fig. 5-6, we find that the slope of *IS* increases (*IS* becomes steeper) as the MPC c and therefore k_e decreases, provided that investment spending is responsive to changes in the rate of interest.

5.6 THE *IS* SCHEDULE FOR A FOUR-SECTOR MODEL

We now add a government and foreign trade sector, where $G = \bar{G}$, $Tn = \bar{T}x + tY - \bar{T}r$, and $X = \bar{X} - xY$, to the earlier two-sector model $(Y = \bar{C} + cYd + \bar{I} - bi)$. Equilibrium income is now

$$Y = \frac{\bar{C} + \bar{I} + \bar{G} + \bar{X} - c\bar{T}x + c\bar{T}r - bi}{1 - c + ct + x}$$

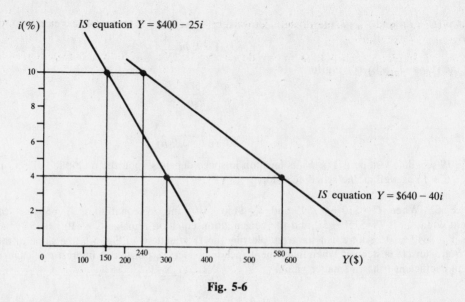

Fig. 5-6

A schedule of equilibrium income still exists for the goods market because planned investment is related to the rate of interest. The *IS* schedule for this four-sector model now shifts when there are changes in autonomous spending ($\bar{C}$, $\bar{I}$, $\bar{G}$, or $\bar{X}$) and autonomous net tax revenues ($\bar{T}x$ or $\bar{T}r$), with the magnitude of the shift dependent upon the autonomous change and the applicable multiplier (Example 8). In expanding the model to four sectors, the slope of the *IS* schedule depends on the interest sensitivity of investment spending b, the marginal propensity to consume c, the income tax rate t and the marginal propensity to import x. Investment spending which is negatively related to the rate of interest remains a necessary condition for a negatively sloped *IS* schedule.

EXAMPLE 8.   Shifts of the *IS* schedule for a four-sector model are illustrated in the situations below.

Situation 1: In Fig. 5-7 schedule *IS* shifts rightward by $k_e\,\Delta\bar{G}$ to *IS'* for a $\Delta\bar{G}$ increase in autonomous government spending, *ceteris paribus*.

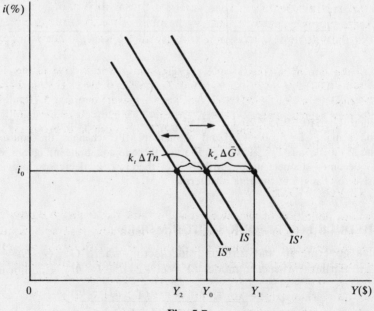

Fig. 5-7

Situation II: In Fig. 5-7 schedule *IS* shifts leftward by $k_t \Delta \bar{T}n$ to *IS"* for a $\Delta \bar{T}n$ increase in autonomous net tax revenues, *ceteris paribus*.

Situation III: In Fig. 5-8 schedule *IS* shifts rightward by $k_e \Delta \bar{X}$ to *IS"* for a $\Delta \bar{X}$ increase in autonomous net exports, *ceteris paribus*.

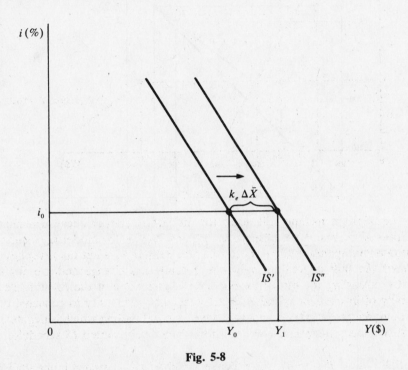

Fig. 5-8

5.7 THE *IS* SCHEDULE AND DISEQUILIBRIUM

Because *IS* represents a schedule of equilibrium spending, points off the curve are positions of disequilibrium. Excess supply exists for points to the right of the *IS* curve (supply exceeds aggregate spending); points to the left represent income levels where aggregate spending exceeds supply.

EXAMPLE 9. When the rate of interest is 10%, equilibrium income is $395 in Fig. 5-9(*a*) for a 4-sector economy where $C = \$40 + 0.80Yd$, $I = \$55 - 2i$, $G = \$20$, $Tn = \$20$ and $X = 0$. This equilibrium position appears as point *A* on the *IS* schedule in Fig. 5-9(*b*). Note that when aggregate output is $350 in Fig. 5-9(*a*), aggregate spending is $359 and excess aggregate demand exists. The existence of excess demand at the $350 output level is represented by point *B'* in Fig. 5-9(*b*). Point *C'* in Fig. 5-9(*b*) is a position of excess supply; the $450 level of output exceeds the $439 level of aggregate spending.

5.8 THE DEMAND FOR MONEY

We shall use as our definition of money currency outside banks plus the private sector's checking account balances. Money is demanded because of its transactions use and its quality as a store of value. Transactions are effected in a market economy through the exchange of money, with this transaction need related to current income and spending (Example 10). Money is also a component of investors' portfolios. In comparison to bonds, equity and real assets, money is normally a better store of value, since its market value is unrelated to interest rate levels. However, money's inclusion in a portfolio of assets is influenced by interest rate levels in that the higher the rate of return on

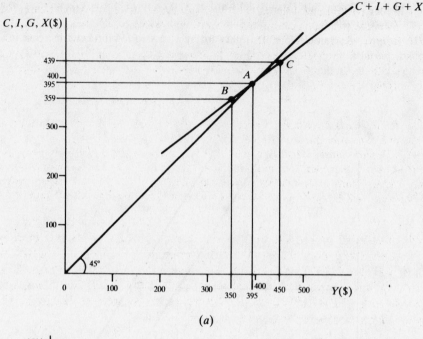

(a)

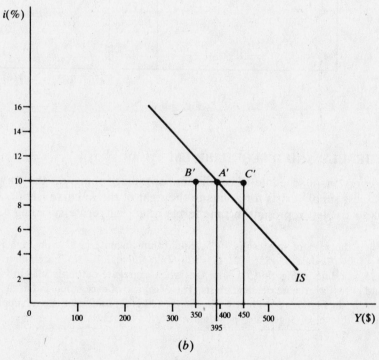

(b)

Fig. 5-9

nonmonetary assets is, the greater the opportunity cost of holding money (Example 11). This transaction and portfolio need for money balances can be specified as

$$L = kY - hi$$

where k is the fraction of income held as an average money balance to facilitate transactions and h is the interest sensitivity of holding money balances in one's portfolio.

EXAMPLE 10. Money receipts and disbursements rarely coincide, necessitating that households and businesses hold transaction balances to meet disbursement needs. For example, a household may be paid (money is received) monthly, yet expenditures are more or less continual throughout the month. Thus, the monthly money income which a household intends to spend must be budgeted—and money must be held—to meet planned monthly expenditure flows. In doing so, the household holds an average money balance during the month which is related to its income level, i.e., $L_t = kY$.

EXAMPLE 11. There exists an inverse relationship between the market rate of interest and the price of securities (bonds and stocks) in the secondary financial markets. Bonds and stocks are therefore less liquid (an inferior store of value) and must offer a greater rate of return than money. As the return on bonds and stocks increases (market interest rates increase) and there is no change in the return from money, investors respond to the increasingly higher return from less liquid assets by reducing their money holdings. With other variables constant, portfolios are less liquid (smaller money balances are held) as the market rate of interest increases.

On a two-dimensional graph, the demand for money appears as a series of demand schedules because of its dependency upon two independent variables, the rate of interest and the level of income. In Fig. 5-10 the $L_1(Y_1)$ demand for money schedule negatively relates the money balance held to the rate of interest for a Y_1 income level. $L_2(Y_2)$ represents the demand for money at a higher Y_2 income level. The shift in the money demand schedule from $L_1(Y_1)$ to $L_2(Y_2)$ equals $k\,\Delta Y$, where ΔY is the difference between income levels Y_2 and Y_1.

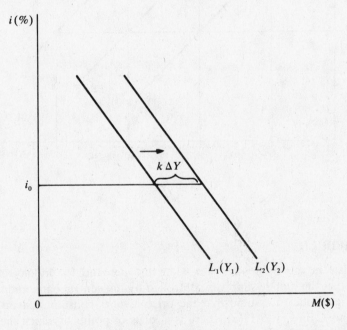

Fig. 5-10

EXAMPLE 12. Suppose the demand for money is specified as $L = kY - hi$, with $k = 0.20$ and $h = 5$. Tables 5-1 and 5-2 give values for kY and hi at various income levels and interest rates. The data from Tables 5-1 and 5-2 are plotted in Fig. 5-11 with L_1 representing the demand for money when income is \$500, L_2 when it is \$600 and L_3 when it is \$700. Note that L_1 is derived by subtracting values for hi at different rates of interest (Table 5-2) from \$100, the value for kY when the income level is \$500.

<table>
<tr><th colspan="2">Table 5-1</th></tr>
</table>

Income	kY (when $k = 0.20$)
$500	$100
600	120
700	140
800	160
900	180
1000	200

<table>
<tr><th colspan="2">Table 5-2</th></tr>
</table>

Rate of interest (%)	hi (when $h = 5$)
10	$50
9	45
8	40
7	35
6	30
5	25

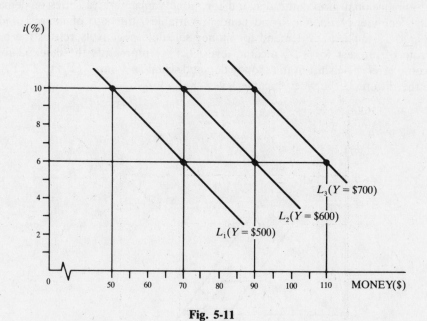

Fig. 5-11

5.9 THE *LM* SCHEDULE

Equilibrium exists in the money market when the demand for money equals the supply of money. We assume that the money supply is controlled by the central bank and is thereby exogenous (constant); we also continue to assume that the price level is constant. Given demand for money schedules L_1, L_2, and L_3 in Fig. 5-12(a), there is a locus of points at which the demand for money equals the money supply. This locus of points is plotted in Fig. 5-12(b); the resulting positively sloped schedule is labeled *LM* and represents equilibrium positions in the money market. When the demand for money is specified as $L = kY - hi$ and the money supply is $\bar{M}$, the *LM* schedule is

$$Y = \frac{\bar{M}}{k} + \left(\frac{h}{k}\right)i$$

or

$$i = \left(\frac{k}{h}\right)Y - \frac{\bar{M}}{h}$$

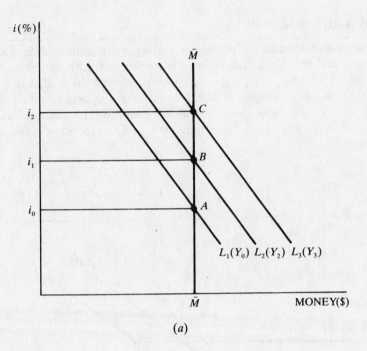

(a)

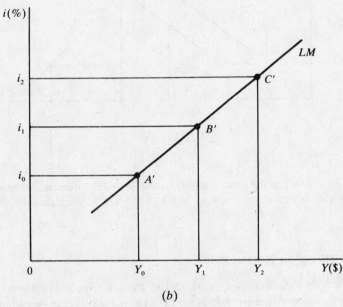

(b)

Fig. 5-12

EXAMPLE 13. Suppose the demand for money is specified as $L = kY - hi$ and the money supply is $\bar{M}$. Monetary equilibrium exists where the demand for money equals the money supply

$$L = M$$
$$kY - hi = \bar{M}$$

Solving for Y, $Y = \bar{M}/h + (h/k)i$, or solving for i, $i = 1/h(kY - \bar{M})$:

$$i = \left(\frac{k}{h}\right)Y - \frac{\bar{M}}{h}$$

5.10   SHIFTS OF THE *LM* SCHEDULE

Changes in either the demand for money or the supply of money shift the *LM* schedule. It is customary to assume that the demand for money is stable, with *LM* shifts caused by changes in the money supply. Increases in the money supply cause rightward shifts of $\Delta \bar{M}(1/k)$ (see Fig. 5-13), whereas decreases cause leftward shifts of $\Delta \bar{M}(1/k)$. Changes in behavioral coefficients h and k also affect the *LM* schedule's location in space. Rightward shifts result from a decrease in k (a reduction in the transactions need for money) and/or an increase in h (an increase in the interest sensitivity of the demand for money).

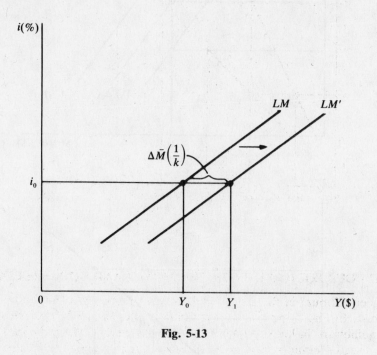

Fig. 5-13

EXAMPLE 14. $\bar{M} = kY - hi$ when the money supply equals $\bar{M}$ and the demand for money is $kY - hi$. Holding the rate of interest constant as well as parameters k and h, $\Delta \bar{M} = k \, \Delta Y$. Money supply changes thereby shift *LM* by $(1/k) \, \Delta \bar{M}$.

5.11   SLOPE OF THE *LM* SCHEDULE

The slope of the *LM* schedule is k/h when the money supply is exogenous, the demand for money is $kY - hi$, and the equation for *LM* is $i = (k/h)Y - \bar{M}/h$. Decreases in h increase the slope of *LM*, with the curve becoming vertical when $h = 0$. As h takes larger values, *LM* is less steeply sloped (*LM* is flatter).

EXAMPLE 15. Suppose the money supply is \$200 and the demand for money is $kY - hi$. When $k = 0.20$ and $h = 5$, the *LM* equation is $i = 0.04Y - \$40$; the *LM* equation is $i = 0.02Y - \$20$ when $k = 0.20$ and $h = 10$. These *LM* equations are plotted in Fig. 5-14. Note that the *LM* schedule is less steeply sloped when $h = 10$ than when $h = 5$, i.e., *LM* is less steeply sloped when the demand for money is more responsive to the rate of interest.

EXAMPLE 16. Suppose the money supply is \$200 and the demand for money is $kY - hi$. When $k = 0.20$ and $h = 5$, the *LM* equation is $i = 0.04Y - \$40$; the *LM* equation is $i = 0.02Y - \$40$ when $k = 0.10$ and $h = 5$. These *LM* equations are plotted in Fig. 5-14. Note that the *LM* schedule is less steeply sloped when there is a smaller transaction demand for money ($k = 0.10$).

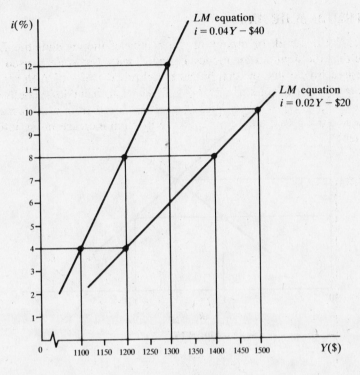

Fig. 5-14

5.12 SIMULTANEOUS EQUILIBRIUM IN THE MONEY AND GOODS MARKETS

Simultaneous equilibrium in the money and goods markets exists at only one income level and one rate of interest. In Fig. 5-15, i_0 is the only rate of interest and Y_0 the only level of income at which there is equilibrium in both the money and goods market. Other interest rates and income levels represent disequilibrium in one or both markets. For example, at interest rate i_1, there is equilibrium in the money market at Y_1 income but in the goods market at income Y_2. The equilibrium position for both markets is found by solving the *IS* and *LM* equations simultaneously.

EXAMPLE 17.   In a two-sector model, suppose $C = \$60 + 0.80Y$, $I = \$116 - 2i$, $L = 0.20Y - 5i$ and $M = \$120$.

The *IS* equation:
$$Y = C + I$$
$$Y = \$60 + 0.80Y + \$116 - 2i$$
$$0.2Y = \$176 - 2i$$
$$i = -0.10Y + \$88$$

The *LM* equation:
$$M = L$$
$$\$120 = 0.20Y - 5i$$
$$5i = 0.20Y - \$120$$
$$i = 0.04Y - \$24$$

Simultaneous equilibrium for *IS* and *LM* is:
$$i = -0.10Y + \$88$$
$$\underline{-i = 0.04Y - \$24}$$
$$0 = -0.14Y + \$112$$
$$Y = \$800$$
$$i = 8\%$$

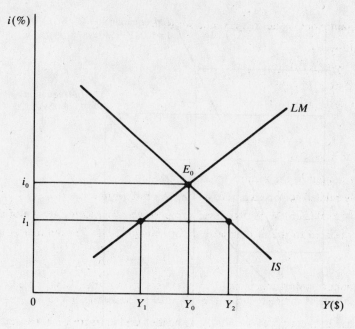

Fig. 5-15

Review Questions

1. When investment spending is negatively related to the rate of interest, equilibrium income in the goods market

    (a) Is unrelated to the rate of interest
    (b) Is inversely related to the rate of interest
    (c) Is positively related to the rate of interest
    (d) Falls as the rate of interest decreases

    Answer: (b)

2. A $10 increase in autonomous investment spending shifts *IS*

    (a) Rightward by $10
    (b) Leftward by $10
    (c) Rightward by k_e ($10)
    (d) Leftward by k_e ($10)

    Answer: (c)

3. Given the *IS* equation $Y = k_e \bar{A} - k_e bi$, the *IS* slope decreases (the *IS* schedule becomes flatter) when

    (a) k_e increases and b increases.
    (b) k_e decreases and b increases.
    (c) k_e increases and b decreases.
    (d) k_e decreases and b decreases.

    Answer: (a)

4.   An increase in autonomous net tax revenue shifts *IS*

   (*a*)   Rightward by $k_r(\Delta \bar{T}n)$
   (*b*)   Leftward by $k_r(\Delta \bar{T}n)$
   (*c*)   Rightward by $k_e(\Delta \bar{T}n)$
   (*d*)   Leftward by $k_e(\Delta \bar{T}n)$

   Answer: (*b*)

5.   The demand for money is

   (*a*)   Positively related to the income level and the rate of interest
   (*b*)   Negatively related to the income level and the rate of interest
   (*c*)   Negatively related to the income level and positively related to the rate of interest
   (*d*)   Positively related to the income level and negatively related to the rate of interest

   Answer: (*d*)

6.   Suppose the money supply and price level are constant, and the demand for money is a function of income and the rate of interest. When the income level increases, there is

   (*a*)   An increase in the quantity of money demanded and an increase in the rate of interest
   (*b*)   An increase in the quantity of money demanded and a decrease in the rate of interest
   (*c*)   A decrease in the quantity of money demanded and a decrease in the rate of interest
   (*d*)   A decrease in the quantity of money demanded and an increase in the rate of interest

   Answer: (*a*)

7.   When the *LM* equation is $Y = \$750 + 20i$, there is equilibrium between the supply of and the demand for money when

   (*a*)   The rate of interest is 10% and income level is \$750.
   (*b*)   The rate of interest is 10% and income level is \$800.
   (*c*)   The rate of interest is 10% and income level is \$950.
   (*d*)   The rate of interest is 10% and income level is \$900.

   Answer: (*c*)

8.   When there is an increase in the autonomous money supply, *ceteris paribus*, *LM* shifts

   (*a*)   Rightward by $\Delta \bar{M}$
   (*b*)   Rightward by $k(\Delta \bar{M})$
   (*c*)   Rightward by $(\Delta \bar{M})/k$
   (*d*)   Rightward by $k/(\Delta \bar{M})$

   Answer: (*c*)

9.   Equilibrium in the money markets can be expressed by the equation $i = (k/h)Y - \bar{M}/h$. The slope of *LM* decreases (the *LM* schedule becomes flatter) when

   (*a*) k increases and h increases.
   (*b*) k increases and h decreases.
   (*c*) k decreases and h increases.
   (*d*) k decreases and h decreases.

   Answer: (*c*)

10. Simultaneous equilibrium in the money (*LM*) and goods (*IS*) markets exists

   (*a*) At an unlimited number of income levels and rates of interest
   (*b*) At only one income level and rate of interest
   (*c*) At an unlimited number of income levels and only one rate of interest
   (*d*) At only one income level and an unlimited number of rates of interest

   Answer: (*b*)

Solved Problems

INVESTMENT AND THE RATE OF INTEREST

5.1 Suppose planned investment is $I = \bar{I} - bi$. (*a*) Find the level of investment when $\bar{I} = \$250$, $b = 5$, and the rate of interest is 10%, 8% and 6%. Plot the data in Fig. 5-16 with the rate of interest on the *y* axis and investment on the *x* axis. Label the schedule *I*. (*b*) Find the level of investment when $\bar{I} = \$250$, $b = 10$ and the rate of interest is 10%, 8% and 6%. Plot the data in Fig. 5-17 and label the schedule *I'*. (*c*) Explain the effect that an increase in behavioral coefficient *b* has upon the investment demand schedule in Fig. 5-16.

   (*a*) When $I = \$250 - 5i$, investment is \$200 when the rate of interest is 10% [$I = \$250 - 5(10)$; $I = \$200$], \$210 when the rate of interest is 8% and \$220 when the rate of interest is 6%. The data are plotted in Fig. 5-16 and labeled *I*.

   (*b*) When $I = \$250 - 10i$, investment is \$150 when the rate of interest is 10%, \$170 when the rate of interest is 8% and \$190 when it is 6%. The data are plotted in Fig. 5-16 and labeled *I'*.

   (*c*) A larger value for *b* indicates that a change in the rate of interest has a greater effect upon the level of investment. Thus, an increase in behavioral coefficient *b* causes the investment demand schedule to shift rightward and become less steeply sloped.

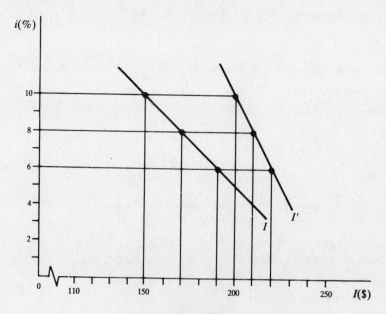

Fig. 5-16

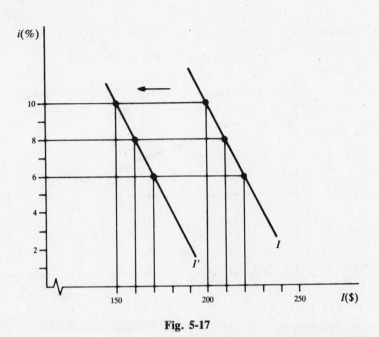

Fig. 5-17

5.2 (*a*) Plot the investment equation $I = \$250 - 5i$ [Problem 5-1(*a*)] in Fig. 5-17 and label the schedule *I*. (*b*) Find investment when $I = \$200 - 5i$ and the rate of interest is 10%, 8% and 6%. Plot the data in Fig. 5-17 and label the schedule *I'*. (*c*) Explain the effect that a $50 decrease in autonomous investment has on the investment demand schedule's location in space.

(*a*) See Fig. 5-17.

(*b*) Investment is $150, $160 and $170 when the rate of interest is 10%, 8% and 6%; the data are plotted in Fig. 5-18 with the schedule labeled *I'*.

(*c*) A change in autonomous investment ($\Delta \bar{I}$) causes a parallel shift of the investment demand schedule. Thus, a $50 decrease in autonomous investment shifts the investment demand schedule in Fig. 5-17 by $50 from *I* to *I'*.

THE *IS* SCHEDULE FOR A TWO-SECTOR MODEL

5.3 (*a*) Find the level of investment for investment equation $I = \$100 - 5i$ when the interest rate is 4%, 5%, 6% and 7%. (*b*) Find equilibrium income for the investment levels found in part (*a*) when saving is $S = -\$40 + 0.25Y$. (*c*) With *i* on the vertical axis and *Y* on the horizontal axis, plot in Fig. 5-18 the equilibrium income levels found in part (*b*); label the schedule *IS*.

(*a*) When the rate of interest is 4%, investment spending is $80. [$I = \$100 - 5(4); I = \$80$]. Investment spending is $75 when $i = 5\%$, planned investment is $70 when $i = 6\%$ and $65 when $i = 7\%$.

(*b*) Equilibrium income is found by equating planned saving and planned investment. When $i = 4\%$, planned investment equals $80. Thus,

$$S = I$$
$$-\$40 + 0.25Y = \$80$$
$$Y = \$480$$

When $i = 5\%$, $I = \$75$ and equilibrium income is $460; when $i = 6\%$, $I = \$70$ and equilibrium income is $440; when $i = 7\%$, $I = \$65$ and equilibrium income is $420.

(*c*) See Fig. 5-18.

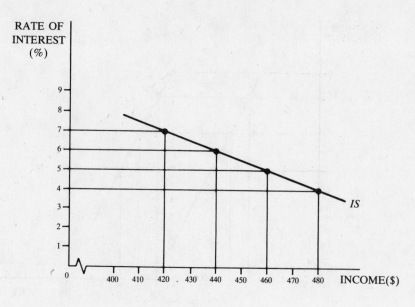

Fig. 5-18

5.4   (*a*) Find an equation that represents equilibrium between planned saving and planned investment for saving and investment equations, $S = -\$40 + 0.25Y$ and $I = \$100 - 5i$, from Problem 5.3. (*b*) Find equilibrium income when the interest rate is 4%, 5%, 6% and 7%. Compare these answers to those found in Problem 5.3(*b*).

(*a*)   The equation equates planned saving and planned investment

$$-\$40 + 0.25Y = \$100 - 5i$$
$$0.25Y = \$140 - 5i$$
$$Y = \$560 - 20i$$

or, solving for *i*, $$i = \$28 - 0.05Y$$

(*b*)   When the rate of interest is 4%, equilibrium income is $480; $Y = \$460$ when $i = 5\%$; $Y = \$440$ when $i = 6\%$ and $Y = \$420$ when $i = 7\%$. The association of the rate of interest and equilibrium income is the same as that found in Problem 5.3(*b*).

5.5   Why is there a schedule of equilibrium income for the goods market?

In a two-sector model, equilibrium income varies directly with the level of investment, given the parameters of the saving (and consumption) function. When investment in turn varies inversely with the rate of interest, so too will equilibrium income. For a family of interest rates, then, there is a schedule of equilibrium income, an *IS* schedule.

5.6   An *IS* equation is also found by equating output *Y* and planned spending $C + I$. (*a*) Find the *IS* equation when $C = \$40 + 0.80Y$ and $I = \$70 - 2i$. (*b*) Find equilibrium income when the rate of interest is 10% and 5%. (*c*) Plot the *IS* equation in Fig. 5-19.

(*a*)   Equilibrium exists where $Y = C + I$:

$$Y = \$40 + 0.80Y + \$70 - 2i$$
$$0.20Y = \$110 - 2i$$
$$Y = \$550 - 10i$$

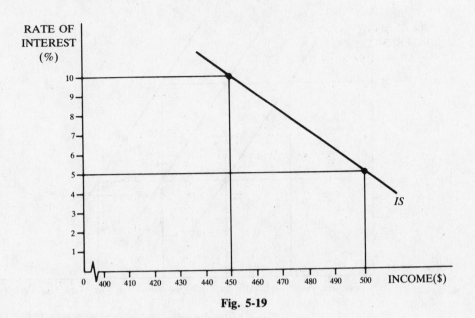

Fig. 5-19

(b) When $i = 10\%$, equilibrium income is $450 [$Y = \$550 - 10(10)$]. Equilibrium income is $500 when $i = 5\%$.

(c) Fig. 5-19.

5.7 (a) Find an equation for equilibrium income when $C = \bar{C} + cY$ and $I = \bar{I} - bi$. (b) Present the *IS* equation where $k_e = 1/(1 - c)$.

(a)
$$Y = C + I$$
$$Y = \bar{C} + cY + \bar{I} - bi$$
$$Y - cY = \bar{C} + \bar{I} - bi$$
$$Y(1 - c) = \bar{C} + \bar{I} - bi$$
$$Y = \frac{\bar{C} + \bar{I} - bi}{1 - c}$$

(b) Letting $k_e = 1/(1 - c)$,

$$Y = k_e(\bar{C} + \bar{I} - bi)$$
or
$$Y = k_e(\bar{C} + \bar{I}) - k_e bi$$

SHIFTS OF THE *IS* SCHEDULE FOR A TWO-SECTOR MODEL

5.8 (a) Find an equation for equilibrium income in the goods market when $C = \$40 + 0.80Y$ and investment spending is (1) $I = \$70 - 2i$; (2) $I = \$80 - 2i$; and (3) $I = \$90 - 2i$. (b) Find equilibrium income when the rate of interest is 10%. (c) What accounts for the change in equilibrium? (d) Plot in Fig. 5-20 the *IS* equations from part (a). (e) What happens to an *IS* schedule when there is a change in autonomous spending?

(a) Equilibrium exists where $Y = C + I$.

(1)
$$Y = \$40 + 0.80Y + \$70 - 2i$$
$$Y - 0.80Y = \$110 - 2i$$
$$Y = \frac{\$110 - 2i}{0.20}$$

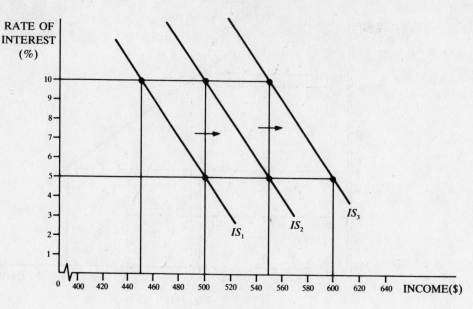

Fig. 5-20

$$Y = \$550 - 10i$$
(2) $$Y = \$600 - 10i$$
(3) $$Y = \$650 - 10i$$

(b)   When the rate of interest is 10%, equilibrium income is (1) \$450 [$Y = \$550 - 10(10) = \$450$]; (2) \$500; (3) \$550.

(c)   Autonomous investment increases from (1) \$70 to (2) \$80 to (3) \$90; i.e., there is a \$10 change in autonomous spending from (1) to (2) and from (2) to (3). Holding the interest rate constant, equilibrium income should therefore change by $k_e \, \Delta \bar{I}$; since k_e is 5, equilibrium income increases \$50 for each situation.

(d)   See Fig. 5-20.

(e)   An *IS* schedule shifts by the multiplier times the change in antonomous spending; thus, *IS* shifts rightward in Fig. 5-20 by \$50 which equals $k_e \, \Delta \bar{I}$.

5.9   Equilibrium income in the goods market is $Y = k_e(\bar{C} + \bar{I}) - k_e b$. (a) Find an expression for ΔY when $\Delta \bar{C} > 0$, *ceteris paribus* and when $\Delta \bar{I} > 0$, *ceteris paribus*. (b) Find the shift of *IS* due to $\Delta \bar{C}$ and $\Delta \bar{I}$.

(a)   When $\Delta \bar{C} > 0$, *ceteris paribus* (i.e., autonomous consumption increases but there is no change in autonomous investment, the rate of interest or behavioral coefficients b or c), $\Delta Y = k_e \, \Delta \bar{C}$. When $\Delta \bar{I} > 0$, *ceteris paribus*, $\Delta Y = k_e \, \Delta \bar{I}$.

(b)   The *IS* schedule shifts rightward by $k_e \, \Delta \bar{C}$ and $k_e \, \Delta \bar{I}$, respectively.

5.10   A change in autonomous spending causes *IS* to shift by the expenditure multiplier times the change in autonomous spending. What happens to *IS* when a behavioral coefficient such as the marginal propensity to consume changes?

In Fig. 5-21, *IS* is the goods equilibrium schedule for a two-sector model with behavioral equations $C = \$50 + 0.75Y$ and $I = \$150 - 5i$. When the MPC increases to 0.80, the *IS* schedule shifts rightward to *IS'*. The rightward shift of *IS* is \$150 at a 10% rate of interest and \$175 at a 5% rate of interest. Thus, a change in a behavioral coefficient causes a nonparallel shift of *IS* and a change in its slope.

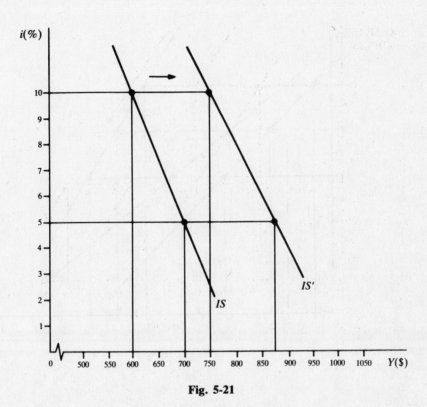

Fig. 5-21

SLOPE OF THE *IS* SCHEDULE FOR A TWO-SECTOR MODEL

5.11　Equilibrium income in the goods market is $Y = k_e(\bar{C} + \bar{I}) - k_e bi$. (a) Plot the equilibrium schedule for the goods market in Fig. 5-22 and label it *IS* when $\bar{C} = \$50$; $\bar{I} = \$100$; $c = 0.80$; $b = 5$. (b) Plot *IS* in Fig. 5-22 and label it *IS'* when $\bar{C} = \$50$; $\bar{I} = \$100$; $c = 0.80$; $b = 10$. (c) What happens to the slope of *IS* when the interest sensitivity of investment spending increases from $b = 5$ [part (a)] to $b = 10$ [part (b)]? (d) Plot *IS* in Fig. 5-22 and label it *IS"* when $\bar{C} = \$50$; $\bar{I} = \$100$; $c = 0.75$; $b = 10$. (e) Compare the slope of *IS'* and *IS"* when the marginal propensity to consume decreases from $c = 0.80$ (for *IS'*) to 0.75 (for *IS"*).

(a)　The *IS* equation is $Y = 5(\$150) - 5(5i)$ which is plotted in Fig. 5-22 for a 10%, 8% and 6% rate of interest.

(b)　The *IS* equation is $Y = 5(\$150) - 5(10)i$ which is plotted in Fig. 5-22 and labeled *IS'*.

(c)　*IS* has a greater slope than *IS'* in Fig. 5-22. An increase in behavioral coefficient b decreases the slope of the *IS* schedule.

(d)　The *IS* equation becomes $Y = 4(\$150) - 4(10)i$; it is plotted in Fig. 5-22 and labeled *IS"*.

(e)　*IS"* is less steeply sloped than *IS'*. A reduction in the marginal propensity to consume reduces the expenditure multiplier, causing the *IS* schedule to become more steeply sloped.

5.12　The *IS* equation is $Y = k_e(\bar{C} + \bar{I}) - k_e bi$. (a) Solve the *IS* equation for i and find the slope of *IS*. (b) Find numerical values for and compare the slope of *IS* when $k_e = 5$ and $b = 10$; $k_e = 5$ and $b = 2$; $k_e = 2$ and $b = 5$. (c) What happens to the slope of *IS* as k_e or b increases?

(a)
$$Y = k_e(\bar{C} + \bar{I}) - k_e bi$$
$$k_e bi = k_e(\bar{C} + \bar{I}) - Y$$

$$i = \frac{k_e(\bar{C} + \bar{I})}{k_e b} - \frac{Y}{k_e b}$$

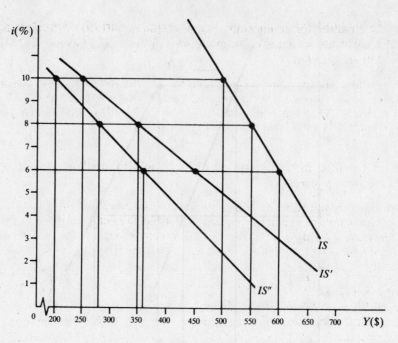

Fig. 5-22

$$i = \frac{1}{b}(\bar{C} + \bar{I}) - \left(\frac{1}{k_e b}\right) \cdot Y$$

The slope of *IS* is $1/k_e b$, the behavioral coefficient for *Y*.

(b) The slope of *IS* is 0.02 when k_e is 5 and *b* is 10 because $1/50 = 0.02$, the slope is 0.10 when k_e is 5 and *b* is 2, and the slope is 0.10 when k_e is 2 and *b* is 5.

(c) The slope of *IS* decreases as k_e and/or *b* increases, i.e., the *IS* schedule is flatter for larger values of k_e and/or *b*.

THE *IS* SCHEDULE FOR A FOUR-SECTOR MODEL

5.13 (a) Derive an *IS* equation given the following specified behavior: $C = \bar{C} + cYd$, $I = \bar{I} - bi$, $Tn = \bar{T}x + tY$, $G = \bar{G}$, $X = \bar{X} - xY$. (b) Find the slope of *IS* by solving the *IS* equation for *i*.

(a)
$$Y = C + I + G + X$$
$$Y = \bar{C} + c(Y - \bar{T}x - tY) + \bar{I} - bi + \bar{G} + \bar{X} - xY$$
$$Y - cY + ctY + xY = \bar{C} - c\bar{T}x + \bar{I} - bi + \bar{G} + \bar{X}$$
$$Y = \frac{\bar{C} - c\bar{T}x + \bar{I} - bi + \bar{G} + \bar{X}}{1 - c + ct + x}$$

or
$$Y = k_e(\bar{C} - c\bar{T}x + \bar{I} + \bar{G} + \bar{X}) - k_e bi$$

where
$$k_e = 1/(1 - c + ct + x)$$

(b) Solving the equation for *i*,

$$Y = k_e(\bar{C} - c\bar{T}x + \bar{I} + \bar{G} + \bar{X}) - k_e bi$$
$$k_e bi = k_e(\bar{C} - c\bar{T}x + \bar{I} + \bar{G} + \bar{X}) - Y$$
$$i = \frac{\bar{C} - c\bar{T}x + \bar{I} + \bar{G} + \bar{X}}{b} - \left(\frac{1}{k_e b}\right)Y$$

The slope of *IS* is $1/k_e b$.

5.14 Using the equation for equilibrium income found in part (*a*) of Problem 5.13, find the shift of *IS* when there are changes in autonomous (1) taxes, (2) government spending and (3) net exports, *ceteris paribus*.

When there are autonomous changes in the variables specified, the *IS* equation $Y = k_e(\bar{C} - c\bar{T}x + \bar{I} + \bar{G} + \bar{X}) - k_e bi$ becomes (1) $\Delta Y = k_e(-c\,\Delta\bar{T}x)$, (2) $\Delta Y = k_e\,\Delta\bar{G}$, and (3) $\Delta Y = k_e\,\Delta\bar{X}$. The shift of *IS* for a change (1) in autonomous taxes is $-ck_e(\Delta\bar{T}x)$, (2) in autonomous government spending is $k_e(\Delta\bar{G})$, and (3) in autonomous net exports is $k_e(\Delta\bar{X})$.

5.15 Using the equation found in part (*b*) of Problem 5.13, establish what happens to the slope of *IS* when *c*, *t* or *x* increases.

Behavioral coefficients *c* (marginal propensity to consume), *t* (household income tax rate) and *x* (marginal propensity to import) determine the expenditure multiplier k_e. An increase in *c* increases k_e, and an increase in *t* and/or *x* decreases the expenditure multiplier. The *IS* slope thereby decreases (i.e., the schedule becomes flatter) when *c* increases; the slope increases when *t* and/or *x* increase.

5.16 Suppose $C = \$40 + 0.75(Y - tY)$, $t = 0.20$, $\bar{T}x = 0$, $\bar{G} = \$90$ and $I = \$150 - 5i$. (*a*) Find the equation for equilibrium in the goods market; plot the equation in Fig. 5-23 and label it *IS*. (*b*) Explain the direction and magnitude of the shift in *IS* when there is a \$40 increase in $\bar{G}$, \$40 increase in $\bar{T}x$, or \$40 increase in $\bar{G}$ and $\bar{T}x$. (*c*) Plot the *IS* schedules associated with the shifts in part (*b*) in Fig. 5-23 and label them IS_1, IS_2 and IS_3.

(*a*)
$$Y = C + I + G$$
$$Y = \$40 + 0.75(Y - 0.20Y) + \$150 - 5i + \$90$$
$$Y - 0.60Y = \$280 - 5i$$
$$Y = \frac{\$280 - 5i}{1 - 0.60}$$
$$Y = \$700 - 12.5i$$

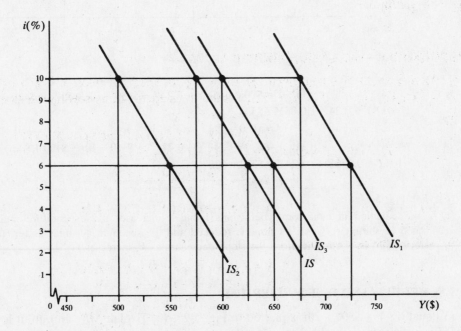

Fig. 5-23

(b) The expenditure multiplier is 2.5 $[k_e = 1/(1 - 0.75 + 0.15) = 2.5]$, and the net tax revenue multiplier is -1.875 $[k_t = -0.75/(1 - 0.75 + 0.15) = -1.875]$. Therefore, a \$40 increase in $\bar{G}$ shifts *IS* rightward \$100, a \$40 increase in $\bar{T}x$ shifts *IS* leftward \$75, and a \$40 increase in $\bar{G}$ and $\bar{T}x$ shifts *IS* rightward by \$25.

(c) See Fig. 5-23.

5.17 Find the *IS* equation when (1) $C = \$20 + 0.80Yd$, $Tn = 0.3Y$, $G = \$120$, $I = \$150 - 10i$ and $X = \$40 - 0.06Y$; (2) $C = \$20 + 0.80Yd$, $Tn = 0.22Y$, $G = \$120$, $I = \$150 - 10i$ and $X = \$40 - 0.024Y$. (b) Plot these *IS* schedules in Fig. 5-24 for a 10% and 5% interest rate and label them IS_1 and IS_2. (c) What effect does a decrease in income taxes from 0.30 to 0.22 and a decrease in the marginal propensity to import from 0.06 to 0.024 have upon *IS*?

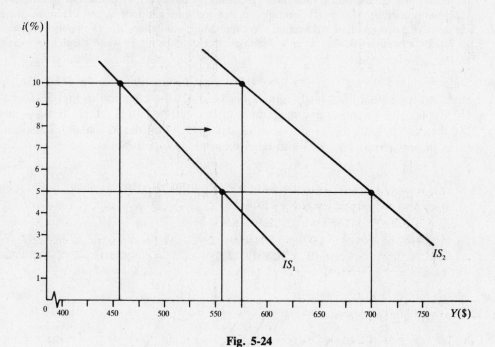

Fig. 5-24

(a)
$$\text{(1)} \quad Y = \$20 + 0.80(Y - 0.3Y) + \$150 - 10i + \$120 + \$40 - 0.06Y$$
$$Y - 0.8Y + 0.24Y + 0.06Y = \$330 - 10i$$
$$Y = \$660 - 20i$$
$$\text{(2)} \quad Y = \$20 + 0.80(Y - 0.22Y) + \$150 - 10i + \$120 + \$40 - 0.024Y$$
$$Y - 0.8Y + 0.176Y + 0.024Y = \$330 - 10i$$
$$Y = \$825 - 25i$$

(b) See Fig. 5-24.

(c) The reduction in behavioral coefficients t and x increases the expenditure multiplier. The *IS* schedule shifts rightward; its slope is reduced and the schedule becomes flatter. (Recall that the slope of *IS* is $1/k_e b$; therefore the slope decreases as k_e increases.)

THE *IS* SCHEDULE AND DISEQUILIBRIUM

5.18 *IS* equation $Y = \$800 - 20i$ is plotted in Fig. 5-25. (a) Explain why an output level of \$550 or \$650 represents disequilibrium when the rate of interest is 10%. (b) Is there excess spending or excess output to the right or left of *IS*?

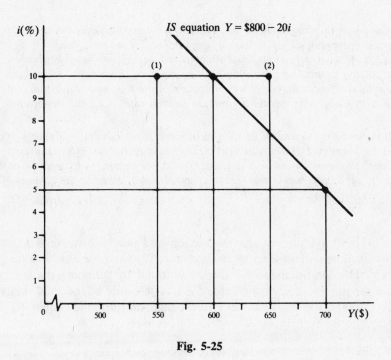

Fig. 5-25

(a)   When the rate of interest is 10%, equilibrium income exists at a $600 production level; production of $550 or $650 thereby represents disequilibrium. There is a deficiency of output when production is $550 and excess supply when production is $650.

(b)   Positions off *IS* and to the left of the schedule represent income levels where planned aggregate spending exceeds output; positions off *IS* and to the right represent excess output, i.e., output is greater than planned aggregate spending.

THE DEMAND FOR MONEY

5.19   (*a*) Why is there a transaction demand for money? (*b*) Does the private sector hold constant transaction money balances over time?

(*a*)   Households and corporations hold transaction balances because money receipts and disbursements rarely coincide. Private sector money receipts normally lead disbursements, with the lead time dependent on "typical" payment patterns. For example, households may be paid weekly, biweekly, or monthly; their money receipts must be budgeted over the pay period, resulting in an average holding of money balances for transactions.

(*b*)   The average holding of money balances for transactions depends on the length of the pay period, timing of expenditures and the income level. Therefore, it is highly unlikely that the private sector will hold constant money balances for transactions over time. In macroeconomic theory, it is customary to assume that pay periods and timing of expenditures do not change in the short run, with income the sole determinant of transaction money holdings. The transaction demand for money is presented as $L_t = f(Y)$.

5.20   (*a*) Why is there a portfolio demand for money? (*b*) Is this portfolio demand constant over time?

(*a*)   Those who possess wealth allocate their accumulated savings among four asset categories: liquid assets (which include money), long-term bonds, equities, and real assets. Individual allocations depend on the magnitude of accumulated savings, willingness to assume risk and market interest rates. For example, an investor whose portfolio of assets is relatively small or who is risk averse may hold a large percentage of accumulated wealth as a money balance because of uncertainties about the future and a possible need to draw on this wealth. Individuals with a relatively large portfolio of assets may hold a combination of the four asset categories, with the actual percentage in each category influenced by market interest rates, i.e., the opportunity cost of holding liquid assets.

(b) It is customary to assume that the distribution of wealth and willingness to assume risk is constant in the short run. Hence, the portfolio demand for money is a stable function of market interest rates. Money balances held in portfolios do not change as long as the market rate of interest is unchanged; increases in market rates, however, will decrease the quantity of money held in private sector portfolios, i.e., $L_p = f(i)$.

5.21 Tables 5-3 and 5-4 present the transaction and portfolio demand for money. (a) Find the quantity of money demanded when income is $700 and the market rate of interest is 8% and 10%. (b) The total demand for money is found by summing the transaction and portfolio demand for money. Present in Table 5-5 is a schedule of the total demand for money when income is $600, $700 and $800. (c) Plot the demand for money schedules derived in part (b) in Fig. 5-26 and label them L, L' and L'' respectively.

Table 5-3   Transaction Demand for Money

Income Level, $	Quantity of Money Demanded, $
500	100
600	120
700	140
800	160
900	180

Table 5-4   Portfolio Demand for Money

Market Rate of Interest, %	Quantity of Money Demanded, $
12	30
10	50
8	70
6	90
4	110

(a) The total demand for money is the sum of the balances demanded for transactions and those held in portfolios. When the income level is $700, transaction holdings are $140, and portfolio holdings are $70 at an 8% market rate of interest and $50 at a 10% rate. The total demand for money at a $700 income level and 8% market rate of interest is $210; total demand is $190 when the income level is $700 and the market rate is 10%.

(b)

Table 5-5 Total Demand for Money

Rate of Interest (%)	Quantity of Money Demanded When		
	$Y = \$600$	$Y = \$700$	$Y = \$800$
12	$150	$170	$190
10	170	190	210
8	190	210	230
6	210	230	250
4	230	250	270

(c) See Fig. 5-26.

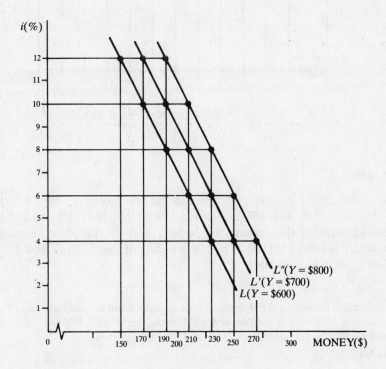

Fig. 5-26

5.22 Suppose the total demand for money is specified as $L = kY - hi$ and the value of behavioral coefficient k is 0.20 and $h = 5$. (a) Plot the demand for money schedule in Fig. 5-27 when income is $600 and the rate of interest is 12%, 10%, 8% and 6%; label the demand schedule L. (b) Plot and label L' and L'' in Fig. 5-27 the demand for money schedule when income is $800 and $1000. (c) What happens to the demand for money schedules in Fig. 5-27 when the income level increases from $600 to $800 to $1000?

(a) and (b) See Fig. 5.27.

(c) The demand for money schedule shifts rightward $40 as a result of $200 increases in the income level; the shift is equal to $k \Delta Y$.

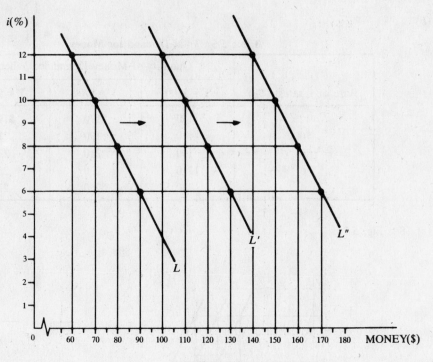

Fig. 5-27

THE *LM* SCHEDULE

5.23 Suppose $L = 0.20Y - 5i$. (*a*) Plot the demand for money in Fig. 5-28(*a*) when the rate of interest is 10%, 8% and 6% and income is (1) \$800, (2) \$900 and (3) \$1000. (*b*) Find equilibrium between the demand for money and the supply of money when the nominal money supply is \$150. (*c*) Derive an *LM* schedule in Fig. 5-28(*b*) from the data in Fig. 5-28(*a*). (*d*) What is an *LM* schedule?

(*a*)   See Fig. 5-28(*a*).

(*b*)   Equilibrium between a \$150 nominal money supply and demand for money schedules *L*, *L'* and *L"* exists at a 10% rate of interest and a \$1000 income level, a 6% rate of interest and a \$900 income level and a 2% rate of interest and an \$800 income level.

(*c*)   See Fig. 5-28(*b*).

(*d*)   An *LM* schedule is a locus of points at which the demand for money is equal to the supply of money.

5.24 (*a*) Find an equation for equilibrium between the demand for money and the supply of money when the demand for money is $L = kY - hi$ and the money supply is $\bar{M}$. (*b*) Find a numerical equation for monetary equilibrium when $k = 0.20$, $h = 5$ and $\bar{M} = \$200$. (*c*) Find the income level associated with interest rates 10%, 8% and 6% when there is equilibrium in the money market.

(*a*)   Equilibrium in the money market exists where the demand for money equals the money supply.

$$L = M$$
$$kY - hi = \bar{M}$$
$$kY = \bar{M} + hi$$

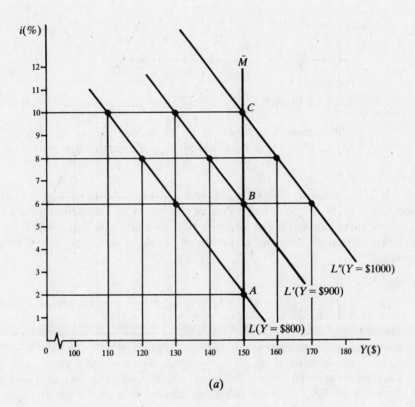

(a)

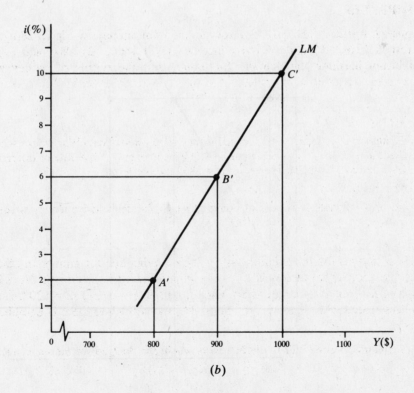

(b)

Fig. 5-28

$$Y = \frac{\bar{M} + hi}{k}$$

or

$$Y = \frac{\bar{M}}{k} + \frac{hi}{k}$$

(b) Substituting $k = 0.20$, $h = 5$, and $\bar{M} = \$200$ into the equation $Y = (\bar{M} + hi)/k$, we have $Y = \$1000 + 25i$.

(c) When $i = 10\%$, there is equilibrium in the money market when Y is \$1250. $[Y = (\$200 + 5(10))/0.20.]$ (2) When $i = 8\%$, Y is \$1200 at equilibrium; and Y must equal \$1150 when $i = 6\%$.

5.25 The *LM* schedule is $Y = \$1000 + 25i$ when $L = 0.20Y - 5i$ and $\bar{M} = \$200$. (a) Plot the *LM* schedule in Fig. 5-29. (b) What is true of the supply of and demand for money at a 10% rate of interest and a \$1100 level of income? 10% rate of interest and a \$1350 level of income? (c) What generalizations can one make about positions to the right and to the left of the *LM* schedule?

(a) Fig. 5-29.

(b) L is \$170 when $i = 10\%$ and $Y = \$1100$; i.e., the demand for money is \$170, less than the \$200 money supply. L equals \$220 when $i = 10\%$ and $Y = \$1350$; a \$220 money demand exceeds a \$200 money supply.

(c) Positions to the left of *LM* represent positions where the demand for money is less than the money supply; there is therefore downward pressure on interest rates. Positions to the right of *LM* exist when money demand exceeds the money supply, and there is upward pressure on interest rates. Points on the *LM* schedule represent equilibrium between the supply of and demand for money.

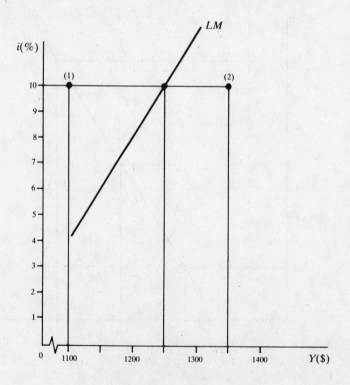

Fig. 5-29

SHIFTS OF THE *LM* SCHEDULE

5.26 The equation for the *LM* schedule is $Y = \bar{M}/k + hi/k$. (*a*) Find the change in income associated with a $\Delta \bar{M}$ increase in money, holding behavioral coefficients *k* and *h* and the rate of interest constant. (*b*) What happens to the *LM* schedule when there is an increase in the money supply of $\Delta \bar{M}$?

(*a*) With the rate of interest held constant, $\Delta Y = \Delta \bar{M}(1/k)$.

(*b*) The $\Delta \bar{M}$ increase in the money supply shifts *LM* rightward by $\Delta \bar{M}(1/k)$.

5.27 (*a*) Find an equation for the *LM* schedule when the money supply is $200 and the demand for money is specified as $L = 0.20Y - 4i$. (*b*) Plot the schedule in Fig. 5-30 and label it *LM*. (*c*) Find an equation for *LM* when the money supply increases from $200 to $210; plot the new *LM* schedule in Fig. 5-30 and label it *LM'*. (*d*) What happens to *LM* as a result of a $10 increase in the money supply?

(*a*)
$$M = L$$
$$\$200 = 0.20Y - 4i$$
$$0.20Y = \$200 + 4i$$
$$Y = \$1000 + 20i$$

(*b*) See Fig. 5-30.

(*c*) The new *LM* equation is $Y = \$1050 + 20i$; the new schedule is *LM'* in Fig. 5-30.

(*d*) The $10 increase in the money supply shifts *LM* rightward $50 from *LM* to *LM'*; the shift equals $\Delta \bar{M}(1/k)$, i.e., $10/0.20.

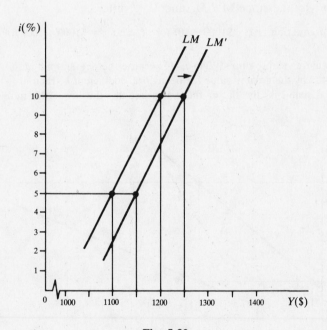

Fig. 5-30

5.28 Establish the direction and magnitude of the shift of *LM* when (*a*) $k = 0.20$ and there is a $20 increase in the money supply, (*b*) $k = 0.50$ and there is a $20 decrease in the money supply, (*c*) $k = 0.25$ and there is a $20 increase in the money supply.

(a) The *LM* schedule shifts rightward \$100; \$20/0.20 = \$100.

(b) The *LM* schedule shifts leftward \$40; $-\$20/0.50 = -\$40$.

(c) The *LM* schedule shifts rightward \$80; \$20/0.25 = \$80.

SLOPE OF THE *LM* SCHEDULE

5.29 (a) Find an equation for *LM* in terms of the rate of interest *i* when the money supply equals $\bar{M}$ and the demand for money is $kY - hi$. (b) Find the slope of the *LM* equation. (c) Find the slope of *LM* when $k = 0.20$ and $h = 10$; $k = 0.20$ and $h = 20$; $k = 0.10$ and $h = 10$. (d) What happens to the slope of *LM* when the value for behavioral coefficient *k* decreases? What happens to the slope of *LM* when the value for behavioral coefficient *h* increases?

(a)
$$M = L$$
$$\bar{M} = kY - hi$$
$$hi = kY - \bar{M}$$
$$i = \left(\frac{k}{h}\right)Y - \frac{\bar{M}}{h}$$

(b) The slope of *LM* is the behavioral coefficient for *Y* (*k/h*).

(c) When $k = 0.20$ and $h = 10$, the slope for *LM* is 0.02; when $k = 0.20$ and $h = 20$, the slope for *LM* is 0.01; when $k = 0.10$ and $h = 10$, the slope is 0.01.

(d) When the value for *k* decreases, the slope of *LM* decreases; the slope of *LM* also decreases when the value for *h* increases.

5.30 Suppose the money supply is \$200 and the demand for money is $kY - hi$. (a) Plot in Fig. 5-31, *LM* when (1) $k = 0.20$ and $h = 10$ and label it *LM'* (2) $k = 0.10$ and $h = 20$ and label it *LM"*. (b) Explain why the slope of *LM'* and *LM"* differ.

(a) The *LM* equation is $Y = \$1000 + 50i$ for (1) and $Y = \$1000 + 100i$ for (2); they are plotted in Fig. 5-31.

(b) *LM'* is more steeply sloped than *LM"* because the demand for money is more interest sensitive in (2) (noted by the greater value for behavioral coefficient *h*) than in (1). The more interest sensitive money demand is, the flatter the *LM* schedule (the lower the numerical value of the slope for *LM*).

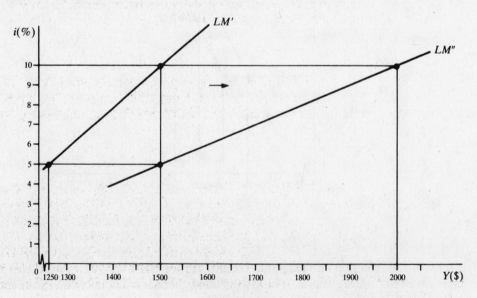

Fig. 5-31

5.31 Suppose the demand for money is \$200 and the demand for money is $kY - hi$. (*a*) Plot in Fig. 5-32 *LM* when k is 0.20 and h is zero. (*b*) Why is the *LM* schedule vertical?

(*a*) The *LM* equation is $Y = \$1000$ and is plotted in Fig. 5-32.

(*b*) *LM* has no relationship to the rate of interest because the demand for money is not influenced by interest levels. Hence, when h is zero or takes a very small value, the *LM* schedule is vertical or steeply sloped.

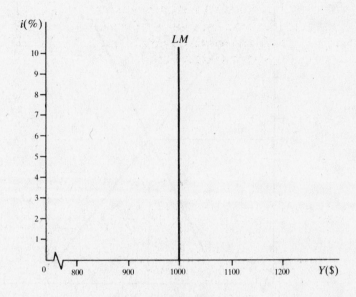

Fig. 5-32

SIMULTANEOUS EQUILIBRIUM IN THE MONEY AND GOODS MARKETS

5.32 Posit a two-sector model where $C = \$100 + 0.80Y$ and $I = \$150 - 6i$, $M = \$150$ and $L = 0.20Y - 4i$. (*a*) Find an equation for equilibrium in the goods market (*IS*) and for the money market (*LM*). (*b*) Find the income level and rate of interest at which there is simultaneous equilibrium in the money and goods markets. (*c*) Plot the *IS* and *LM* equations in Fig. 5-33 and find equilibrium income and the rate of interest.

(*a*) The *IS* equation:

$$Y = C + I$$
$$Y = \$100 + 0.80Y + \$150 - 6i$$
$$Y = \$1250 - 30i$$

The *LM* equation:

$$M = L$$
$$\$150 = 0.20Y - 4i$$
$$Y = \$750 + 20i$$

(*b*) Simultaneous equilibrium income occurs where $IS = LM$.

$$Y = \$1250 - 30i$$
$$-(Y = \$\ 750 + 20i)$$
$$\overline{\qquad 0 = \$\ 500 - 50i \qquad}$$

$$i = 10\%$$
$$Y = \$ \ 950$$

(*c*) Simultaneous equilibrium exists at the intersection of the *IS* and *LM* schedules. In Fig. 5-33, this
occurs at a $950 income level and a 10% rate of interest.

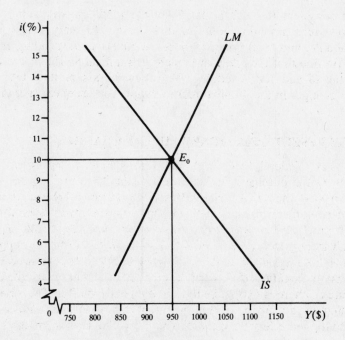

Fig. 5-33

5.33 Find simultaneous equilibrium income for the goods and money market when $C = \$100 +
0.80Yd$, $I = \$150 - 6i$, $Tn = 0.25Y$, $G = \$100$, $L = 0.20Y - 2i$ and $M = \$150$.

The *IS* equation:

$$Y = C + I + G$$
$$Y = \$100 + 0.80(Y - 0.25Y) + \$150 - 6i + \$100$$
$$Y = \$350 + 0.6Y - 6i$$
$$Y = \$875 - 15i$$

The *LM* equation:

$$M = L$$
$$\$150 = 0.20Y - 2i$$
$$Y = \$750 + 10i$$

Simultaneous equilibrium for *IS* and *LM*:

$$IS = LM$$
$$\$875 - 15i = \$750 + 10i$$
$$25i = \$125$$
$$i = 5\%$$
$$Y = \$800$$

Chapter 6

Monetary and Fiscal Policy in an *IS-LM* Framework

This chapter considers the effect that a change in the money supply, government spending and/or net tax revenues has upon equilibrium income. Monetary policy (money supply changes) shifts the *LM* schedule, and fiscal policy (changes in government spending or net tax revenues) shifts the *IS* schedule. We find that the effect of monetary and fiscal policy on equilibrium income depends on the slope of the *IS* and *LM* schedules. We retain the assumptions that the price level remains constant and that changes in the nominal money supply represent changes in the real money supply.

6.1 TWO-STAGE EFFECT OF A MONEY SUPPLY CHANGE

The central bank (Federal Reserve in the United States) implements money supply changes (monetary policy) by the purchase and sale of Treasury securities (open market operations). The money supply expands when the Federal Reserve purchases Treasury securities in the financial markets and exchanges them for newly issued paper currency and/or bank deposits at the Federal Reserve. Security purchases increase the money supply from M_0 to M_1 in Fig. 6-1 and cause the interest rate to fall from i_0 to i_2. (See Example 1.) An M_0 to M_1 money supply increase is presented in Fig. 6-2 as a $\Delta \bar{M}(1/k)$ rightward shift of *LM* from *LM'* to *LM''*. At income level Y_0, the increased money supply causes a *liquidity effect* which lowers the rate of interest from i_0 to i_2. At income level Y_0 and interest rate i_2, there is excess demand in the goods market. This disequilibrium in the goods market is remedied by an *income effect*; a lower rate of interest induces additional investment spending and a multiplied effect on income. The money and goods markets return to simultaneous equilibrium at an i_1 rate of interest and a Y_1 level of income.

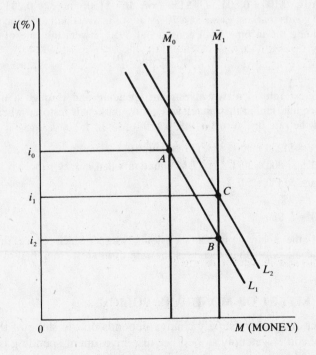

Fig. 6-1

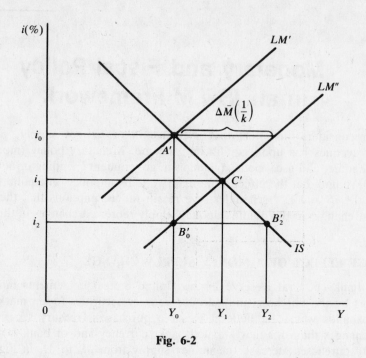

Fig. 6-2

EXAMPLE 1. Suppose the Federal Reserve purchases Treasury securities from the private sector which increases the money supply in Fig. 6-1 from M_0 to M_1. Movement along demand for money schedule L_1 causes a *liquidity effect* which reduces the rate of interest from i_0 to i_2. The lowered rate of interest, however, increases investment spending and equilibrium income. The resulting *income effect* shifts the demand for money schedule upward from L_1 to L_2, and the rate of interest increases from i_2 to i_1.

EXAMPLE 2. The equation for equilibrium in the goods market is $Y = \$1250 - 30i$ and in the money market is $Y = \$750 + 20i$ when $C = \$100 + 0.80Y$, $I = \$150 - 6i$, $M = \$150$, and $L = 0.20Y - 4i$. Simultaneous equilibrium in the money and goods markets exists at a 10% rate of interest and $950 income level. A $10 increase in the money supply, holding the income level constant at $950, lowers the rate of interest from 10 to 7.50%.

$$\$160 = 0.20(\$950) - 4i$$
$$4i = \$30 \qquad i = 7.50\%$$

However, a lower interest rate increases investment spending and through a multiplier effect equilibrium income. Simultaneous equilibrium in the money and goods markets is restored when the income level increases from $950 to $980 and the rate of interest is 9%.

$$
\begin{array}{ll}
Y = \$1250 - 30i & \text{(\textit{IS} equation)} \\
\underline{(Y = \quad 800 + 20i)} & \text{(\textit{LM} equation when money supply is \$160)} \\
0 = \$ \ 450 - 50i & \\
i = 9\% & \\
Y = \$ \ 980 &
\end{array}
$$

Thus, the $10 increase in the money supply causes a liquidity effect which reduces the rate of interest from 10 to 7.50%; the resulting income effect then increases the rate of interest from 7.50 to 9.00%.

6.2   THE INCOME EFFECT OF MONETARY POLICY

The income effect of a money supply change depends on the slope of the *IS* and *LM* schedules. In Fig. 6-3, the *IS* schedule is steeply sloped because investment spending is somewhat unresponsive to the rate of interest and/or there is a low value for the expenditure multiplier. (Our discussion will

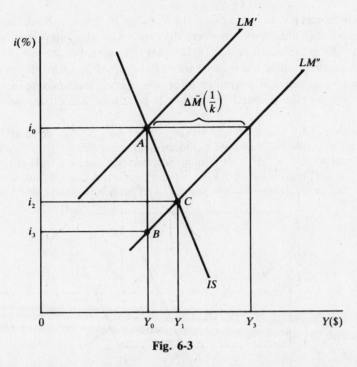

Fig. 6-3

focus upon the interest sensitivity of investment spending.) A money supply increase in Fig. 6-3 shifts *LM* rightward from *LM'* to *LM"*, which at interest rate i_0 equals Y_0 to Y_3. At income level Y_0, the rate of interest decreases from i_0 to i_3. The income effect, however, is only Y_0 to Y_1, because investment spending is relatively insensitive to the rate of interest. There is an equal money supply increase of $\Delta \bar{M}$ in Fig. 6-4 with a similar liquidity effect which reduces the rate of interest from i_0 to i_3. Because investment spending is more interest sensitive, there is a larger income effect and therefore larger increase in equilibrium income. The Y_0 to Y_3 shift of *LM* in Fig. 6-4 has an income

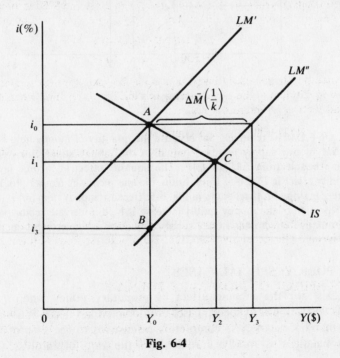

Fig. 6-4

effect of Y_0 to Y_2, which is greater than the Y_0 to Y_1 effect in Fig. 6-3. Note that the liquidity effect is the same in Fig. 6-3 and Fig. 6-4; however, differences in the interest sensitivity of investment spending result in a different income effect. Examples 6.3 and 6.4 relate the effect that an increase in the money supply has on equilibrium income when there are differences in the slope of *LM*. We find that a money supply increase has a greater effect on equilibrium income when *LM* is flatter than when it is steeply sloped (the demand for money is relatively interest insensitive).

EXAMPLE 3. Schedule *LM'* in Fig. 6-5 is steeply sloped because the demand for money is relatively insensitive to the rate of interest (the amount of money held in the private sector's portfolio of assets is little affected by interest rate levels). A $\Delta \bar{M}$ money supply increase results in a $\Delta \bar{M}(1/k)$ rightward shift of the *LM* schedule from *LM'* to *LM''* (equivalent to a Y_0 to Y_3 shift at interest rate i_0). The liquidity effect is i_0 to i_4 at income level Y_0. Equilibrium income increases from Y_0 to Y_2 which is slightly less than the *LM* shift.

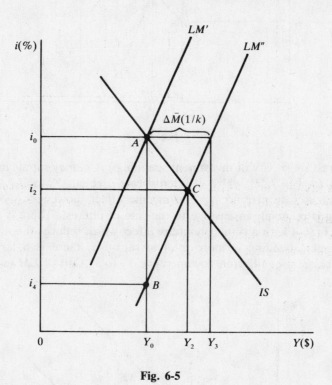

Fig. 6-5

EXAMPLE 4. In Fig. 6-6 *LM'* is relatively flat because the quantity of money held is highly responsive to the rate of interest. A $\Delta \bar{M}$ money supply increase (equal to the money supply increase in Fig. 6-5) shifts the monetary equilibrium schedule from *LM'* to *LM''*. The liquidity effect at income level Y_0 is i_0 to i_3 which is smaller than the liquidity effect in Fig. 6-5. Equilibrium income increases from Y_0 to Y_1, which is less than that found for the more steeply sloped *LM* schedule in Fig. 6-5. Because money demand is highly sensitive to interest rate changes, a larger portion of the money supply increase is held in private sector portfolios; a small liquidity effect reduces the stimulative effect of a money supply expansion on investment spending.

6.3 MONETARY POLICY: SPECIAL CASES

Special cases exist for the income effect of monetary policy when *LM* is vertical, *LM* is horizontal, and *IS* is vertical. These special cases are depicted in Figs. 6-7, 6-8 and 6-9. A vertical *LM* exists when the demand for money is completely insensitive to the rate of interest, i.e., portfolio holding of money balances is totally unrelated to the rate of interest. In the *LM* equation,

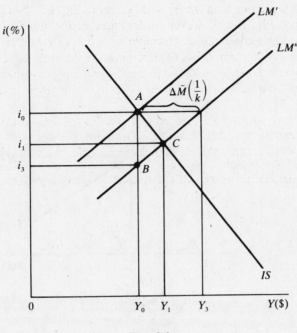

Fig. 6-6

$\bar{M} = kY - hi$; such a situation arises when $h = 0$ so that $\bar{M} = kY$. A money supply increase of $\Delta \bar{M}$ in Fig. 6-7 shifts *LM* from *LM'* to *LM''*; the Y_0 to Y_1 increase in equilibrium income is equal to the $\Delta \bar{M}(1/k)$ shift, regardless of the slope of *IS*.

   LM is horizontal (Fig. 6-8) when there is a liquidity trap. A liquidity trap arises when portfolio holders have an infinite demand for money because they do not want to hold bonds. The entirety of a money supply increase is held in portfolios; therefore there is no liquidity effect and no change in

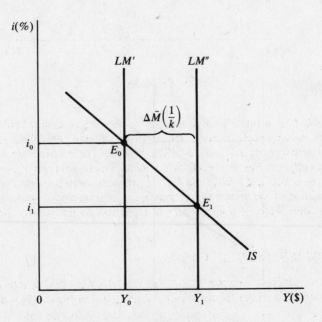

Fig. 6-7

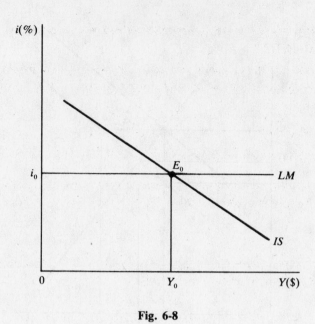

Fig. 6-8

income. Money supply changes do not affect the location of *LM* in space and therefore leave interest rates and income levels unchanged.

IS is vertical (Fig. 6-9) when investment spending is unrelated to the rate of interest. Suppose the *IS* equation for a two-sector model is $Y = (\bar{C} + \bar{I} - bi)/(1 - c)$. When behavioral coefficient b equals zero, interest rates have no effect on investment spending. The *IS* equation is then $Y = (\bar{C} + \bar{I})/(1 - c)$, and the *IS* schedule is vertical. Shifts of monetary equilibrium from *LM'* to *LM''* in Fig. 6-9 have a liquidity effect of i_0 to i_1 but do not change equilibrium income because investment is unrelated to the rate of interest.

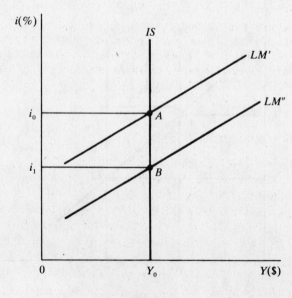

Fig. 6-9

6.4 THE MULTIPLIER EFFECT OF A MONEY SUPPLY CHANGE IN AN *IS-LM* FRAMEWORK

Simultaneous equilibrium in the goods and money markets exists at the intersection of the *IS* and *LM* schedules. For a negatively sloped *IS* and positively sloped *LM*, this intersection is given by

$$Y = \bar{A}\left(\frac{hk_e}{h + kbk_e}\right) + \bar{M}\left(\frac{bk_e}{h + kbk_e}\right)$$

where $\bar{A}$ represents the sum of autonomous spending ($\bar{C} + \bar{I} - b\overline{Tn} + \bar{G} + \bar{X}$). (See Problem 6.13 for derivation.)

Assuming no change in autonomous spending $\bar{A}$ or behavioral coefficients h, k, b and k_e, a change in the money supply is associated with the following change in equilibrium income.

$$\Delta Y = \Delta \bar{M}\left(\frac{bk_e}{h + kbk_e}\right)$$

The rate of change in income due to a change in the money supply—the multiplier effect of a money supply change, or $\Delta Y/\Delta \bar{M}$—is therefore written as

$$\frac{\Delta Y}{\Delta \bar{M}} = \frac{bk_e}{h + kbk_e}$$

Note that the multiplier effect is larger as the value for h is smaller. (Recall that small values for h are associated with a steeply sloped *LM*; money supply changes have a greater effect on equilibrium income when *LM* is steeply sloped.) The larger the value for coefficients b and/or k_e—the less steeply sloped *IS*—the greater the multiplier effect of $\Delta \bar{M}$ on ΔY.

EXAMPLE 5. When there is a stable *IS* schedule, changes in equilibrium income due to a change in the money supply is written as

$$\Delta Y = \Delta \bar{M}\left(\frac{bk_e}{h + kbk_e}\right)$$

Situation I A money supply change has a greater effect on equilibrium income when the value of behavioral coefficient h is smaller—the responsiveness of holding money balances to the rate of interest. Suppose $b = 5$, $k_e = 4$ and $k = 0.20$. When $h = 5$ and there is a $20 increase in the money supply, equilibrium income increases: $\Delta Y = \$20\{5(4)/[5 + (0.20)(5)(4)]\} = \$74.07$. However, when $h = 0$ and the money supply increases $20, equilibrium income increases: $\Delta Y = \$20\{5(4)/[0 + (0.20)(5)(4)]\} = \$100$.

Situation II A money supply change has a smaller effect on equilibrium income when behavioral coefficient b is small—spending is largely unresponsive to the rate of interest—than when b has a larger value. Suppose $k_e = 4$, $k = 0.20$, and $h = 5$. When $b = 5$ and the money supply increases $20, equilibrium income increases $74.07 as calculated above. However, when $b = 1$ and the money supply increases $20, equilibrium income increases: $\Delta Y = \$20\{1(4) / [5 + (0.20)(1)(4)]\} = \$13.79$.

6.5 THE INCOME EFFECT OF FISCAL POLICY

Discretionary fiscal policy involves changes in government spending, taxes and/or transfers to affect the economy's equilibrium income. In Fig. 6-10, simultaneous equilibrium is initially at Y_0 and i_0. A $\Delta \bar{G}$ increase in government spending shifts *IS* rightward by $k_e\Delta \bar{G}$, equal to Y_0 to Y_3 at interest rate i_0. In Fig. 6-10, this $k_e\Delta \bar{G}$ multiplied effect of fiscal policy is not realized. Increased government spending causes movement along *LM*—and an increase in the rate of interest—until simultaneous equilibrium is reached at Y_2 and i_1. Because of the increase in the rate of interest from i_0 to i_1, some investment spending is *crowded out* reducing the stimulative effect of the fiscal action.

The income effect of an increase in government spending (and other fiscal measures) depends on the slope of the *IS* and *LM* schedules. The *LM* schedule is steeply sloped in Fig. 6-11(a), largely the result of a demand for money which is relatively unresponsive to interest rate levels. A $\Delta \bar{G}$ increase

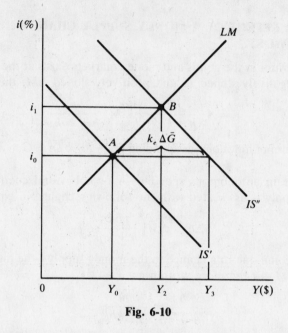

Fig. 6-10

in government spending shifts *IS* rightward by $k_e \Delta \bar{G}$, raising the interest rate from i_0 to i_2. Because the demand for money is insensitive to the rate of interest, a larger increase in the rate of interest is needed to accommodate the increased income demand for money. Equilibrium income increases from Y_0 to Y_1, although the projected income change would be Y_0 to Y_3 in the absence of a change in the interest rate. Private sector spending of Y_1 to Y_3 is crowded out by the i_0 to i_2 increase in the rate of interest. In Fig. 6-11(*b*), a $\Delta \bar{G}$ increase in government spending results in less crowding out of private sector spending. The rightward shift of *IS* from *IS'* to *IS''* is the same as that in Fig. 6-11(*a*), but the *LM* schedule is less steeply sloped because the demand for money is more interest sensitive. The shift from *IS'* to *IS''* results in a smaller increase in the interest rate (i_0 to i_1) in Fig. 6-11(*b*) and a larger increase in equilibrium income (Y_0 to Y_2) than in Fig. 6-11(*a*), where the interest rate rises from i_0 to i_2 and equilibrium income increases from Y_0 to Y_1. Examples 5 and 6 show that there is

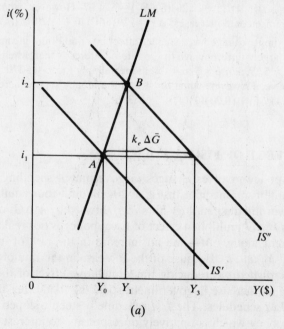

(*a*)

Fig. 6-11

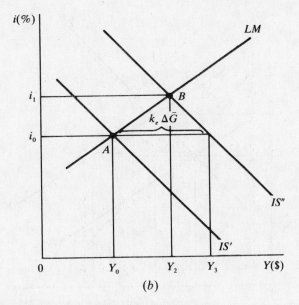

Fig. 6-11 *(continued)*

less crowding out when *IS* is steeply sloped (spending is less affected by the rate of interest) than when *IS* is relatively flat and spending is highly responsive to the rate of interest.

EXAMPLE 6.   Schedule *IS'* is steeply sloped in Fig. 6-12(a) because spending is largely unresponsive to the rate of interest. Increased government spending shifts *IS* from *IS'* to *IS''*, by $k_e \Delta \bar{G}$ which equals Y_0 to Y_3. Equilibrium income increases from Y_0 to Y_2 with a crowding out of private sector spending of Y_2 to Y_3.

EXAMPLE 7.   Schedule *IS'* is less steeply sloped in Fig. 6-12(b) because of the greater interest sensitivity of investment spending. The shift from *IS'* to *IS''*, which is the same as the Y_0 to Y_3 shift in Fig. 6-12(a), increases equilibrium income from Y_0 to Y_1. Because private sector spending is highly sensitive to higher interest rates, there is crowding out of Y_1 to Y_3 of private sector spending as the rate of interest increases from i_0 to i_1.

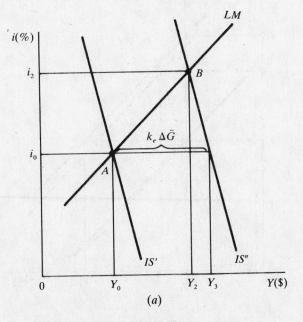

Fig. 6-12

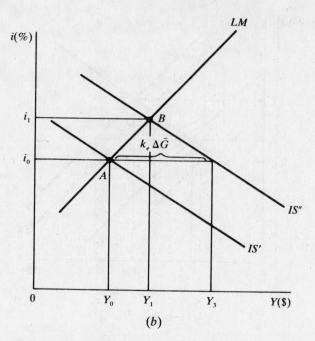

Fig. 6-12 (*continued*)

6.6 FISCAL POLICY: SPECIAL CASES

Special cases exist for the income effect of fiscal policy when *LM* is vertical, *LM* is horizontal and *IS* is vertical. In comparing this analysis with that in Section 6.4 on monetary policy, one finds that a fiscal action has a full multiplier effect when monetary policy has no effect on income and fiscal policy has no effect on equilibrium income when monetary policy is most effective.

The *LM* schedule in Fig. 6-13(*a*) is vertical because the demand for money is unrelated to the rate of interest (in the demand for money function $L = kY - hi$, h equals 0). The rightward shift of

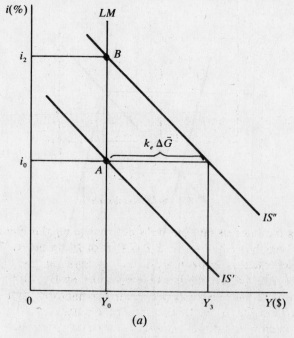

Fig. 6-13

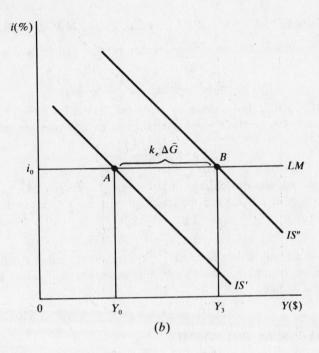

(b)

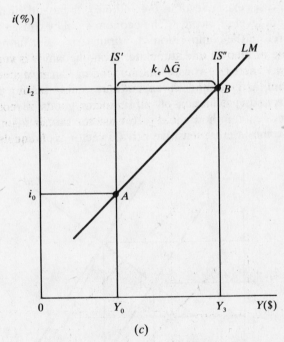

(c)

Fig. 6-13 (*continued*)

IS from *IS'* to *IS"* raises the interest rate but does not change equilibrium income; there is complete crowding out of Y_0 to Y_3 which is equal to the $k_e \Delta \bar{G}$ shift of *IS*. In Fig. 6-13(b), there is no crowding out because the *LM* schedule is horizontal; a $\Delta \bar{G}$ increase in government spending increases equilibrium income by $k_e \Delta \bar{G}$ (Y_0 to Y_3) because investors have an infinite demand for money at interest rate i_0. The complete multiplier effect of a fiscal stimulus ($k_e \Delta \bar{G} = Y_0$ to Y_3) is also realized in the rightward shift of *IS* in Fig. 6-13(c). Increased government spending raises the rate of interest, but the higher rate has no crowding out effect because investment spending is unrelated to the rate of interest.

6.7 THE MULTIPLIER EFFECT OF FISCAL POLICY IN AN *IS-LM* FRAMEWORK

Simultaneous equilibrium in the goods and money market can be written as

$$Y = \bar{A}\left(\frac{hk_e}{h + kbk_e}\right) + \bar{M}\left(\frac{bk_e}{h + kbk_e}\right)$$

Assuming a stable *LM* schedule (no change in $\bar{M}$ or behavioral coefficients k_e and b), a change in autonomous spending $\Delta\bar{A}$ causes the following change in equilibrium income

$$\Delta Y = \Delta\bar{A}\left(\frac{hk_e}{h + kbk_e}\right)$$

where $\Delta\bar{A}$ represents an autonomous change in government spending $\Delta\bar{G}$, taxes $c\Delta\bar{T}x$ and transfers $c\Delta\bar{T}r$. The multiplier effect of a fiscal action, specified here as $\Delta\bar{A}$, is written as

$$\frac{\Delta Y}{\Delta\bar{A}} = \frac{hk_e}{h + kbk_e}$$

The multiplier effect of a fiscal action is greater the smaller the value for b and/or the larger the value for h. A small value for b makes the *IS* schedule steeply sloped, and a large value for h results in a relatively flat *LM* schedule.

6.8 THE MONETARY-FISCAL POLICY MIX

Except when special cases exist (Sections 6.4 and 6.6), fiscal and/or monetary policy can be used to increase the equilibrium level of income. The economic policy chosen has a selective impact upon sector spending and therefore the composition of output. An easier monetary policy, in shifting *LM* rightward, lowers the rate of interest and stimulates spending which is interest sensitive. A reduction in household income taxes increases consumption spending, an investment tax credit increases the profitability of new plant and equipment expenditures and thereby investment, and increased government spending expands production of public sector goods. Because a fiscal stimulus causes higher interest rates, a reduction in household sector income taxes and/or an increase in government spending "crowds out" some interest-sensitive private sector spending.

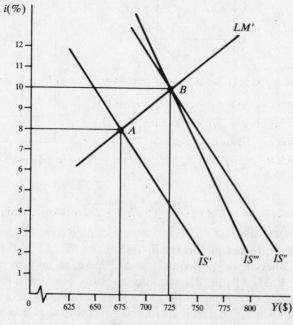

Fig. 6-14

EXAMPLE 8. Posit an economy where schedules *IS'* and *LM'* in Fig. 6-14 determine an 8% rate of interest and a \$675 equilibrium level of income. Sector spending behavior in the goods market is specified as $C = \$20 + 0.80(Y - 0.25Y)$, $I = \$130 - 5i$, and $G = \$160$. At a \$675 income level, consumption is \$425, investment is \$90, and government spending is \$160. Suppose income taxes are lowered from 0.25 to 0.20 with the consumption equation now specified as $C = \$20 + 0.80(Y - 0.20Y)$. Assuming no other parameter change, *IS* shifts rightward to *IS'''* (note that there is both a shift and a change in slope), causing interest rates to rise to 10% and income to increase to \$722. At this higher income level consumption has increased to \$482 from its \$425 previous level, investment has fallen to \$80 from \$90, and government spending has remained at \$160. An alternative fiscal action might have called for a \$28.80 increase in government spending with no change in taxes. *IS* would have shifted to *IS''* also resulting in a 10% rate of interest and a \$722 income level. Consumption spending would be \$453.20 rather than \$482 when there was a decrease in household income taxes, investment would continue at its reduced level of \$80, and government spending has increased from \$160 to \$188.80.

Review Questions

1. A liquidity effect occurs when

    (a) A reduction in government spending lowers the rate of interest.

    (b) A money supply increase lowers the rate of interest.

    (c) An increase in government spending increases the rate of interest.

    (d) A money supply increase raises the rate of interest.

    Answer: (b)

2. A liquidity effect will normally result in an income effect because

    (a) Lower interest rates will increase the portfolio demand for money.

    (b) Lower interest rates will cause less crowding out.

    (c) Lower interest rates will increase interest-sensitive spending.

    (d) Lower interest rates will cause more crowding out.

    Answer: (c)

3. A change in the money supply has a greater effect upon equilibrium income

    (a) The more interest-sensitive private sector spending is

    (b) The less interest-sensitive private sector spending is

    (c) The smaller the expenditure multiplier is

    (d) The more interest-sensitive money holdings are to the rate of interest

    Answer: (a)

4. A money supply increase shifts *LM* rightward by $\Delta \bar{M}(1/k)$, with the actual change in equilibrium income closely approximating the shift of *LM* when

    (a) *LM* is steeply sloped and *IS* is steeply sloped.

    (b) *LM* is relatively flat as is *IS*.

    (c) *LM* is steeply sloped and *IS* is relatively flat.

    (d) *LM* is relatively flat and *IS* is steeply sloped.

    Answer: (c)

5. In which of the following situations will an increase in the money supply have no effect upon equilibrium income?

    (*a*) *LM* is steeply sloped and *IS* is relatively flat.

    (*b*) *LM* is vertical and *IS* is steeply sloped.

    (*c*) *LM* is steeply sloped and *IS* is vertical.

    (*d*) *LM* is relatively flat as is *IS*.

    Answer: (*c*)

6. k_e is the expenditure multiplier, *b* the interest sensitivity of private sector spending, *h* the interest sensitivity of the demand for money and *k* is the transaction demand for money. From the following sets of values for k_e, *b*, *h* and *k*, find the one in which a change in the money supply will have the larger multiplying effect on equilibrium income.

    (*a*) $k_e = 5$, $b = 5$, $h = 5$, $k = 0.20$

    (*b*) $k_e = 4$, $b = 1$, $h = 5$, $k = 0.20$

    (*c*) $k_e = 5$, $b = 10$, $h = 1$, $k = 0.20$

    (*d*) $k_e = 4$, $b = 5$, $h = 10$, $k = 0.10$

    Answer: (*c*)

7. An increase in government spending shifts *IS* rightward by $k_e \Delta \bar{G}$, with the actual change in equilibrium income closely approximating the schedule's shift when

    (*a*) The *LM* is relatively flat and *IS* is steeply sloped.

    (*b*) The *LM* is vertical and *IS* is steeply sloped.

    (*c*) The *LM* is relatively flat as is *IS*.

    (*d*) The *LM* is steeply sloped and the *IS* is relatively flat.

    Answer: (*a*)

8. Crowding out is more likely to occur when

    (*a*) The demand for money is interest sensitive, and private sector spending is largely interest insensitive.

    (*b*) The demand for money is interest sensitive, and private sector spending is interest sensitive.

    (*c*) The demand for money is interest insensitive, and private sector spending is interest insensitive.

    (*d*) The demand for money is interest insensitive, and private sector spending is interest sensitive.

    Answer: (*d*)

9. Crowding out will occur when

    (*a*) A decrease in the money supply raises interest rates which crowd out interest-sensitive private sector spending.

    (*b*) An increase in taxes for the private sector reduces private sector disposable income and spending.

    (*c*) A reduction in income taxes causes higher interest rates, which crowd out interest-sensitive private sector spending.

    (*d*) A reduction in government spending causes induced consumption spending to fall.

    Answer: (*c*)

10. From the following sets of values for k_e, *b*, *h* and *k*, find the set in which a change in government spending has the largest multiplier effect on equilibrium income.

    (*a*) $k_e = 5$, $b = 5$, $h = 5$, $k = 0.20$

(b) $k_e = 10$, $b = 5$, $h = 10$, $k = 0.20$

(c) $k_e = 5$, $b = 10$, $h = 1$, $k = 0.20$

(d) $k_e = 5$, $b = 5$, $h = 1$, $k = 0.20$

Answer: (b)

Solved Problems

TWO-STAGE EFFECT OF A MONEY SUPPLY CHANGE

6.1   Suppose the Federal Reserve purchases Treasury securities from the household sector. (*a*) Show in Fig. 6-15 what happens to the supply of Treasury securities held by the private sector and thereby the price of Treasury securities as a result of this purchase. What is happening to the yield on Treasury securities? (*b*) Show through a T-account what has happened to the reserves of the banking system, assuming the household sector deposits funds received from security sales in a checking account. (*c*) Assume that the banking system, as a result of holding excess reserves, purchases Treasury securities. Explain and show in Fig. 6-15 the effect additional purchases of Treasury securities by the banking system has upon the price of Treasury securities.

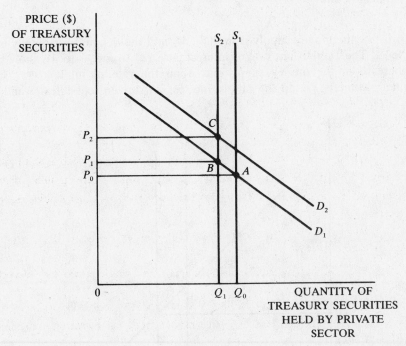

Fig. 6-15

(*a*)   When the Federal Reserve purchases Treasury securities from households, it reduces the supply of Treasury securities held by the private sector; the supply of Treasury securities available to the private sector decreases from S_1 to S_2 in Fig. 6-15. The price of Treasury securities increases from P_0 to P_1; the yield on Treasury securities thereby falls from i_0 to i_1.

(b) When households place funds from the sale of Treasury securities in checking accounts, the reserve assets of the banking system increase as does the bank's checking account liability to households. The banking system has excess reserves because it is required to hold only a fraction of checking deposits as reserves.

Banking System

Δ Assets		Δ Liabilities	
Reserves	+	Checking deposits	+

(c) The banking system reduces its excess reserve position by expanding checking deposits; the banking system pays for newly purchased Treasury securities by expanding checking deposit liabilities. (We shall assume that households are the sellers of Treasury securities to the banking system.) The demand for Treasury securities would increase in Fig. 6-15 from D_1 to D_2, causing the price of Treasury securities to increase from P_1 to P_2. The yield on Treasury securities falls from i_1 to i_2.

6.2   Holding the price level constant, why does an increase in the money supply cause a liquidity effect which reduces the rate of interest?

An increase in the money supply decreases the quantity of Treasury securities held by the private sector and creates an imbalance in private sector portfolios, given the initial rate of interest. Thus, money expansion results in households holding larger money balances (greater liquidity) than they desire at the initial rate of interest; they restore balance between their holding of liquid (money) and illiquid financial assets by increasing their demand for Treasury securities, which causes downward pressure on interest rates.

6.3   In Fig. 6-16(a), the money supply is initially M_0 and the demand for money is L_1, given a Y_0 income level. The equilibrium rate of interest is i_0. (a) In Fig. 6-16(a), show the effect an M_0 to M_1 increase in the money supply has upon the rate of interest. (b) In Fig. 6-16(b), equilibrium income is Y_0 and the rate of interest is i_0, given schedules *IS* and *LM*. Assuming

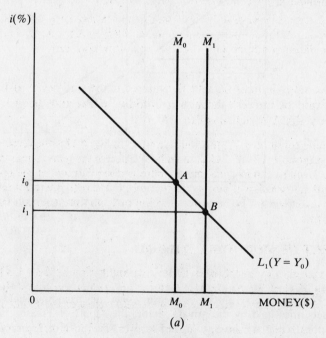

(a)

Fig. 6-16

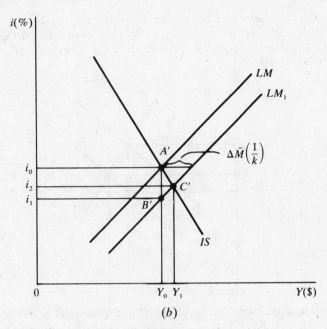

(b)

Fig. 6-16 (*continued*)

no change in income level Y_0 and an increase in the money supply from M_0 to M_1, what happens to the *LM* schedule and the rate of interest? (*c*) Does the liquidity effect from an expansion of the money supply result in a new equilibrium position?

(*a*) The M_0 to M_1 increase in the money supply causes the rate of interest to decrease from i_0 to i_1 in Fig. 6-16(*a*).

(*b*) The M_0 to M_1 increase in the money supply shifts *LM* rightward by $\Delta \bar{M}(1/k)$ to LM_1. With no change in income, the rate of interest falls from i_0 to i_1.

(*c*) Simultaneous equilibrium in the money and goods market does not exist at income level Y_0 and interest rate i_1. A lower interest rate induces additional spending, i.e., an income effect, that increases equilibrium income to Y_1 and the rate of interest to i_2.

6.4 Equilibrium income is initially Y_0 and the rate of interest i_0 in Fig. 6-17 for schedules *IS* and *LM*. Find the rate of interest through a liquidity effect and income effect when a money supply increase shifts *LM* rightward to LM_1.

Holding income constant at Y_0, the liquidity effect in Fig. 6-17 is the reduction in the rate of interest caused by *LM*'s rightward shift to LM_1; the liquidity effect is the reduction in the rate of interest from i_0 to i_1. At income level Y_0 and interest rate i_1, there is disequilibrium in the goods market. The income effect is the resulting expansion of income and increase in the rate of interest on the economy's return to equilibrium; the income effect is the increase in the rate of interest from i_1 to i_2 and the expansion of income from Y_0 to Y_1.

THE INCOME EFFECT OF MONETARY POLICY

6.5 In Fig. 6-18 a money supply increase shifts *LM* rightward by $\Delta \bar{M}(1/k)$ to LM_1. (*a*) Find the new equilibrium level of income in Fig. 6-18 (*a*) and (*b*) as a result of the Y_0 to Y_3 shift of *LM*. (*b*) Why is the income level change in Fig. 6-18(*a*) greater than that in Fig. 6-18(*b*)?

(*a*) The Y_0 to Y_3 shift of *LM* raises the income level from Y_0 to Y_2 in Fig. 6-18(*a*) and from Y_0 to Y_1 in Fig. 6-18(*b*).

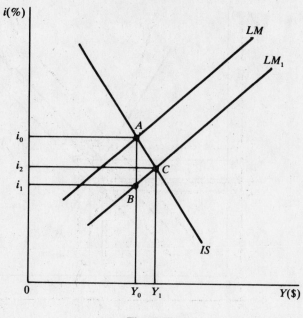

Fig. 6-17

(b) There is a greater increase in the income level in Fig. 6-18(a) because *IS* is less steeply sloped, indicating a greater responsiveness of investment spending to changes in the rate of interest. Note that the decline in the rate of interest (the combined liquidity and income effect) in Fig. 6-18(a) is less than that in Fig. 6-18(b), although the increase in income is greater.

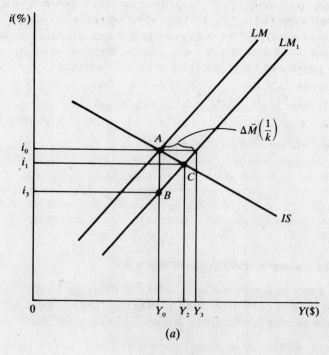

(a)

Fig. 6-18

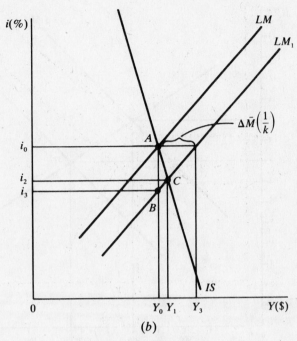

Fig. 6-18 (*continued*)

6.6 Suppose the *LM* equation for a two-sector model is $Y = \$750 + 20i$; money demand is specified as $L = 0.20Y - 4i$; the exogenous money supply is $150. (*a*) Plot the *LM* equation in Fig. 6-19(*a*) and 6-19(*b*); and the *IS* equation in Fig. 6-19(*a*) when it is specified as $Y = \$1250 - 30i$ when $C = \$100 + 0.80Y$ and $I = \$150 - 6i$ and in Fig. 6-19(*b*) when it is specified as $Y = \$1100 - 15i$ when $C = \$100 + 0.80Y$ and $I = \$120 + 3i$. (*b*) Find simultaneous equilibrium for the money and goods markets when the *IS* equation is specified as (1) $Y = \$1250 - 30i$ and (2) $Y = \$1100 - 15i$. (*c*) Plot a new *LM* equation in Fig. 6-19(*a*) and Fig. 6-19(*b*) and label it LM_1 for a $20 increase in the money supply $20. (*d*) Use the *IS* equations specified in part (*c*) and find equilibrium income when the money supply increases from $150 to $170. For which *IS* equation is there a greater decrease in the rate of interest? (*e*) Find investment and consumption spending when the money supply is $150 [part (*b*)] and when the money supply is $170 [part (*d*)].

(*a*) Fig. 6-19(*a*) & (*b*)

(*b*) Equilibrium income is $950 for situation (1)

$$
\begin{array}{ll}
Y = \$1250 - 30i & (IS) \\
-(Y = 750 + 20i) & (LM) \\
\hline
0 = \$500 - 50i \\
\end{array}
$$

$$i = 10\%$$

$$Y = \$950$$

Equilibrium income is also $950 for situation (2)

$$
\begin{array}{ll}
Y = \$1100 - 15i & (IS) \\
-(Y = 750 + 20i) & (LM) \\
\hline
0 = \$350 - 35i \\
\end{array}
$$

$$i = 10\%$$

$$Y = \$950$$

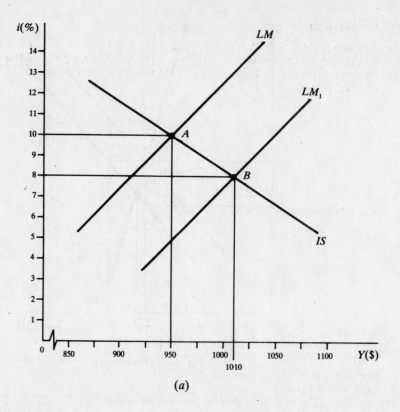

(a)

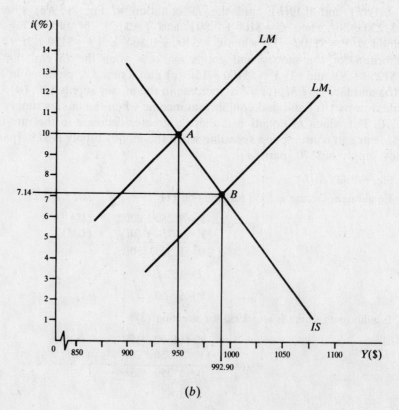

(b)

Fig. 6-19

(c) See Fig. 6-19.

(d) The new *LM* schedule is $Y = \$850 + 20i$. The rate of interest falls from 10% to 8% for situation (1) and to 7.143% for situation (2). There is a greater increase in equilibrium income for situation (1), although there is a greater decrease in the rate of interest for situation (2). Equilibrium income is now $1010 for situation (1)

$$
\begin{array}{ll}
Y = \$1250 - 30i & (IS) \\
-(Y = \quad 850 + 20i) & (LM) \\
\hline
0 = \$\ 400 - 50i &
\end{array}
$$

$$i = 8\%$$

$$Y = \$1010$$

Equilibrium income is $992.90 for situation (2)

$$
\begin{array}{ll}
Y = \$1100 - 15i & (IS) \\
-(Y = \quad 850 + 20i) & (LM) \\
\hline
0 = \$\ 250 - 35i &
\end{array}
$$

$$i = 7.143\%$$

$$Y = \$\ 992.50$$

(e) Investment is $90 for both (1) and (2) in part (b). The $20 money supply increase raises investment spending in situation (1) in part (d) to $102 ($I = \$150 - 6i$; $I = \$150 - 48$; $I = \$102$) and to $98.57 for (2): $I = \$120 - 3i$; $I = \$120 - 21.43$; $I = \$98.57$. Consumption in part (b) is $860 for both (1) and (2). As a result of the $20 money supply increase, consumption in (d) is $908 for (1) and $894.33 for (2).

6.7   The *IS* schedules in Fig. 6-20(a) & (b) have the same slope. Schedule LM_1 in Fig. 6-20(a) is more steeply sloped than LM_2 in Fig. 6-20(b). In Fig. 6-20(a) & (b) equilibrium income is initially Y_0 and the rate of interest is i_0. (a) In Fig. 6-20(a) & (b) find equilibrium income and the rate of interest resulting from a money expansion that shifts *LM* rightward from Y_0 to Y_3

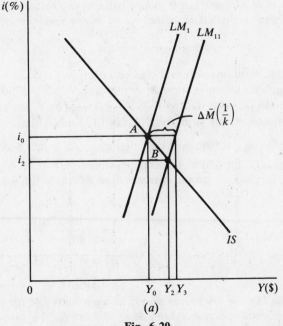

(a)

Fig. 6-20

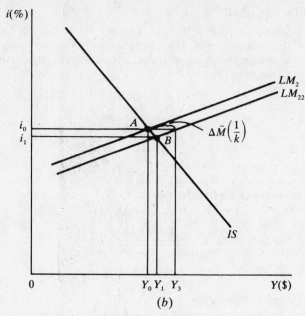

Fig. 6-20 (*continued*)

at interest rate i_0. (*b*) Is there a greater change in equilibrium income in Fig. 6-20(*a*) or (*b*)? Why? (*c*) Why is there a smaller change in the rate of interest in Fig. 6-20(*b*) than in Fig. 6-20(*a*)?

(*a*) Equilibrium income increases from Y_0 to Y_2 and the rate of interest decreases from i_0 to i_2 in Fig. 6-20(*a*), whereas equilibrium income increases from Y_0 to Y_1 in Fig. 6-20(*b*) with the rate of interest decreasing from i_0 to i_1.

(*b*) Because of the greater decline in the rate of interest in Fig. 6-20(*a*), there is a greater response from interest-sensitive spending and therefore a larger increase in equilibrium income.

(*c*) The less steeply sloped *LM* schedule in Fig. 6-20(*b*) indicates that the demand for money is more interest sensitive. Because larger money balances are held as interest rates fall, the money supply expansion has a smaller effect on the rate of interest and therefore on interest-sensitive investment spending.

6.8 Posit a two-sector economy where the *IS* equation is $Y = \$1250 - 30i$. (*a*) Given a \$150 money supply, find equilibrium when the *LM* equation is (1) $Y = \$750 + 20i$ (where $L = 0.20Y - 4i$) and (2) $Y = \$600 + 35i$ (where $L = 0.25Y - 8.75i$). (*b*) What happens to equilibrium income and the rate of interest for situations (1) and (2) when the money supply increases \$20?

(*a*) Equilibrium income is \$950, and the rate of interest is 10% for situations (1) and (2).

(*b*) For situation (1), the \$20 money supply increase shifts *LM* rightward \$100, that is, $\Delta\bar{M}(1/k) = \$20/(0.20)$. Equilibrium income increases from \$950 to \$1010; the rate of interest falls from 10% to 8%.

$$Y = \$1250 - 30i$$
$$\underline{-(Y = \quad 850 + 20i)}$$
$$0 = \$\ 400 - 50i$$

$$i = 8\%$$

$$Y = \$1010$$

For situation (2), the \$20 money supply increase shifts *LM* rightward \$80 or $\Delta\bar{M}(1/k) = 20/0.25$. Equilibrium income increases from \$950 to \$986.90; the rate of interest declines from 10 to 8.769%.

6.9   What determines the effect of an increase in the money supply upon equilibrium income?

The effect of a money supply increase on equilibrium income depends on the transaction need for money balances, the interest sensitivity of the demand for money, the interest sensitivity of investment spending, and the expenditure multiplier. When the transaction need is large, greater incremental money holdings are associated with increases in equilibrium income. Therefore, for example, when $k = 0.50$, a $20 money supply increase can be associated with no more than a $40 increase in equilibrium income $[\Delta Y = \Delta \bar{M}(1/k)]$. However, when $k = 0.20$, a $20 money supply increase can be associated with up to a $100 increase in equilibrium income. The interest sensitivity of the demand for money determines the extent to which money supply changes affect interest rates and thereby aggregate spending. For example, money demand which is highly interest sensitive indicates that a money supply expansion will be less successful in reducing interest rates than when money demand is highly interest insensitive. The interest sensitivity of investment spending determines the extent to which a change in the rate of interest affects the level of investment spending. For example, a money supply increase has a greater effect upon equilibrium income, *ceteris paribus*, the larger the value of behavioral coefficient b in the investment demand equation. And the value of k_e determines the extent to which investment spending has a multiplied effect upon equilibrium income. Larger values for k_e have greater effects on equilibrium income for a given increase in investment spending due to a decrease in the rate of interest.

MONETARY POLICY: SPECIAL CASES

6.10   (a) Find the change in equilibrium income in Fig. 6-21(a), (b) and (c) when a $\Delta \bar{M}$ increase in the money supply shifts *LM* rightward to LM_1. (b) Explain the changes in equilibrium income found in part (a).

(a)   The $\Delta \bar{M}$ money supply increase in Fig. 6-21(a) shifts *LM* rightward to LM_1. The rate of interest declines from i_0 to i_1 with equilibrium income increasing from Y_0 to Y_1. The change in equilibrium income (Y_0 to Y_1) is equal to the *LM* shift. The $\Delta \bar{M}$ money supply increase in Fig. 6-21(b) shifts *LM* rightward to LM_1. The rate of interest declines from i_0 to i_2 with equilibrium income remaining at its initial Y_0 level. The $\Delta \bar{M}$ money supply increase in Fig. 6-21(c) has no effect on the *LM* schedule, since it is horizontal at interest rate i_0. There is neither a change in the rate of interest nor equilibrium income.

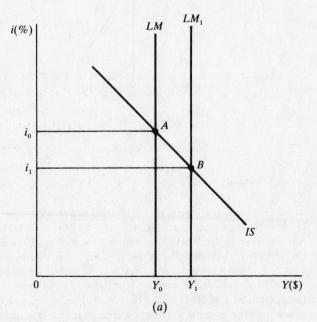

(a)

Fig. 6-21

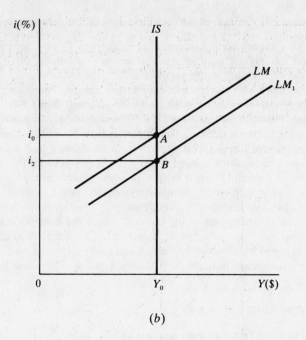

(b)

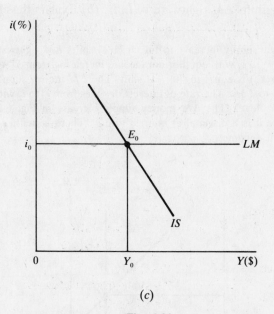

(c)

Fig. 6-21

(b) *LM* is vertical [Fig. 6-21(a)] when the demand for money is unrelated to the rate of interest. Because the demand for money is not affected by the rate of interest, a money expansion must be met by a $k\Delta Y$ increase in the transaction demand for money. Hence, ΔY must equal $\Delta \bar{M}(1/k)$. In contrast, the vertical *IS* schedule in Fig. 6-21(b) indicates that aggregate spending is unrelated to the rate of interest. The rightward shift of *LM* to LM_1, while lowering the rate of interest from i_0 to i_2, does not increase equilibrium income because of the insensitivity of spending to the rate of interest. The horizontal *LM* schedule in Fig. 6-21(c) indicates that the private sector is willing to hold an infinite quantity of money without a change in the rate of interest. Thus, a money supply increase has no effect upon either the rate of interest or equilibrium income.

6.11 Suppose the demand for money is specified $L = 0.20Y$, the money supply is $200, and, for a two-sector model, $C = \$100 + 0.80Y$ and $I = \$140 - 5i$. (*a*) From these data, derive an *IS* and *LM* equation; plot *IS* and *LM* in Fig. 6-22. What effect does an increase in the money supply have on equilibrium income? (*b*) Find the rate of interest, equilibrium income, consumption and investment from the *IS* and *LM* equations derived in part (*a*). (*c*) In Fig. 6-22 plot and label LM_1 the monetary equilibrium schedule resulting from a $20 increase in the money supply. (*d*) Find equilibrium income, the rate of interest, consumption and investment when the money supply increases $20. (*e*) What is the relationship of the shift of *LM* in Fig. 6-22 and the change in equilibrium income?

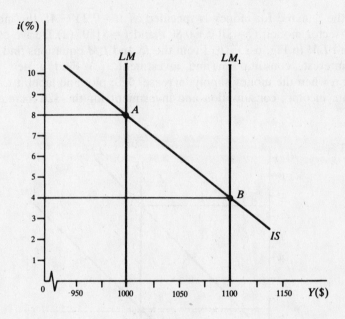

Fig. 6-22

(*a*) The *LM* equation:
$$L = M$$
$$0.20Y = \$200$$
$$Y = \$1000$$

The *IS* equation:
$$Y = C + I$$
$$Y = \$100 + 0.80Y + \$140 - 5i$$
$$Y = \$1200 - 25i$$

Because the *LM* schedule is vertical, we would expect equilibrium income to change by $\Delta \bar{M}(1/k)$.

(*b*) Simultaneous equilibrium $LM = IS$:
$$\$1000 = \$1200 - 25i$$
$$25i = \$ 200$$
$$i = 8\%$$
$$Y = \$1000$$
$$C = \$ 900$$
$$I = \$ 100$$

(*c*) An increase in the money supply shifts *LM* rightward by $\Delta \bar{M}(1/k)$. Thus, *LM* shifts rightward $100 to LM_1: $\Delta \bar{M}(1/k) = \$20(1/0.20) = \$100$.

(d) The *LM* equation is now $Y = \$1100$.

Simultaneous equilibrium

$$LM = IS$$
$$\$1100 = \$1200 - 25i$$
$$i = 4\%$$
$$Y = \$1100$$
$$C = \$\ 980$$
$$I = \$\ 120$$

(e) The \$100 increase in equilibrium income equals the \$100 rightward shift of *LM*.

6.12 Suppose the demand for money is specified as $L = 0.2Y - 4i$, the money supply is \$200, and for a two-sector model, $C = \$100 + 0.80Y$ and $I = \$150$. (a) Derive equations for *IS* and *LM*; plot *IS* and *LM* in Fig. 6-23. (b) From the *IS* and *LM* equations find equilibrium income, the rate of interest, consumption and investment. (c) Find a new equation for monetary equilibrium when the money supply increases \$20; plot and label it LM_1 in Fig. 6-23. (d) Find equilibrium income, consumption and investment for the \$20 increase in the money supply.

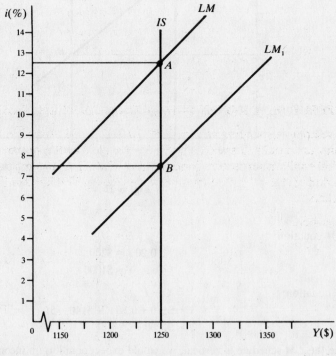

Fig. 6-23

(a) The *LM* equation:

$$L = M$$
$$0.20Y - 4i = \$200$$
$$Y = \$1000 + 20i$$

The *IS* equation:

$$Y = C + I$$
$$Y = \$\ 100 + 0.80Y + \$1.50$$
$$Y = \$1250$$

(b)
$$LM = IS$$
$$\$1000 + 20i = \$1250$$
$$20i = 250$$
$$i = 12.5\%$$
$$Y = \$1250$$
$$C = \$1100$$
$$I = \$150$$

(c) LM equation for a $220 money supply:

$$0.20Y - 4i = \$220$$
$$Y = \$1100 + 20i$$

(d) There is no change in equilibrium income because consumption and investment spending are unrelated to the rate of interest. The $20 money supply expansion causes interest rates to fall from 12.50 to 7.50%.

$$LM = IS$$
$$\$1100 + 20i = \$1250$$
$$20i = 150$$
$$i = 7.50\%$$
$$Y = \$1250$$
$$C = \$1100$$
$$I = \$150$$

MULTIPLIER EFFECT OF A MONEY SUPPLY CHANGE IN AN *IS-LM* FRAMEWORK

6.13 Suppose spending is specified as $C = \bar{C} + cYd$, $I = \bar{I} - bi$, $Tn = \bar{T}x$, $G = \bar{G}$, and $X = \bar{X} - xY$. The demand for money is specified as $L = kY - hi$, and the money supply is $\bar{M}$. (a) Find an equation for equilibrium in the goods market. (b) Find an equation for equilibrium in the money market. (c) Find an equation that represents equilibrium income in the money and goods markets.

(a) *LM* equation:

$$L = M$$
$$kY - hi = \bar{M}$$
$$Y = \frac{\bar{M}}{k} + \frac{hi}{k}$$

or,
$$i = \frac{kY}{h} - \frac{\bar{M}}{h}$$

(b) *IS* equation:

$$Y = C + I + G + X$$
$$Y = \bar{C} + c(Y - \bar{T}x) + \bar{I} - bi + \bar{G} + \bar{X} - xY$$
$$Y - cY + xY = \bar{C} - c\bar{T}x + \bar{I} - bi + \bar{G} + \bar{X}$$
$$Y = \frac{\bar{C} + \bar{I} + \bar{G} + \bar{X} - c\bar{T}x}{1 - c + x} - \frac{bi}{1 - c + x}$$

Letting $\bar{A} = \bar{C} + \bar{I} + \bar{G} + \bar{X} - c\bar{T}x$ and $k_e = (1/(1 - c + x)$:

$$Y = k_e\bar{A} - k_ebi$$

(c) We can find simultaneous equilibrium in the money and goods markets by substituting the *LM* equation $i = kY/h - \bar{M}/h$ into the *IS* equation. Thus,

$$Y = k_e\bar{A} - k_eb\left(\frac{kY}{h} - \frac{\bar{M}}{h}\right)$$

$$Y = k_e\bar{A} - \left(\frac{k_ebkY}{h} + \frac{k_eb\bar{M}}{h}\right)$$

$$hY = hk_e\bar{A} - k_ebkY + k_eb\bar{M}$$

$$hY + k_ebkY = hk_e\bar{A} + k_eb\bar{M}$$

$$Y = hk_e\bar{A}\left(\frac{1}{h + kbk_e}\right) + k_eb\bar{M}\left(\frac{1}{h + k_ebk}\right)$$

or

$$Y = \bar{A}\left(\frac{hk_e}{h + kbk_e}\right) + \bar{M}\left(\frac{bk_e}{h + kbk_e}\right)$$

6.14   (*a*) Holding variables constant other than Y and $\bar{M}$, find an expression that relates the change in equilibrium income to a change in the money supply. (*b*) Find an expression for the multiplying effect μ that a change in the money supply has on equilibrium income.

(*a*)

$$\Delta Y = k_eb\Delta\bar{M}\left(\frac{1}{h + k_ebk}\right)$$

$$\Delta Y = \Delta\bar{M}\left(\frac{k_eb}{h + k_ebk}\right)$$

(*b*)   Dividing both sides of the equation in part (*a*) by $\Delta\bar{M}$, we derive μ, the multiplying effect that a change in the money supply has on equilibrium income.

$$\frac{\Delta Y}{\Delta\bar{M}} = \frac{k_eb}{h + k_ebk}$$

letting

$$\mu = \frac{\Delta Y}{\Delta\bar{M}}$$

$$\mu = \frac{k_eb}{h + k_ebk}$$

6.15   Find the value of $\mu(\Delta Y/\Delta\bar{M})$ for the values of k_e, b, h and k given in situations (1) through (5) in Table 6-1. (*b*) What generalization can one make about the multiplying effect of a money supply change upon equilibrium income when there is an increase in the value of k_e, b, h, or k? (*c*) Relate your answer in (*b*) to the slope of *IS* and/or *LM* and how the slope of these schedules influences the multiplying effect of a money supply change upon equilibrium income.

Table 6-1

Situation	k_e	b	h	k
(1)	5	4	4	0.20
(2)	10	4	4	0.20
(3)	5	10	4	0.20
(4)	5	4	10	0.20
(5)	5	4	4	0.25

(*a*)   The values for μ are (1) 2.500, (2) 3.333, (3) 3.571, (4) 1.429 and (5) 2.222.

(b) A larger value for the expenditure multiplier k_e and the interest sensitivity of investment spending b increases the multiplying effect of a money supply change on equilibrium income. An increase in the interest sensitivity of the demand for money h and the desire to hold transaction balances k reduces the multiplying effect of a money supply change on equilibrium income.

(c) An increase in k_e and/or b reduces the slope of *IS* (*IS* becomes flatter), indicating that an interest rate change induced by a change in the money supply has a greater effect on equilibrium income. That is, a money supply change has a greater multiplying effect on equilibrium income when there is a small slope for *IS*. An increase in h or k decreases the slope of *LM* (*LM* becomes flatter), indicating that a money supply change brings about a smaller change in the rate of interest. The multiplying effect of a money supply change on equilibrium income is thereby lessened by a smaller-sloped *LM*.

THE INCOME EFFECT OF FISCAL POLICY

6.16 The *LM* equation is $Y = \$500 + 25i$; money demand is specified $L = 0.20Y - 5i$; the exogenous money supply is \$100. The *IS* equation is $Y = \$950 - 50i$; $C = \$40 + 0.80Yd$; $Tn = \$50$; $G = \$50$; $I = \$140 - 10i$. (a) Find equilibrium income, the rate of interest, consumption and investment. (b) Find the *IS* equation when government spending increases from \$50 to \$80. (c) Find equilibrium income, the rate of interest, consumption and investment when government spending is \$80 rather than \$50. (d) Why has equilibrium income increased by less than $k_e \Delta \bar{G}$—an amount equal to the shift of *IS*?

(a)
$$Y = \$950 - 50i$$
$$\underline{-(Y = 500 + 25i)}$$
$$0 = \$450 - 75i$$
$$i = 6\%$$
$$Y = \$650$$
$$C = \$520$$
$$I = \$80$$

(b)
$$Y = C + I + G$$
$$Y = \$40 + 0.80(Y - \$50) + \$140 - 10i + \$80$$
$$Y = \$1100 - 50i$$

(c)
$$Y = \$1100 - 50i$$
$$\underline{-(Y = 500 + 25i)}$$
$$0 = \$600 - 75i$$
$$i = 8\%$$
$$Y = \$700$$
$$C = \$560$$
$$I = \$60$$

(d) A \$30 expansion of government spending has increased the rate of interest from 6 to 8% and crowded out private sector investment. With a higher 8% interest rate, investment spending falls from \$80 to \$60. Thus, the total net effect of increased government spending on equilibrium income is \$50 rather than \$150 $[k_e \Delta \bar{G} = 5(\$30) = \$150]$.

6.17 (a) Explain the crowding-out effect. (b) What determines the magnitude of the crowding-out effect?

(a) A crowding-out effect occurs when increased government spending causes a higher interest rate which results in a lower level of investment spending, i.e., government spending "crowds out" interest-insensitive private sector spending.

(*b*) The magnitude of the crowding-out effect depends on (1) the increase in the interest rate associated with an expansion in government spending and (2) the interest sensitivity of private sector spending. The interest sensitivity of the demand for money determines the rise in the rate of interest, which results from an expansion in government spending; interest rates experience a smaller increase from expanded government spending when the demand for money is interest sensitive. A given increase in the rate of interest has a larger crowding-out effect when private sector investment spending is highly sensitive to the rate of interest.

6.18 In Fig. 6-24(*a*) and (*b*), IS_1 is the initial *IS* schedule which shifts rightward by $k_e \Delta \bar{G}$ (Y_0 to Y_3) to IS_2 as a result of a $\Delta \bar{G}$ increase in government spending. (*a*) What is equilibrium income after the $\Delta \bar{G}$ increase in government spending? (*b*) Explain why the increases in equilibrium income in Fig. 6-24(*a*) and (*b*) differ.

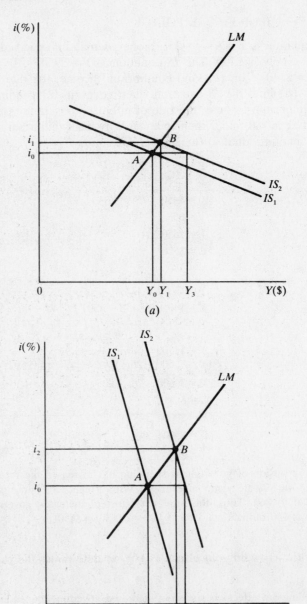

(*a*)

(*b*)

Fig. 6-24

(a) Equilibrium income increases from Y_0 to Y_1 in Fig. 6-24(a) and Y_0 to Y_2 in Fig. 6-24(b).

(b) There is a larger increase in equilibrium income in Fig. 6-24(b) than in Fig. 6-24(a), although the rise in the rate of interest is greater in Fig. 6-24(b). Investment spending is more interest sensitive in Fig. 6-24(a), indicated by a flatter *IS* schedule; thus, although the rise in the interest rate is smaller in (a), the $\Delta \bar{G}$ increase in government spending has a greater crowding-out effect on investment spending.

6.19 In Fig. 6-25, IS_1 shifts rightward to IS_2 when government spending increases by $\Delta \bar{G}$. (a) Find equilibrium income after the $\Delta \bar{G}$ increase in government spending for monetary equilibrium schedules LM_1 and LM_2. (b) Contrast the increase in equilibrium income for monetary equilibrium schedule LM_1 and LM_2.

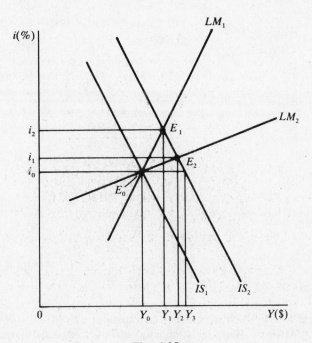

Fig. 6-25

(a) Equilibrium income increases from Y_0 to Y_1 for LM_1 and from Y_0 to Y_2 for LM_2.

(b) The demand for money is less interest sensitive for monetary equilibrium schedule LM_1; hence, the rightward shift of *IS* causes a greater increase in the rate of interest (from i_0 to i_2) along LM_1. It therefore follows that increased government spending crowds out more investment spending along LM_1 than along LM_2.

6.20 The *LM* equation is $Y = \$500 + 25i$; money demand is specified as $L = 0.20Y - 5i$; the exogenous money supply is $100. (a) Find equilibrium income, the rate of interest and investment when the *IS* equation is (1) $Y = \$950 - 50i$, given $C = \$40 + 0.80Yd$, $I = \$140 - 10i$, $Tx = \$50$, $G = \$50$; (2) $Y = \$800 - 25i$, given $C = \$40 + 0.80Yd$, $I = \$110 - 5i$, $Tx = \$50$, $G = \$50$. (b) Recalculate the *IS* equation for part (a) when government spending increases from $50 to $80. (c) Find equilibrium income, the rate of interest and investment when government spending is $80. (d) Explain why the increase in government spending to $50 to $80 has a different effect on equilibrium income for situation (1) and situation (2). (Hint: look at the value for behavioral coefficient *b*.)

(*a*) (1)
$$Y = \$950 - 50i$$
$$-(Y = 500 + 25i)$$
$$0 = \$450 - 75i$$
$$i = 6\%$$
$$Y = \$650$$
$$I = \$80$$

(2)
$$Y = \$800 - 25i$$
$$-(Y = 500 + 25i)$$
$$0 = \$300 - 50i$$
$$i = 6\%$$
$$Y = \$650$$
$$I = \$80$$

(*b*) (1)
$$Y = C + I + G$$
$$Y = \$40 + 0.80(Y - \$50) + \$140 - 10i + \$80$$
$$Y = \$1100 - 50i$$

(2)
$$Y = C + I + G$$
$$Y = \$40 + 0.80(Y - \$50) + \$110 - 5i + \$80$$
$$Y = \$950 - 25i$$

(*c*) (1)
$$Y = \$1100 - 50i$$
$$-(Y = 500 + 25i)$$
$$0 = \$600 - 75i$$
$$i = 8\%$$
$$Y = \$700$$
$$I = \$60$$

(2)
$$Y = \$950 - 25i$$
$$-(Y = 500 + 25i)$$
$$0 = \$450 - 50i$$
$$i = 9\%$$
$$Y = \$725$$
$$I = \$65$$

(*d*) Investment is more interest sensitive in situation (1) where $I = \$140 - 10i$ than in situation (2) where $I = \$110 - 5i$. Thus, the stimulative effect of increased government spending has a larger crowding-out effect in (1) than (2) when the rate of interest increases. The \$30 increase in government spending causes investment spending to decline from \$80 to \$60 in (1), whereas investment spending declines from \$80 to \$65 in (2).

FISCAL POLICY: SPECIAL CASES

6.21 Find the change in equilibrium income in Fig. 6-26(*a*), (*b*) and (*c*) when government spending increases by $\Delta \bar{G}$ and shifts *IS* rightward by $k_e \Delta \bar{G}$.

In Fig. 6-26(*a*) the $\Delta \bar{G}$ increase in government spending shifts *IS* rightward to IS_2. The rate of interest increases from i_0 to i_2; however, equilibrium income remains at Y_0. There is complete crowding out, i.e., the decline in investment spending equals the increase in government spending.

In Fig. 6-26(*b*) the $\Delta \bar{G}$ increase in government spending shifts *IS* rightward to IS_2. Although the rate of interest increases from i_0 to i_1, equilibrium income increases from Y_0 to Y_1, which equals the $k_e \Delta \bar{G}$ shift of *IS*. There is no crowding out because private sector spending is unrelated to the rate of interest.

There is no crowding out in Fig. 6-26(*c*) as *IS* shifts rightward from IS_1 to IS_2. The horizontal *LM* schedule indicates that the private sector is willing to supply additional money balances for transaction needs without a change in the rate of interest.

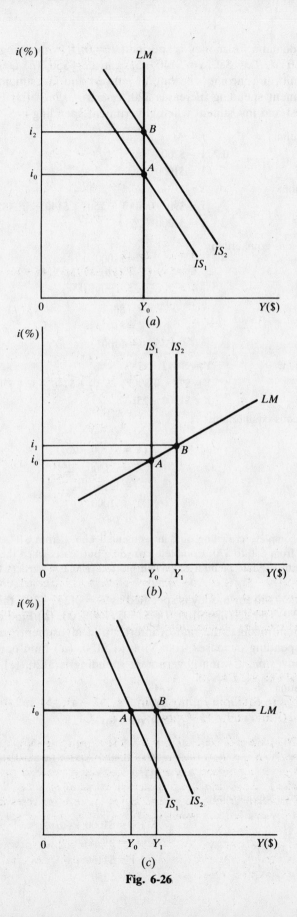

Fig. 6-26

6.22 Suppose the demand for money is specified $L = 0.20Y$, the exogenous money supply is \$200, $C = \$90 + 0.80Yd$, $Tx = \$50$, $I = \$140 - 5i$, and $G = \$50$. (*a*) Derive an *IS* and *LM* equation. (*b*) Find equilibrium income, the rate of interest and investment. (*c*) Derive the *IS* equation when government spending increases \$20, *ceteris paribus*. (*d*) Find equilibrium income, the rate of interest and investment when government spending is \$70. (*e*) Is there crowding out?

(*a*)   *LM* equation: $L = M$

$$0.20Y = \$200$$
$$Y = \$1000$$

        IS equation: $Y = C + I + G$

$$Y = \$90 + 0.80(Y - \$50) + \$140 - 5i + \$50$$
$$Y = \$1200 - 25i$$

(*b*)   Simultaneous equilibrium:

$$Y = \$1000$$
$$-(Y = \ 1200 - 25i)$$
$$\overline{0 = -\$200 + 25i}$$
$$i = 8\%$$
$$Y = \$1000$$
$$I = \$100$$

(*c*)   *IS* equation: $Y = C + I + G$

$$Y = \$90 + 0.80(Y - \$50) + \$140 - 5i + \$70$$
$$Y = \$1300 - 25i$$

(*d*)   Simultaneous equilibrium:

$$Y = \$1000$$
$$-(Y = \$1300 - 25i)$$
$$\overline{0 = -\$300 + 25i}$$
$$i = 12\%$$
$$Y = \$1000$$
$$I = \$80$$

(*e*)   There is complete crowding out; investment declines from \$100 to \$80 as government spending increases from \$50 to \$70. Complete crowding out exists when the portfolio demand for money is unrelated to the rate of interest. When plotted, *LM* is a vertical line.

6.23 Suppose the demand for money is specified as $L = 0.2Y - 10i$, the exogenous money supply is \$200, $C = \$60 + 0.8Yd$, $Tn = \$100$, $I = \$150$, $G = \$100$. (*a*) Find equations for *IS* and *LM*. (b) Find equilibrium income, the rate of interest and investment. (*c*) Find the *IS* equation when government spending increases from \$100 to \$120. (*d*) Find equilibrium income, the rate of interest and investment when government spending is \$120. (*e*) Is there crowding out?

(*a*)   *LM* equation: $L = M$

$$0.20Y - 10i = \$200$$
$$Y = \$1000 + 50i$$

        IS equation: $Y = C + I + G$

$$Y = \$60 + 0.80(Y - \$100) + \$150 + \$100$$
$$Y = \$1150$$

(*b*)   Simultaneous equilibrium:

$$IS = LM$$
$$\$1150 = \$1000 + 50i$$
$$i = 3\%$$
$$Y = \$1150$$
$$I = \$150$$

(c) *IS* equation:

$$Y = C + I + G$$
$$Y = \$60 + 0.80(Y - \$100) + \$150 + \$120$$
$$Y = \$1250$$

(d) Simultaneous equilibrium:

$$IS = LM$$
$$\$1250 = \$1000 + 50i$$
$$i = 5\%$$
$$Y = \$1250$$
$$I = \$150$$

(e) There is no crowding out. Although the interest rate increases from 3 to 5%, investment spending remains at \$150, since it is not influenced by the rate of interest. Money balances are released from portfolios at the higher interest rate (3 to 5%) to meet the increased transaction need for money at the higher \$1250 equilibrium level of income.

THE MULTIPLIER EFFECT OF FISCAL POLICY IN AN *IS-LM* FRAMEWORK

6.24 Simultaneous equilibrium in the money and goods markets can be presented as

$$Y = \bar{A}\left(\frac{hk_e}{h + kbk_e}\right) + \bar{M}\left(\frac{k_e b}{h + k_e bk}\right)$$

(a) Holding variables constant other than Y and $\bar{G}$, find an expression that relates the change in equilibrium income to the change in government spending. (b) Find an expression for the multiplying effect γ that a change in government spending has upon equilibrium income.

(a)

$$\Delta Y = \Delta \bar{G}\left(\frac{hk_e}{h + kbk_e}\right)$$

(b) Dividing both sides of the equation in part (a) by $\Delta \bar{G}$, we derive γ, the multiplying effect that a change in government spending has on equilibrium income.

$$\frac{\Delta Y}{\Delta \bar{G}} = \frac{hk_e}{h + kbk_e}$$

Letting $\gamma = \Delta Y/\Delta \bar{G}$,

$$\gamma = \frac{hk_e}{h + kbk_e}$$

6.25 (a) Find the value of γ for the values of k_e, b, h and k given in situations (1) through (5) in Table 6-2. (b) What multiplier effect would a change in government spending have on equilibrium income in the simple $(C + I + G)$ model? (c) What generalizations can one make about the multiplying effect of a change in government spending on equilibrium income where there is an increase in the value of k_e, b, h and/or k?

Table 6-2

Situation	k_e	b	h	k
(1)	5	4	4	0.20
(2)	10	4	4	0.20
(3)	5	10	4	0.20
(4)	5	4	10	0.20
(5)	5	4	4	0.25

(a) The values for γ are (1) 2.500, (2) 3.333, (3) 1.429, (4) 3.571 and (5) 2.222.

(b) The multiplier effect associated with increased government spending in the simple $(C + I + G)$ model is k_e; hence, in the absence of a monetary sector, the value for the multiplying effect of government spending is 5 when $k_e = 5$ and 10 when k_e is 10.

(c) An increase in the expenditure multiplier k_e and the interest sensitivity of the demand for money h results in a larger value for γ; thus, larger values for k_e and/or h increase the multiplying effect that a change in government spending has on equilibrium income. An increase in the interest sensitivity of spending b and in the desire to hold transaction balances k reduce the value of γ; increased values for b and/or k reduce the multiplying effect that a change in government spending has on equilibrium income.

THE MONETARY-FISCAL POLICY MIX

6.26 Suppose equilibrium output is initially Y_0 for schedules IS_1 and LM_1 in Fig. 6-27; full employment exists at output Y_1. (a) Establish in Fig. 6-27 how monetary or fiscal policy can be used to reach full employment. (b) Explain how the choice of monetary or fiscal policy has a selective impact on sector spending and the composition of output.

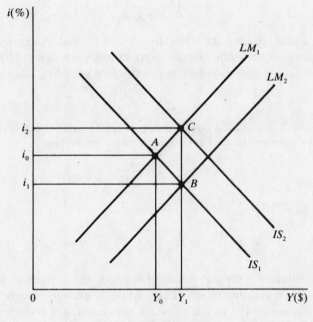

Fig. 6-27

(a) A money supply increase that shifts LM to LM_2 will achieve output Y_1, with the interest rate decreasing to i_1. An alternative economic policy would be an expansion of government spending which shifts IS to IS_2, with equilibrium output increasing to Y_1 and the interest rate increasing to i_2.

(b) A stimulative monetary policy lowers the rate of interest and increases interest-sensitive spending which in turn has a multiplier effect on equilibrium income. Private sector goods and services become a larger percentage of aggregate output. However, should increased government spending be the policy choice, the interest rate increase would crowd out some interest-sensitive investment spending. The composition of output would be weighted incrementally toward public sector goods and services as interest-sensitive private sector spending falls.

6.27 The multiplying effect β of a money supply change upon equilibrium income equals $k_e b/(h + k_e bk)$, whereas the multiplying effect α of a change in government spending on equilibrium income is $hk_e/(h + kbk_e)$. In Problems 6.15 and 6.25 respectively, we find that β and α equal 2.5 when $k_e = 5$, $b = 4$, $h = 4$ and $k = 0.20$. (*a*) What increase in (1) the money supply or (2) government spending is needed to increase equilibrium income \$100? (*b*) Find the change in investment spending as a result of policy (1) and policy (2) in part (*a*).

(*a*)   Policy (1)

$$\beta \Delta \bar{M} = \Delta Y$$
$$2.5 \Delta \bar{M} = \$100$$
$$\Delta \bar{M} = \$40$$

Policy (2)

$$\alpha \Delta \bar{G} = \Delta Y$$
$$2.5 \Delta \bar{G} = \$100$$
$$\Delta \bar{G} = \$40$$

(*b*)   (1) The \$100 increase in equilibrium income can be presented as $k_e \Delta \bar{I} = \$100$; since $k_e = 5$, the money supply expansion must lower the rate of interest to a level that causes investment spending to increase \$20. (2) In the absence of a monetary sector, a \$40 increase in government spending would increase equilibrium income \$200. Since income expands only \$100, the interest rate increases to a level which causes a \$20 decrease in investment spending.

Chapter 7

Equilibrium in the Money and Goods Market in an Open Economy

7.1 INTRODUCTION

This chapter integrates foreign trade and capital flows into the analysis of equilibrium in the money and goods markets. In an open economy, trade flows impact the slope of and location of the *IS* schedule. International capital flows are related to domestic and international interest rates; equilibrium not only requires equilibrium in the money and goods markets but necessitates portfolio equilibrium between the domestic (internal) and foreign (external) financial markets as well. Throughout this chapter, the United States is the domestic economy; foreign economies are those that the United States exports to and imports from.

7.2 NET EXPORTS IN AN *IS-LM* FRAMEWORK

The U.S export function can be presented as $X = \bar{X} - xY$ (see Section 4.8) where $\bar{X}$ represents autonomous net exports (autonomous exports less autonomous imports) and x is the U.S. marginal propensity to import foreign-made goods. Autonomous net exports are largely influenced by the foreign exchange value of the dollar and aggregate economic activity of major trading partners. When the U.S. dollar devalues, autonomous exports increase as foreigners find that they can buy more U.S.-made goods with a given quantity of their currency. Autonomous exports also increase when major U.S. trading partners increase purchases of U.S.-made goods due to increased economic activity in their country; U.S. autonomous imports decline when the foreign exchange value of the dollar falls due to the increased cost of foreign-made goods in the United States. In the export function, $X = \bar{X} - xY$, behavioral coefficient x measures the direct relationship of imports to economic activity Y in the United States. Behavioral coefficient x is a leakage from the spending flow, since x represents a demand for foreign- rather than domestic-made goods and services. In an *IS-LM* framework, variable x influences the slope of *IS*, and changes in net autonomous exports cause parallel shifts of *IS*.

EXAMPLE 1. The export function $X = \$50 - 0.10Y$ is plotted in Fig. 7-1 and labeled X. We find that the economy's net export balance is zero (exports equal imports) when income is $500. When autonomous net exports rise $10, because of increased economic activity in foreign countries, the export function becomes $X = \$60 - 0.10Y$, X' in Fig. 7-1. A zero net export balance exists for $X = \$60 - 0.10Y$ when output is $600. An increased value for the U.S. dollar might cause autonomous imports to rise $15 while autonomous exports fall $5; the export function would then be $X = \$40 - 0.10Y$, represented by X'' in Fig. 7-1. For $X = \$40 - 0.10Y$, a zero net export balance occurs when aggregate output is $400.

EXAMPLE 2. When $C = \bar{C} + cYd$, $Yd = Y - Tn$, $Tn = tY$, $I = \bar{I} - bi$, $G = \bar{G}$, $X = \bar{X} - xY$, the *IS* equation is $Y = (\bar{C} + \bar{I} + \bar{G} + \bar{X} - bi)/(1 - c + ct + x)$ and is represented by schedule *IS* in Fig. 7-2. A $\Delta \bar{X}$ increase in autonomous net exports shifts the goods equilibrium schedule *IS* rightward by $k_e \Delta \bar{X}$ to *IS'*. An increase in x, *ceteris paribus*, reduces the expenditure multiplier; schedule *IS* shifts leftward to *IS''* and becomes more steeply sloped.

7.3 MARKET-DETERMINED EXCHANGE RATES

A foreign exchange rate is the price of one currency in terms of another, e.g., the West German *deutschemark* price of U.S. dollars. The equilibrium exchange rate is E_0 for the international supply

130

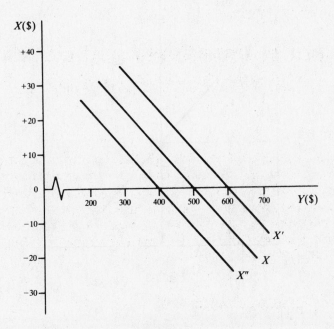

Fig. 7-1

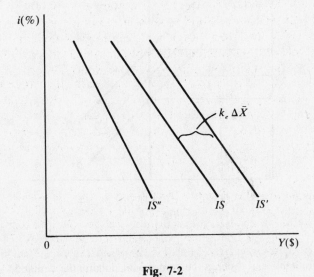

Fig. 7-2

S and demand D for U.S. dollars in Fig. 7-3. Holding the supply of dollars constant, foreign exchange rates change when there are shifts in the demand for dollars. Factors which can cause such demand shifts are a change in (1) interest rates in the United States i_{US}, (2) interest rates in foreign countries i_F, (3) the U.S. price level relative to the price level in foreign countries p_{US}/p_F and (4) productivity in the United States relative to that in foreign countries.

EXAMPLE 3. The equilibrium exchange rate for the U.S. dollar is E_0 in Fig. 7-4 for supply and demand schedules S and D. Holding other variables constant, higher interest rates in the United States i_{US} increase U.S. capital inflows, shift the demand for dollars schedule upward to D' and cause the dollar's exchange rate to rise to E_1. Starting from an initial E_0 exchange rate in Fig. 7-4, an increase in i_F, *ceteris paribus*, makes investments

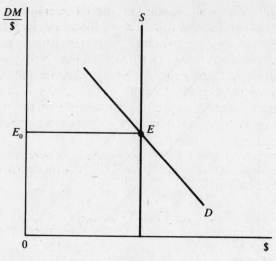

Fig. 7-3

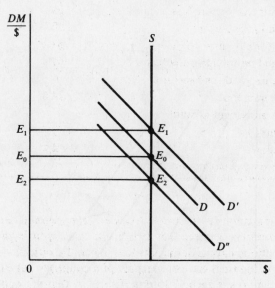

Fig. 7-4

in other countries more profitable and reduces the demand for dollars; the demand for dollars shifts downward to D'' and reduces the exchange rate to E_2. An increase in the U.S. price level, *ceteris paribus*, reduces U.S. competitiveness; autonomous net exports decline, the demand schedule shifts downward, and the value of the dollar falls. Increased productivity in the United States, *ceteris paribus*, improves U.S. competitiveness; greater demand for U.S.-made goods shifts the demand schedule upward, and the dollar appreciates.

7.4 BALANCE OF PAYMENTS

A balance-of-payments statement is a record of all economic transactions between the residents of a country and the residents of foreign countries for a specific period. A debit entry ($-$) represents a home country's payment to another country, and a credit entry ($+$) represents a payment received by the home country. Subsets of these international transactions usually have a net debit or net credit balance, categorized to measure a country's balance of trade, balance on goods and services, balance on current account, balance on capital account and official reserve transactions. A country's trade balance is the difference between its total commodity exports and its total commodity imports. The current account balance includes all international trade transactions, international service transactions (tourism, transportation, and royalty fees) and international unilateral transfers (gifts and foreign aid). Financial transactions (consisting of direct investment and purchases of interest-bearing financial instruments, non-interest-bearing demand deposits and gold) comprise the capital account balance. Official reserve transactions consist of movements of international reserves by governments and official agencies to accommodate imbalances arising from the current and capital accounts.

EXAMPLE 4. Table 7-1 presents a hypothetical balance-of-payments statement for the United States. As the table shows, the United States has a $124.3 billion trade deficit and a net capital inflow of $117.4 billion. The official reserve transaction balance is zero.

Table 7-1   ($ billions)

Exports of goods	+214.0	
Imports of goods	−338.3	
Balance on merchandise trade		−124.3
Income from current services	+55.2	
Income on foreign assets	+90.5	
Payments for current services	−58.2	
Interest paid on foreign-owned assets	−65.8	
Balance on goods and services		−102.6
Unilateral transfers	−14.8	
Balance on current account		−117.4
Capital outflows	−29.5	
Capital inflows	+146.9	
Balance on capital account		+117.4

A country's balance of payments is the net balance on its combined current and capital accounts; it is a debit (−) entry when official reserve transactions have a credit balance and a credit (+) entry when official reserve transactions have a debit balance. When the official reserve transactions balance is zero, the capital account is the financial counterpart of a country's balance on current account, and the country's balance of payments is zero. (Note in Table 7-1 that the debit current account balance (−$117.4) is offset by the credit (+$117.4) balance on capital account.) In the discussion that follows, the official reserve transaction balance is zero unless otherwise specified. It is also assumed that current account imbalances are due to imbalances in the import and export of goods.

7.5 THE CAPITAL INFLOW SCHEDULE

When there is risk associated with the holding of foreign financial assets (domestic and foreign financial assets are not perfect substitutes), interest rates in foreign countries i_F must be greater than those in the United States i_{US} to encourage capital to flow out of the United States. It follows that $i_{US} > i_F$ for capital to flow into the United States. Fig. 7-5 presents a capital inflow schedule CF for the United States, given an interest rate of i_F in foreign financial markets. There is a capital outflow (the capital account has a debit balance) of −X when the interest rate in the United States is 2% below those in foreign financial markets. The capital account has a credit balance (there is a capital inflow) of +X when the interest rate is 3% above those in foreign financial markets. The slope of the capital flow schedule depends on the perceived risk in holding foreign financial assets.

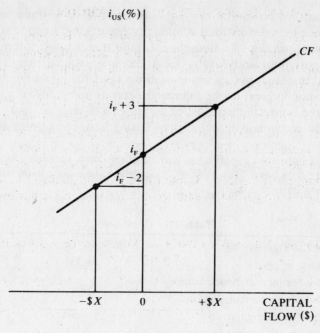

Fig. 7-5

EXAMPLE 5. Three capital inflow schedules for the United States are plotted in Fig. 7-6, representing different foreign perceptions of risk in holding U.S. financial assets. CF_1 is steeply sloped, indicating high perceived risk and thereby low substitutability between U.S. and foreign financial assets. The risk premium required by foreigners to hold U.S. financial assets is considerably smaller for CF_2; horizontal schedule CF_3 indicates that foreigners perceive no risks in holding U.S. financial assets; hence, U.S. and foreign financial assets are perfect substitutes.

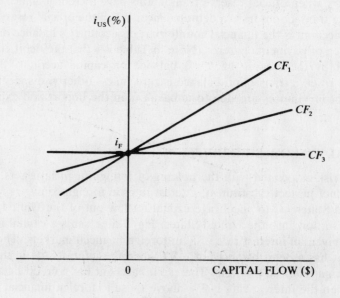

Fig. 7-6

7.6   SCHEDULE OF BALANCE-OF-PAYMENTS EQUILIBRIUM

When the export function $(X = \bar{X} - xY)$ is stable and there is a zero balance for official reserve transactions, capital inflows must vary with output for balance-of-payments equilibrium. Table 7-2 presents the U.S. trade balance and the required capital account balance for balance-of-payments equilibrium when the export function is $X = \$50 - 0.10Y$. There is a zero trade balance at a $500 output level; capital flows, therefore, are not needed to achieve a 0 balance of payments. However, when output is $600, a $10 trade deficit necessitates a $10 capital inflow for a zero balance of payments. A positively sloped schedule for balance-of-payments equilibrium BP, derived from the data in Table 7-2, is presented in Fig. 7-7. The BP schedule is upward sloping because foreign financial assets are not perfect substitutes for U.S. financial assets; capital inflows occur above the $500 income level prompted by higher U.S. interest rates to offset the U.S. trade deficit. When U.S. and foreign financial assets are perfect substitutes, the BP schedule is horizontal at a rate of interest of $i_{US} = i_F$.

Table 7-2   Balance-of-Payments Equilibrium for the Net Export Function
$$X = \$50 - 0.10Y$$

Income Level ($)	Trade Surplus (Deficit) ($)	Required Capital Flow ($)
200	+30	−30
300	+20	−20
400	+10	−10
500	0	0
600	−10	+10
700	−20	+20
800	−30	+30

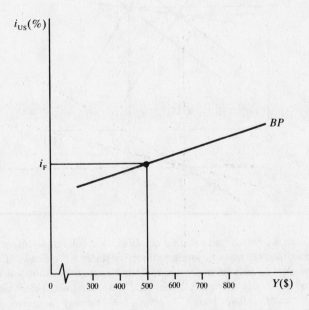

Fig. 7-7

There is a surplus in the U.S. balance of payments to the left of BP in Fig. 7-7. The United States has a surplus balance on current and capital account along with negative official reserve transactions; foreign central banks are providing the dollars which are needed to make the required excess dollar payments to the United States. The United States has a balance-of-payments deficit for positions to the right of BP in Fig. 7-7. The Federal Reserve and other official foreign institutions are supplying the foreign currency needed for U.S. payments to foreigners. (We are assuming in this section that balance-of-payments disequilibrium does not change foreign exchange rates or the money supply in the United States or foreign countries.)

Over time, a country cannot rely on central bank foreign exchange intervention and thereby must have a zero balance of payments, i.e., balance-of-payments equilibrium. Most governments are also committed to full employment of their labor resources. Monetary and fiscal policy must be coordinated not only to bring output to its full employment level but in doing so to achieve balance-of-payments equilibrium. Suppose monetary equilibrium, goods equilibrium and balance-of-payments equilibrium schedules are initially at LM, IS, and BP in Fig. 7-8; full employment output exists at output level Y_f. Although there is equilibrium in the specified markets at Y_0, aggregate economic activity is below its Y_f full employment level. The monetary and fiscal policy mix, necessary to expand output to its full employment level, is now dictated by external factors. With reference to Fig. 7-8, monetary and fiscal policy must shift the IS and LM schedules rightward to IS' and LM' in order to achieve output Y_f and balance-of-payments equilibrium at interest rate i_1.

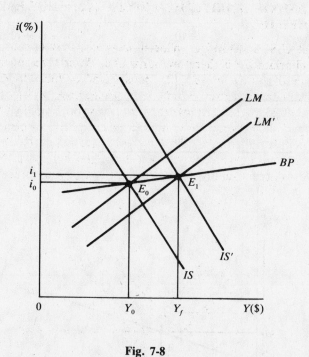

Fig. 7-8

EXAMPLE 6. Suppose there is internal and external equilibrium at full employment output Y_f and interest rate i_0 in Fig. 7-9. A decrease in interest rates in foreign countries shifts BP downward to BP'. The United States now has a balance-of-payments surplus at interest rate i_0 and output Y_f, although there is equilibrium in the money and goods markets. An easier monetary policy and a tighter fiscal policy must be implemented which shifts LM rightward to LM' and IS leftward to IS' to return the economy to internal and external equilibrium at full employment output Y_f.

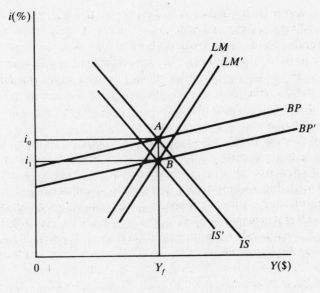

Fig. 7-9

7.7 BALANCE-OF-PAYMENTS EQUILIBRIUM: FIXED EXCHANGE RATES AND CAPITAL MOBILITY

We shall assume that U.S. and foreign financial assets are perfect substitutes; the schedule of balance-of-payments equilibrium BP is therefore horizontal. When foreign exchange rates are fixed, the central bank is required to buy or sell U.S. dollars (sell or buy foreign exchange) whenever balance-of-payments disequilibrium exists. From a U.S. perspective, positions above BP in Fig. 7-10 represent a U.S. balance-of-payments surplus; there is an excess supply of foreign currency and a shortage of U.S. dollars. The Federal Reserve intervenes in the foreign exchange markets by purchasing the excess supply of foreign currency and expanding the supply of U.S. dollars. Balance-of-payments deficits exist below BP in Fig. 7-10. When the United States has a balance-of-payments deficit, there is an excess supply of dollars and a shortage of foreign currency; the Federal

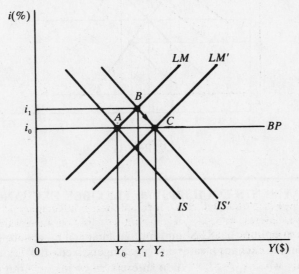

Fig. 7-10

Reserve intervenes to keep exchange rates fixed by purchasing U.S. dollars and selling foreign exchange, which reduces the supply of U.S. dollars.

Equilibrium is initially at Y_0 and i_0 in Fig. 7-10, for schedules BP, IS and LM. Increased government spending shifts IS rightward to IS'; equilibrium in the money and goods markets now exists at a Y_1 output and i_1 interest rate. Interest rate i_1 is now above those in foreign countries, and increased capital inflows put upward pressure on the value of the dollar. To maintain fixed exchange rates, the Federal Reserve intervenes in the foreign exchange markets, purchasing the excess supply of foreign exchange and expanding the supply of U.S. dollars. Foreign exchange rate intervention to prevent an appreciation of the dollar increases the U.S. money supply, and LM shifts rightward in Fig. 7-10 until LM' is reached and there is no longer disequilibrium in the U.S. balance of payments. To avert a balance-of-payments surplus and the need for foreign exchange rate intervention, the Federal Reserve could have initiated an expansive monetary policy to accompany the fiscal stimulus. IS and LM would shift rightward to IS' and LM', and equilibrium income would increase from Y_0 to Y_2 with the rate of interest remaining at i_0. In the absence of a fiscal action, however, money supply changes are incapable of changing equilibrium output when exchange rates are fixed and BP is horizontal (Example 7).

EXAMPLE 7. Suppose equilibrium is initially at Y_0 and i_0 in Fig. 7-11 for schedules BP, IS and LM. A money supply increase shifts LM rightward to LM'. Equilibrium in the money and goods markets now exists at Y_1 and i_1. Because U.S. interest rates are now below those in other countries, U.S. capital outflows increase, and there is a balance-of-payments deficit. To prevent the dollar from devaluing, the Federal Reserve purchases the excess supply of dollars in the market place. The U.S. money supply falls as a result of central bank intervention in the foreign exchange market, and the LM schedule shifts leftward until it returns to LM and balance-of-payments equilibrium is restored at Y_0 and i_0. When exchange rates are fixed and U.S. and foreign financial assets are perfect substitutes, monetary policy alone is unable to change the economy's equilibrium level of output.

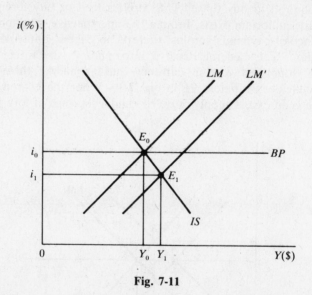

Fig. 7-11

7.8 BALANCE-OF-PAYMENTS EQUILIBRIUM: FLEXIBLE EXCHANGE RATES AND CAPITAL MOBILITY

We continue the assumption that U.S. and foreign financial assets are perfect substitutes and the BP schedule is horizontal. Exchange rates are no longer fixed; the U.S. dollar appreciates when $i_{US} > i_F$ and depreciates when $i_{US} < i_F$. When interest rates in the United States exceed those in foreign countries, capital flows into the United States; the dollar appreciates, since the demand for

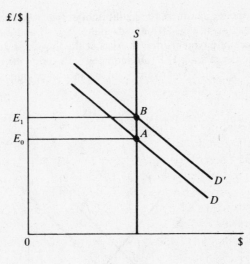

Fig. 7-12

U.S. dollars has increased from D to D' in Fig. 7-12. An increased value for the U.S. dollar causes autonomous net exports to decline as autonomous imports rise and autonomous exports fall; IS shifts leftward by $k_e \Delta \bar{X}$.

When exchange rates are flexible and capital is mobile, fiscal policy, *ceteris paribus*, cannot change equilibrium output. In Fig. 7-13, equilibrium output is initially Y_0, given schedules IS, LM and BP. Increased government spending shifts the IS schedule from IS to IS'; equilibrium output expands to Y_1, but at interest rate i_1 there is a balance-of-payments surplus. Expanded capital inflows increase the demand for U.S. dollars, and the dollar appreciates; autonomous net exports decline, and IS' shifts leftward. The U.S. dollar depreciates in value until balance-of-payments equilibrium is restored, which occurs when the goods market schedule returns to its initial IS position. Fiscal policy completely "crowds out" private sector spending. Crowding out could have been avoided if monetary policy was accommodative, shifting LM to LM'; at output Y_2 and interest rate i_0 there is balance-of-payments equilibrium as well as equilibrium in the money and goods markets.

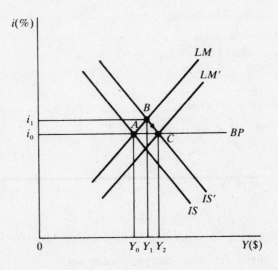

Fig. 7-13

EXAMPLE 8. Only monetary policy can increase equilibrium output when exchange rates are flexible. Y_0 and i_0 are the initial equilibrium positions in Fig. 7-14 for schedules IS, LM and BP. A money supply increase shifts LM rightward to LM'; a balance-of-payments deficit exists at the lower i_1 rate of interest. An excess supply of U.S. dollars causes the dollar to depreciate; U.S. autonomous net exports increase, and IS shifts rightward. The U.S. dollar falls in value, and IS shifts rightward until balance-of-payments equilibrium is restored at the intersection of LM', IS' and BP at output Y_2.

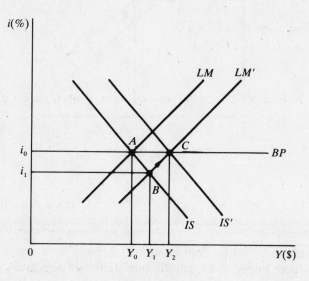

Fig. 7-14

Review Questions

1. Which of the following does not result in an increase in U.S. autonomous net exports?

    (a) The U.S. dollar depreciates.

    (b) Major trading partners stimulate their economy.

    (c) Foreign currencies depreciate.

    (d) Foreign trading partners lift tariff barriers.

    Answer: (c)

2. An increase in autonomous net exports

    (a) Shifts IS rightward by $k_e \Delta \bar{X}$

    (b) Shifts IS leftward by $k_e \Delta \bar{X}$

    (c) Increases the slope of IS

    (d) Decreases the slope of IS

    Answer: (a)

3. Which of the following results in an increase in the value of the dollar:

    (a) Interest rates in the United States decrease, *ceteris paribus*.

    (b) Interest rates in foreign countries increase, *ceteris paribus*.

(c) Price level in the United States increases, *ceteris paribus*.

(d) Productivity in the United States increases, *ceteris paribus*.

Answer: (d)

4. When there is no change in central banking holdings of international reserve balances, a country's

(a) Trade balance always equals 0.

(b) Current account balance always equals 0.

(c) Capital account balance always equals 0.

(d) Balance of payments always equals 0.

Answer: (d)

5. When the export function is $100 - 0.2Y$, net exports are 0 when income is

(a) $300

(b) $400

(c) $500

(d) $600

Answer: (c)

6. Which of the following statements is true when the U.S. export function is $80 - 0.1Y$ and there is no change in central bank holding of international reserve balances?

(a) The United States has a $20 current account deficit when aggregate output is $1000.

(b) The U.S. capital account balance has a $30 deficit balance when aggregate output is $1100.

(c) The United States has a balance-of-payments surplus when aggregate output is $1200.

(d) The United States has a zero balance of payments when aggregate output is $1300.

Answer: (a)

7. The *BP* schedule

(a) Is horizontal when domestic and foreign financial assets are perfect substitutes

(b) Is positively sloped when domestic and foreign financial assets are perfect substitutes

(c) Is a schedule where the domestic economy's trade balance is zero

(d) Is a schedule where the domestic economy's capital account balance is zero

Answer: (a)

8. When equilibrium in the money and goods markets occurs at a rate of interest below the *BP* schedule, internal and external equilibrium for the United States can be achieved by

(a) Expanding the U.S. money supply

(b) Increasing government spending

(c) Increasing taxes

(d) Lowering interest rates in the United States

Answer: (b)

9. When the economy is initially at a position of internal and external equilibrium, exchange rates are fixed, and domestic and foreign financial assets are perfect substitutes, an increase in government spending causes

(a) External imbalance and a decrease in the value of the dollar

(b) External imbalance and a decrease in autonomous net exports

(c) External imbalance and necessitates an expansion of the money supply to restore internal and external equilibrium

(d) Internal imbalance and necessitates a reduction of the money supply to restore internal and external equilibrium

Answer: (c)

10. When the economy is initially at a position of internal and external equilibrium, exchange rates are flexible, and domestic and foreign financial assets are perfect substitutes, an increase in government spending causes external imbalance and

(a) A decrease in autonomous net exports as the dollar appreciates

(b) A decrease in autonomous net exports as the dollar depreciates

(c) An increase in autonomous net exports as the dollar appreciates

(d) An increase in autonomous net exports as the dollar depreciates

Answer: (a)

Solved Problems

NET EXPORTS IN AN *IS-LM* FRAMEWORK

7.1 (a) Why are U.S. exports exogenous in a model of the U.S. economy? (b) What variables influence U.S. exports? (c) What variables influence autonomous imports? (d) In the export function $X = \bar{X} - xY$, $\bar{X}$ represents autonomous net exports. What are autonomous net exports?

(a) Exports are exogenous because their level is not explained by economic conditions in the United States, i.e., by the interest rate, the income level, and the price level in the United States.

(b) U.S. exports are influenced by tehnological change in the United States and foreign countries, foreign demand for U.S.-made goods, tariff barriers to U.S.-made goods and the exchange rate between the dollar and foreign currencies (which in turn is related to the rate of interest, the price level and relative economic growth in the U.S. and foreign countries).

(c) Autonomous U.S. imports are influenced by technological change in the United States and foreign countries, U.S. demand for foreign-made goods, U.S. import restrictions and the dollar's foreign exchange rate.

(d) Autonomous net exports equal gross autonomous exports less gross autonomous imports.

7.2 (a) From the export schedule X_1 in Fig. 7-15, find the income level at which the net export balance is 0. (b) Suppose foreign countries impose trade restrictions, U.S. exports decrease, and the export schedule in Fig. 7-15 shifts to X_2. At what income level is there now a zero net export balance? (c) Find the income level at which the net export balance is zero when technological change in the United States lowers production costs, autonomous net exports increase, and the export schedule shifts to X_3. (d) What effect does a change in autonomous net exports have on the *IS* schedule?

(a) The net export balance is zero at an $800 income level.

(b) The decrease in autonomous net exports causes the net export balance to be zero at a $700 income level.

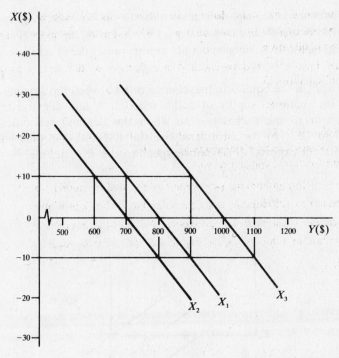

Fig. 7-15

(c)   Increased autonomous net exports cause the net export blance to be zero at a $1000 income level.

(d)   A change in autonomous net exports causes the IS schedule to shift by $k_e \, \Delta \bar{X}$.

7.3   (a) Explain behavioral coefficient x in the export function $X = \bar{X} - xY$. (b) What happens to the IS schedule when there is an increase in x?

(a)   Behavioral coefficient x relates the change in exports to a change in income ($\Delta X / \Delta Y$); as such, x represents the marginal propensity to import foreign-made goods and services.

(b)   Behavioral coefficient x represents a leakage from the spending flow and has an effect on IS similar to that of a change in the marginal propensity to save. Hence, an increase in x causes IS to become more steeply sloped as it shifts leftward.

MARKET-DETERMINED EXCHANGE RATES

7.4   (a) What is a foreign exchange rate? (b) What happens to the U.S. dollar price of Japanese-made goods when the yen-dollar foreign exchange rate falls, *ceteris paribus*? (c) What happens to the price of U.S.-made goods in Japan when the yen-dollar foreign exchange rate falls, *ceteris paribus*? (d) What happens to U.S. autonomous net exports (autonomous U.S. exports less autonomous U.S. imports) when the yen-dollar foreign exchange rate falls? (e) What happens to the IS schedule when the yen-dollar foreign exchange rate falls?

(a)   A foreign exchange rate is the rate at which one country's currency is exchanged for that of another. For example, $1 (U.S. currency) may purchase ¥130 (Japan's currency).

(b)   Holding other variables constant, a decrease in the yen-dollar foreign exchange rate makes the price of Japanese-made goods more expensive in the United States.

(c)   The price of U.S.-made goods in Japan declines as the U.S. dollar falls in value relative to the Japanese yen.

(d) U.S. autonomous net exports increase when the yen-dollar exchange rate falls. This is because U.S. autonomous exports to Japan increase while U.S. autonomous imports from Japan fall.

(e) The increase in U.S. autonomous net exports causes the IS schedule to shift rightward by $k_e \Delta \bar{X}$.

7.5 In Fig. 7-16, E_0 is the equilibrium exchange rate between the Japanese yen and the U.S. dollar given the international supply of dollar schedule S and demand for dollar schedule D. (a) What happens to the exchange rate when the demand schedule shifts upward to D' or downward to D''? (b) As a result of the shifts specified in part (a), what happens to U.S. autonomous net exports? (c) What happens to the IS schedule?

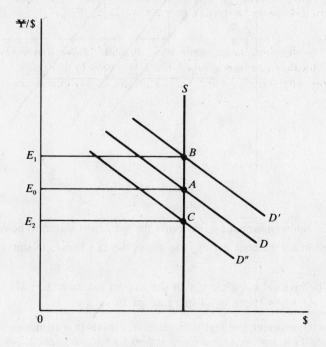

Fig. 7-16

(a) The exchange rate increases to E_1 when demand shifts upward to D'; the dollar has appreciated relative to the Japanese yen. The exchange rate falls to E_2 when demand shifts downward to D''; the dollar has depreciated relative to the Japanese yen.

(b) Autonomous net exports in the United States fall when the demand for dollars shifts upward to D' because U.S.-made goods are more expensive in Japan and Japanese-made goods cost less in the United States. The downward shift to D'' increases U.S. autonomous net exports.

(c) The IS schedule shifts leftward by $k_e \Delta \bar{X}$ ($\Delta \bar{X}$ is the net decrease in autonomous net exports) when the dollar appreciates and rightward by $k_e \Delta \bar{X}$ ($\Delta \bar{X}$ is the increase in autonomous net exports) when the dollar depreciates.

7.6 Assume that the exchange rate is initially E_0 (Fig. 7-16) for each of the following situations. What happens to the exchange rate when (a) interest rates in the United States i_{US} increase, *ceteris paribus*; (b) interest rates in foreign countries i_F increase, *ceteris paribus*; (c) the price level in the United States increases 5% while the price level of major trading partners increases 2%, *ceteris paribus*; (d) productivity increases in the United States exceed those of its major trading countries, *ceteris paribus*?

(a) An increase in interest rates in the United States, holding those in foreign countries constant, expands capital inflows into the United States, and there is an increased demand for dollars. The dollar appreciates as the exchange rate exceeds E_0.

(b) An increase in interest rates in foreign countries, holding interest rates in the United States constant, expands capital outflows from the United States. The demand for dollars shifts downward; the dollar depreciates with the exchange rate falling below E_0.

(c) United States' goods and services become less competitive as the United States experiences a greater rate of price increase. The demand for U.S.-made goods declines. The demand for dollars shifts downward, and the exchange rate falls below E_0.

(d) Productivity increases reduce per-unit production costs in the United States, and U.S.-made goods become more price competitive. Autonomous net exports increase. The demand for dollars shifts rightward, and the exchange rate rises above E_0.

7.7   In Fig. 7-17, equilibrium income is initially Y_0 and the rate of interest i_0. (a) Find equilibrium income and the rate of interest when a $\Delta \bar{G}$ increase in government spending shifts IS to IS', *ceteris paribus*. (b) Why does the fiscal stimulus in (a) affect autonomous net exports?

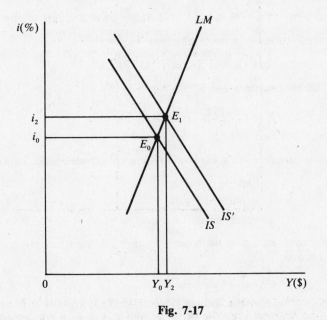

Fig. 7-17

(a) Equilibrium in the money and goods markets exists at output Y_2 and rate of interest i_2 after the $\Delta \bar{G}$ increase in government spending.

(b) The i_0 to i_2 increase in the U.S. interest rate stimulates capital inflows into the United States. The demand for dollars shifts upward, and there is an appreciation of the dollar. Autonomous net exports decrease because of the appreciation of the dollar, and the goods equilibrium schedule shifts leftward from IS'. Increased government spending crowds out autonomous exports due to an increase in the U.S. rate of interest.

BALANCE OF PAYMENTS

7.8   What is a balance-of-payments statement?

A balance-of-payments statement is a record of all economic transactions between the residents of a country and the residents of foreign countries for a specific period of time. These international transactions can be categorized according to type of transaction. In doing so, the statement records a country's trade balance (net balance for a country's commodity exports and imports), current account balance (net balance on international trade, services and unilateral transfers), capital account balance (net balance on capital inflows and outflows) and official reserve transactions (changes in the international reserves held by governments and official agencies). When there are no statistical discrepancies and no change in official reserve transactions, the capital account balance is the financial counterpart of a country's balance on current account. Thus, in the absence of a change in official reserve assets, a country's net balance on current account and capital account is zero, i.e., its balance of payments is zero.

7.9   Use the following data to measure a country's balance on merchandise trade, balance on current account, balance on capital account and balance of payments. There is no change in reserve assets held by governments and official agencies.

(1)   The United States exports goods valued at $19,650.

(2)   The United States imports merchandise valued at $21,758.

(3)   U.S. citizens receive interest income of $3621 from foreign investments.

(4)   Interest income of $1394 is paid on foreign-owned assets in the United States.

(5)   U.S. citizens' travel expenditures equal $1919.

(6)   Foreign travel in the United States is $1750.

(7)   U.S. unilateral transfers are $2388.

(8)   U.S. capital outflow is $4174

(9)   U.S. capital inflow is $6612.

The balance on merchandise trade is the difference between goods imported and goods exported:

Exports of goods	+$19,650
Imports of goods	−$21,758
Balance on merchandise trade	−$2,108

The balance on current account is the balance on merchandise trade, interest paid and received, travel and unilateral transfers

Exports of services		+$5,371
Interest income	+$3,621	
Travel	+$1,750	
Imports of services		−$3,313
Interest income	−$1,394	
Travel	−$1,919	
U.S. government unilateral transfers		−$2,388
Balance on current account		−$2,438

The balance on capital account is the difference between capital inflows and capital outflows

U.S. capital outflows	−$4,174
U.S. capital inflows	+$6,612
Balance on capital account	+$2,438

The balance of payments equals the net balance on current account and capital account: Balance of payments = 0.

7.10 (*a*) What are official reserve transaction balances? (*b*) Explain why the capital account is the financial counterpart of a country's balance on current account when there is no change in official reserve transaction balances.

(*a*) Official reserve transaction balances consist of international reserves held by government or official government agencies. International reserves include a government's holdings of gold, balances in the International Monetary Fund, and foreign currencies.

(*b*) International transactions are recorded on a system of double-entry accounting where each debit entry necessitates a credit entry. Thus, the sum of all debit items in the balance of payments must equal the sum of all credit items. When there is no change in official reserve assets held by governments, the balance on current account plus the balance on capital account must equal zero. Hence, a deficit (−) current account balance must be countered by a surplus (+) capital account balance, i.e., the capital account is the financial counterpart of a country's balance on current account when there is no change in the holding of official reserve transaction balances.

THE CAPITAL INFLOW SCHEDULE

7.11 (*a*) Suppose the U.S. current account balance is given by the export function $X = \$100 - 0.10Y$. Present in Table 7-3 the current account balance and the balance on capital account (assuming no change in international reserves) when equilibrium income is $800, $900, $1000, $1100 and $1200. (*b*) Plot the capital account balance from Table 7-3 in Fig. 7-18 and (1) label the schedule CF_1 when domestic and foreign financial assets are perfect substitutes; (2) label the schedule CF_2 when domestic and foreign financial assets are not perfect substitutes and i_F is 5%. (*c*) Why is CF_2 upward sloping while CF_1 is horizontal?

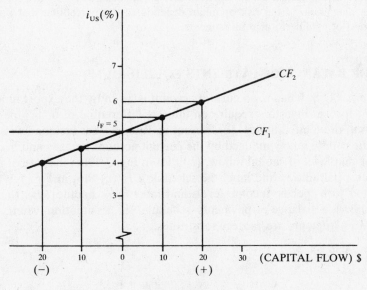

Fig. 7-18

(*a*) See Table 7-3.

(*b*) See Fig. 7-18.

(*c*) When domestic and foreign financial assets are imperfect substitutes (there is risk in holding foreign financial assets), i_{US} must exceed i_F for a capital inflow into the United States, and i_{US} must be less than i_F for a capital outflow to occur. Hence, CF_2 is upward sloping from $i_F = 5\%$ for capital inflows to occur. When domestic and foreign financial assets are perfect substitutes, an unlimited capital inflow and outflow exists when $i_F = i_{US}$. CF_1 is horizontal at interest rate $i_F = 5\%$.

Table 7-3

Income Level ($)	Current Account Balance ($)	Capital Account Balance ($)
800	+20	−20
900	+10	−10
1000	0	0
1100	−10	+10
1200	−20	+20

7.12 (*a*) What risk is there in holding foreign financial assets?

(*b*) What is the relationship of domestic and foreign interest rates when there is risk in holding foreign financial assets?

(*a*) Risks associated with holding foreign financial assets include the possibility that the domestic currency will appreciate relative to foreign currencies (the return on foreign-held assets falls when the domestic currency appreciates), the possibility that a country will impose restrictions on capital outflows (capital may not be allowed to leave a foreign country) and the possibility that the foreign entity may be unable to meet interest payments or repay the amount borrowed.

(*b*) When investors perceive that there are risks in holding foreign financial assets, they require a higher return (a risk premium) from foreign financial assets than from domestic financial assets. The magnitude of the risk premium depends on the perception that risks may occur during the period of holding foreign investments.

SCHEDULE OF BALANCE-OF-PAYMENTS EQUILIBRIUM

7.13 Suppose the U.S. balance on current account is given by the export function $C = \$70 - 0.10Y$; $i_F = 5\%$; foreign investors require an interest differential of 0.50% per \$10 additional capital inflow into the United States. (*a*) Present in Table 7-4 for income levels \$800, \$900, \$1000 and \$1100 the capital inflow induced by the current account balance and the interest rate that must exist for that level of capital inflow. (*b*) Plot in Fig. 7-19(*a*) the rate of interest associated with specific capital inflows and label the schedule *CF*. (*c*) Plot in Fig. 7-19(*b*) the rate of interest associated with specific income levels and label the schedule BP_1. (*d*) Plot and label BP_2 in Fig. 7-19(*b*) a balance-of-payments schedule for a situation where domestic and foreign financial instruments are perfect substitutes.

(*a*) See Table 7-4.

Table 7-4

Income Level ($)	Capital Inflow ($)	Required i_{US} (%)
800	−10	5.50
900	−20	6.00
1000	−30	6.50
1100	−40	7.00

(*b*), (*c*), (*d*) See Fig. 7-19.

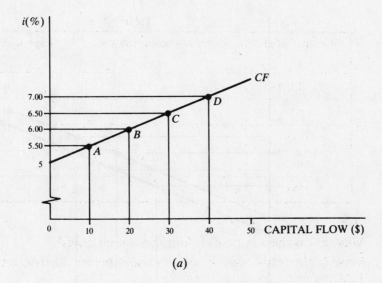

(a)

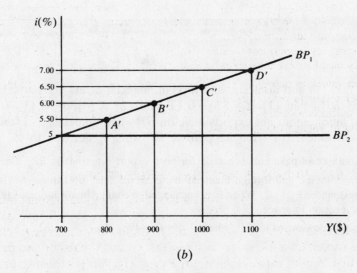

(b)

Fig. 7-19

7.14 Suppose $i_F = 5\%$ and foreign investors require a 0.50% interest differential per \$10 capital inflow into the United States. (a) Plot the balance-of-payments schedule in Fig. 7-20 and label it BP_1 when $X = \$70 - 0.1Y$, BP_2 when $X = \$80 - 0.1Y$. (b) When the BP schedule is upward sloping, what effect does a change in autonomous net exports have on the schedule's location in space? (c) What happens to balance-of-payments schedule BP_1 when i_F declines from 5% to 4%?

(a) See Fig. 7-20. For equation $X = \$70 - 0.10Y$, X is zero when Y equals \$700. For equation $X = \$80 - 0.10Y$, X is zero when Y equals \$800. Thus, $i_{US} = i_F = 5\%$ when $Y = \$700$ for schedule BP_1 and when $Y = \$800$ for schedule BP_2.

(b) The \$10 increase in autonomous net exports shifts BP rightward \$100. When BP is upward sloping, an autonomous change in net exports shifts BP by the change in autonomous net exports divided by the marginal propensity to import or by $\Delta \bar{X}(1/x)$.

(c) When BP is upward sloping, net capital flows equal zero when $i_F = i_{US}$. With no change in the export function, a 1% decline in the foreign interest rate shifts BP downward 1%.

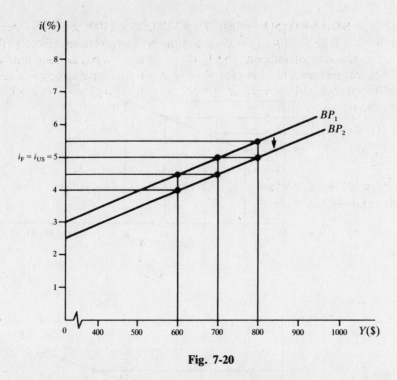

Fig. 7-20

7.15 Suppose $i_F = 5\%$ and domestic and foreign financial assets are perfect substitutes. (*a*) In Fig. 7-21, plot *BP* when (1) $X = \$70 - 0.1Y$ and (2) $X = \$80 - 0.1Y$. (*b*) What effect does a change in autonomous net exports have on *BP* when domestic and foreign financial assets are perfect substitutes? (*c*) What happens to *BP* when i_F declines to 4%.

(*a*)   The balance-of-payments schedule for both export functions is BP_1. See Fig. 7-21.

(*b*)   When domestic and foreign financial assets are perfect substitutes, *BP* is horizontal at the rate of interest where $i_{US} = i_F$. When i_F is unchanged, a change in autonomous net exports has no effect on *BP*'s location in space.

(*c*)   *BP* shifts downward to BP_2 where $i_{US} = i_F = 4\%$.

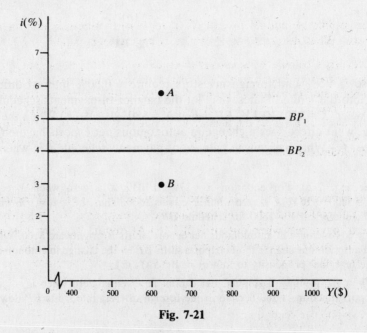

Fig. 7-21

7.16 Suppose $C = \$47.50 + 0.85(Y - Tn)$; $Tn = \$100$; $G = \$100$; $I = \$100 - 5i$; $X = \$50 - 0.10Y$; $M = \$100$; $L = 0.20Y - 10i$. $i_F = 5\%$, and there is capital mobility. (*a*) Find equilibrium income and the rate of interest. (*b*) Is there balance-of-payments equilibrium? What is the balance on current account and capital account at equilibrium income found in part (*a*)? (*c*) What effect will a \$10 increase in government spending have on equilibrium income? on balance-of-payments equilibrium?

(*a*) *IS* equation:

$$Y = C + I + G + X$$
$$Y = \$47.50 + 0.85(Y - \$100) + \$100 - 5i + \$100 + \$50 - 0.10Y$$
$$Y - 0.85Y + 0.10Y = \$850 - 20i = \$212.50 - 5i$$

LM equation:

$$M = L$$
$$\$100 = 0.20Y - 10i$$
$$0.20Y = \$100 + 10i$$
$$Y = \$500 + 50i$$

Goods and money market equilibrium:

$$IS = LM$$
$$\$850 - 20i = \$500 + 50i$$
$$i = 5\%$$
$$Y = \$750$$

(*b*) At a 5% rate of interest, there is balance-of-payments equilibrium ($i_F = i_{US} = 5\%$) as well as equilibrium in the money and goods markets. The balance on current account is found by substituting equilibrium income into the export function $X = \$50 - 0.10Y$. The balance on current account is $-\$25$, i.e., the economy has a \$25 deficit on its current account. Because there is balance-of-payments equilibrium, there is a \$25 surplus on capital account.

(*c*) The *IS* equation is $Y = \$890 - 20i$ as a result of the \$10 increase in government spending. Simultaneous equilibrium in the goods and money markets exist when $Y = \$778.57$ and $i = 5.57\%$. Because there is capital mobility and i_{US} (5.57%) is now greater than i_F (5%), there is balance of payments disequilibrium.

7.17 Why do points *A* and *B* in Fig. 7-21 represent disequilibrium in a country's balance of payments? What do positions above or below *BP* represent?

A country's balance of payments (balance on current and capital account) is zero along a *BP* schedule. A country has a credit (+) balance on its current and capital accounts at point *A*, i.e., a country has a surplus balance of payments—official reserve transactions are a negative entry to offset a positive balance on current and capital account. A country has a debit (−) balance on its current and capital accounts at point *B*; the balance of payments is in deficit, and the country is acquiring official reserve assets. Positions above *BP*, therefore, indicate a balance-of-payments surplus, and positions below *BP* indicate a deficit.

7.18 Posit an economy in Fig. 7-22 where schedules *LM*, *IS* and *BP* represent equilibrium in the money and goods markets and the balance of payments. (*a*) What is true of this economy's balance of payments when output is Y_0? (*b*) At output Y_0, what is happening to the country's holding of official reserve transaction balances? (*c*) How can the balance-of-payments disequilibrium be remedied when full employment output exists at a Y_1 level of output?

(*a*) The economy has a balance-of-payments surplus. Equilibrium in the money and goods markets exists at a rate of interest above balance-of-payments equilibrium, and there is an excess capital inflow into the country.

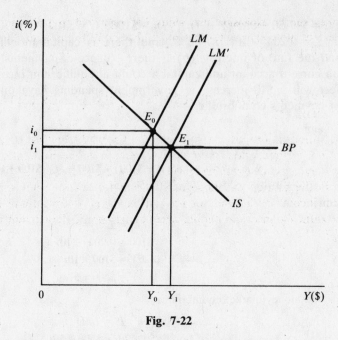

Fig. 7-22

(b) The economy is losing official reserve transaction balances at a rate of interest above balance-of-payments equilibrium. (The surplus balance of payments is offset by a deficit in official reserve balances held.)

(c) An increase in the money supply that shifts LM rightward to LM' would bring about internal and external equilibrium at a Y_1 level of output.

7.19 In Fig. 7-23, there is internal and external equilibrium at output Y_f. Suppose foreign economies enter a recession; their imports and rate of interest decline. U.S. autonomous net exports fall; IS shifts leftward to IS_1, and the balance-of-payments schedule shifts downward from BP to BP_1 due to a decrease in i_F. What monetary and fiscal policy mix must the United States implement to reinstate internal and external equilibrium at full employment?

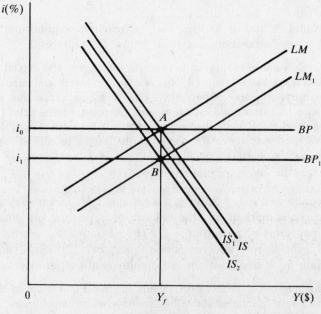

Fig. 7-23

A money supply expansion that shifts LM rightward to LM_1 and a reduction in government spending and/or increase in taxes that shifts IS leftward from IS_1 to IS_2 would reinstate internal and external equilibrium at Y_f.

BALANCE-OF-PAYMENTS EQUILIBRIUM: FIXED EXCHANGE RATES AND CAPITAL MOBILITY

7.20 Suppose equilibrium output is Y_0 in Fig. 7-24, for schedules LM, IS and BP. (*a*) What happens to equilibrium income when there is a $\Delta \bar{G}$ increase in government spending? (*b*) Why is there balance-of-payments disequilibrium at this new income level? (*c*) Why must the central bank intervene in the foreign exchange market when exchange rates are fixed? What happens to equilibrium income as a result of foreign exchange intervention? (*d*) What happens to the current account balance and capital account balance if the current account balance is zero at output Y_0?

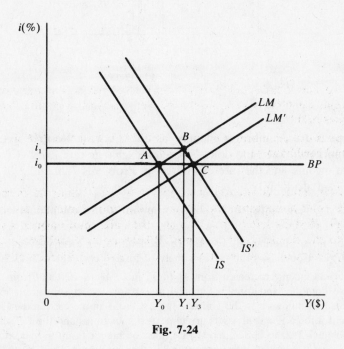

Fig. 7-24

(*a*) IS shifts upward to IS', and equilibrium income increases to Y_1.

(*b*) External disequilibrium exists because equilibrium in the money and goods markets exists at a rate of interest above the BP schedule; there is a balance-of-payments surplus at interest rate i_1.

(*c*) There is an increased capital inflow into the United States. To keep exchange rates from changing, the Federal Reserve must purchase the excess supply of foreign currency with U.S. dollars. (The Fed must match the excess demand for dollars with an increased supply of dollars.) In doing so, the U.S. money supply increases, and LM shifts rightward from LM to LM'. Foreign exchange intervention by the Fed causes equilibrium income to increase to Y_3.

(*d*) Because imports expand with output and there is no change in autonomous net exports, the current account is in deficit, but the capital account shows a surplus balance.

7.21 Suppose equilibrium output is initially Y_0 in Fig. 7-25, for schedules LM, IS and BP. (*a*) What happens to equilibrium income when there is a $\Delta \bar{G}$ increase in government spending? (*b*)

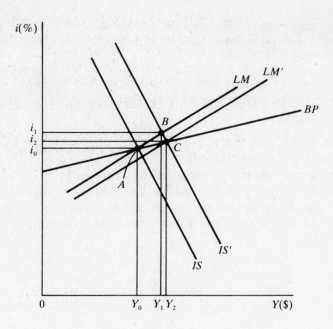

Fig. 7-25

What happens to equilibrium income as the Federal Reserve intervenes in the foreign exchange market to keep the dollar's foreign exchange rate fixed? (c) Compare the change in equilibrium income and the rate of interest in Problems 7.20 and 7.21, which differ only with respect to capital mobility.

(a) Increased government spending shifts *IS* upward to *IS'*; equilibrium income increases from Y_0 to Y_1.

(b) Equilibrium income increases to Y_2. The Federal Reserve expands the money supply, shifting *LM* to *LM'*, as it purchases the excess supply of foreign currency with U.S. dollars.

(c) Equilibrium income increases from Y_0 to Y_3 in Problem 7.20 and from Y_0 to Y_2 in Problem 7.21. Because domestic and foreign financial assets are perfect substitutes in Problem 7.20, there are larger capital inflows into the United States without an increase in the U.S. rate of interest. When U.S. and foreign financial assets are imperfect substitutes and the *BP* schedule is positively sloped in Problem 7.21, the U.S. interest rate must be higher to attract additional foreign capital. Some interest-sensitive private sector spending is thereby crowded out by the higher U.S. interest rate which is necessary to attract additional foreign capital inflows.

7.22 Suppose equilibrium output is initially Y_0 in Fig. 7-26, for schedules *IS*, *LM* and *BP*. (a) What happens to equilibrium income when the Federal Reserve increases the money supply by $\Delta \bar{M}$? (b) What happens to equilibrium income when the Federal Reserve intervenes in the foreign exchange markets to keep the dollar's foreign exchange rate fixed?

(a) A $\Delta \bar{M}$ increase in the money supply shifts *LM* rightward to *LM'*; equilibrium income increases from Y_0 to Y_1.

(b) A balance-of-payments deficit exists at output Y_1 and interest rate i_1. There is an excess supply of dollars (shortage of foreign exchange) at output Y_1; to keep exchange rates fixed, the Federal Reserve sells foreign exchange (buys dollars). In doing so, the U.S. money supply declines, and *LM'* shifts left to *LM*; equilibrium output returns to Y_0. Monetary policy is unable to change the income level at which there is internal and external equilbrium.

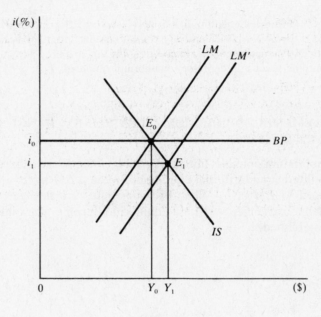

Fig. 7-26

7.23 Suppose equilibrium output is Y_0 in Fig. 7-27, for schedules *IS*, *LM* and *BP*. (*a*) What happens to internal and external equilibrium when autonomous net exports decline, *ceteris paribus*? (*b*) What policy options does the United States have to return the economy to internal and external equilibrium when exchange rates are fixed?

(*a*)   A decrease in autonomous net exports shifts *IS* leftward to *IS'* in Fig. 7-27; equilibrium output falls to Y_1 and the U.S. rate of interest declines to i_1. External disequilibrium exists; a lower interest rate in the United States induces capital outflows and a balance-of-payments deficit.

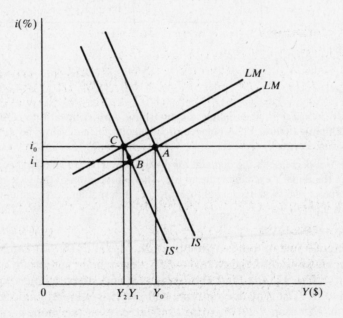

Fig. 7-27

(b) Internal and external equilibrium can be reestablished by increased government spending and/or reduced taxes which shift commodity equilibrium back to *IS*, with equilibrium output returning to Y_0. A tighter monetary policy, which shifts *LM* to *LM'*, is an alternative; however, such a policy is less plausible because it depresses equilibrium output to Y_2.

BALANCE-OF-PAYMENTS EQUILIBRIUM: FLEXIBLE EXCHANGE RATES AND CAPITAL MOBILITY

7.24   Suppose equilibrium output is initially Y_0 in Fig. 7-28, for schedules *LM*, *IS* and *BP*. (a) What happens to internal and external equilibrium when a $\Delta \bar{M}$ increase in the money supply shifts *LM* rightward to *LM'*? (b) When exchange rates are flexible, what happens to the U.S. dollar's foreign exchange rate? Find equilibrium income when internal and external equilibrium is reestablished.

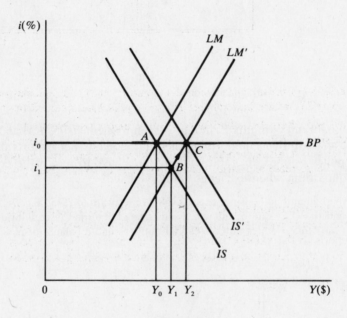

Fig. 7-28

(a) A $\Delta \bar{M}$ increase in the money supply shifts *LM* rightward to *LM'* in Fig. 7-28, increasing equilibrium output to Y_1. A balance-of-payments deficit develops because of the decline in the U.S. rate of interest to i_1.

(b) There is a decrease in the demand for dollars; the leftward shift of the demand-for-dollars schedule causes the dollar's exchange rate to fall. The depreciation of the U.S. dollar increases autonomous net exports, which shifts *IS* rightward to *IS'*. Internal and external equilibrium is reestablished at output Y_2.

7.25   Suppose equilibrium output is Y_0 in Fig. 7-29, schedules *IS*, *LM* and *BP*. A $\Delta \bar{M}$ increase in the money supply shifts *LM* rightward to *LM'*, increasing equilibrium income in the money and goods markets to Y_1. (a) Find equilibrium income after depreciation of the dollar shifts *IS* rightward to *IS"*. (b) Why does internal and external equilibrium occur at a higher output level in Problem 7.25 than 7.24 when the $\Delta \bar{M}$ increase in the money supply is the same in both problems?

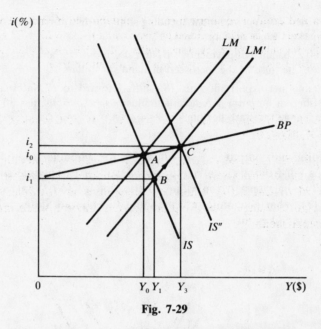

Fig. 7-29

(a) Depreciation of the dollar increases autonomous net exports and shifts the goods market schedule from *IS* to *IS'''*, where internal and external equilibrium occurs at output Y_2.

(b) Internal and external equilibrium occurs at a higher interest rate (i_2) in Fig. 7-29 because of the upward-sloping *BP* schedule (domestic and foreign financial assets are not perfect substitutes); while interest-sensitive spending falls in Problem 7.25, expansion of autonomous exports more than offsets the decrease and raises output above the Y_2 level in Problem 7.24.

7.26 Suppose equilibrium output is Y_0 in Fig. 7-30, for schedules *IS*, *LM* and *BP*. (a) Find equilibrium income when a $\Delta \bar{G}$ increase in government spending shifts *IS* rightward to *IS'*. (b) What happens to the value of the dollar as a result of the change in the income level in part (a)? (c) At what income level are internal and external equilibrium established?

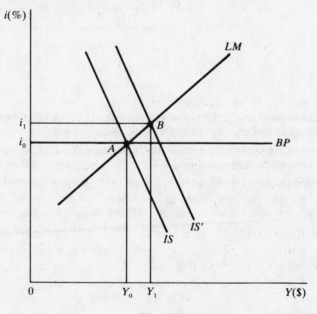

Fig. 7-30

(a) The $\Delta \bar{G}$ increase in government spending shifts *IS* rightward to *IS'*; equilibrium in the money and goods markets exists at output level Y_1.

(b) There is a balance-of-payments surplus at output Y_1 and interest rate i_1. The U.S. dollar appreciates because of the increased demand for dollars.

(c) Autonomous net exports decline. *IS'* shifts leftward to *IS*; internal and external equilibrium is reestablished at output Y_0. A fiscal stimulus, *ceteris paribus*, has no effect on equilibrium income when exchange rates are flexible.

7.27 Suppose equilibrium output is Y_0 in Fig. 7-31, for schedules *IS*, *LM* and *BP*. Suppose foreign interest rates fall from i_0 to i_1, *ceteris paribus*; the *BP* schedule shifts downward from *BP* to *BP'*. (a) What happens to the value of the dollar? (b) What happens to the *IS* and *LM* schedules? (c) What economic policy should the United States follow to reestablish internal and external equilibrium?

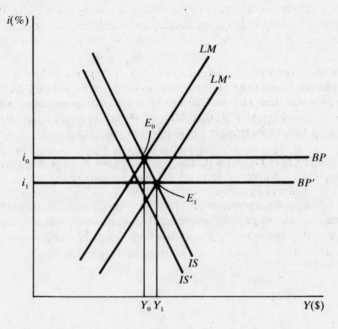

Fig. 7-31

(a) A balance-of-payments surplus develops since the U.S. interest rate remains at i_0, above the i_1 rate now existing in foreign countries. The U.S. dollar appreciates.

(b) Autonomous net exports fall because of the stronger dollar; *IS* shifts leftward from *IS* to *IS'*. There is no change in the *LM* schedule.

(c) The United States must expand the domestic money supply, shift *LM* rightward and bring the U.S. interest rate into parity with foreign rates at i_1. But in doing so, *IS'* shifts back to *IS* since the exchange rate returns to its initial level as do autonomous exports. Internal and external equilibrium are reestablished at output Y_1 and interest rate i_1 for schedules *IS* and *LM'*.

Chapter 8

Schedules of Aggregate Demand
and Aggregate Supply

8.1 THE PRICE LEVEL AND EQUILIBRIUM INCOME

The real money supply is a function of the price level and the nominal money supply; $m = \bar{M}/p$, where m is the real money supply, $\bar{M}$ is the nominal money supply, and p is the price level (Example 1). Changes in the real money supply shift the schedule of monetary equilibrium; increases in the real money supply shift LM rightward, and decreases shift it leftward. Thus, holding the nominal money supply constant, an increase in the price level decreases the real money and shifts LM leftward. Price-level changes thereby have the same effect on aggregate spending as do changes in the nominal money supply. A decrease in the nominal money supply and/or an increase in the price level reduce the real money supply and aggregate spending, whereas an increase in the nominal money supply and/or decrease in the price level expand spending levels (Example 2).

EXAMPLE 1. The real money supply increases from $100 to $200 when the price level remains at 1.0 and the nominal money supply increases from $100 to $200: $m = \bar{M}/p$; $100 = \$100/1.0$ and $\$200 = \$200/1.0$. The real money supply also increases from $100 to $200 when the nominal money supply is $100 and the price level falls from 1.0 to 0.5: $m = \bar{M}/p$; $100 = \$100/1.0$ and $\$200 = \$100/0.5$. Obviously, the real money supply is unchanged when there is an equal relative increase in the nominal money supply and the price level.

EXAMPLE 2. Schedule LM in Fig. 8-1 is derived from schedules of the demand for real money balances and of the real money supply m_0, given price level p_0 and nominal money supply $\bar{M}$. Equilibrium income is y_0 for schedules LM and IS. A doubling of the price level from p_0 to $2p_0$, *ceteris paribus*, reduces the real money supply from m_0 to $0.5m_0$; LM shifts leftward to LM', and equilibrium income declines from y_0 to y_1. Thus, an increase in the price level, *ceteris paribus*, lowers equilibrium income while a decrease in the price level, *ceteris paribus*, increases equilibrium income.

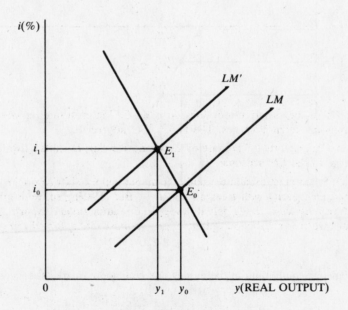

Fig. 8-1

8.2 A SCHEDULE OF AGGREGATE DEMAND

An aggregate demand schedule relates the price level to equilibrium output in the money and goods markets. In Fig. 8-2(a), the nominal money supply is constant; increases in the price level from p_0 to $1.1p_0$ to $1.2p_0$ shift monetary equilibrium from LM to LM' to LM''. (LM is associated with price level p_0, LM' with price level $1.1p_0$, and LM'' with $1.2p_0$.] These leftward shifts of LM, due to a reduction in the real money supply, lower equilibrium income and raise the rate of interest from y_0 and i_0 to y_1 and i_1 to y_2 and i_2, respectively. In Fig. 8-2(b) we derive an aggregate demand schedule by plotting equilibrium income y_0 with the associated price level p_0, y_1 with the associated price level $1.1p_0$, and y_2 with $1.2p_0$. The slope of aggregate demand depends on the value of behavioral coefficients b (the interest sensitivity of investment), k_e (the expenditure multiplier), h (the interest sensitivity of the demand for money) and k (the transaction demand for money).

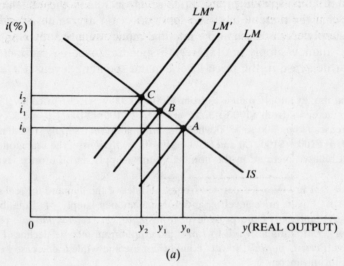

(a)

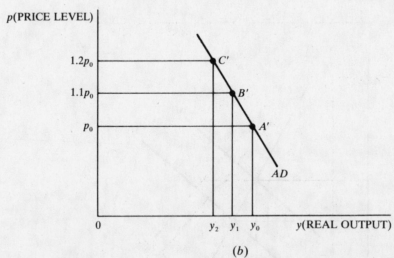

(b)

Fig. 8-2

EXAMPLE 3. Simultaneous equilibrium in the money and commodity markets is given by the equation

$$y = \frac{hk_e}{h + kbk_e}(\bar{A}) + \frac{bk_e}{h + kbk_e}\left(\frac{\bar{M}}{p}\right)$$

where y represents real output, $\bar{A}$ autonomous spending, $\bar{M}$ the nominal money supply, p the price level, h the sensitivity of the demand for money to the rate of interest, k_e the spending multiplier, b the sensitivity of investment spending to the rate of interest and k the transactions demand for money. A change in the price level, *ceteris paribus*, has the following effect on equilibrium output:

$$\Delta y = \frac{bk_e}{h + kbk_e} \Delta\left(\frac{\bar{M}}{p}\right)$$

With price on the vertical axis and output on the horizontal axis, the slope of the derived aggregate demand schedule is $(h + kbk_e)/(bk_e)$. (See Problem 8.7.) Aggregate demand is less steeply sloped (flatter), the larger the value of b and k_e and/or the smaller the value of h and k.

8.3 SHIFTING THE AGGREGATE DEMAND SCHEDULE

Changes in autonomous spending and/or the nominal money shift the aggregate demand schedule. An increase in the nominal money supply and/or autonomous spending shifts aggregate demand to the right, and decreases shift it to the left. Equilibrium income is y_0 in Fig. 8-3(a), given

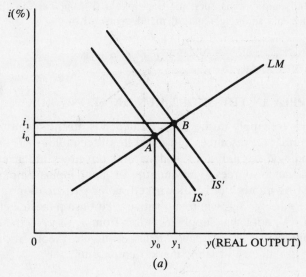

(a)

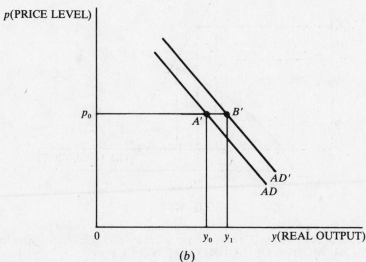

(b)

Fig. 8-3

schedules LM, IS and price level p_0. This y_0 equilibrium position appears on aggregate demand schedule AD in Fig. 8-3(b) as point A'. An increase in government spending, *ceteris paribus*, shifts IS rightward to IS' with equilibrium output increasing from y_0 to y_1. With the price level remaining at p_0 in Fig. 8-3(b), equilibrium output y_1 is point B' on aggregate demand schedule AD'. Increases in autonomous spending ($\Delta\bar{A} > 0$) shift the aggregate demand schedule rightward by $[hk_e/(h + kbk_e)]\Delta\bar{A}$, while autonomous increases in the nominal money supply shift aggregate demand rightward by $[bk_e/(h + kbk_e)](\Delta\bar{M}/\bar{p})$.

EXAMPLE 4. Simultaneous equilibrium in the money and commodity markets is given by the equation

$$y = \frac{hk_e}{h + kbk_e}(\bar{A}) + \frac{bk_e}{h + kbk_e}\left(\frac{\bar{M}}{\bar{p}}\right)$$

Holding the price level and nominal money supply constant, a $\Delta\bar{A}$ increase in autonomous spending increases equilibrium income and shifts aggregate demand rightward by

$$\Delta y = \frac{hk_e}{h + kbk_e}(\Delta\bar{A})$$

Holding the price level and autonomous spending constant, a $\Delta\bar{M}$ increase in the nominal money supply increases equilibrium income and shifts aggregate demand rightward by

$$\Delta y = \frac{bk_e}{h + kbk_e}\left(\frac{\Delta\bar{M}}{\bar{p}}\right)$$

8.4   AGGREGATE SUPPLY IN THE SHORT RUN AND LONG RUN

The economy's ability to supply in the long run depends on the quantity and quality of human (N), capital (K) and natural (L) resources and the state of technology (T), i.e., $y = y(N, K, L; T)$. In the short run, technology, capital stock and natural resources are fixed; supply is altered by varying the inputs of human resources. The quantity of labor inputs employed in the short run is variable and depends on the number of hours worked, labor participation rates and the demand for labor inputs. This is noted in Fig. 8-4, where a positive relationship exists between the supply of real output y and labor inputs N; note that supply increases from y_1 to y_2 as the quantity of labor inputs employed increases from N_1 to N_2. Because macroeconomic theory focuses on the short run, aggregate supply theory is a theory of labor market equilibrium.

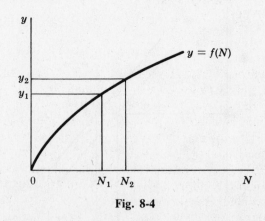

Fig. 8-4

8.5   A NEOCLASSICAL MODEL OF AGGREGATE SUPPLY

The Demand for Labor Inputs. The demand for labor inputs is derived from the marginal revenue generated by employing labor inputs. The incremental revenue associated with an increase in the use of labor inputs, called the marginal revenue product of labor MRP_N in microeconomic theory, depends upon the price at which goods are sold and the marginal physical product of labor MPP_N. The marginal physical product of labor, the incremental output associated with an increase in the quantity of labor inputs, is derived from the short-run supply of output schedule. According to the law of diminishing returns, the marginal physical product of labor falls as the quantity of labor inputs increases. Thus, the marginal revenue product of labor is negatively related to the quantity of labor inputs.

EXAMPLE 5. Suppose that the price level is 1 and the marginal physical product of labor is given by $750 - 20N$. Incremental revenue is $MPP \times p = 1(750 - 20N) = \$750 - 20N$. A schedule of incremental revenue from increasing quantities of labor inputs is given in Table 8-1.

Table 8-1

Labor Inputs	10	12	14	16	18	20
Marginal Revenue ($)	550	510	470	430	390	350

Assuming profit maximization, labor inputs are added as long as the incremental revenue $(MPP \cdot p)$ per unit of labor input exceeds per-unit incremental cost. That is, additional units of labor are demanded until $MPP \cdot p = W$, where W is the dollar cost per unit of labor input, or until $MPP = W/p$. This last equation states that labor inputs are added until the real value of their incremental output is equal to their real wage. The inverse relationship between the quantity of labor inputs demanded and the real wage is presented in Fig. 8-5 and is labeled N_d, the aggregate demand for labor inputs.

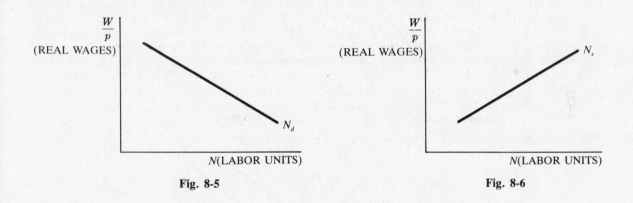

Fig. 8-5   Fig. 8-6

The Supply of Labor Inputs. Work competes with leisure. When workers attach a positive value to leisure, greater disutility is associated with each additional hour of labor input. We shall assume that the increasing disutility of work can be overcome by increased material reward, i.e., by a higher real wage. This behavior is presented in Fig. 8-6 as a positively sloped labor supply schedule where a higher real wage is necessary to increase the quantity of labor inputs supplied.

Labor Market Equilibrium and Aggregate Supply. Equilibrium in the market for labor services exists in Fig. 8-7 when N_0 labor inputs are employed and the real wage is W_0/p_0. When the supply of and demand for labor immediately adjust to changes in the price level (for example, supply and demand shift upward proportionally by the increase in the price level), the real wage is unaffected by any price-level change. For example, in Fig. 8-8(a), the quantity of labor units employed remains at N_0 as the price level increases from p_0 to $1.1p_0$ to $1.2p_0$. This equilibrium condition in the market for N_0 labor inputs determines a fixed y^* output in Fig. 8-8(b) which is designated the full employment level of output. When equilibrium in the labor markets is unaffected by the price level, aggregate supply is vertical [Fig. 8-8(c)] which is classified in macroeconomic theory as a neoclassical aggregate supply schedule.

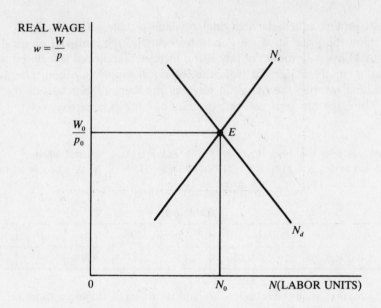

Fig. 8-7

EXAMPLE 6. Suppose the price level is initially p_0, given the demand N_d for and supply N_s of labor in Fig. 8-8(a). Equilibrium in the labor markets occurs at a W_0 nominal wage. An increase in the price level to $1.1p_0$ or $1.2p_0$ shifts the demand for labor schedule upward to N'_d and N''_d, respectively. (The marginal revenue product of labor equals the price at which goods are sold times the marginal physical product of labor; hence, a 10% or 20% increase in price causes the marginal revenue product of labor, and therefore the demand for labor, to shift upward accordingly.) When we assume that labor's nominal wage is adjusted immediately for any increase (or decrease) in the price level, the labor supply schedule shifts upward to N'_s when the price level increases 10%

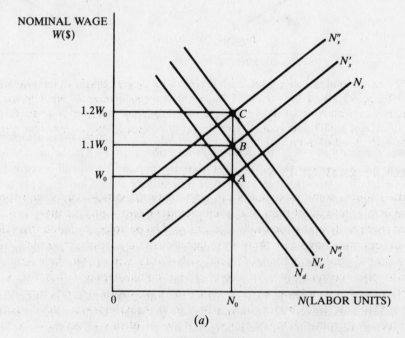

(a)

Fig. 8-8

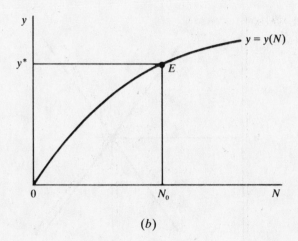

(b)

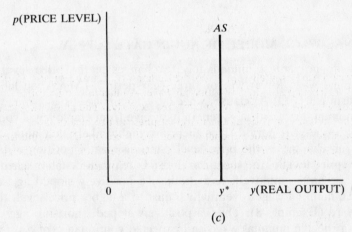

(c)

Fig. 8-8 (*continued*)

and to N_s'' for a 20% increase in the price level. Such proportional upward shifts of supply and demand keep the real wage intact—$W_0/p_0 = 1.1W_0/1.1p_0 = 1.2W_0/1.2p_0$—and the employment of labor inputs remains at N_0. Labor market equilibrium with N_0 labor units employed determines a y^* full employment level of output in Fig. 8-8(b). When labor market equilibrium is unaffected by the price level, aggregate supply is vertical [Fig. 8-8(c)] at a y^* full employment level of output.

8.6   THE NATURAL RATE OF UNEMPLOYMENT

During normal times, some labor units are frictionally or structurally unemployed; thus, even when there is labor market equilibrium, the unemployment rate is greater than zero. Schedule N_s in Fig. 8-9 excludes frictionally and structurally unemployed labor units; excluded from the labor supply schedule are workers who have lost their jobs because of industrial shrinkage, workers who are seasonally unemployed and workers who have voluntarily withdrawn their services because of dissatisfaction with their current position. Labor market equilibrium and therefore full employment exist at a natural rate of unemployment. The actual unemployment rate can be above or below the natural rate. When the unemployment rate is greater than the natural rate, the economy is operating below full employment output; when the actual unemployment rate is less than the natural rate, the economy is operating above normal capacity and inflationary pressures exist.

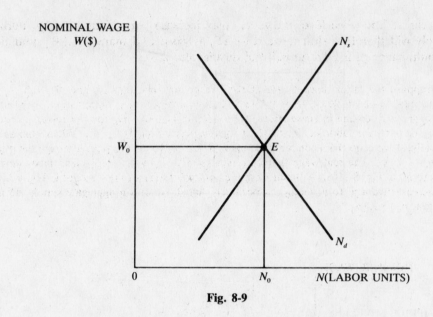

Fig. 8-9

8.7 A "STICKY" NOMINAL WAGE MODEL OF AGGREGATE SUPPLY

Nominal wages usually do not adjust immediately to changes in the price level. Unionized workers contract for a nominal wage for a two- or three-year period. Even when labor contracts include a cost of living adjustment (COLA) clause, wage adjustments are usually made annually or semiannually. In addition, nonunionized workers generally receive from employers a commitment to a specific nominal wage for a one-year period. It is therefore highly likely that nominal wages lag (and often adapt to) short-run changes in the price level. Starting from a position of labor market equilibrium, increases in the price level in the short run shift the demand-for-labor schedule upward, increase the quantity of labor units employed, and produce a positively sloped aggregate supply schedule (Example 7). When nominal wages eventually adjust to a higher price level, the short-run aggregate supply shifts upward (Example 8). Thus, a positively sloped, short-run aggregate supply schedule is associated with a specific nominal wage and expected continuance of a price level. For example, schedule AS_1 in Fig. 8-10 is associated with a W_1 nominal wage and continuance of a p_1

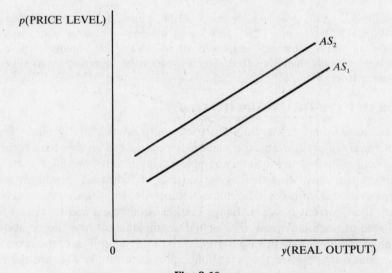

Fig. 8-10

price level in year 1. The price level, however, may increase ten percent to $1.1p_1$ during year 1. Aggregate supply will therefore shift upward to AS_2 as workers demand a $1.1W_1$ nominal wage, if they assume continuance of a $1.1p_1$ price level during year 2.

EXAMPLE 7. Suppose the labor markets are at equilibrium for schedules N_d and N_s with N_0 labor units employed and the real wage at W_0/p_0 [Fig. 8-11(a)]; full-employment real output equals y_0 [Fig. 8-11(b)]. During the year aggregate demand increases from AD to AD' in Fig. 8-11(c). The price level increases from p_0 to $1.1p_0$, and the demand for labor in Fig. 8-11(a) shifts upward from N_d to N_d'. When nominal wages are determined annually, there is no change in labor supply schedule N_s during the year, although the price level has increased from p_0 to $1.1p_0$. The real wage therefore falls from W_0/p_0 to $W_1/1.1p_0$, and labor units employed increase from N_0 to N_1 in Fig. 8-11(a). N_1 labor units are associated with a y_1 real output in Fig. 8-11(b). In Fig. 8-11(c) output increases from y_0 to y_1 along the positively sloped, short-run aggregate supply AS as the price level increases from p_0 to $1.1p_0$.

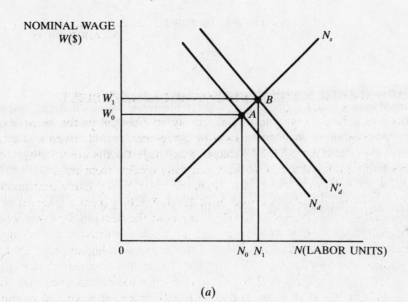

(a)

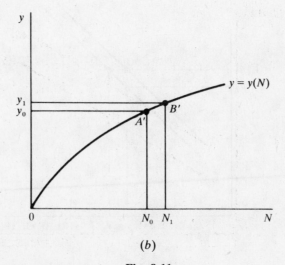

(b)

Fig. 8-11

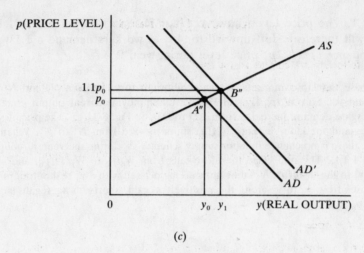

(c)

Fig. 8-11 (*continued*)

EXAMPLE 8. Aggregate supply schedule AS in Fig. 8-11(c) is reproduced in Fig. 8-12. The labor supply schedule is unchanged during year 1 although the price level increases from p_0 to $1.1p_0$; real output increases from y_0 to y_1 during year 1. Thus, in the short run, it is possible to move along the short-run aggregate supply schedule when there are changes in the price level and nominal wage demands remain unchanged. When labor incorporates the 10% price increase into the labor supply schedule during year 2, the nominal wage increases to $1.1W_0$, and the aggregate supply schedule shifts upward from AS to AS'. A y_0 real output is consistent with a W_0/p_0 real wage along schedule AS and a $1.1W_0/1.1p_0$ real wage along schedule AS'. Thus, an increase in the price level, *ceteris paribus*, causes movement along a positively sloped aggregate supply schedule, whereas an increase in nominal wage demands, *ceteris paribus*, shifts the positively sloped aggregate supply schedule upward.

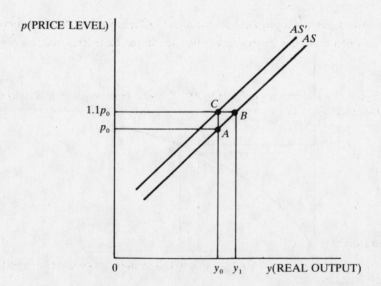

Fig. 8-12

Review Questions

1.   Which of the following statements is not true?

   (a)   When the relative increase in the price level is greater than the relative increase in the nominal money supply, the real money supply decreases.

   (b)   When the relative increase in the nominal money supply is greater than the relative increase in the price level, the real money supply increases.

   (c)   When the price level decreases, *ceteris paribus*, the real money supply decreases.

   (d)   When the price level increases, *ceteris paribus*, the real money supply decreases.

   Answer: (c)

2.   An increase in the price level

   (a)   Reduces the real money supply and shifts the *LM* schedule to the right

   (b)   Reduces the real money supply and shifts the *LM* schedule to the left

   (c)   Increases the real money supply and shifts the *LM* schedule to the right

   (d)   Increases the real money supply and shifts the *LM* schedule to the left

   Answer: (b)

3.   The short-run labor supply function is

   (a)   Positively sloped because of the increasing disutility of work

   (b)   Negatively sloped because of the decreasing disutility of work

   (c)   Positively sloped because of the decreasing disutility of leisure

   (d)   Negatively sloped because of the increasing disutility of leisure

   Answer: (a)

4.   Given a demand for labor schedule, the quantity of labor units demanded

   (a)   Falls as the price level rises

   (b)   Increases as the price level rises

   (c)   Increases when there is a proportionate increase in the price level and the nominal wage

   (d)   Decreases when there is a proportionate increase in the price level and the nominal wage

   Answer: (b)

5.   When the marginal physical product of labor is $800 - 2N$, the price of goods is \$2, and the cost of labor is \$4 per unit, the quantity of labor employed is

   (a)   20 units

   (b)   399 units

   (c)   800 units

   (d)   80 units

   Answer: (b)

6.   Aggregate demand is

   (a)   Negatively related to the price level because a decline in the price level has a negative effect on the demand for output

   (b)   Negatively related to the price level because a decline in the price level has a positive effect on the demand for output

(c) Positively related to the price level because a decline in the price level has a negative effect on the demand for output

(d) Positively related to the price level because a decline in the price level has a positive effect on the demand for output

Answer: (b)

7. The slope of aggregate demand becomes flatter

(a) The more sensitive investment spending is to the rate of interest

(b) The more sensitive the demand for money is to the rate of interest

(c) The smaller the value of the expenditure multiplier

(d) The larger the nominal money supply

Answer: (a)

8. Aggregate demand shifts to the

(a) Right when government spending decreases, *ceteris paribus*

(b) Left when the price level increases, *ceteris paribus*

(c) Left when there is a decrease in taxes, *ceteris paribus*

(d) Right when the nominal money supply increases, *ceteris paribus*

Answer: (d)

9. A neoclassical aggregate supply schedule exists

(a) At an output rate greater than the natural rate of unemployment

(b) At an output level determined by the supply of and demand for labor

(c) When the demand-for-labor and supply-of-labor schedules adjust immediately to a change in the price level

(d) When equilibrium in the labor markets is unaffected by shifts in the supply of labor schedule

Answer: (c)

10. Aggregate supply is positively related to the price level when

(a) Frictional and structural unemployment exists.

(b) The supply of labor schedule adjusts immediately to changes in the demand for labor.

(c) The demand for labor schedule adjusts immediately to the price level, and the labor supply schedule does not.

(d) The supply of labor schedule adjusts immediately to the price level, and the demand for labor does not.

Answer: (c)

Solved Problems

THE PRICE LEVEL AND EQUILIBRIUM INCOME

8.1 (a) What is the real money supply when the price level is 1, 1.5 and 2 and the nominal money supply is $450? (b) Explain why there is a negative relationship between the price level and the real money supply, *ceteris paribus*.

(a) The real money supply equals the nominal money supply divided by the price level. When the nominal money supply is $450, the real money supply is $450 for a price level of 1, $300 for a price level of 1.5 and $225 for a price level of 2.

(b) The nominal money supply is a stock of spending power whose value falls as the price level increases. Thus, the spending power of the nominal money supply, and therefore the real money supply, is inversely related to the price level.

8.2 The money market is in equilibrium when the real money supply equals the demand for real money balances. (a) Find an equation for LM when the nominal money supply is $150, the price level is 1, and the demand for real money balances is given by the equation $0.20y - 4i$. (b) Plot in Fig. 8-13 and label LM the monetary equilibrium equation found in part (a). (c) Suppose the price level increases to 1.2, *ceteris paribus*. Find the new equation for LM, plot it in Fig. 8-13 and label it LM'. (d) What happens to the monetary equilibrium schedule when the price level increases, *ceteris paribus*?

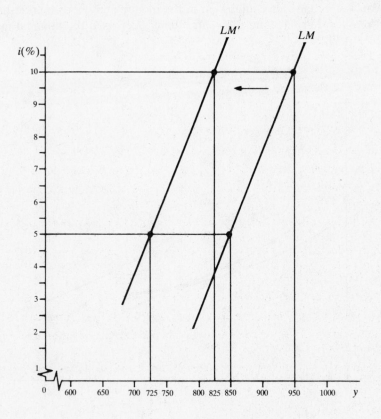

Fig. 8-13

(a) Monetary equilibrium occurs when $\bar{M}/p = L$ or $m = L$, where m is the real money supply:

$$\frac{\bar{M}}{p} = L$$

$$\$150/1 = 0.20y - 4i$$

$$y = \$750 + 20i \qquad (LM \text{ equation})$$

(b) See Fig. 8-13.

(c)
$$\frac{\bar{M}}{p} = L$$

$$\$150/1.20 = 0.20y - 4i$$
$$\$125 = 0.20y - 4i$$
$$y = \$625 + 20i \qquad (LM \text{ equation})$$

(d) An increase in the price level reduces the real money supply and shifts LM upward.

8.3 The IS equation is $y = \$1250 - 30i$ when $C = \$100 + 0.80Yd$, $I = \$150 - 6i$, $Tx = \$50$ and $G = \$40$. When the nominal money supply is $150 and the demand for money is $0.20y - 4i$, the LM equation is $y = \$750 + 20i$ when the price level is 1.00; $y = \$625 + 20i$ when the price level is 1.20; $y = \$500 + 20i$ when the price level is 1.50. (a) Find simultaneous equilibrium for the money and goods market when the price level is 1.00, 1.20, and 1.50. (b) In Fig. 8-14, put the price level on the vertical axis and real output on the horizontal axis; from part (a) plot the equilibrium output associated with price levels 1.00 1.20 and 1.50 and label the schedule AD. (c) Would simultaneous equilibrium in the money and goods market have differed if the price level remained at 1.00 and the central bank decreased the nominal money supply from $150 to $125 to $100?

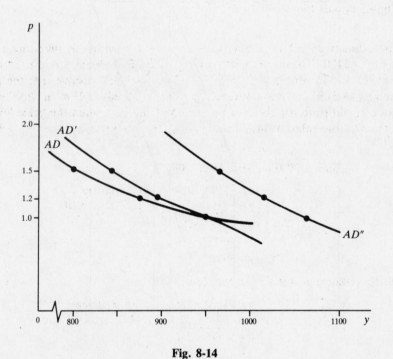

Fig. 8-14

(a) Equilibrium income is $950 for price level 1.00:

$$y = \$1250 - 30i \qquad (IS \text{ equation})$$
$$-(y = \quad 750 + 20i) \qquad (LM \text{ equation})$$
$$\overline{\quad 0 = \$ \ 500 - 50i}$$
$$i = 10\%$$
$$y = \$950$$

Equilibrium income is $875 for price level 1.20:

$$
\begin{aligned}
y &= \$1250 - 30i \quad &(IS \text{ equation})\\
-(y &= 625 + 20i) \quad &(LM \text{ equation})\\
\hline
0 &= \$625 - 50i\\
i &= 12.5\%\\
y &= \$875
\end{aligned}
$$

Equilibrium income is $800 for price level 1.50:

$$
\begin{aligned}
y &= \$1250 - 30i \quad &(IS \text{ equation})\\
-(y &= 500 + 20i) \quad &(LM \text{ equation})\\
\hline
0 &= \$750 - 50i\\
i &= 15\%\\
y &= \$800
\end{aligned}
$$

(b)   Fig. 8-14.

(c)   The real money supply declines from $150 to $125 to $100 when the price level increases from 1.00 to 1.20 to 1.50 and the nominal money remains at $150. When the price level remains at 1.00, the real money supply undergoes a similar decline if the monetary authority reduces the nominal money supply from $150 to $125 to $100. A decrease in the real money supply from $150 to $125 to $100, due to an increase in the price level and/or a reduction in the nominal money supply, lowers equilibrium income from $950 to $875 to $800.

8.4   Suppose investment spending is less interest sensitive with the investment equation now presented as $I = \$120 - 3i$ instead of $I = \$150 - 6i$ from Problem 8.3. The IS equation would then be $y = \$1100 - 15i$ instead of $y = \$1250 - 30i$. We shall assume that the nominal money supply remains at $150 and the demand for money is $0.20y - 4i$ as in Problem 8.3. (a) Find simultaneous equilibrium for the money and goods market when the price level is 1.00, 1.20 and 1.50. (b) Plot the relationship of real output and the price level in Fig. 8-14 and label the schedule AD'.

(a)   Equilibrium income is $950 for price level 1.00:

$$
\begin{aligned}
y &= \$1100 - 15i \quad &(IS \text{ equation})\\
-(y &= 750 + 20i) \quad &(LM \text{ equation})\\
\hline
0 &= \$350 - 35i\\
i &= 10\%\\
y &= \$950
\end{aligned}
$$

Equilibrium income is $896.43 for price level 1.20:

$$
\begin{aligned}
y &= \$1100 - 15i \quad &(IS \text{ equation})\\
-(y &= 625 + 20i) \quad &(LM \text{ equation})\\
\hline
0 &= \$475 - 35i\\
i &= 13.57\%\\
y &= \$896.43
\end{aligned}
$$

Equilibrium income is $842.86 for price level 1.50:

$$
\begin{aligned}
y &= \$1100 - 15i \quad &(IS \text{ equation})\\
-(y &= 500 + 20i) \quad &(LM \text{ equation})\\
\hline
0 &= \$600 - 35i\\
i &= 17.14\%\\
y &= \$842.86
\end{aligned}
$$

(b)   See Fig. 8-14.

8.5   Suppose the demand for money becomes more interest sensitive, changing from $0.20y - 4i$ to $0.20y - 10i$. When the nominal money supply is unchanged at \$150, the *LM* equation is $y = \$750 + 50i$ when the price level is 1.0; $y = \$625 + 50i$ when the price level is 1.20; $y = \$500 + 50i$ when the price level is 1.50. The *IS* schedule is $y = \$1250 - 30i$ (Problem 8.3). (*a*) Find simultaneous equilibrium in the money and goods market when the price level is 1.00, 1.20 and 1.50. (*b*) Plot the relationship of the price level and real output in Fig. 8-14 and label the schedule *AD"*.

(*a*)   Equilibrium income is \$1062.50 for price level 1.00:

$$
\begin{aligned}
y &= \$1250 - 30i \qquad &\text{(IS equation)} \\
-(y &= 750 + 50i) \qquad &\text{(LM equation)} \\
\hline
0 &= \$500 - 80i \\
i &= 6.25\% \\
y &= \$1062.50
\end{aligned}
$$

Equilibrium income is \$1015.62 for price level 1.20:

$$
\begin{aligned}
y &= \$1250 - 30i \qquad &\text{(IS equation)} \\
-(y &= 625 + 50i) \qquad &\text{(LM equation)} \\
\hline
0 &= \$625 - 80i \\
i &= 7.81\% \\
y &= \$1015.62
\end{aligned}
$$

Equilibrium income is \$968.75 for price level 1.50:

$$
\begin{aligned}
y &= \$1250 - 30i \qquad &\text{(IS equation)} \\
-(y &= 500 + 50i) \qquad &\text{(LM equation)} \\
\hline
0 &= \$750 - 80i \\
i &= 9.375\% \\
y &= \$968.75
\end{aligned}
$$

(*b*)   See Fig. 8-14.

8.6   Compare the aggregate demand schedules *AD*, *AD'* and *AD"* in Fig. 8-14. Why is there a difference in the slope of these aggregate demand schedules?

Changes in the price level affect the real money supply and thereby the rate of interest. *LM* shifts leftward, and the rate of interest increases when the price level increases and the real money supply declines; higher interest rates have a smaller effect on equilibrium income when investment spending is less sensitive to the rate of interest. Hence, a given increase in the price level (1.0 to 1.2) has a smaller effect upon equilibrium income in Problem 8.4 (real output declines from \$950 to \$896) than in Problem 8.3 (real output falls from \$950 to \$875). Because investment spending is less interest sensitive in Problem 8.3, *AD'* is more steeply sloped than *AD*. The interest sensitivity of the demand for money also affects the change in equilibrium income for a given change in the price level. A 20% increase in the price level causes real output to decline from \$1062.50 to \$1015.625 in Problem 8.5 and from \$950 to \$875 in Problem 8.3. *AD"* is more steeply sloped than *AD* because the demand for money is more interest sensitive for schedule *AD"*.

8.7   Simultaneous equilibrium in the money and goods markets is given by the equation

$$
y = \frac{hk_e}{h + kbk_e} (\bar{A}) + \frac{bk_e}{h + kbk_e} \left(\frac{\bar{M}}{p} \right)
$$

(*a*) Find an expression which relates the change in equilibrium income to a change in the price level. (*b*) What does the equation in part (*a*) represent? (*c*) What is the slope of the aggregate demand schedule?

(a) Holding the values of $\bar{A}$, $\bar{M}$ and the behavioral coefficients constant, $\Delta y = [bk_e/(h + kbk_e)]\Delta(\bar{M}/p)$, where $\Delta(\bar{M}/p)$ represents a change in the real money supply due to a change in the price level.

(b) The equation in part (a) measures movement along an aggregate demand schedule for a change in the price level.

(c) The slope of a straight line is $\Delta y/\Delta x$. With price p on the y axis and output y on the x axis, the slope of aggregate demand is $(h + kbk_e)/bk_e$.

8.8 What happens to the slope of the aggregate demand schedule when there is an increase in b, the interest sensitivity of investment; k_e, the expenditure multiplier; h, the interest sensitivity of the demand for money and k, the income responsiveness of the demand for money.

The slope of aggregate demand decreases (the curve becomes flatter) when b, the interest sensitivity of investment, and k_e, the expenditure multiplier, increase; the slope increases (the curve is steeper) when h, the interest sensitivity of the demand for money, and k, the transaction need for money balances, increase.

SHIFTING THE AGGREGATE DEMAND SCHEDULE

8.9 Find the shift in aggregate demand when there is an increase in the nominal money supply, *ceteris paribus*, and simultaneous equilibrium in the money and commodity markets is given by the equation

$$y = \frac{hk_e}{h + kbk_e}(\bar{A}) + \frac{bk_e}{h + kbk_e}\left(\frac{\bar{M}}{p}\right)$$

An increase in the nominal money supply, holding other variables constant, shifts aggregate demand rightward by $\Delta y = [bk_e/(h + kbk_e)](\Delta\bar{M}/\bar{p})$ where $\Delta\bar{M}$ represents a change in the nominal money supply with the price level held constant.

8.10 Find the shift in aggregate demand when there is an increase in government spending, *ceteris paribus*, and simultaneous equilibrium in the money and commodity markets is given by the equation

$$y = \frac{hk_e}{h + kbk_e}(\bar{A}) + \frac{bk_e}{h + kbk_e}\left(\frac{\bar{M}}{p}\right)$$

Holding other variables constant, an increase in autonomous government spending shifts aggregate demand rightward by $\Delta y = [hk_e/(h + kbk_e)]\Delta\bar{G}$.

AGGREGATE SUPPLY IN THE SHORT RUN AND LONG RUN

8.11 What is the difference between an economy's short-run and long-run capacity to produce?

An economy's short-run and long-run productive capacity depends on the quantity and quality of economic resources and the state of technology. Hence, productive capacity (ability to supply) depends on human resources N, capital resources K and natural resources R as well as technology T. In the long run, technology and the quantity and quality of economic resources are variable and therefore a means of expanding productive capacity. In the short run, there exists a given state of technology, and the quantity and quality of capital and natural resources—factories, machines, tools, land—are fixed. Although the quality of human resources is also constant in the short run, the quantity of human resources can vary. Labor inputs in the short run depend on labor participation rates (proportion of the population in the labor force) and the number of hours a given labor supply is willing to work. Thus, short-run aggregate supply depends on the equilibrium condition in the labor markets.

A NEOCLASSICAL MODEL OF AGGREGATE SUPPLY

8.12 (*a*) From the short-run schedule of aggregate output in Table 8-2, find the incremental output associated with an additional unit of labor input. (*b*) Find the incremental revenue from each additional unit of labor input when the price level is 1.0, 1.1 and 1.2. (*c*) Plot the data from part (*b*) in Fig. 8-15. What happens to incremental revenue from additional labor inputs when there is an increase in the price level?

Table 8-2

Quantity of Labor Inputs	100	101	102	103	104	105	106
Aggregate Output	950	1000	1040	1075	1105	1130	1152

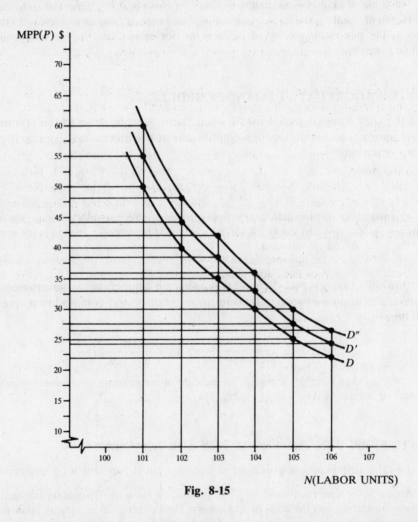

Fig. 8-15

(*a*) In adding the 101st labor input, aggregate output increases 50. Thus, the incremental output for the 101st labor input is 50, 40 for the 102d labor input, 35 for the 103d labor input, 30 for the 104th labor input, 25 for the 105th labor input and 22 for the 106th labor input.

(*b*) Incremental revenue from each additional labor input equals MPP times p, where MPP (marginal physical product) is the incremental output and p is the price level. When the price level is 1.0, incremental revenue of the 101st labor input is $50, $40 for the 102d labor input, $35 for the 103d labor input, $30 for the 104th labor input, $25 for the 105th and $22 for the 106th. When the price level is 1.1, incremental revenue of the 101st through 106th labor input is, respectively, $55, $44, $38.50, $33, $27.50 and $24.20. When the price level is 1.2, incremental revenue of the 101st through 106th labor input is, respectively, $60, $48, $42, $36, $30 and $26.40.

(c)   The incremental revenue from additional labor inputs is plotted in Fig. 8-15. The schedule of incremental revenue shifts to the right when the price level increases from 1.0 to 1.1 to 1.2.

8.13   (a) Why is the labor supply schedule positively sloped? (b) What happens to the labor supply schedule when there is less disutility associated with work or there is an increase in labor participation rates (the labor supply increases)?

(a)   Work competes with leisure. It is generally postulated that labor prefers leisure to work; a higher real wage, though, is sufficient incentive for labor to supply additional labor inputs (hours of work). Thus, the supply of labor inputs is positively related to the real wage.

(b)   The labor supply schedule shifts to the right when there is either a decrease in the disutility of work (labor is more willing to offer its services for a given real wage) or an increase in labor participation rates (a larger percentage of the population seeks employment).

8.14   (a) Suppose the marginal physical product of labor is given by the equation $14 - 0.08N$, where N is the quantity of labor inputs. Find the quantity of labor units demanded when the price level is 1 and the nominal wage per labor unit is $4, $3, $2 or $1. (b) Find an expression for the demand for labor, given the equation for incremental revenue and incremental cost in part (a). (c) From the demand for labor schedule in part (b), find the quantity of labor demanded when the price level is 1 and the nominal wage is $4, $3, $2 and $1. Plot the data in Fig. 8-16 and label the schedule N_d. (d) From the demand for labor schedule in part (b), find the quantity of labor demanded when the price level is 2 and the nominal wage is $4, $3, $2 and $1. Plot the data in Fig. 8-16 and label the schedule N_d'. (e) What happens to the demand for labor when the price level increases, ceteris paribus?

(a)   In a competitive market, labor units are added until the incremental revenue equals the incremental cost of each additional labor unit. The equation for incremental revenue is $p(14 - 0.08N)$. Incremental cost equals W, the nominal wage per labor unit. The quantity of labor units employed is found by solving the equation $p(14 - 0.08N) = W$ for N. When the price level is 1 and the nominal wage is $4,

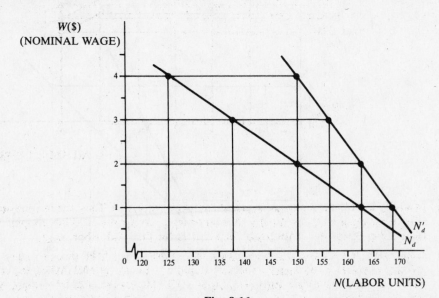

Fig. 8-16

$$1(14 - 0.08N) = \$4$$
$$0.08N = 14 - 4$$
$$N = 125$$

137.5 labor units are employed when the nominal wage is $3, 150 when it is $2 and 162.5 when it is $1.

(b)   We derive an equation for the demand for labor by solving the equation $p(14 - 0.08N) = W$ from part (a) for N:

$$p(14 - 0.08N) = W$$
$$0.08pN = 14p - W$$
$$N = 14/(0.08) - \left(\frac{W}{0.08p}\right)$$
$$N = 175 - 12.5\left(\frac{W}{p}\right)$$

(c)   When the price level is 1, 125 labor units are employed at a $4 nominal wage, 137.5 at a $3 nominal wage, 150 at a $2 nominal wage, and 162.5 at a $1 nominal wage. The data are plotted in Fig. 8-16, and the schedule is labeled N_d.

(d)   When the price level is 2, 150 labor units are employed at a $4 nominal wage, 156.25 are employed at a $3 nominal wage, 162.5 at a $2 nominal wage and 168.75 at a $1 nominal wage. The data are plotted in Fig. 8-16, and the schedule is labeled N_d'.

(e)   The demand for labor shifts upward when there is an increase in the price level, *ceteris paribus*.

8.15   Suppose the equation for the supply of labor is $140 + 5(W/p)$. (a) Find the quantity of labor supplied when the price level is 1 and the nominal wage is $4, $3, $2, $1. Plot the data in Fig. 8-17 and label the schedule N_s. (b) Find the quantity of labor units supplied when the price level is 2 and the nominal wage is $4, $3, $2 and $1. Plot the data in Fig. 8-17 and label the schedule N_s'. (c) What happens to the labor supply schedule when the price level increases, *ceteris paribus*?

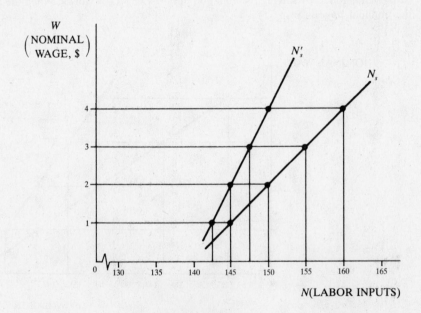

Fig. 8-17

(a) Substituting into the equation $N_s = 140 + 5(W/p)$, 160 labor units are supplied when the price level is 1 and the nominal wage is $4: $140 + 5(4) = 160$. With the price level remaining at 1, 155 labor units are supplied at a $3 nominal wage, 150 at a $2 nominal wage and 145 at a $1 nominal wage.

(b) When the price level is 2 and the nominal wage is $4, 150 labor units are supplied; 147.5 labor units are supplied when the nominal wage is $3; 145 are supplied when the nominal wage is $2; 142.5 when the nominal wage is $1.

(c) The labor supply schedule shifts upward to the left when the price level increases, *ceteris paribus*.

8.16 (a) The demand for labor equation, $N_d = 125 - 12.5(W/p)$, and labor supply equation, $N_s = 140 + 5(W/p)$, are plotted in Fig. 8-18(a) when the price is 1 and 2. What happens to the

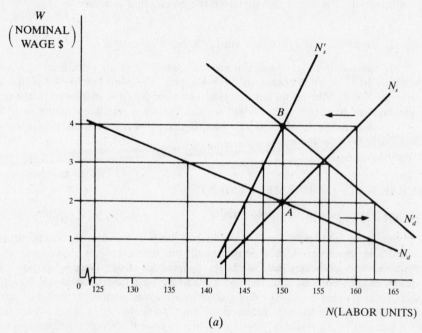

(a)

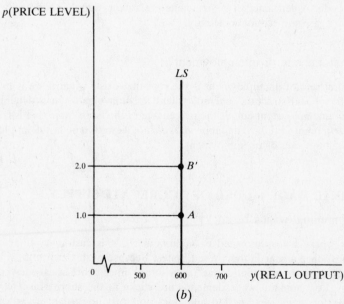

(b)

Fig. 8-18

labor units employed (equilibrium in the labor markets) when the labor demand and labor supply schedules adapt immediately to changes in the price level? (b) Suppose a $600 real output level is associated with the employment of 150 labor units. Put the price level on the vertical axis and real output on the horizontal axis; present and label LS in Fig. 8-18(b) an aggregate supply schedule which represents equilibrium in the labor markets when the labor demand and labor supply schedules adjust immediately to changes in the price level.

(a)   The equilibrium nominal wage is $2 when the price level is 1 and $4 when the price level is 2. The real wage (nominal wage/price level) is unaffected by an increase in the price level. One hundred and fifty labor units are employed before and after the increase in the price level.

(b)   The aggregate supply schedule is vertical because price level changes have no effect on the quantity of labor units employed and therefore the equilibrium condition in the labor market.

8.17   Why is the neoclassical aggregate supply schedule vertical?

Neoclassical analysis of the labor market assumes that all price-level changes are incorporated immediately into the labor demand and labor supply schedules. Because of such immediate price-level adjustments, the equilibrium quantity of labor units employed is unaffected by the price level. Thus, the full employment condition in the labor markets, which is unrelated to the price level, results in an aggregate supply schedule which is also independent of the price level. Aggregate supply is therefore vertical.

THE NATURAL RATE OF UNEMPLOYMENT

8.18   What are the causes of unemployment?

Unemployed labor units can be placed into three categories: frictional, structural, and cyclical. Frictional unemployment is short-term, usually up to six months; it consists of temporary layoffs (perhaps due to a temporary decrease in the demand for labor), labor which has voluntarily left a job, reentrants and new entrants into the labor force who have a longer job search. Structural unemployment is longer term; it exists because of skill and/or location mismatching in the labor markets. For example, a job applicant may not have the required skill for a particular job; a job may exist in another region but labor is unaware of its availability or is unwilling to relocate. Cyclical unemployment exists because of the business cycle. A deficiency of labor demand relative to supply periodically develops when there are fluctuations in aggregate economic activity.

8.19   What is a natural rate of unemployment?

The natural rate of unemployment is the rate that exists when there is no cyclical unemployment. Because frictional and structural unemployment are unavoidable in a dynamic market economy, the natural rate of unemployment equals the percentage of the labor force that is frictionally and structurally unemployed at a point in time. The labor markets are viewed to be at full employment when equilibrium exists at the natural rate of unemployment.

A STICKY NOMINAL WAGE MODEL OF AGGREGATE SUPPLY

8.20   Why might nominal wages be sticky?

Whether workers are unionized or nonunionized, it is customary to review and change nominal wages (salaries) once a year in the United States. Because of this institutional behavior, labor's demand for a nominal wage is not continuous (as assumed in a neoclassical view of aggregate supply) but discontinuous; i.e., nominal wage demands are sticky in the short run. The labor supply schedule is thereby stable for a one-year period and does not shift upward or downward when the price level changes by more or less than what was expected at the time labor agreed to work for a specific nominal wage.

8.21 Suppose labor agrees to work for a specific nominal wage structure for a one-year period. (*a*) Explain what happens to labor supply schedule N_s in Fig. 8-19 when the price level increases during the year from p_0 to $1.05p_0$ to $1.1p_0$. (*b*) Explain what happens to labor demand schedule N_d in Fig. 8-19 when the price level increases during the year from p_0 to $1.05p_0$ to $1.1p_0$. (*c*) What happens to the quantity of labor units employed when the price level increases from p_0 to $1.05p_0$ to $1.1p_0$?

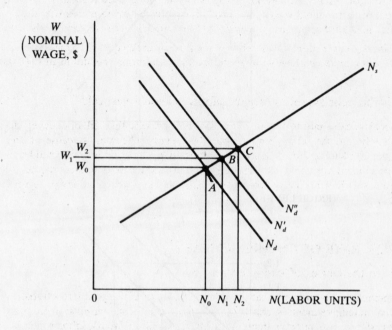

Fig. 8-19

(*a*) Labor has agreed to supply its services at the nominal wage rates depicted by N_s for a one-year period. There is therefore no shift of schedule N_s during the year, although the price level is increasing.

(*b*) Labor's marginal revenue increases with the price level. Hence, labor demand schedule N_d shifts upward to N_d' when the price level increases to $1.05p_0$ and to N_d'' when the price level is $1.1p_0$.

(*c*) Labor units employed increases from N_0 to N_1 to N_2 as the price level increases from p_0 to $1.1p_0$.

8.22 Suppose nominal wage demands change annually. In Fig. 8-20(*a*), the demand for labor schedule shifts upward when there are increases in the price level, whereas the labor supply schedule N_s remains unchanged. The productivity of labor is assumed constant. (*a*) Suppose labor demand schedules N_d, N_d' and N_d'' are associated with a p_0, $1.1p_0$ and $1.2p_0$ price level. From Fig. 8.20(*a*), find the units of labor employed when the price level is p_0, $1.1p_0$, and $1.2p_0$. (*b*) Suppose labor units N_0, N_1 and N_2 are associated with real output levels y_0, y_1 and y_2. With price level on the vertical axis and real output on the horizontal axis, plot a short-run aggregate supply schedule and label it AS in Fig. 8-20(*b*) for price levels p_0, $1.1p_0$ and $1.2p_0$ and associated output levels y_0, y_1 and y_2.

(*a*) N_0 labor units are employed at price level p_0; N_1 and N_2 units are employed at price level $1.1p_0$ and $1.2p_0$, respectively.

(*b*) Aggregate supply schedule AS relates price level p_0 and output level y_0, $1.1p_0$ and y_1 and $1.2p_0$ and y_2. With a stable labor supply schedule in the short run, aggregate supply is positively related to the price level.

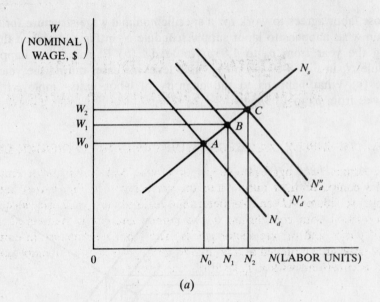

(a)

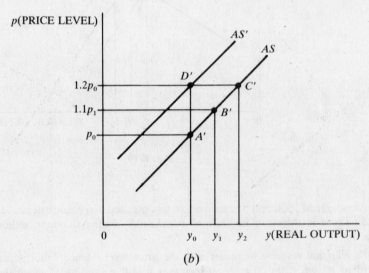

(b)

Fig. 8-20

8.23 What happens to aggregate supply schedule AS in Fig. 8-20(b) when one year later labor increases its demand for nominal wages because the price level has increased from p_0 to $1.2p_0$?

Aggregate supply schedule AS in Fig. 8-20(b) shifts upward to AS' one year later as labor demands a higher nominal wage because of the p_0 to $1.2p_0$ increase in the price level. Thus, along schedule AS' output y_0 is now associated with price level $1.2p_0$, whereas output y_0 was associated with price level p_0 one year earlier.

Chapter 9

Aggregate Supply and Aggregate Demand Analysis

9.1 AGGREGATE SUPPLY, AGGREGATE DEMAND AND THE PRICE LEVEL

Aggregate demand and aggregate supply determine real output, labor units employed, the rate of interest, the composition of output and the price level. In Fig. 9-1(a), aggregate demand and aggregate supply schedules AD and AS determine real output y_o and price level p_o. In Fig. 9-1(b), y_o and p_o are consistent with equilibrium in the money and goods markets at interest rate i_o and a specific mix of public and private sector goods. The labor markets are in equilibrium [Fig. 9-1(c)] when N_o labor units are employed at a w_o real wage ($w_o = W_o/p_o$); the employment of N_o labor units in Fig. 9-1(d) is consistent with a y_0 level of real output.

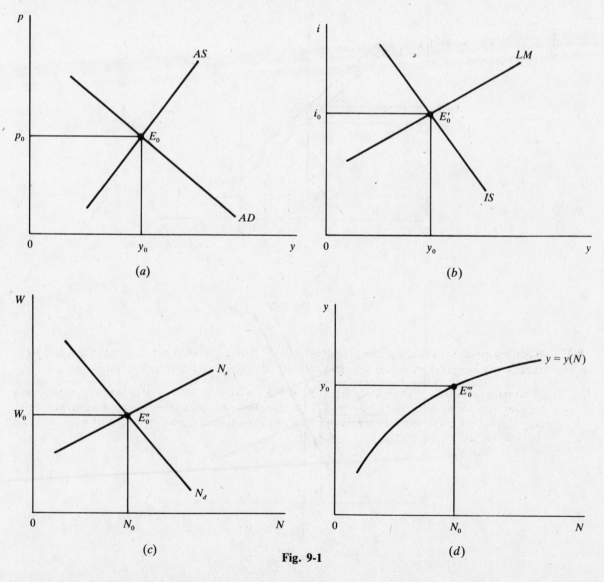

Fig. 9-1

183

9.2 NEOCLASSICAL AGGREGATE SUPPLY: DEMAND CHANGES

A neoclassical (vertical) aggregate supply exists when price level changes are immediately incorporated into the labor demand and labor supply schedules. In the absence of economic policy, the price level can theoretically overcome a disequilibrium created by a change in aggregate demand and/or aggregate supply. In Fig. 9-2(a), real output falls from full employment output y_e to output y_1 when there is a leftward shift of aggregate demand from AD to AD' and the price level remains at p_o. A decline in the price level from p_o to p_1 (and movement along aggregate demand schedule AD') returns output to its y_e full employment level. Distribution and/or expectation problems can develop, however, when the price system is relied on to correct disequilibrium. Price expectations can influence spending decisions and thereby contribute to a movement away from full employment output (see Example 2). In addition, price level changes have redistribution effects when they are unanticipated (Problem 9.9). Such problems lend support to interventionist economic policies which seek to stabilize aggregate demand whenever changes in aggregate demand and/or aggregate supply move output away from its full employment level.

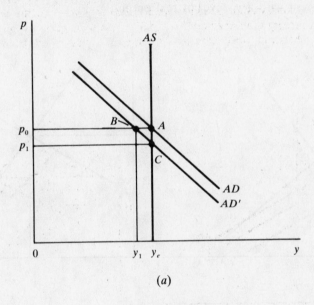

(a)

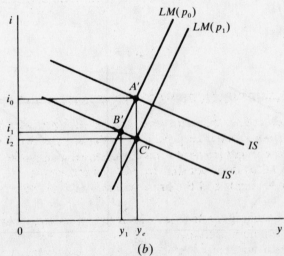

(b)

Fig. 9-2

EXAMPLE 1.   Output is at its full employment level y_e and the price level is p_o in Fig. 9-2(a) for aggregate demand and aggregate supply schedules AD and AS. A decrease in autonomous net exports, *ceteris paribus*, shifts aggregate demand leftward from AD to AD' and output falls to y_1 when the price level remains at p_o. A decline in the price level from p_o to p_1 returns economic activity to full employment output y_e. The events in Fig. 9-2(a) are presented in Fig. 9-2(b) through an analysis of the money and goods markets. The economy is initially at full employment output y_e for schedules IS and $LM(p_o)$. The decrease in autonomous net exports shifts IS leftward to IS'. At price level p_o, output falls from y_e to y_1, and the rate of interest declines from i_o to i_1. LM shifts rightward to $LM(p_1)$ as a result of the decrease in the price level and the increase in the real money supply. At price level p_1, output is at the y_e full employment level, and the interest rate has fallen to i_2.

EXAMPLE 2.   Output is at the full employment level y_e and the price level is p_o in Fig. 9-3(a) for aggregate demand and aggregate supply schedules AD and AS. A reduction in autonomous net exports, *ceteris paribus*, shifts aggregate demand leftward to AD'. At price level p_o, real output is y_1. Deflationary expectations develop because output is below the full employment level. Expecting lower prices in the near future, some private sector spending is postponed, but postponed purchases in the current period shift aggregate demand further to the left to, say, AD'' and output declines to y_2. These events are also presented in Fig. 9-3(b). IS initially shifts from IS to IS' due to the decline in autonomous net exports. Expecting the price level to fall, the household and business sectors postpone nonessential spending, which shifts IS further to the left to IS'', and real output declines to y_2. Economic activity eventually returns to full employment output y_e and price level p_1 as analyzed in Example 1. But in the short run, price expectations cause real output to fall below the level indicated by the analysis in Example 1.

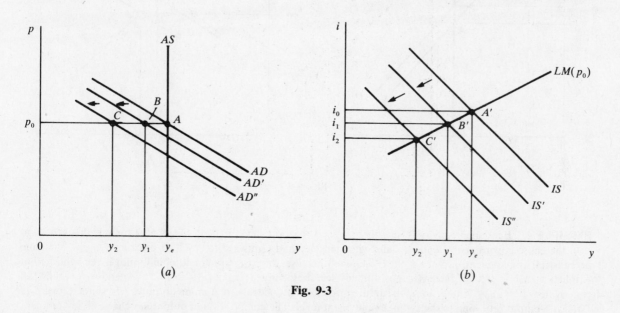

Fig. 9-3

9.3   NEOCLASSICAL AGGREGATE SUPPLY: MONETARY AND FISCAL POLICY

Aggregate demand as well as the price level can be stabilized through monetary and/or fiscal policy. A decrease in autonomous net exports, such as the one assumed in Example 1, can be offset, for example, by an increase in government spending of equal magnitude. In doing so, the aggregate demand schedule in Fig. 9-2(a) does not shift to AD' but remains at AD. Hence, real output would not deviate from full employment, and the price system would not be relied on to correct aggregate demand imbalances.

In the absence of an autonomous change in aggregate spending, a change in the nominal money supply, taxes and/or government spending, *ceteris paribus*, has no effect on the output level when aggregate supply is vertical and output is initially at full employment. A change in the nominal money supply in a full employment economy is neutral; the change in the price level is proportional to the change in the nominal money supply, and there is no effect on either the level or composition of real output. A change in taxes and/or government spending in a full employment economy is not neutral in that there is a change in the composition of output as well as the price level.

EXAMPLE 3.   The economy is initially at full employment output y_e and the price level is p_o in Fig. 9-4(a) for schedules AS and AD. An increase in the nominal money supply shifts aggregate demand rightward from AD to AD'. At price level p_o, y_1 demand exceeds the economy's y_e capacity to supply; the price level increases to p_1 to bring aggregate supply and aggregate demand into equilibrium at full employment. In Fig. 9-4(b), the expanded nominal money supply shifts LM rightward from LM to LM'; equilibrium in the money and goods markets increases from y_e to y_1. Because y_1 exceeds full employment y_e, the price level increases to p_1; the decline in the real money supply shifts LM from LM' back to LM, its original position. The increase in the nominal money supply is neutral: the rate of interest, employment and real output are unchanged, and the increase in the price level is proportional to the increase in the nominal money supply.

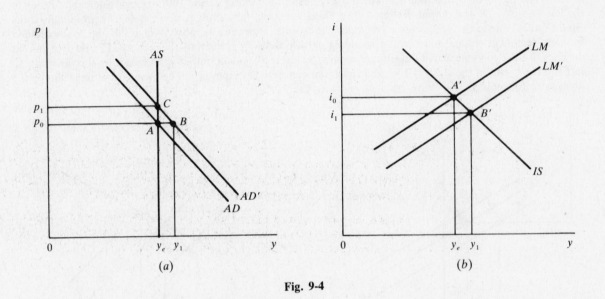

Fig. 9-4

EXAMPLE 4.   Economic activity is initially at y_e and the price level is p_o in Fig. 9-5(a) for schedules AS and AD. Increased government spending shifts aggregate demand rightward to AD'. At price level p_o, y_1 spending exceeds full employment output y_e; the price level increases from p_o to p_1, and equilibrium is reestablished at output y_e. In Fig. 9-5(b), increased government spending shifts IS rightward to IS'; y_1 spending exceeds full employment output y_e. The p_o to p_1 rise in the price level reduces the real money supply; LM shifts leftward to LM' with output returning to the y_e full employment level. The composition of output has changed; government spending has crowded out interest-sensitive private sector spending as a result of the i_o to i_2 rise in the rate of interest.

9.4   POSITIVELY SLOPED AGGREGATE SUPPLY: DEMAND CHANGES

Aggregate supply is positively sloped when price level changes are not immediately and/or completely incorporated into the labor supply schedule. (See Section 8.7.) When aggregate supply is positively sloped, changes in aggregate demand impact not only the price level but real output in the short run. Economic activity is initially at full employment output y_e and the price level is p_o for schedule AS and AD in Fig. 9-6(a). Increased government spending shifts aggregate demand from AD to AD' in Fig. 9-6(a), the price level increases from p_o to p_1, and real output increases from y_e to y_1. (See Example 5.) Output y_1 is not an equilibrium level. Because output y_1 exceeds full

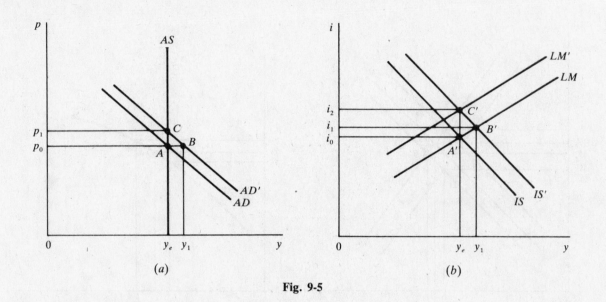

Fig. 9-5

employment output y_e, the rate of unemployment is below the natural rate. The price level is also above the initial p_o level, which labor expected to continue when it agreed to supply labor services. Thus, labor demands and receives a higher nominal wage in the next time period and aggregate supply shifts leftward to AS'. The aggregate supply shifts leftward in successive periods as long as the price level at the end of the period exceeds that which workers expected at the beginning of the period and the rate of unemployment is below the natural rate. Eventually, aggregate supply comes to rest at AS'' in Fig. 9-6(a); the price level has increased to p_3 and real output has returned to y_e. (See Example 6.)

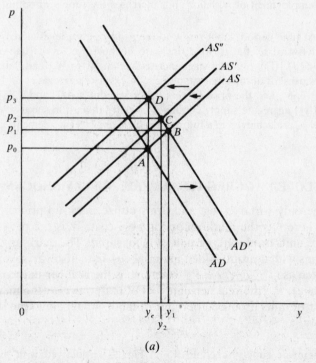

(a)

Fig. 9-6

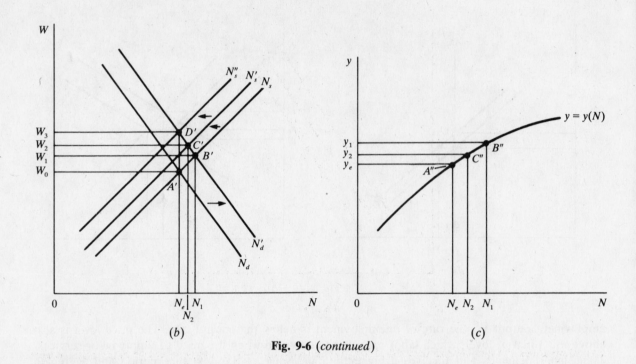

Fig. 9-6 (*continued*)

EXAMPLE 5. Economic activity is initially at full employment output y_e in Fig. 9-6(a), for aggregate demand and aggregate supply schedules AD and AS. Increased government spending shifts aggregate demand rightward to AD'; the price level increases from p_o to p_1 and real output expands from y_e to y_1. In Fig. 9-6(b), the labor markets are initially at equilibrium with N_e workers employed at a W_o nominal wage. The price level increase in Fig. 9-6(a) causes the demand for labor schedule to shift rightward from N_d to N_d'; the labor supply schedule remains at N_s, since nominal wage agreements are fixed in the short run. N_1 labor units are now employed at a W_1 nominal wage. The employment of N_1 labor units increases the supply of output [Fig. 9-6(c)] from y_e to y_1.

EXAMPLE 6. In the next time period, labor reacts to the p_o to p_1 price level increase in Example 5 as the labor supply schedule shifts leftward by the p_o to p_1 increase in the price level. [Labor supply schedule N_s shifts leftward to N_s' in Fig. 9-6(b).] The nominal wage increases from W_1 to W_2; and, labor units employed decrease from N_1 to N_2. The leftward shift of the labor supply schedule causes aggregate supply to shift from AS to AS' in Fig. 9-6(a). Real output is y_2, and the price level is p_2 for schedules AD' and AS'. Because output y_2 exceeds full employment output y_e, aggregate supply continues to shift leftward in successive periods. Full employment output y_e and price level p_3 are achieved in a future period when aggregate demand is AD' and aggregate supply is AS''.

9.5 POSITIVELY SLOPED AGGREGATE SUPPLY: SUPPLY SHOCKS

When labor is the only variable cost and firms utilize mark-up pricing, per-unit supply price P equals $(1 + \theta)W/a$, where θ is the mark-up on variable cost, W is the per-labor unit nominal wage, and a is the number of units produced per unit of labor input. The mark-up on labor cost covers fixed costs and provides firms with a profit. When material costs are also variable in the short run, per-unit supply price P is written as $(1 + \theta)W/a + P_n$, where P_n is the real per-unit cost of materials. A change in W (the nominal wage), P_n (the real per-unit cost of materials), θ (the mark-up over variable cost) and/or a (the number of units produced per unit of labor input) alters the supply cost of output and shifts aggregate supply.

EXAMPLE 7. The aggregate supply schedule AS in Fig. 9-7 is derived with the following variables held constant: the nominal wage W, the mark-up on variable cost θ, the productivity of labor a, and the real per-unit

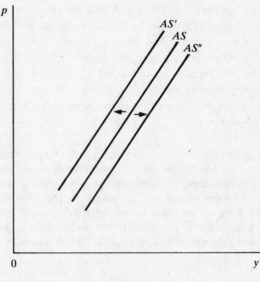

Fig. 9-7

cost of materials P_n. An increase in nominal wages *or* mark-up on costs *or* real per-unit cost of materials, *ceteris paribus*, shifts aggregate supply leftward to AS'. An increase in labor productivity (the number of units produced per unit of labor input) lowers production costs and shifts aggregate supply rightward to AS''.

OPEC's ability to substantially raise oil prices in the 1970s increased the real per-unit cost of materials. Because oil price increases were sustained and the level became permanent, aggregate supply was shifted leftward, for example from AS to AS' in Fig. 9-8. Movement along aggregate demand schedule AD in Fig. 9-8 raises the price level from p_o to p_1 and real output falls from full employment y_e to y_1. Because y_1 is less than full employment output y_e, the actual rate of unemployment is greater than the natural rate. (The association of rising prices and unemployment

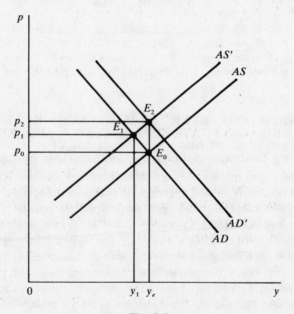

Fig. 9-8

was classified as "stagflation" during the 1970s.) When government does not initiate an economic policy to alleviate the unemployment caused by higher material prices, the disequilibrium must be remedied eventually in the labor markets. The nominal wage must be reduced by a rightward shift of the labor supply schedule, which causes aggregate supply schedule AS' to shift rightward to AS; economic activity returns to full employment output y_e and the price level to p_o. A stimulative economic policy which shifts aggregate demand rightward to AD' is an alternative to unemployed labor units in the short run. Economic activity returns more quickly to output y_e, but the price level rises to p_2 rather than returns to p_o.

EXAMPLE 8. The economy is initially at full employment output y_e, for aggregate demand and aggregate supply schedules AD and AS in Fig. 9-9. Suppose oil prices fall substantially due to a surplus in oil production, i.e., the real per-unit cost of materials declines. Aggregate supply shifts rightward from AS to AS'; real output rises to y_1 and exceeds full employment output y_e. "Tightness" in the labor markets causes a leftward shift of the labor supply schedule and a higher nominal wage. Aggregate supply shifts from AS' back to AS, and economic activity returns to y_e. A restrictive economic policy, which shifts aggregate demand leftward from AD to AD', is an alternative measure; the positive supply shock then results in a lower p_2 price level.

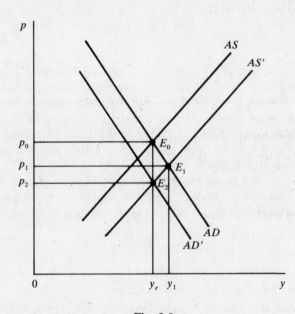

Fig. 9-9

9.6   THE NEW CLASSICAL AND KEYNESIAN MACROECONOMICS

The effect of aggregate demand changes on output depends on the slope and location of aggregate supply. Since the late 1960s, there has been considerable discussion about and reformulation of Keynes' original rigid nominal wage model (see Problem 9.20) The "new classical" macroeconomics views a positively sloped aggregate supply schedule as a short-run phenomenon. An imperfect knowledge model contends that aggregate supply is positively sloped because nominal wages "adapt" to price-level changes; however, in the long run, aggregate supply is vertical. A rational expectations model attributes the short-run, positively sloped aggregate supply schedule to forecasting errors. Because forecasting errors have a zero expected value, aggregate supply is vertical over longer periods. Contemporary Keynesian macroeconomics bases the positively sloped aggregate supply schedule on institutional patterns where wage contracts exist over a one to three-year period. In contemporary Keynesian analysis of the labor markets, a positively sloped aggregate supply schedule persists for longer periods and is less steeply sloped than the one perceived by the new classical view.

Review Questions

1. Suppose there is full employment and aggregate supply is vertical. A decrease in taxes

    (*a*) Increases the price level and real output
    (*b*) Increases the price level but has no effect on real output
    (*c*) Increases real output but has no effect on the price level
    (*d*) Has no effect on the price level or real output

    Answer: (*b*)

2. Suppose there is full employment and a neoclassical aggregate supply schedule. A 10% increase in the nominal money supply

    (*a*) Has no effect upon the price level
    (*b*) Increases the rate of interest
    (*c*) Increases the nominal wage 10%
    (*d*) Increases the real money supply 10%

    Answer: (*c*)

3. Suppose there is full employment and a neoclassical aggregate supply schedule. An increase in government spending

    (*a*) Causes higher interest rates, which change the composition of output
    (*b*) Causes the real money supply to increase, which changes the composition of output
    (*c*) Has no effect on the real money supply or the composition of output
    (*d*) Has no effect on the rate of interest or the composition of output

    Answer: (*a*)

4. Suppose there is full employment and a vertical aggregate supply schedule. An increase in the nominal money supply

    (*a*) Causes the real money supply to increase, which changes the composition of output
    (*b*) Has no effect on the real money supply or the composition of output
    (*c*) Causes a proportional increase in real output
    (*d*) Reduces the rate of interest and changes the composition of output

    Answer: (*b*)

5. Suppose there is full employment and a positively sloped aggregate supply schedule. A decrease in taxes increases

    (*a*) The price level and real output
    (*b*) The price level but has no effect on real output
    (*c*) Real output but has no effect on the price level
    (*d*) The nominal and real wage

    Answer: (*a*)

6. Suppose there is full employment and a positively sloped aggregate supply schedule. An increase in government spending raises

    (*a*) The equilibrium level of output and the price level
    (*b*) The equilibrium level of output and the real wage

(c) The equilibrium level of output and the nominal wage

(d) The level of output and the price level

Answer: (d)

7. Suppose there is full employment and a positively sloped aggregate supply schedule. A rightward shift of aggregate demand increases

(a) The real wage, labor units employed and real output

(b) The nominal wage, labor units employed and real output

(c) The productivity of labor and real output

(d) The demand for labor, labor units employed and the real wage

Answer: (b)

8. When aggregate supply is positively sloped and there is an increase in the real per unit cost of materials, aggregate supply shifts to the

(a) Right, the price level falls, and real output increases

(b) Left, the price level falls, and real output increases

(c) Right, the price level increases, and real output decreases

(d) Left, the price level increases, and real output decreases

Answer: (d)

9. When aggregate supply is positively sloped and there is a decrease in the mark-up on variable cost, aggregate supply shifts to the

(a) Left, the price level falls, and real output increases

(b) Right, the price level falls, and real output increases

(c) Left, the price level increases, the real output decreases

(d) Right, the price level increases, and real output decreases

Answer: (b)

10. Which of the following statements about the labor markets is false?

(a) The imperfect knowledge model contends that nominal wages adapt to changes in the price level.

(b) In a rational expectations model, aggregate supply may be positively sloped in the short run because of forecasting errors.

(c) In the "new classical" macroeconomics, aggregate supply is positively sloped in the long run.

(d) Contemporary Keynesian macroeconomics attributes the positively sloped aggregate supply schedule to nominal wage contracts that last for extended periods.

Answer: (c)

Solved Problems

AGGREGATE SUPPLY, AGGREGATE DEMAND AND THE PRICE LEVEL

9.1 The *IS* equation is $y = \$1300 - 30i$ when $C = \$90 + 0.80Yd$, $I = \$150 - 6i$, $Tx = \$100$, $G = \$100$; *LM* is $y = \$800 + 20i$ when the nominal money supply is \$160, the price level is 1 and the demand for money is $0.20y - 4i$; *LM* is $y = \$640 + 20i$ when the nominal money supply is \$160, the price level is 1.25 and the demand for money is $0.20y - 4i$. Find the output level at which there is simultaneous equilibrium in the money and goods markets for price level (a) 1.00 (b) 1.25.

(a) When the price level is 1.00, simultaneous equilibrium in the money and goods markets exists when $y = \$1000$ and $i = 10\%$.

$$
\begin{array}{ll}
y = \$1300 - 30i & \text{(IS equation)} \\
-(y = \quad 800 + 20i) & \text{(LM equation)} \\
\hline
0 = \$ \ 500 - 50i \\
i = 10\% \\
y = \$1000
\end{array}
$$

(b) When the price level is 1.25, simultaneous equilibrium in the money and goods markets exists when $y = \$904$ and $i = 13.2\%$.

$$
\begin{array}{ll}
y = \$1300 - 30i & \text{(IS equation)} \\
-(y = \quad 640 + 20i) & \text{(LM equation)} \\
\hline
0 = \$ \ 660 - 50i \\
i = 13.2\% \\
y = \$ \ 904
\end{array}
$$

9.2 Suppose the economy's short-run production equation is $y = 14N - 0.04N^2$, the demand for labor equation is $N_d = 175 - 12.5(W/p)$, and the labor supply equation is $N_s = 70 + 5(W/p)$. (a) Find labor market equilibrium when the price level is 1.00 and 1.25. (b) Find short-run supply when there is labor market equilibrium at price level 1.00 and 1.25.

(a) When the price level is 1.00, labor market equilibrium exists when $N = 100$ and $W = \$6$.

$$
\begin{array}{ll}
N = 175 - 12.5\left(\dfrac{W}{1.0}\right) & \text{(Labor demand)} \\[2mm]
-\left(N = \ 70 + \ 5\left(\dfrac{W}{1.0}\right)\right) & \text{(Labor supply)} \\
\hline
0 = 105 - 17.5W \\
W = \$6 \\
N = 100
\end{array}
$$

When the price level is 1.25, and the equations for the supply and demand for labor adjust immediately to price-level changes, labor market equilibrium exists when $N = 100$ and $W = \$7.50$.

$$
\begin{array}{ll}
N = 175 - 12.5\left(\dfrac{W}{1.25}\right) & \text{(Labor demand)} \\[2mm]
-\left(N = \ 70 + \ 5\left(\dfrac{W}{1.25}\right)\right) & \text{(Labor supply)} \\
\hline
0 = 105 - 17.5\left(\dfrac{W}{1.25}\right) \\[2mm]
W = \$7.50 \\
N = 100
\end{array}
$$

(b) Labor market equilibrium is unaffected by the price level; 100 labor units are employed when the price level is 1.00 or 1.25. Hence, short-run supply is $1000 at both price levels:

$$
y = 14N - 0.04N^2
$$
$$
y = 1400 - 400 = 1000
$$

9.3 Utilize the solutions in Problems 9.1 and 9.2 to explain why there is equilibrium in the money, goods and labor markets at only one price level.

Because the labor demand and supply equations in Problem 9.2 are immediately affected by changes in the price level, labor market equilibrium is unaffected by the price level. However, the price level affects the real money supply in Problem 9.1; money and goods market equilibrium exists at output $y = \$1000$ when the price level is 1.00 and at output $y = \$904$ when the price level is 1.25. When the price level is 1.00, aggregate demand ($y = \$1000$) equals aggregate supply ($y = \$1000$); however, when the price level is 1.25, aggregate demand ($y = \$904$) is less than aggregate supply ($y = \$1000$). When the price level affects the real money supply (and therefore the location of the *LM* schedule in space), there is only one price level at which there is equilibrium in the money, goods and labor markets.

9.4 The aggregate demand schedule *AD* [Fig. 9-10(*a*)] is derived from money and goods market equilibrium schedules [Fig. 9-10(*b*)]. Explain why there is not equilibrium at price level p_o. What must happen to the price level to achieve equilibrium?

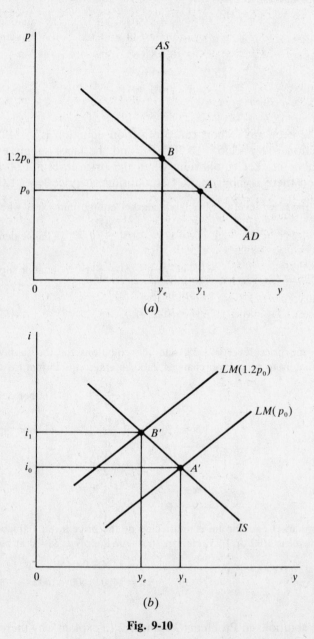

Fig. 9-10

Schedules IS and $LM(p_o)$ are in equilibrium at output y_1 in Fig. 9-10(b). However, aggregate demand of y_1 at price level p_o exceeds aggregate supply y_e in Fig. 9-10(a). The price level must increase to $1.2p_o$, which decreases the real money supply and shifts LM in Fig. 9-10(b) leftward to $LM(1.2p_o)$. This movement to equilibrium is seen in Fig. 9-10(a) as a movement along schedule AD from price level p_o to $1.2p_o$ where aggregate demand equals aggregate supply.

NEOCLASSICAL AGGREGATE SUPPLY: DEMAND CHANGES

9.5   Schedules AD and AS in Fig. 9-11(a) are in equilibrium at full employment output y_e and price level p_o. This equilibrium condition is also depicted in Fig. 9-11(b) for goods and money market schedules IS and $LM(p_o)$. (a) Explain what happens to the IS, LM and AD schedules and the equilibrium condition when taxes are increased, *ceteris paribus*. (b) Explain how the price level corrects for the disequilibrium caused by a tax increase.

(a)   Increased taxes shift IS leftward to IS' in Fig. 9-11(b) and aggregate demand leftward to AD' in Fig. 9-11(a). Aggregate demand is now y_1 at price level p_o, which is below full employment output y_e.

(b)   When prices are flexible, the price level declines when aggregate spending is less than full employment output. The price level falls from p_o to p_1; there is movement along schedule AD' [Fig. 9-11(a)] until full employment output y_e is reached. In Fig. 9-11(b), the decline in the price level increases the real money supply which shifts LM rightward to $LM(p_1)$; IS' and $LM(p_1)$ intersect at full employment output y_e.

9.6   The goods market equation, plotted and labeled IS in Fig. 9-12(a), is $y = \$1300 - 30i$ when $C = \$90 + 0.80Yd$, $I = \$150 - 6i$, $Tx = \$100$, and $G = \$100$. The money market equation, plotted and labeled LM in Fig. 9-12(a), is $y = \$800 + 20i$ when the nominal money supply is $\$160$, the price level is 1.00 and the demand for money is $0.20y - 4i$. The neoclassical aggregate supply schedule AS in Fig. 9-13(b) is derived from the short-run production function $y = 14N - 0.04N^2$ and the supply and demand for labor equations $N_s = 70 + 5(W/p)$ and $N_d = 175 - 12.5(W/p)$. Equilibrium output is initially $\$1000$, the price level 1.00, and rate of interest 10%. (a) Find simultaneous equilibrium in the money and goods market when taxes increase $\$20$ and there is no change in the price level. Explain what should happen to the

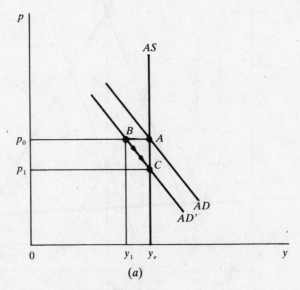

Fig. 9-11

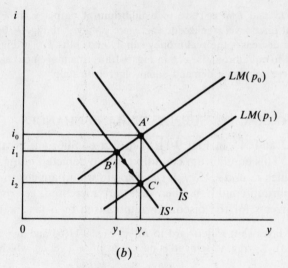

(b)

Fig. 9-11 (*continued*)

price level. (b) A \$20 increase in taxes shifts aggregate demand leftward to AD'; the price level at equilibrium is 0.9374. What happens to the real money supply when the price level declines from 1.00 to 0.9374? Find the new LM equation. (c) Find the rate of interest when the price level is 0.9374. (d) Compare C, I and G when the price level is 1.00 and 0.9374. (e) Find the nominal and real wage when the price level is 1.00 and 0.9374.

(a) When taxes increase \$20, the IS equation becomes $y = \$1220 - 30i$.

$$y = \$90 + 0.80(Y - \$120) + \$150 - 6i + \$100$$
$$y = \$1220 - 30i$$

Simultaneous equilibrium in the money and goods markets exists when output is \$968.

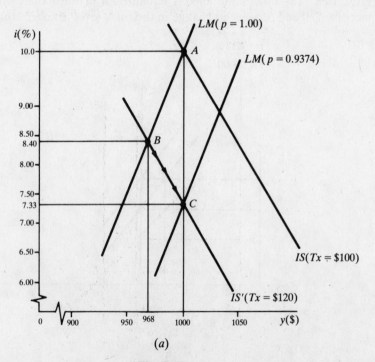

(a)

Fig. 9-12

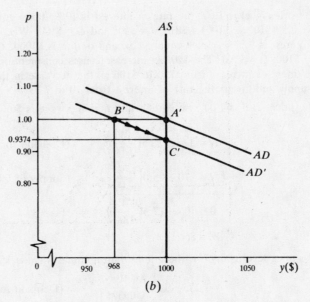

(b)

Fig. 9-12

$$y = \$1220 - 30i \qquad (IS \text{ equation when } Tx = \$120)$$
$$\underline{-(y = \quad 800 + 20i) \qquad (LM \text{ when price level is } 1.00)}$$
$$0 = \$ \ 420 - 50i$$
$$i = 8.40\%$$
$$y = \$ \ 968$$

(b)   The real money supply increases from \$160, or 160/1.00, to \$170.68, or \$160/0.9374. The *LM* equation is $y = \$853.40 + 20i$. ($\$170.68 = 0.20y - 4i$; $\$853.40 = y - 20i$.)

(c)   When the price level is 0.9374, simultaneous equilibrium in the money and goods markets exists at a \$1000 output and 7.33% rate of interest:

$$y = \$1220.00 - 30i \qquad (IS \text{ equation when } Tx = \$120)$$
$$\underline{-(y = \quad 853.40 + 20i) \qquad (LM \text{ when price level is } 0.9374)}$$
$$0 = \$ \ 366.60 + 50i$$
$$i = 7.33\%$$
$$y = \$1000$$

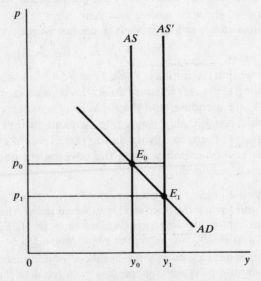

Fig. 9-13

(d) When the price level is 1.00, the rate of interest is 10%, taxes equal $100, and output is $1000, $C = \$90 + 0.80(\$1000 - \$100) = \$810$; $I = \$90$; and $G = \$100$. When the price level is 0.9374, the rate of interest is 7.33%, taxes equal $120, and output is $1000, $C = \$90 + 0.80(\$1000 - \$120) = \$794$; $I = \$106$; $G = \$100$. The $20 tax increase causes consumption to decline from $810 to $794 and investment to increase from $90 to $106 as the decrease in the price level expands the real money supply and lowers the rate of interest from 10 to 7.33%.

(e) When the price level is 1.00, the equilibrium nominal wage is $6.

$$N = 175 - 12.5\left(\frac{W}{1.00}\right) \qquad \text{(Demand for labor)}$$

$$-\left(N = 70 + 5.0\left(\frac{W}{1.00}\right)\right) \qquad \text{(Supply of labor)}$$

$$\overline{0 = 105 - 17.5\left(\frac{W}{1.00}\right)}$$

$$W = \$6$$

When the price level is 0.9374, the equilibrium nominal wage is $5.62.

$$N = 175 - 12.5\left(\frac{W}{0.9374}\right) \qquad \text{(Demand for labor)}$$

$$-\left(N = 70 + 5.0\left(\frac{W}{0.9374}\right)\right) \qquad \text{(Supply of labor)}$$

$$\overline{0 = 105 - 17.5\left(\frac{W}{0.9374}\right)}$$

$$0 = 98.427 - 17.5W$$

$$W = \$5.62$$

The real wage is unaffected by the change in the price level and remains at $6.

9.7 Full employment equilibrium is initially y_e in Fig. 9-13, for schedules AD and AS. Suppose technological change shifts aggregate supply rightward to AS'. (a) Explain how the economy adjusts to its increased capacity through changes in the price level. (b) What happens to the composition of aggregate output?

(a) With increased capacity, full employment output y_1 exceeds y_e aggregate spending at price level p_o. The price level declines from p_o to p_1; the real money supply increases, and LM shifts to the right; the rate of interest falls and interest-sensitive private sector spending increases.

(b) When taxes are unrelated to income and there is no change in government spending, interest-sensitive private sector spending expands as does consumption.

9.8 Full employment output is initially y_e in Fig. 9-14, for schedules AD and AS. Reduced government spending shifts AD leftward to AD'. At price level p_o, full employment output y_e now exceeds aggregate spending, and the price level is expected to fall. (a) Explain why price expectations would probably shift aggregate demand further to the left, e.g., to AD''. (b) What disadvantages are there to relying on the price level to correct a situation of insufficient demand? (c) What economic policy might the government implement to avert the destabilizing effect of a price-level decline?

(a) Deflation (a decline in the price level) means that goods and services can be purchased at lower prices in the future. When the price level is expected to fall, the private sector will postpone some expenditures to future spending periods. Decreases in $(C + I)$ will further depress aggregate demand (shift it to AD''), and aggregate output would fall to y_2 rather than to y_1 in Fig. 9-14.

(b) The disadvantages include not only the likelihood of postponed spending but less responsiveness from interest-sensitive private sector spending to increases in the real money supply. Recall that a

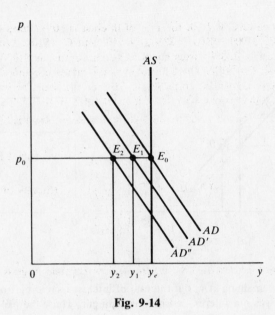

Fig. 9-14

decrease in the price level increases the real money supply, which lowers the rate of interest. In a period of declining economic activity, private sector spending may become less interest sensitive. Aggregate demand would not only shift to the left due to expected deflation but would become steeper as well. The required decline in the price level to reach full employment might become substantial, which would further feed deflationary expectations, deepen the contraction and prolong the recession.

(c) Rather than rely on deflation, government can initiate stimulative economic policies (increase the nominal money supply, expand government spending, and/or decrease taxes which would shift aggregate demand back to AD in Fig. 9-14. Economic contractions would be not only moderated but shortened as well.

9.9 Explain why unexpected deflation might have redistribution effects which could further dampen aggregate demand.

Unexpected deflation increases the real indebtedness of borrowers (debtors) and the real wealth of lenders (creditors). Since debtors are more likely to have a higher marginal propensity to consume than creditors, unexpected deflation is likely to reduce aggregate consumption and shift aggregate demand to the left, further contracting economic activity.

NEOCLASSICAL AGGREGATE SUPPLY: MONETARY AND FISCAL POLICY

9.10 An economy is initially at full employment output y_e, for schedules AD and AS in Fig. 9-15(a) and IS and $LM(p_o)$ in Fig. 9-15(b). (a) What effect does an increase in government spending have on equilibrium output, the price level, and the rate of interest, *ceteris paribus*? (b) What effect does increased government spending have on sector output in this full employment economy?

(a) IS shifts rightward to IS' in Fig. 9-15(b) with aggregate demand shifting from AD to AD' in Fig. 9-15(a). Because aggregate spending y_1 exceeds full employment output y_e, the price level increases from p_0 to p_1, which shifts LM leftward from $LM(p_o)$ to $LM(p_1)$. Real output remains at full employment output y_e, the price level increases from p_o to p_1, and the rate of interest increases from i_o to i_1.

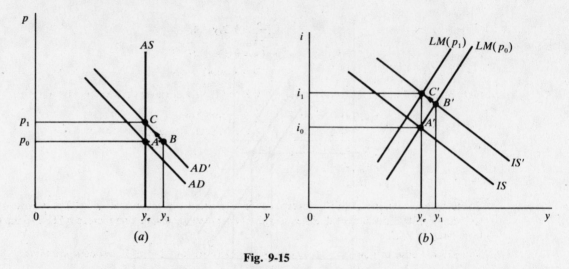

Fig. 9-15

(b) With output remaining at y_e but the rate of interest increasing from i_o to i_1, increased government spending crowds out interest-sensitive investment. Thus, the expansion of public sector output is achieved by an equal decrease in interest-sensitive private sector output.

9.11 Economic activity is at the $700 full employment output level, and the price level is 2.00 in Fig. 9-16 for schedules AD and AS. The equation for IS is $y = \$1000 - 30i$ with $C = \$30 + 0.80yd$, $I = \$150 - 6i$, $Tx = \$100$, and $G = \$100$. The LM equation is $y = \$500 + 20i$ with a $200 nominal money supply; the price level is 2.00, and the demand for money is $0.20y - 4i$. (a) Find equations for IS and LM when a $15 increase in government spending shifts aggregate demand rightward in Fig. 9-16 to AD' and the price level increases to 2.22. (b) Find the rate of interest, C and I when the price level is 2.00 and 2.22. (c) What effect does the $15 increase in government spending have on the composition of output?

(a) The IS equation is $y = \$1075 - 30i$ when government spending increases from $100 to $115.

$$y = \$30 + 0.8(y - \$100) + \$150 - 6i + \$115$$
$$y = \$1075 - 30i$$

The LM equation is $y = \$450.45 + 20i$ when the price level is 2.22.

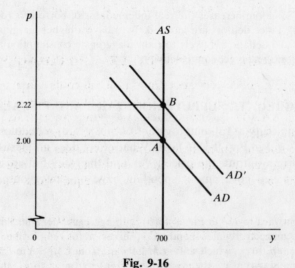

Fig. 9-16

$$\frac{\$200}{2.22} = 0.20y - 4i$$

$$\$90.09 = 0.20y - 4i$$

$$y = \$450.45 + 20i$$

(b) Output remains at the $700 full employment level; the rate of interest increases from 10 to 12.5%.

$$
\begin{array}{ll}
y = \$1075.00 - 30i & \text{(\textit{IS} equation when \textit{G} is \$115)} \\
-(y = \quad 450.45 + 20i) & \text{(\textit{LM} equation when price level is 2.22)} \\
\hline
0 = \$624.55 + 50i & \\
i = 12.50\% & \\
y = \$700 & \\
\end{array}
$$

Consumption remains at $510. Investment is $90 when the price level is 2.00 and government spending is $100; investment declines to $75 when government spending increases $15 and the price level rises to 2.22.

(c) The $15 increase in government sector spending crowds out $15 of investment spending.

9.12 The initial parameters of Problem 9.11 are retained, but we now assume that aggregate demand AD in Fig. 9-16 shifts rightward to AD' because the nominal money supply increases from $200 to $222. (a) What effect does the $22 increase in the nominal money supply have on the real money supply when the rightward shift of aggregate demand raises the price level from 2.00 to 2.22? (b) What has happened to the composition of sector output in this full employment economy?

(a) There is no change in the real money supply. The real money supply is $100 when the nominal money supply is $200, and the price level is 2.00 and $100 when the nominal money supply is $222 and the price level is 2.22.

(b) With the real money supply constant, the rate of interest is unchanged as is the composition of sector output.

9.13 Why is a change in the nominal money supply neutral when aggregate supply is vertical?

When aggregate supply is vertical, changes in the nominal money supply cause proportional changes in the price level. Because the real money supply remains unchanged, nominal money supply changes have no effect on the rate of interest or the composition of output. Thus, nominal money changes are neutral in their effect on the compositon and level of real output.

POSITIVELY SLOPED AGGREGATE SUPPLY: DEMAND CHANGES

9.14 Suppose the money, goods and labor markets are in equilibrium at full employment output y_e: schedules AD and AS in Fig. 9-17(a) determine output y_e and price level p_o; schedules IS and $LM(p_o)$ in Fig. 9-17(b) determine output y_e and interest rate i_o; and N_e labor units are employed for schedules N_d and N_s in Fig. 9-17(c) at nominal wage W_o. Assume that the labor supply schedule does not immediately adjust for changes in the price level. (a) What happens to the price level, real output and labor units employed when the nominal money supply increases, *ceteris paribus*? (b) Is output at an equilibrium level after the money supply expansion?

(a) In Fig. 9-17(a) aggregate demand shifts rightward to AD'; the price level and real output increase to p_1 and y_2 respectively. $LM(p_o)$ in Fig. 9-17(b) shifts rightward to $LM'(p_o)$ initially, but the rise in the price level to p_1 shifts LM leftward to $LM(p_1)$; the rate of interest declines to i_2 and real output expands to y_2. The p_o to p_1 increase in the price level shifts labor demand rightward to N_d' in

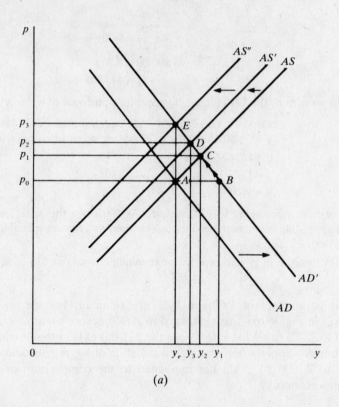

(a)

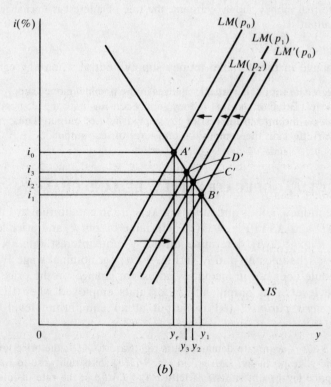

(b)

Fig. 9-17

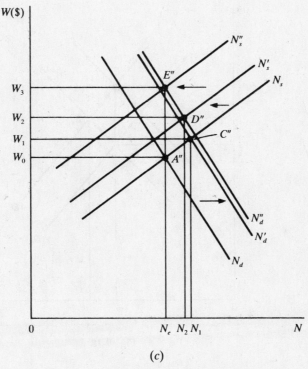

(c)

Fig. 9-17 (*continued*)

Fig. 9-17(c) with the labor supply schedule remaining at N_s; the nominal wage increases to W_1 with labor units employed increasing from N_e to N_1.

(b)   The economy is not in equilibrium. Schedule AS in Fig. 9-17(a) is derived from labor market equilibrium where price level p_o is expected to continue and the nominal wage is W_o; and real output y_2 and labor units employed N_1 exceed the level associated with full employment. Because the price level is above p_o and N_1 exceeds N_e, labor is able to demand and receive higher nominal wages, which shift the labor supply schedule N_s in Fig. 9-17(c) leftward to N_s'. Aggregate supply in Fig. 9-17(a) shifts leftward to AS' with the price level rising to p_2 and real output declining to y_3. Money equilibrium schedule $LM(p_1)$ in Fig. 9-17(b) shifts leftward to $LM(p_2)$ with the rate of interest rising to i_3. And in Fig. 9-17(c), the labor demand schedule shifts rightward to N_d'' with schedules N_s' and N_d'' determining a W_2 nominal wage and N_2 labor units employed. Labor continues to demand higher nominal wages, which shift aggregate supply leftward, as long as labor units employed and real output exceeds N_e and y_e, respectively. The economy returns to equilibrium when AD' and AS'' determine full employment output y_e and price level p_3.

9.15   In Fig. 9-18, an economy is at full employment output y_e for schedules AS and AD with the price level at p_o. An increase in the nominal money supply shifts aggregate rightward to AD' with real output increasing to y_1. Explain and show what happens to real output as the economy returns to an equilibrium position.

Because price level p_1 is higher than the expected p_o level and output y_1 exceeds full employment output y_e, labor demands higher nominal wages, which shift aggregate supply to the left. Higher nominal wage demands persist until aggregate supply and aggregate demand intersect at output y_e and price level p_2. Hence, real output increases from y_e to y_1 and then declines over a number of periods as aggregate supply shifts to the left and moves along AD' until price level p_2 is reached. The path of real output is indicated by the arrows in Fig. 9-18.

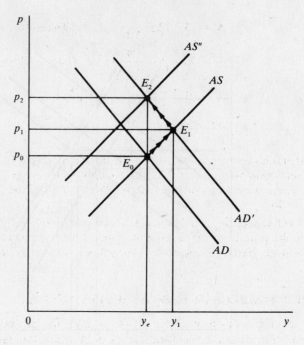

Fig. 9-18

9.16 Suppose the equation for short-run supply is $y = 14N - 0.04N^2$, and the demand for labor equation is $N_d = 175 - 12.5(W/p)$. The labor supply equation is $N_s = 70 + 5W$; labor expects the 1.00 price level to continue. Economic activity is initially at the $1000 full employment level of output; the price level is 1.00; the nominal wage is $6; the real wage is $6; and 100 labor units are employed. (*a*) What happens to the quantity of labor units employed, the nominal wage and the real wage when increased government spending shifts aggregate demand rightward, real output expands to $1011.40, and the price level increases to 1.10? (*b*) What happens to the nominal wage, the real wage and labor units employed when labor's demand for a 10% increase in the nominal wage (because of the 10% increase in the price level) shifts aggregate supply leftward, which causes real output to decline to $1005.96 and the price level to increase to 1.15? (*c*) What real output, real wage and labor units employed prevail in the long run? (*d*) Why did real output exceed the $1000 full employment level?

(*a*) Labor units employed increase from 100 to 102, the nominal wage increases from $6.00 to $6.42 and the real wage declines from $6.00 to $5.84 [the real wage w equals W/p; when $W = \$6.42$ and $p = 1.10$, $w = (\$6.42/1.10) = \$5.84$].

$$N = 175 - 12.5\left(\frac{W}{1.10}\right) \qquad \text{(Demand for labor)}$$
$$\underline{- (N = 70 + 5.0W)} \qquad \text{(Supply of labor)}$$
$$0 = 105 - 12.5\left(\frac{W}{1.10}\right) - 5W$$
$$W = \$6.42$$
$$N = 102.08$$

(*b*) Labor units employed decrease from 102 to 101, the nominal wage increases from $6.42 to $6.81, and the real wage increases from $5.84 to $5.92.

$$N = 175 - 12.5\left(\frac{W}{1.15}\right) \qquad \text{(Demand for labor)}$$

$$-\left(N = 70 + 5.0\left(\frac{W}{1.10}\right)\right) \qquad \text{(Supply of labor)}$$

$$0 = 105 - 12.5\left(\frac{W}{1.15}\right) - 5\left(\frac{W}{1.10}\right)$$

$$W = \$6.81$$

$$N = 101$$

(c)   Labor demands higher nominal wages as long as the real wage is below its initial equilibrium level and labor units employed exceeds the 100 labor units employed at the $1000 full employment level of output. Thus, in the long run, real output returns to $1000, labor units employed to 100 and the real wage to $6.

(d)   Labor did not expect the initial increase in the price level and therefore did not immediately incorporate the price level increase into its demand for nominal wages. The result is a decline in labor's real wage, pushing labor units employed and real output beyond full employment.

POSITIVELY SLOPED AGGREGATE SUPPLY: SUPPLY SHOCKS

9.17   Explain how an increase in variable W, θ, a and Pn in the mark-up pricing formula $P = W/a(1 + \theta) + Pn$ affects the supply cost of output and the aggregate supply schedule.

W is the nominal wage; an increase in the nominal wage increases per-unit supply cost and therefore shifts aggregate supply to the left. θ is the mark-up on variable cost; an increase in mark-up increases per-unit supply cost and shifts aggregate supply to the left. Variable a represents the productivity of labor; an increase in labor productivity, the number of units produced per unit of labor input, decreases per-unit supply cost and shifts aggregate supply to the right. An increase in the real per-unit cost of materials, Pn, increases per-unit supply cost and shifts aggregate supply to the left.

9.18   Economic activity is initially at full employment output y_e in Fig. 9-19 for schedules AD and AS. (a) What happens to equilibrium output and the price level when the real per-unit cost of materials increases, *ceteris paribus*? (b) What happens to the disequilibrium in part (a) when nominal wages are "sticky" downward? Is labor able to bargain for higher nominal wages because of the p_o to p_1 increase in the price level? (c) When prices and wages are flexible and there is no demand-stabilizing economic policy, what eventually happens to nominal wages and/or prices to reestablish equilibrium at full employment? (d) What demand-stabilizing economic policies could the government implement to eliminate the disequilibrium in (a)? (e) What is true of the disequilibrium in (a) when the increase in per-unit materials cost is temporary?

(a)   Aggregate supply in Fig. 9-19 shifts leftward from AS to AS'. There is movement along schedule AD with output declining from y_e to y_1 and the price level increasing from p_o to p_1.

(b)   When nominal wages remain at their initial W_o level and there is no demand-stabilizing economic policy, output remains at the y_1 disequilibrium level, which is below full employment output. Although the price level has increased from p_o to p_1 and the real wage has fallen, labor in unable to bargain for a higher nominal wage because employment and real output is below the full employment level.

(c)   When labor markets are competitive and nominal wages are flexible, the nominal wage should decline, since output and employment is below full employment. The decline in the nominal wage reduces the per-unit cost of output and shifts aggregate supply rightward from AS' to AS. There is a return to output y_e and price level p_o.

(d)   Rather than rely on the labor markets to correct the disequilibrium, government could increase its expenditures, reduce taxes and/or increase the nominal money supply to shift aggregate demand

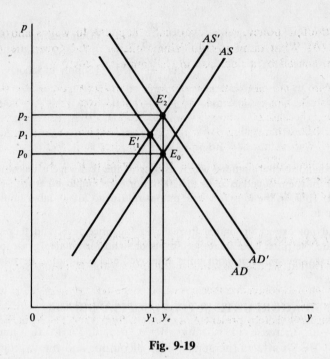

Fig. 9-19

rightward to AD'. Demand-stimulating policies could return output to the y_e full employment level but would cause a further increase in the price level to p_2.

(e)   When material cost increases are only temporary, aggregate supply shifts leftward to AS' in Fig. 9-19 but returns to AS in a future period. The decline in real output is temporary as is the increase in the price level.

9.19   Economic activity is initially at full employment output y_e in Fig. 9-20 for schedules AD and AS. Suppose a decrease in per-unit materials cost occurs. (a) In the absence of a demand-

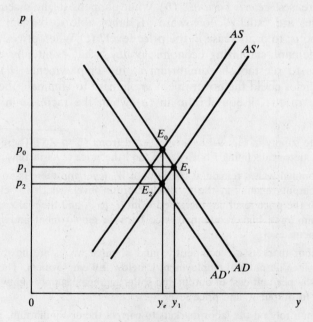

Fig. 9-20

stabilizing economic policy, what eventually happens to wages and/or prices to reestablish equilibrium? (*b*) What demand-stabilizing policies could government utilize to correct the disequilibrium caused by a decrease in real materials cost?

(*a*) The decrease in per-unit materials cost shifts aggregate supply in Fig. 9-20 rightward from *AS* to *AS'*. Movement along *AD* causes output to expand from y_e to y_1 with the price level decreasing from p_o to p_1 because of a lower per-unit production cost. Since output y_1 exceeds full employment output y_e, labor's bargaining power is enhanced. Nominal wages increase; aggregate supply shifts back to *AS* with output and the price level returning to y_e and p_o.

(*b*) The government could shift aggregate demand leftward from *AD* to *AD'* in Fig. 9-20 by reducing government spending, increasing taxes and/or decreasing the nominal money supply. Output would return to y_e at a lower p_2 price level.

THE NEW CLASSICAL AND KEYNESIAN MACROECONOMICS

9.20 Explain the original Keynesian analysis of labor market equilibrium and aggregate supply.

Keynesian analysis contended that a nominal wage floor existed; the nominal wage would not fall below a specific level and tended to remain constant until real output reached its full employment level. The nominal wage was thereby presented as constant, for example, at W_o in Fig. 9-21(*a*) and remained at

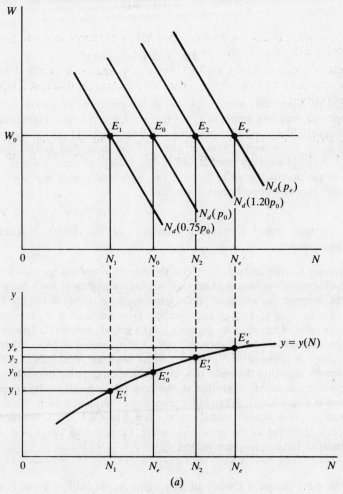

Fig. 9-21

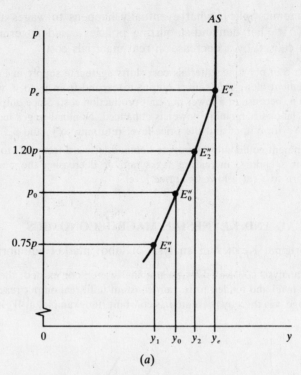

Fig. 9-21 (*continued*)

that level until N_e labor units were employed at full employment output y_e. In Fig. 9-21(a), N_o labor units are employed, and real output is y_o at price level p_o; N_1 labor units are employed, and real output is y_1 for price level $0.75p_o$; and N_2 labor units are employed, and real output is y_2 for price level $1.20p_o$. Upon reaching N_e, the nominal wage increases at the same rate as the price level, and real output remains at y_e. Aggregate supply schedule AS in Fig. 9-21(b) presents the effect of labor's money illusion with respect to the nominal wage in Fig. 9-21(a); aggregate supply is positively sloped until output y_e, where aggregate supply's slope becomes vertical.

9.21   How does contemporary Keynesian analysis of the labor markets differ from earlier Keynesian analysis?

Contemporary Keynesian analysis rejects the contention of a wage floor but views nominal wages as "sticky" in the short run because workers sign contracts agreeing to work for a specific nominal wage for the term of the contract. For example, in the labor supply schedule $N_s(p_o)$ in Fig. 9-22(a), labor expects continuance of price level p_o and agrees to supply labor units for a W_o nominal wage. The demand for labor during the term of the contract depends on the actual price level. Thus, a change in the price level shifts the labor demand schedule rightward to $N_d(1.20p_o)$ in Fig. 9-22(a), when the price level increases from p_o to $1.20p_o$, or leftward to $N_d(0.80p_o)$ when the price level falls to $0.80p_o$. Aggregate supply is therefore positively sloped in the short run, but its location in space depends on the price level expected when labor contracts to supply labor inputs. We note this dependency by appending p_o to the aggregate supply schedule in Fig. 9-22(b). When labor contracts expect and thereby include the higher $1.20p_o$ price level, aggregate supply is located to the left of $AS(p_o)$ at $AS(1.20p_o)$. When the price level included in labor contracts is the same as the price level which exists during the period of the contract, aggregate supply is vertical at full employment output y_e.

9.22   How does the new classical theory of aggregate supply differ from contemporary Keynesian theory?

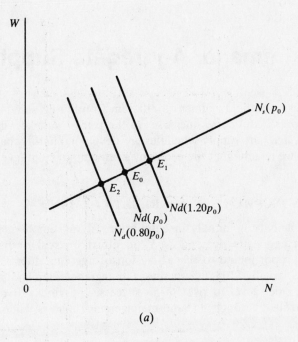

(a)

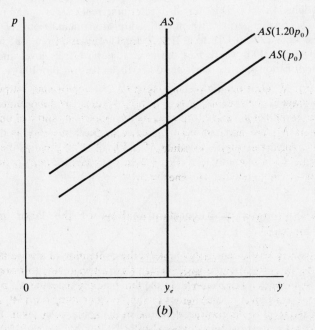

(b)

Fig. 9-22

Both recognize that aggregate supply may be positively sloped in the short run. In the new classical aggregate supply models, the nominal wage adapts to changes in the price level and, in more recent models, uses information which may be incomplete in setting the nominal wage. Hence, the nominal wage may be above or below the market-clearing real wage for a time, but the period is shorter than the one assumed in contemporary Keynesian models. As more complete information becomes available, aggregate supply becomes more steeply sloped and is vertical over longer periods.

Chapter 10

Aggregate Demand, Aggregate Supply and Inflation

This chapter focuses on the dynamics of inflation. Continuous shifts in aggregate demand and/or aggregate supply result in continuous increases in the price level, i.e., inflation. Dynamic aggregate demand and dynamic aregate supply schedules are developed in this chapter to analyze inflation. To simplify the analysis, we assume that the economy's full employment level of output does not change.

10.1 CONTINUOUS INCREASES IN AGGREGATE DEMAND

When economic activity is initially in equilibrium at full employment and aggregate supply is vertical, increases in aggregate demand have no effect on real output but result in price level increases which are proportionate to the expansion of aggregate demand. For example, when full employment output is initially $100, 5% increases in aggregate demand from $100 to $105 to $110.25 to $115.76 cause the price level to rise 5% in successive periods; there is a 5% rate of inflation. Inflation can be controlled through demand-management policies when increases in the price level are demand related.

EXAMPLE 1. Schedules AS and AD in Fig. 10-1 determine real output y_e and price level 1.0; 10% increases in aggregate demand in successive periods, which shift aggregate demand from AD to AD_1 to AD_2 to AD_3, cause the price level to rise from 1.00 to 1.10 to 1.21 to 1.33. The inflation rate (π) for each period is found by the formula $\pi = [(p - p_{-1})/p_{-1}]100$, where p is the current period price level and p_{-1} is the price level in the previous period. The inflation rate for each period is 10%: $(0.10/1.00)(100) = 10\%$; $(0.11/1.10)(100) = 10\%$; $(0.12/1.21)(100) = 10\%$.

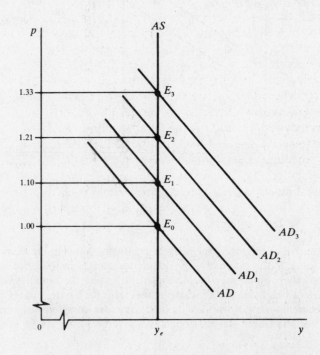

Fig. 10-1

EXAMPLE 2.   *LM* is vertical when the demand for money is unrelated to the rate of interest; fiscal policy is ineffective and shifts of aggregate demand are solely the result of changes in the nominal money supply. The central bank controls aggregate demand's location in space and thereby inflation through its management of the nominal money supply.

10.2   INFLATION AND UNEMPLOYMENT: THE PHILLIPS CURVE

When aggregate supply is positively sloped, sustained expansions of aggregate demand cause continuous increases in both the price level (inflation) and real output. (See Section 9.4.) Increases in real output are associated with lower unemployment rates. The Phillips curve traces the inverse relationship between the rate of inflation and the rate of unemployment; its slope and location in space depend on the inflation expectations of labor. When labor expects a higher inflation rate, the short-run Phillips curve shifts rightward. When labor correctly anticipates price-level changes, aggregate supply is vertical at the full employment level of output; and the long-run Phillips curve is vertical at the natural rate of unemployment.

EXAMPLE 3.   The economy is initially at full employment output y_e in Fig. 10-2(a) for schedules *AD* and *AS*. Continuous increases in the nominal money supply shift aggregate demand rightward to AD_1, AD_2 and AD_3; output and the price level increase to y_1, y_2 and y_3 and to p_1, p_2 and p_3, respectively. Price level increases from p_0 to p_3 are associated with π_1, π_2 and π_3 inflation rates, and output increases y_e to y_3 are associated with unemployment rates of 6%, 5% and 4%. The Phillips curve *SPC* in Fig. 10-2(b) is derived from the decreasing unemployment rates and increasing inflation rates caused by the rightward shifts of aggregate demand in Fig. 10-2(a).

10.3   SCHEDULE OF DYNAMIC AGGREGATE DEMAND

In Section 8.2, the equation for aggregate demand is $y = [hk_e/(h + kbk_e)](\bar{A}) + [bk_e/(h + kbk_e)](\bar{M}/p)$. Increases in autonomous spending and/or the nominal money supply, with the price level held constant, shift the aggregate demand rightward by $\Delta y = [hk_e/(h + kbk_e)]\Delta\bar{A} + [bk_e/(h + kbk_e)](\Delta\bar{M}/\bar{p})$. Growth in the level of aggregate demand (the dynamic aggregate demand schedule) can be presented as $y = y_{-1} + \Delta y$, where y is the current period's level of aggregate demand, y_{-1} is the previous period's level of aggregate demand, and Δy is the change in aggregate demand between the current and previous period. When growth in the level of aggregate demand is due to increases in the nominal money supply and/or a fiscal expansion, the equation for dynamic aggregate demand is $y = y_{-1} + \beta(\dot{M} - \pi) + \alpha f$, where β and α are the multipliers of money and fiscal expansion, $\dot{M}$ is the growth rate of the nominal money supply, π is the current inflation rate, $(\dot{M} - \pi)$ is the rate of expansion of the real money supply, and f is the fiscal stimulus. (See Example 4.) Holding $\dot{M}$ and f constant, there is an inverse relationship between the rate of inflation and the level of aggregate demand, depicted by schedule *DAD* in Fig. 10-3. (Since we are now analyzing the growth of aggregate demand, the inflation rate π replaces the price level p on the vertical axis.) Increases in the growth rate of the nominal money supply, *ceteris paribus*, shift *DAD* rightward, and decreases shift it leftward. (See Example 5.) Increases in the previous period's output (y_{-1}) shift *DAD* to the right, and decreases shift it to the left (Example 6).

EXAMPLE 4.   The equation for dynamic aggregate demand is $y = y_{-1} + \Delta y$. When monetary and/or fiscal policy is the source of increasing aggregate demand, $\Delta y = [bk_e/(h + kbk_e)](\Delta\bar{M}/p) + [hk_e/(h + kbk_e)]\Delta\bar{G}$. Letting $\beta = [bk_e/(h + kbk_e)]$, $\alpha = [hk_e/(h + kbk_e)$, $\dot{M} = $ the rate of growth of the nominal money supply, $\pi = $ the current rate of inflation, and $f = $ the fiscal stimulus, $\Delta y = \beta(\dot{M} - \pi) + \alpha f$. The equation for *DAD* is then $y = y_{-1} + \beta(\dot{M} - \pi) + \alpha f$.

EXAMPLE 5.   When the demand for money is unrelated to the rate of interest (behavioral coefficient $h = 0$), fiscal expansion has no stimulative effect on aggregate demand. In the equation $\Delta y = \beta(\dot{M} - \pi) + \alpha f$, $\beta = 1/k$

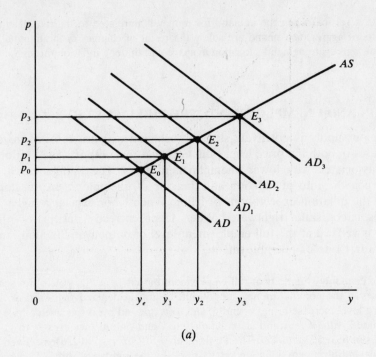

(a)

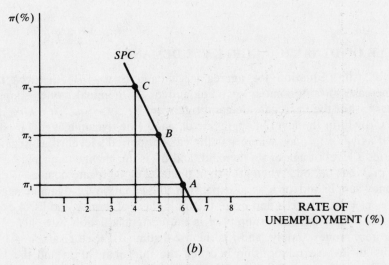

(b)

Fig. 10-2

and $\alpha = 0$. $[\beta = bk_e/(h + kbk_e); \beta = bk_e/(0 + kbk_e); \beta = 1/k$. $\alpha = hk_e/(h + kbk_e); \alpha = 0k_e/(0 + kbk_e); \alpha = 0.]$ The equation for dynamic aggregate demand is then $y = y_{-1} + 1/k(\dot{M} - \pi)$. When y_{-1} equals \$100, nominal money supply growth is 10%, and $k = 0.20$, the level of current period aggregate demand is \$100 when the inflation is 10% $[y = \$100 + 5(10\% - 10\%) = \$100]$, \$115 when the inflation rate is 7% and \$125 when the inflation rate is 5%. The association of a 10%, 7% and 5% rate of inflation with aggregate demand levels \$100, \$115 and \$125 is plotted in Fig. 10-4 with the schedule labeled DAD. When nominal money supply growth is 7% instead of 10%, aggregate demand levels \$85, \$100 and \$110 are associated with inflation rates 10%, 7% and 5%. These data are plotted in Fig. 10-4 with the schedule labeled DAD'. When nominal money supply growth is 13%, inflation rates 10%, 7% and 5% are associated with aggregate demand levels \$115, \$130 and \$140. These data are ploted in Fig. 10-4 with the schedule labeled DAD''. Holding the inflation rate constant, an increase in nominal money supply growth shifts DAD rightward, and a decrease in nominal money supply growth shifts DAD leftward.

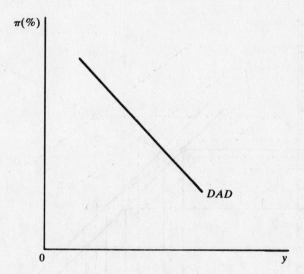

Fig. 10-3

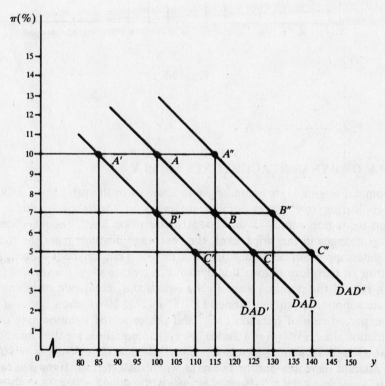

Fig. 10-4

EXAMPLE 6. The dynamic aggregate demand schedule also shifts when the previous period's output y_{-1} changes. In Fig. 10-5, schedule DAD is reproduced from Fig. 10-4. When y_{-1} is $105 rather than $100, the level of aggregate demand is $105 when the inflation rate is 10%, $120 when it is 7% and $130 when it is 5%. These data are plotted in Fig. 10-5 with the schedule labeled DAD'. The dynamic aggregate demand schedule shifts to the right when previous period's output is higher and to the left when the previous period's output is lower, *ceteris paribus*.

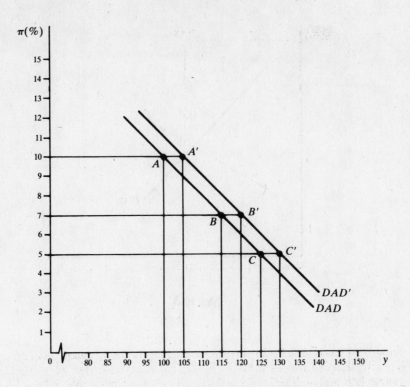

Fig. 10-5

10.4   SCHEDULE OF DYNAMIC AGGREGATE SUPPLY

When the nominal wage adapts immediately to changes in the price level, labor units employed stay at a market-clearing real wage; equilibrium exists in the labor markets; output is at full employment; and aggregate supply is unrelated to the price level. (See Section 8.5.) When the nominal wage lags changes in the price level, the real wage deviates from the market-clearing real wage, and aggregate supply can be higher or lower than full employment output. (See Section 8.7.) In a dynamic setting, it therefore follows that dynamic aggregate supply is vertical (DAS in Fig. 10-6) when the growth rate of the nominal wage (gW) equals the actual rate of inflation (π). However, dynamic aggregate supply is positively sloped (DAS' in Fig. 10-6) when nominal wage growth is a function of the expected rate of inflation (π^e), and the expected inflation rate does not equal the actual rate of inflation, i.e., $gW = f(\pi^e)$ and $\pi^e \neq \pi$. The equation for dynamic aggregate supply is then $\pi = \pi^e + \lambda(y - y_e)$. Dynamic aggregate supply schedule DAS' in Fig. 10-6 shifts to the left when expected inflation increases and to the right when expected inflation decreases.

The dynamic aggregate supply schedule is positively sloped when the labor supply schedule depends on expectations about the rate of inflation [$N_s = f(\pi^e)$], the demand for labor depends on the current rate of inflation [$N_d = f(\pi)$], and the current rate of inflation is not the same as the expected rate of inflation. Economists disagree on how labor arrives at inflationary expectations. The adaptive expectations hypothesis is a backward-looking approach, contending that π^e is derived from past economic behavior. In its most simplified form, inflationary expectations are presented as $\pi^e = \pi_{-1}$; inflationary expectations are a function of the previous period's rate of inflation. A rational expectations approach suggests that inflationary expectations are formed from all current, available information. The adaptive expectations approach ($\pi^e = \pi_{-1}$) is used in this chapter.

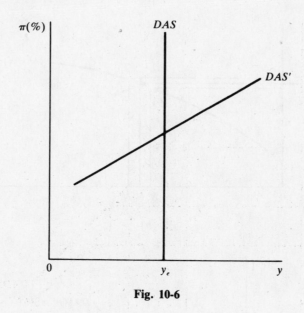

Fig. 10-6

EXAMPLE 7.   Suppose there is no inflation and the labor markets are in equilibrium in Fig. 10-7(a) for labor supply and demand schedules $N_s(\pi^e = 0)$ and $N_d(\pi = 0)$. Labor's expectation of a 5% rate of inflation shifts the labor supply schedule leftward to $N_s(\pi^e = 5\%)$. When the actual inflation rate is 3%, 5% or 7%, the labor demand schedule shifts rightward to $N_d(\pi = 3\%)$, $N_d(\pi = 5\%)$ or $N_d(\pi = 7\%)$, respectively. At a current inflation rate of 3%, 5% or 7%, N_1, N_e and N_2 labor units are employed which are associated in Fig. 10-7(b) with output levels y_1, y_e and y_2. Along dynamic aggregate supply schedule $DAS(\pi^e = 5\%)$ in Fig. 10-7(c), inflation rates 3%, 5% and 7% are associated with output levels y_1, y_e and y_2.

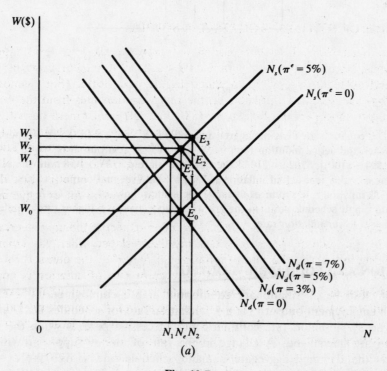

Fig. 10-7

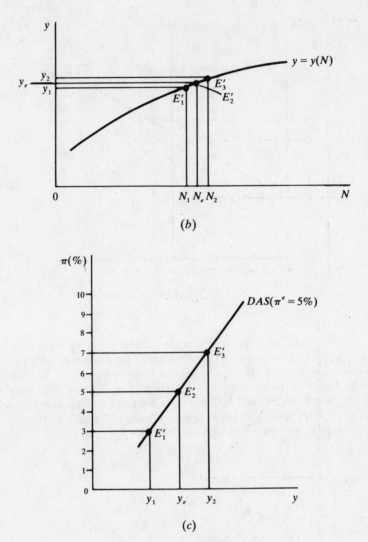

(b)

(c)

Fig. 10-7 (continued)

EXAMPLE 8.   The equation for dynamic aggregate supply is $\pi = \pi^e + \lambda(y - y_e)$. Suppose $\lambda = 0.50$, $\pi^e = 5\%$, and $y_e = \$100$. When the actual inflation rate is 3%, 6% or 7%, real output is \$96 [$3\% = 5\% + 0.5(y - 100)$; $3\% = 5\% + 0.50(\$94 - \$100)$], \$102 or \$104. The data are plotted in Fig. 10-8 with the schedule labeled DAS ($\pi^e = 5\%$). When $\pi^e = 3\%$ and actual inflation is 3%, 6% or 7%, real output is \$100, \$106 or \$108. Labor's expectation of a 3% inflation rate produces dynamic aggregate supply schedule $DAS(\pi^e = 3\%)$ in Fig. 10-8. The dynamic aggregate supply schedule shifts to the left when labor expects a higher rate of inflation and to the right when labor expects a lower inflation rate.

10.5   INFLATION AND EQUILIBRIUM OUTPUT

An economy can be in inflationary equilibrium at full employment. For example, economic activity is at full employment output y_e at a 5% inflation rate for schedules DAD and $DAS(\pi^e = 5\%)$ in Fig. 10-9. The 5% inflation rate continues into successive periods when the variables affecting DAD and DAS are unchanged. A change in the rate of money supply growth and/or the fiscal expansion shifts the dynamic aggregate demand schedule and moves the economy away from equilibrium, impacting output and inflation in successive periods. (See Examples 9 and 10.)

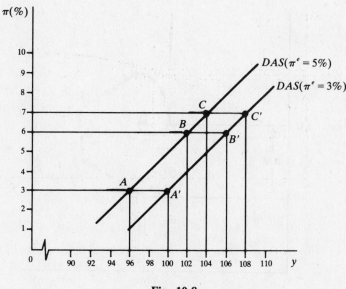

Fig. 10-8

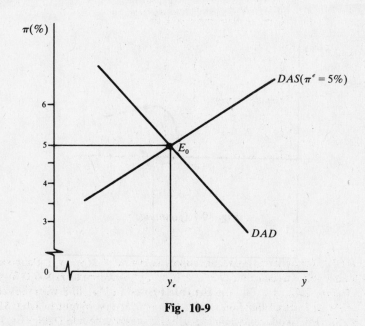

Fig. 10-9

Equilibrium is restored over time as changing inflation rates are incorporated into the dynamic aggregate supply schedule. Fig. 10-10 traces the path of inflation and output which results from an increase in the growth rate of the nominal money supply; there is an eventual return to full employment output but at a higher inflation rate. Fig. 10-11 traces the path of inflation and output which result from a fiscal expansion; note that both output and inflation return to their initial level.

EXAMPLE 9. In period 1, equilibrium output is initially y_e at inflation rate π_1 for schedules DAD_1 and $DAS(\pi^e = \pi_1)$ in Fig. 10-12. An increase in the growth rate of the nominal money supply in period 2 shifts DAD_1 rightward to DAD_2; inflation and output increase to π_2 and y_2, respectively. Because output has increased to y_2, DAD_2 shifts rightward to DAD_3 during period 3. (Recall an increase in previous period output

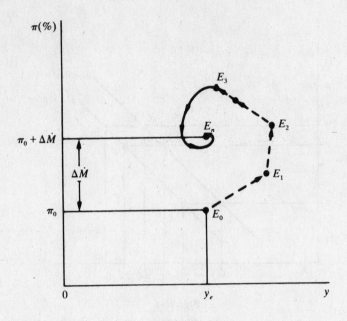

Fig. 10-10

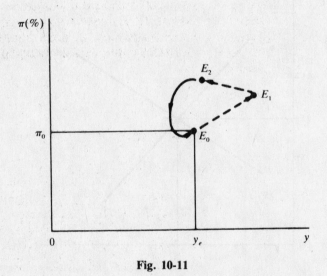

Fig. 10-11

shifts dynamic aggregate demand upward.) Because inflation has increased from π_1 to π_2 during period 2, labor's inflationary expectations increase to π_2 during period 3. [Recall $\pi^e = f(\pi_{-1})$.] Dynamic aggregate supply incorporates inflation rate π_2 during period 3 and shifts to the left from $DAS(\pi^e = \pi_1)$ to $DAS(\pi^e = \pi_2)$. Output and inflation increase to y_3 and π_3 by the end of period 3. In period 4, dynamic aggregate demand has a smaller rightward shift than in period 3 because of the smaller increase in real output (y_2 to y_3). Dynamic aggregate supply shifts leftward to DAS ($\pi^e = \pi_3$) as the inflation rate of period 3 is expected to continue into period 4. Because the upward shift of DAD_4 is less than the leftward shift of $DAS(\pi^e = \pi_3)$, real output falls, and inflation increases during period 4. Beginning in period 5, DAD begins shifting leftward with output and inflation following the path traced out in Fig. 10-10. When economic activity returns to full employment output y_e, inflation has increased from π_1 to π_n, which is equal to the change in the growth rate of the nominal money supply.

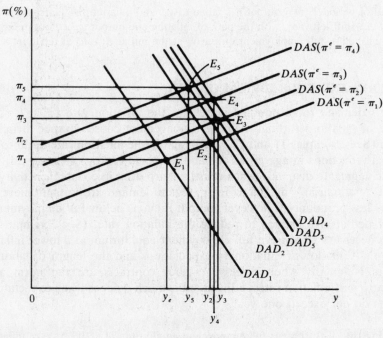

Fig. 10-12

EXAMPLE 10. Equilibrium output is y_e at inflation rate π_1 for schedules DAD_1 and $DAS(\pi^e = \pi_1)$ in Fig. 10-13. A fiscal expansion during period 2 shifts DAD_1 rightward to DAD_2. Output and inflation increase to y_2 and π_2. Although the fiscal expansion is permanent, it is not continuous. Hence, dynamic aggregate demand begins shifting leftward during period 3; however, it does not return to DAD_1 immediately because output during period 2 (y_2) is greater than that in period 1 (y_e). Hence, DAD_2 shifts leftward during period 3 to DAD_3; dynamic aggregate supply shifts leftward to $DAS(\pi^e = \pi_2)$, since labor expects inflation rate π_2 to

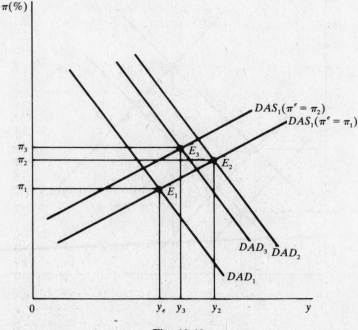

Fig. 10-13

continue. By the end of period 3, real output has fallen to y_3, and inflation has increased to π_3. In successive periods, DAD and DAS shift leftward, with the path of inflation and output traced out in Fig. 10-11. Note that equilibrium is reestablished at full employment output y_e at the initial π_1 rate of inflation.

10.6 DISINFLATION AND EQUILIBRIUM OUTPUT

Because labor's demand for a nominal wage lags the inflation rate $[\pi^e = f(\pi_{-1})]$, disinflation (reducing the rate of inflation) through demand management causes output to fall below the full employment level. (See Examples 11 and 12.) How rapidly the inflation rate declines depends on the magnitude of initial reductions in aggregate demand. A "cold turkey" strategy calls for substantial, initial reductions in aggregate demand, which cause a sharp drop in economic activity. (See Example 11.) In a policy of "gradualism," decreases in aggregate demand are initially more moderate. The decline in output is less pronounced; however, output remains below full employment longer, and a greater number of periods are needed to reduce the inflation rate. (See Example 12.) The actual number of periods necessary to achieve full employment equilibrium at a lower inflation rate is also influenced by labor's formation of inflationary expectations and the length of labor contracts. The adjustment process is lengthy when three-year labor contracts are the norm and inflationary expectations adjust to past inflation rates; adjustment is much quicker when expectations are rational and labor contracts do not exceed one year.

EXAMPLE 11. In Fig. 10-14(a), there is full employment equilibrium at a 10% rate of inflation for schedules DAD_1 and $DAS(\pi^e = 10\%)$. Suppose the central bank is committed to lowering the inflation rate to 2% as soon as possible, nominal money supply growth is reduced from 10% to 2% during period 2, shifting DAD_1 leftward to DAD_2. The inflation rate falls to 6% by the end of period 2, and output declines to y_2. DAD_2 shifts leftward to DAD_3 during period 3, since output fell from y_e to y_2; dynamic aggregate supply shifts rightward to $DAS(\pi^e = 6\%)$, since the inflation rate in period 2 is reduced to 6%. By the end of period 3, output increases to y_3 and the inflation rate is 3%. DAD shifts rightward in future periods, eventually returning to DAD_2, and DAS

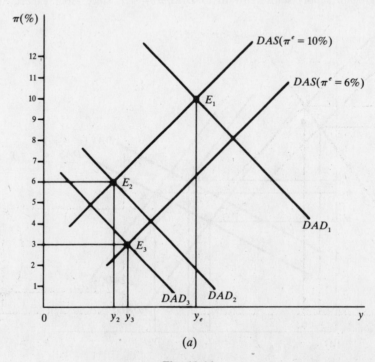

(a)

Fig. 10-14

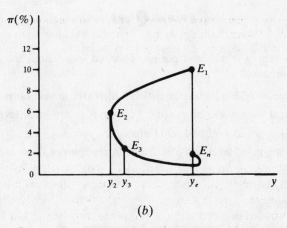

(b)

Fig. 10-14 (*continued*)

shifts rightward until it intersects DAD_2 at output y_e and a 2% inflation rate. The path to full employment equilibrium is traced out in Fig. 10-14(b).

EXAMPLE 12.   There is full employment equilibrium at a 10% inflation rate in Fig. 10-15(a) for schedules DAD_1 and $DAS(\pi^e = 10\%)$. A policy of gradualism calls for 2% decreases in nominal money supply growth during the next four periods, eventually reducing nominal money growth from 10% to 2%. During period 2, DAD_1 shifts leftward to DAD_2, and the inflation rate declines to 9%. In successive periods dynamic aggregate demand continues to shift leftward as nominal money supply growth is further reduced. The dynamic aggregate supply shifts rightward as the inflation rate falls. The path of adjustment from a 10% to a 2% inflation rate is traced out in Fig. 10-15(b).

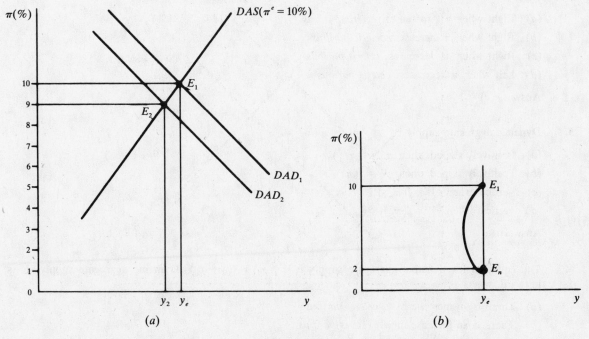

(a)   (b)

Fig. 10-15

Review Questions

1. When the aggregate supply schedule is positively sloped, continuous increases in the nominal money supply, *ceteris paribus*, result in

    (*a*) No change in the price level and proportional increases in real output

    (*b*) No change in real output and proportional increases in the price level

    (*c*) An increase in the price level and real output

    (*d*) An increase in the price level and a decrease in real output

    Answer: (*c*)

2. The Phillips curve shows

    (*a*) An inverse relationship between the real and nominal wage

    (*b*) An inverse relationship between the rate of inflation and the rate of unemployment

    (*c*) A positive relationship between the nominal wage and the rate of unemployment

    (*d*) A positive relationship between the rate of inflation and the nominal wage

    Answer: (*b*)

3. The dynamic aggregate demand schedule shifts rightward when there is an increase in

    (*a*) The expected rate of inflation, *ceteris paribus*

    (*b*) The growth rate of the nominal money supply, *ceteris paribus*

    (*c*) The income tax rate, *ceteris paribus*

    (*d*) The current inflation rate, *ceteris paribus*

    Answer: (*b*)

4. The equation for dynamic aggregate demand is $y = y_{-1} + \beta(\dot{M} - \pi) + \alpha f$. Dynamic aggregate demand shifts to the

    (*a*) Right when y_{-1} increases, *ceteris paribus*

    (*b*) Right when π increases, *ceteris paribus*

    (*c*) Right when $\dot{M}$ decreases, *ceteris paribus*

    (*d*) Left when π decreases, *ceteris paribus*

    Answer: (*a*)

5. Dynamic aggregate supply is

    (*a*) Positively sloped when $\pi^e = f(\pi_{-1})$

    (*b*) Positively sloped when $gW = f(\pi)$

    (*c*) Vertical when $gW = f(\pi_{-1})$

    (*d*) Vertical when $gW = f(\pi^e)$

    Answer: (*a*)

6. The equation for dynamic aggregate supply is $\pi = \pi^e + \lambda(y - y_e)$. Dynamic aggregate supply shifts leftward, when

    (*a*) There is an increase in y, *ceteris paribus*.

    (*b*) There is an increase in π^e, *ceteris paribus*.

    (*c*) There is an increase in π, *ceteris paribus*.

(d) There is a decrease in λ, *ceteris paribus*.

Answer: (b)

7. An economy is in inflationary equilibrium. An increase in the growth rate of the nominal money supply shifts

(a) *DAD* rightward, establishing equilibrium at a higher rate of inflation and level of output

(b) *DAD* and *DAS* rightward, establishing equilibrium at a higher rate of inflation and level of output

(c) *DAD* and *DAS* leftward with a new equilibrium established at a future period at a higher rate of inflation and level of output

(d) *DAD* to the right and *DAS* to the left with a new equilibrium established at a future period at a higher rate of inflation and no change in output

Answer: (d)

8. An economy is in inflationary equilibrium. A sustained increase in government spending shifts

(a) *DAD* rightward for one period

(b) *DAD* rightward permanently

(c) *DAD* and *DAS* rightward permanently

(d) *DAD* rightward, and a new equilibrim is established after successive periods at a higher rate of inflation

Answer: (a)

9. Disinflationary demand-management policies:

(a) Achieve a lower rate of inflation without causing a decrease in output

(b) Reduce output but have no initial effect on the inflation rate

(c) Require an increase in government spending

(d) Require a reduction in the growth rate of the nominal money supply

Answer: (d)

10. The economy is in inflationary equilibrium. A reduction in

(a) Government spending permanently lowers the economy's rate of inflation.

(b) Nominal money supply growth lowers the inflation rate with no effect on output in the short run.

(c) Nominal money supply growth lowers the inflation rate and the level of output in the short run.

(d) Government spending lowers the rate of inflation with no effect on output in the short run.

Answer: (c)

Solved Problems

CONTINUOUS INCREASES IN AGGREGATE DEMAND

10.1 Define the terms *inflation*, *disinflation* and *deflation*.

Inflation exists when there are continuous increases in the price level over time; the rate of inflation is found from the formula $\pi = [(p - p_{-1})/p_{-1}](100)$, where π is the inflation rate, p is the price level in the current period and p_{-1} is the price level in the previous period. When the rate of inflation is declining, there is disinflation. Deflation occurs when there are continuous decreases in the price level.

10.2 During period 1 schedules AS_1 and AD_1 in Fig. 10-16 determine price level 2.00 and full employment output y_e. Suppose continuous increases in aggregate demand shift schedule AD_1 upward to AD_2 in period 2, AD_3 in period 3, AD_4 in period 4 and AD_5 in period 5 with the price level increasing from 2.00 to 2.12, 2.25, 2.38 and 2.52 respectively. Find the economy's inflation rate for each period.

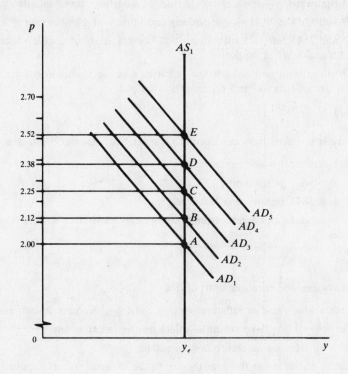

Fig. 10-16

The rate of inflation π is found by solving the equation $\pi = [(p - p_{-1})/p_{-1}](100)$ for π. The rate of inflation between period 1 and period 2 is 6% or $[(2.12 - 2.00)/2.00](100)$; the rate is 6% for each successive period.

10.3 The equation for aggregate demand is $y = \alpha(\bar{A}) + \beta(\bar{M}/p)$, where α is the multiplying effect of autonomous spending $\bar{A}$ and β is the multiplying effect of the real money supply $\bar{M}/p$. Suppose output is $1000 in period 1; investment spending is $200; $\alpha = 2$ and $\beta = 3$. (a) Find the level of aggregate demand in period 2 and in period 3 when there are 5% increases in autonomous investment in each period. (b) If full employment output is $1000, what government spending and/or money supply change can the government implement to keep output at the full employment level?

(a) Investment spending increases from $200 in period 1 to $210 in period 2 to $220.50 in period 3. The multiplier effect on the level of aggregate demand is $\alpha \Delta \bar{I}$. The level of aggregate demand increases $20 during period 2 to $1020 and $21 during period 3 to $1041.

(b) Since a change in autonomous government spending has the same multiplying effect as a change in autonomous investment, government spending must decrease $10 during period 2 and $10.50 during period 3 to keep output at the $1000 level. An alternative economic policy is a reduction in the nominal money supply. With β equal to 3, the nominal money supply must decrease $6.67 during period 1 and $7.00 during period 2 to keep output at the $1000 level.

INFLATION AND UNEMPLOYMENT: THE PHILLIPS CURVE

10.4   What is a Phillips curve?

In studying the relationship between the rate of unemployment and inflation, A.W. Phillips found that a low rate of unemployment was associated with a high rate of inflation, whereas a high rate of unemployment was associated with a low rate of inflation. The curve tracing out this relationship is presented in Fig. 10-17 and labeled *PC*. Some economists used this relationship to support expansive economic policies which increased the rate of inflation and lowered the rate of unemployment. A debate followed regarding the stability and long-run location and shape of the Phillips curve; some economists suggested that the curve shifted over time and/or was vertical in the long run.

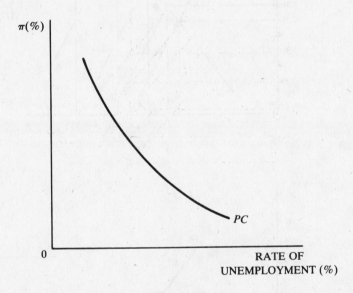

Fig. 10-17

10.5   During period 1, schedules AS_1 and AD_1 in Fig. 10-18(*a*) determine price level 2.00 and full employment output y_1. Continuous increases in aggregate demand shift AD_1 rightward in periods 2 through 5; the price level increases from 2.00 in the initial period to 2.04, 2.12, 2.25 and 2.43 in successive periods with associated output at y_e, y_2, y_3, y_4 and y_5. Output y_e through y_5 are associated with unemployment rates of 7%, 6%, 5%, 4% and 3%. (*a*) Find the rate of inflation associated with aggregate demand schedules AD_1 through AD_5 in Fig. 10-18(*a*). (*b*) What rate of unemployment is associated with each rate of inflation? Plot this association in Fig. 10-18(*b*) and label the curve *PC*. (*c*) Does aggregate supply schedule AS_1 remain stable over time?

(*a*)   Increases in the price level from 2.00 in period 1 to 2.43 in period 5 result in the following inflation rates: 2% in period 2, 4% in period 3, 6% in period 4 and 8% in period 5.

(*b*)   A zero inflation rate in period 1 is associated with output y_e and a 7% rate of unemployment; 2% inflation is associated with a 6% unemployment rate in period 2; 4% with 5% in period 3; 6% with 4% in period 4 and 8% with 3% in period 5. The data are plotted in Fig. 10-18(*b*); the Phillips curve is labeled *PC*.

(*c*)   The location of schedule AS_1 in space depends on the price level expected by labor in supplying labor services. If AS_1 is associated with a 2.00 price level, we can expect AS_1 to shift leftward during some future period. When this occurs, the Phillips curve shifts rightward; with a specific unemployment rate associated with a higher rate of inflation.

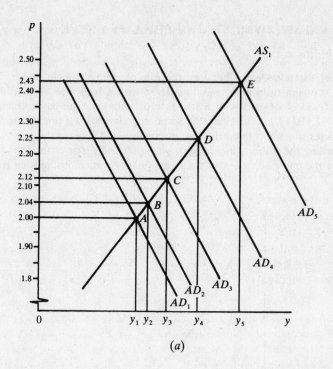

(a)

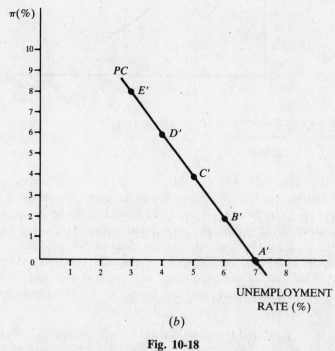

(b)

Fig. 10-18

10.6 Is there an inverse relationship between the rate of unemployment and the rate of inflation in the long run?

   The relationship of the rate of unemployment and inflation depends on labor's ability to recognize and adjust the nominal wage for changes in the price level. Recall that aggregate supply is vertical when the nominal wage adjusts immediately to changes in the price level. Under such circumstances, changes in aggregate demand have no effect on real output; there is no relationship between inflation and unemployment, and the Phillips curve is vertical at the natural rate of unemployment. However, when labor contracts and/or incorrect inflationary expectations cause the growth of the nominal wage to be greater or less than the rate of inflation, aggregate supply is positively sloped, and the Phillips curve shows an inverse relationship between inflation and unemployment rates. It is unlikely that nominal wage growth will consistently differ from inflation over long priods. Hence, the Phillips curve is vertical at the natural rate of unemployment in the long run.

SCHEDULE OF DYNAMIC AGGREGATE DEMAND

10.7 Suppose aggregate demand in period 1 is $y_1 = [hk_e/(h + kbk_e)]\bar{A} + [bk_e/h + kbk_e)]\bar{M}/p$. (*a*) Find an expression for aggregate demand in period 2 when there is a $\Delta\bar{G}$ increase in government spending, *ceteris paribus*. (*b*) Find an expression for aggregate demand in period 3 when the nominal money supply increases by $\Delta\bar{M}$, *ceteris paribus*. (*c*) Find a generalized equation for aggregate demand when there are changes in autonomous spending and/or the nominal money supply. (*d*) Why is the equation in part (*c*) an equation for dynamic aggregate demand?

(*a*) Aggregate demand in period 2 (y_2) equals the level of aggregate demand in period 1 (y_1) plus the increase in aggregate demand (Δy) due to expanded government spending. Hence, $y_2 = y_1 + [hk_e/(h + kbk_e)]\,\Delta\bar{G}$.

(*b*) Aggregate demand in period 3 (y_3) equals the level of aggregate demand in period 2 (y_2) plus the increase in aggregate demand (Δy) due to an expanded nominal money supply. Hence, $y_3 = y_2 + [bk_e/(h + kbk_e)](\Delta\bar{M}/p)$.

(*c*) A generalized equation for aggregate demand is $y = y_{-1} + \Delta y$; current period aggregate demand is the sum of aggregate demand in the previous period plus the increase in aggregate demand due to an increase in autonomous spending and/or an increase in the nominal money supply. Hence, $y = y_{-1} + [hk_e/(h + kbk_e)](\Delta\bar{A}) + [bk_e/(h + kbk_e)](\Delta\bar{M}/p)$.

(*d*) A dynamic aggregate demand schedule represents continuous growth in the level of aggregate spending over time. Growth of the nominal money supply shifts LM and aggregate demand rightward over successive periods. Such continuous increases in aggregate demand are captured by the dynamic aggregate demand equation $y = y_{-1} + [hk_e/(h + kbk_e)(\Delta\bar{A}) + [bk_e/(h + kbk_e)](\Delta\bar{M}/p)$.

10.8 (*a*) Find an equation for dynamic aggregate demand when the sources of incremental spending are permanent increases in government spending and/or increases in the growth rate of the nominal money supply. (*b*) Let $\dot{M}$ = growth rate for the nominal money supply and π = the inflation rate. Explain why $(\dot{M} - \pi)$ can be substituted for $(\Delta\bar{M}/p)$ in the dynamic aggregate demand equation in part (*a*). (*c*) Let $\alpha = hk_e/(h + kbk_e)$ and $\beta = bk_e/(h + kbk_e)$, with the dynamic aggregate demand schedule now presented as $y = y_{-1} + \beta(\dot{M} - \pi) + \alpha(\Delta\bar{G})$. Find α and β when $h = 0$, $k_e = 5$, $b = 5$, and $k = 0.25$.

(*a*) When a permanent expansion of government spending is the only source of increased autonomous spending, and growth of the nominal money supply is the cause of a larger real money supply, the dynamic aggregate demand equation becomes $y = y_{-1} + [hk_e/(h + kbk_e)](\Delta\bar{G}) + [bk_e/(h + kbk_e)](\Delta\bar{M}/p)$.

(*b*) Changes in the real money supply depend on changes in the nominal money supply and in the price level. For example, the real money supply is unchanged when the nominal money supply increases from \$100 to \$110 and the price level increases from 1.00 to 1.10; or restated, the real money supply is unchanged when the nominal money supply and price level increase 10%. Hence, changes in the real money supply can be presented as $(\Delta\bar{M}/p)$ or as $(\dot{M} - \pi)$ where $\dot{M}$ is the growth rate of the nominal money supply and π is the inflation rate.

(c) Substituting into the equation, we find that $\alpha = 0$ and $\beta = 4$:

$$\alpha = \frac{hk_e}{h + kbk_3}$$

$$\alpha = \frac{0(5)}{0 + 0.25(5)5} = 0$$

$$\beta = \frac{bk_p}{h + kbk_e}$$

$$\beta = \frac{5(5)}{0 + 0.25(5)5} = 4$$

10.9 The equation for dynamic aggregate demand is $y = y_{-1} + \beta(\dot{M} - \pi) + \alpha(\Delta\bar{G})$. Suppose $y_{-1} = \$800$, $\alpha = 2$, $\beta = 3$, $\dot{M} = 9\%$ and $\Delta\bar{G} = \$5$. (a) Find the level of aggregate demand when the inflation rate is 7%, 5% or 3%. Plot and label the schedule DAD in Fig. 10-19. (b) Find the level of aggregate demand when $\dot{M} = 9\%$ but $\Delta\bar{G} = \$10$ and the inflation rate is 7%, 5% and 3%. Plot and label the schedule DAD' in Fig. 10-19. (c) Find the level of aggregate demand when $\Delta\bar{G} = \$5$ but $\dot{M} = 5\%$ and the inflation rate is 7%, 5% and 3%. Plot and label the schedule DAD'' in Fig. 10-19. (d) What happens to the dynamic aggregate demand schedule when there is a permanent increase in government spending [part (a) compared with part (b)] or a decrease in the growth rate of the nominal money supply [part (a) compared with part (c)]? (e) Are the shifts in dynamic aggregate demand due to changes in $\bar{G}$ and/or $\bar{M}$, sustained over time?

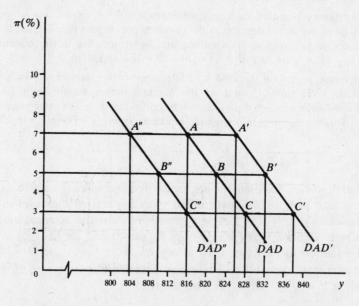

Fig. 10-19

(a) The level of aggregate demand is \$816 when $\pi = 7\%$:

$$y = y_{-1} + \beta(\dot{M} - \pi) + \alpha(\Delta\bar{G})$$
$$y = \$800 + 3(9 - 7) + 2(5) = \$816$$

The level of aggregate demand is \$822 when $\pi = 5\%$; it is \$828 when the inflation rate is 3%. The data are plotted and the schedule is labeled DAD in Fig. 10-19.

(b) The level of aggregate demand is \$826 when the inflation rate is 7%, $\Delta \bar{G} = \$10$ and $\dot{M} = 9\%$; aggregate demand is \$832 when $\pi = 5\%$ and \$838 when $\pi = 3\%$. The data are plotted and the schedule is labeled DAD' in Fig. 10-19.

(c) The level of aggregate demand is \$804 when $\pi = 7\%$, $\dot{M} = 5\%$ and $\Delta \bar{G} = \$5$; it is \$810 when $\pi = 5\%$ and \$816 when $\pi = 3\%$. The data are plotted and the schedule is labeled DAD'' in Fig. 10-19.

(d) An increase in the level of government spending shifts the dynamic aggregate demand schedule rightward. A decrease in the growth rate of the nominal supply shifts the dynamic aggregate demand schedule leftward.

(e) An increase in the level of government spending causes a one-period upward shift of DAD. For the shift to be sustained, government spending must continue to increase in successive periods. An increase in the growth rate of the nominal money supply results in a permanent shift of the dynamic aggregate demand schedule. Nominal money supply expansion is continuous in successive periods when there is an increase in its growth rate.

10.10 The equation for dynamic aggregate demand is $y = y_{-1} + \beta(\dot{M} - \pi) + \alpha(\Delta \bar{G})$. Suppose $\alpha = 2$, $\beta = 3$, $\dot{M} = 9\%$ and $\Delta \bar{G} = \$5$. (a) Find the level of aggregate demand when the inflation rate is 3%, 5% and 7% and previous period output is \$800, \$830 or \$710. Plot the data in Fig. 10-20 and label the schedule DAD when $y_{-1} = \$800$, DAD' when $y_{-1} = \$830$, and DAD'' when $y_{-1} = \$710$. (b) What happens to the dynamic aggregate demand schedule when there is a higher or lower level of aggregate demand in the previous period?

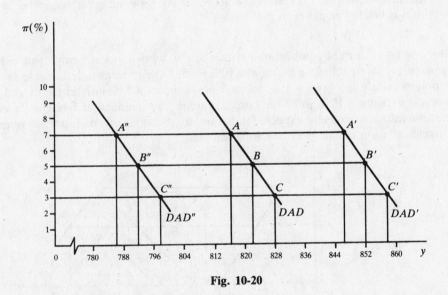

Fig. 10-20

(a) When previous period output is \$800 and $\pi = 3\%$, the level of aggregate demand is \$828; it is \$822 when $\pi = 5\%$ and \$816 when $\pi = 7\%$. The data are plotted in Fig. 10-20; the schedule is labeled DAD. When previous period output is \$830 and $\pi = 3\%$, the level of aggregate demand is \$858; it is \$852 when $\pi = 5\%$ and \$846 when $\pi = 7\%$. The data are plotted in Fig. 10-20; the schedule is labeled DAD'. The level of aggregate demand is \$798 when previous period output is \$770 and $\pi = 3\%$. It is \$792 when $\pi = 5\%$ and \$786 when $\pi = 7\%$. The data are plotted in Fig. 10-20; the schedule is labeled DAD''.

(b) The dynamic aggregate demand schedule shifts rightward when previous period output is higher and leftward when previous period output is lower.

SCHEDULE OF DYNAMIC AGGREGATE SUPPLY

10.11 (*a*) Explain the difference beftween the functions $W = f(p)$, the nominal wage as a function of the price level, and $gW = f(\pi)$, the growth of the nominal wage is a function of the inflation rate. (*b*) What is the difference between an aggregate supply and a dynamic aggregate supply schedule?

(*a*)   The function $W = f(p)$ ties the nominal wage to the price level; hence, the nominal wage increases 5% when the price level increases 5%. In the function $gW = f(\pi)$, we move from one-time changes in the price level to continuous changes. Labor asks for continuous increases in the nominal wage because of inflation.

(*b*)   An aggregate supply schedule is derived from a labor supply function which links the nominal wage to the price level. Price-level changes are continuous for a dynamic aggregate supply schedule where labor's demand for nominal wage growth is tied to inflationary expectations.

10.12 (*a*) Explain the function $\pi^e = f(\pi_{-1})$. (*b*) Are labor markets in equilibrium when $gW = f(\pi^e)$, $\pi^e = f(\pi_{-1})$, and the current inflation rate differs from the previous period's inflation rate?

(*a*)   The function $\pi^e = f(\pi_{-1})$ is an adaptive approach to inflationary expectations; it specifies that inflation is expected to continue at the rate which existed in the previous period.

(*b*) $gW = f(\pi^e)$ specifies that labor's demand for growth in the nominal wage is a function of the expected rate of inflation. When $\pi^e = f(\pi_{-1})$, $gW = f(\pi_{-1})$. Hence, the labor markets are not in equilibrium when current period inflation differs from the inflation rate in the previous period. When $\pi > \pi_{-1}$, the real wage is below the equilibrium real wage, and output exceeds full employment output. The real wage is above the market-clearing real wage when $\pi < \pi_{-1}$; output is then below full employment output.

10.13 Suppose labor market equilibrium exists when N_e labor units are employed in Fig. 10-21. The demand for labor schedule is $N_d(\pi = 10\%)$ when the current inflation rate is 10%; the labor supply schedule is $N_s(\pi^e = 5\%)$ when labor expects a 5% inflation rate and $N_s(\pi^e = 10\%)$ when it expects a 10% inflation rate. Compare the quantity of labor units employed when current inflation exceeds expected inflation to the quantity of labor units employed when current inflation equals expected inflation.

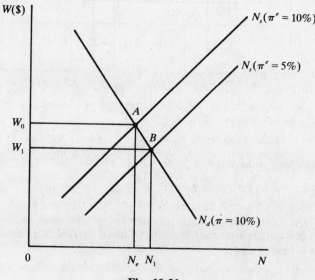

Fig. 10-21

N_1 labor units are employed for schedules $N_d(\pi = 10\%)$ and $N_s(\pi^e = 5\%)$; N_e labor units are employed for schedules $N_d(\pi = 10\%)$ and $N_s(\pi^e = 10\%)$. The labor markets are in equilibrium when the expected inflation rate is the same as the current inflation rate. When labor's inflationary expectations are below the current inflation rate, the labor markets are in disequilibrium; employment exceeds the market-clearing full employment level.

10.14 The equation for dynamic aggregate supply is $\pi = \pi^e + \lambda(y - y_e)$. Suppose $y_e = \$200$ and $\lambda = 0.50$. (a) Find y when π^e is 6% and the current inflation rate is 4%, 6% or 8%. Plot the dynamic aggregate supply schedule in Fig. 10-22 and label it $DAS(\pi^e = 6\%)$. (b) Compare the level of aggregate supply to the \$200 full employment level of output when $\pi^e > \pi$ and $\pi^e < \pi$. (c) Find y when $\pi^e = 4\%$ and the current inflation rate is 4%, 6% and 8%. Plot the dynamic aggregate supply schedule in Fig. 10-22 and label it $DAS(\pi^e = 4\%)$. (d) What happens to the dynamic aggregate supply schedule when inflationary expectations decline from 6% to 4%? (e) When $\pi^e = f(\pi_{-1})$, what happens to the DAS schedule in the next period when current inflation differs from inflation in the previous period?

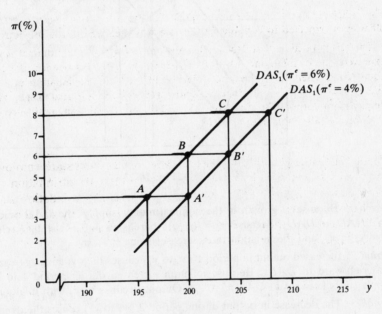

Fig. 10-22

(a) When π^e is 6% and $\pi = 4\%$, y is \$196. $[4\% = 6\% + 0.5(y - \$200); \ y = \$196]$ y is \$200 when $\pi = 6\%$; $y = \$204$ when $\pi = 8\%$. The association of inflation and output is plotted in Fig. 10-22 with the schedule labeled $DAS(\pi^e = 6\%)$.

(b) When $\pi^e > \pi$, the \$196 level of aggregate supply is less than the \$200 full employment level. Aggregate supply is at the \$200 full employment level when $\pi^e = \pi$ and exceeds the full employment level when $\pi^e < \pi$.

(c) When π^e is 4% and $\pi = 4\%$, y equals \$200; y is \$204 when $\pi = 6\%$ and equals \$208 when $\pi = 8\%$. The association of inflation and output are plotted in Fig. 10-22 with the schedule labeled $DAS(\pi^e = 4\%)$.

(d) The dynamic aggregate supply schedule shifts rightward from $DAS(\pi^e = 6\%)$ to $DAS(\pi^e = 4\%)$ when inflationary expectations decline from 6 to 4%.

(e) When $\pi^e = \pi_{-1}$, the DAS schedule shifts leftward in the next period if $\pi > \pi_{-1}$. DAS shifts to the right in the next period when current inflation is less than the inflation rate in the previous period.

INFLATION AND EQUILIBRIUM OUTPUT

10.15 Output is at the full employment level y_e during period 0 for schedules DAD_0 and $DAS(\pi^e = \pi_0)$ in Fig. 10-23. During period 1, the nominal money supply increases $X\%$. What happens to the DAD and DAS schedules during periods 1, 2 and 3? Find output and inflation at the end of periods 1, 2 and 3.

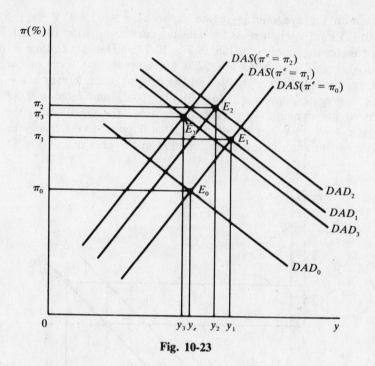

Fig. 10-23

Period 1: Because of growth in the nominal money supply, the DAD schedule shifts to the right from DAD_0 to DAD_1. Because $\pi^e = f(\pi_{-1})$, there is no shift of the DAS schedule. Output expands from y_e to y_1, and the inflation rate increases from π_0 to π_1.

Period 2: Increased output in period 1 (y_e to y_1) causes the dynamic aggregate demand schedule to shift rightward to DAD_2. Because inflation increased during period 1 to π_1, dynamic aggregate supply shifts leftward to $DAS(\pi^e = \pi_1)$. Output declines to y_2 with inflation increasing to π_2.

Period 3: The decrease in output during period 2 (y_1 to y_2) causes the dynamic aggregate demand schedule to shift leftward to DAD_3. DAS shifts leftward to $DAS(\pi^e = \pi_2)$ due to increased inflation during period 2. Output falls to y_3 with inflation declining to π_3.

10.16 The equations for dynamic aggregate demand and dynamic aggregate supply are $y = y_{-1} + \beta(\dot{M} - \pi) + \alpha f$ and $\pi = \pi^e + \lambda(y - y_e)$, respectively. The economy is initially at the \$500 full employment level, the inflation rate is 4%, $\beta = 3$, $\alpha = 2$, $f = 0$, and $\lambda = 0.5$. Suppose the growth rate of the nominal money supply increases from 4 to 10%, *ceteris paribus*. (*a*) Find the inflation rate and output level for periods 1 through 6 which result from more rapid growth of the nominal money supply. (*b*) Plot the output levels and inflation rates found in part (*a*) in Fig. 10-24. (*c*) What is the rate of inflation when the economy eventually returns to full employment output?

(*a*) *Period 1*:

$$y = y_{-1} + \beta(\dot{M} - \pi) + \alpha f \qquad (DAD \text{ equation})$$
$$y = \$500 + 3(10 - \pi) + 0$$

(*b*) See Fig. 10-24.

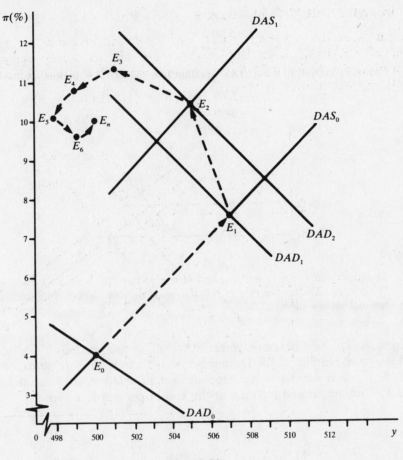

Fig. 10-24

$$\pi = \pi^e + \lambda(y - y_e) \qquad \text{(DAS equation)}$$
$$\pi = 4 + 0.5(y - \$500)$$

Substituting the DAS equation into the DAD equation, we have

$$y = \$500 + 3(10) - 3[4 + 0.5(y - \$500)]$$
$$y = \$500 + 30 - 12 - 1.5y + \$750$$
$$y = \$507.20$$
$$\pi = 7.60\%$$

Period 2:

$$y = y_{-1} + \beta(\dot{M} - \pi) + \alpha f \qquad \text{(DAD equation)}$$
$$y = \$507.20 + 3(10 - \pi) + 0$$
$$\pi = \pi^e + \lambda(y - y_e) \qquad \text{(DAS equation)}$$
$$\pi = 7.60 + 0.5(y - \$500)$$

Substituting the DAS equation into the DAD equation, we have

$$y = \$507.20 + 3(10) - 3[7.6 + 0.5(y - \$500)]$$
$$y = \$505.76$$
$$\pi = 10.48\%$$

Period 3: Substituting the DAS equation into the DAD equation, we have

$$y = \$505.76 + 3(10) - 3[10.48 + 0.5(y - \$500)]$$
$$y = \$501.73$$
$$\pi = 11.345\%$$

Period 4: Substituting the *DAS* equation into the *DAD* equation, we have

$$y = \$501.73 + 3(10) - 3[11.345 + 0.5(y - \$500)]$$
$$y = \$499.08$$
$$\pi = 10.88\%$$

Period 5:

$$y = \$498.58$$
$$\pi = 10.17\%$$

Period 6:

$$y = \$499.23$$
$$\pi = 9.79\%$$

(c)   At equilibrium $y = y_{-1}$, $\pi = \pi_{-1}$ and $\dot{M} = \pi$ so that there are no further shifts of *DAD* or *DAS*. Thus, at equilibrium the rate of inflation must be 10%, which is the increased growth rate of the nominal money supply.

10.17   Output is at the full employment level y_e during period 0 for schedules DAD_0 and $DAS(\pi^e = \pi_0)$ in Fig. 10-25. During period 1, there is an increase in the level of government spending, *ceteris paribus*. What happens to the *DAD* and *DAS* schedules during periods 1, 2 and 3? Find output and inflation at the end of periods 1, 2 and 3.

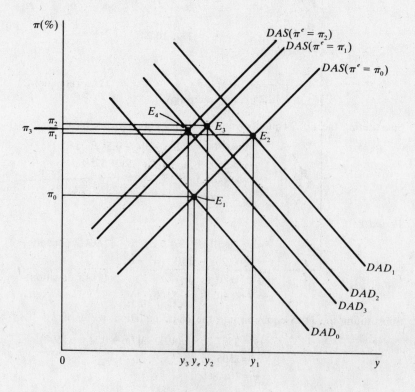

Fig. 10-25

Period 1: The *DAD* schedule shifts rightward to DAD_1. There is no shift of *DAS*, since inflationary expectations are based on the inflation rate in period 0. Output expands from y_e to y_1, and the inflation rate increases from π_0 to π_1 by the end of period 1.

Period 2: The leftward shift of DAD_1 to DAD_2 is the net result of no further additions to the level of government spending in period 2 (a negative influence on further demand growth) and the y_e to y_1 increase in output in period 1 (a positive factor expanding demand growth). *DAS* shifts leftward to $DAS(\pi^e = \pi_1)$. As a result of the leftward shift of *DAD* and *DAS*, output and inflation are y_2 and π_2 by the end of period 2.

Period 3: Dynamic aggregate demand schedule shifts leftward to DAD_3 due to decline in output between period 1 and 2. Dynamic aggregate supply shifts leftward to $DAS(\pi^e = \pi_2)$ due to the increase in inflation during the previous period. Output and inflation fall to y_3 and π_3 by the end of period 3.

10.18 The equation for *DAD* and *DAS* is $y = y_{-1} + \beta(\dot{M} - \pi) + \alpha f$ and $\pi = \pi^e + \lambda(y - y_e)$, respectively. The economy is initially at the \$500 full employment level, the inflation rate is 4%, nominal money supply growth is 4%, $\beta = 3$, $\alpha = 2$, and $\lambda = 0.5$. Suppose there is a \$10 increase in the level of government spending, *ceteris paribus*. (*a*) Find the inflation rate and output level for periods 1 through 4 which result from the \$10 fiscal expansion. (*b*) Plot the output levels and inflation rates found in part (*a*) in Fig. 10-26. (*c*) What is the rate of inflation when the economy returns to the \$500 full employment level?

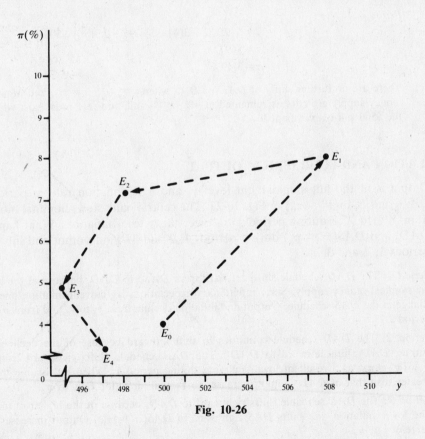

Fig. 10-26

(*a*) *Period 1*:

$$y = y_{-1} + \beta(\dot{M} - \pi) + \alpha f \qquad (DAD \text{ equation})$$
$$y = \$500 + 3(4 - \pi) + 2(10)$$
$$\pi = \pi^e + \lambda(y - y_e) \qquad (DAS \text{ equation})$$
$$\pi = 4 + 0.5(y - \$500)$$

Substituting the DAS equation into the DAD equation, we have

$$y = \$500 + 3(4) - 3[4 + 0.5(y - \$500)] + 2(10)$$
$$y = \$508$$
$$\pi = 8\%$$

Period 2:

$$y = \$508 + 3(4 - \pi) + 0 \qquad (DAD \text{ equation})$$
$$\pi = 8 + 0.5(y - \$500) \qquad (DAS \text{ equation})$$

(*b*)   See Fig. 10-26.

Substituting the DAS equation into the DAD equation, we have

$$y = \$508 + 3(4) - 3[8 + 0.5(y - \$500)] + 0$$
$$y = \$498.40$$
$$\pi = 7.20\%$$

Period 3:

$$y = \$498.40 + 3(4) - 3[7.20 + 0.5(y - \$500)]$$
$$y = \$495.52$$
$$\pi = 4.96\%$$

Period 4:

$$y = \$495.52 + 3(4) - 3[4.96 + 0.5(y - \$500)]$$
$$y = \$497.06$$
$$\pi = 3.49\%$$

(*c*)   There are no further shifts of DAD or DAS when $y = y_{-1}$, $\pi = \pi_{-1}$ and $\dot{M} = \pi$. Because nominal money supply growth has remained at 4%, a 4% inflation rate must exist when output returns to the $500 full employment level.

DISINFLATION AND EQUILIBRIUM OUTPUT

10.19 Output is at the full employment level y_e and a π_0 inflation rate in period 0 for schedules DAD_0 and $DAS(\pi^e = \pi_0)$ in Fig. 10-27. The central bank slows nominal money supply growth from $Y\%$ to $X\%$ during period 1 to lower the rate of inflation. What happens to schedules DAD_0 and $DAS(\pi^e = \pi_0)$ during periods 1, 2 and 3? Find output and inflation at the end of periods 1, 2 and 3.

Period 1: The DAD schedule shifts leftward from DAD_0 to DAD_1 because of the lower growth rate of the nominal money supply. Since inflationary expectations lag current inflation one period, there is no change in the DAS schedule. Output and inflation decline from y_e to y_1 and from π_0 to π_1 by the end of period 1.

Period 2: The DAD schedule continues to shift leftward because of the decline in previous period output; DAD shifts leftward to DAD_2. The DAS schedule shifts rightward from $DAS(\pi^e = \pi_0)$ to $DAS(\pi^e = \pi_1)$ as a result of lower inflation during period 1. When we assume that the DAS shift is greater than that of DAD, output increases to y_2 while inflation falls to π_2.

Period 3: The DAD schedule shifts rightward to DAD_3 because of the higher output level in period 2. The lower inflation rate shifts DAS rightward to $DAS(\pi^e = \pi_2)$. Output increases to y_3 and inflation decreases to π_3.

10.20 The equation for dynamic aggregate demand and dynamic aggregate supply are $y = y_{-1} + \beta(\dot{M} - \pi) + \alpha f$ and $\pi = \pi^e + \lambda(y - y_e)$, respectively. The inflation rate is 10%, full employment output is $1000, nominal money supply growth is 10%, $\beta = 3$, $\alpha = 2$, $f = 0$ and $\lambda = 0.5$.

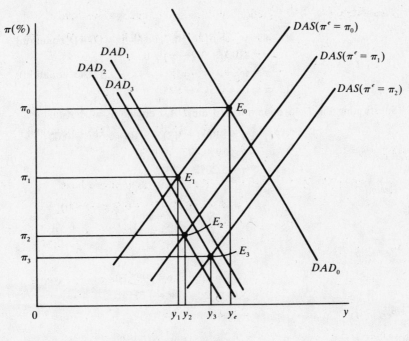

Fig. 10-27

The central bank reduces nominal money supply growth from 10 to 2% during period 1 to reduce inflation. (a) Find inflation and output at the end of periods 1 through 5 which result from a slower growth rate for the nominal money supply. (b) Plot the output and inflation rates found in part (a) in Fig. 10-28.

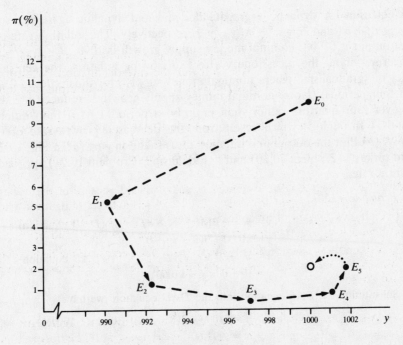

Fig. 10-28

(a) Period 1:

$$y = y_{-1} + \beta(\dot{M} - \pi) + \alpha f \qquad (DAD \text{ equation})$$
$$y = \$1000 + 3(2 - \pi) + 0$$
$$\pi = \pi^e + \lambda(y - y_e) \qquad (DAS \text{ equation})$$
$$\pi = 10 + 0.5(y - 1000)$$

Substituting the DAS equation into the DAD equation, we have

$$y = \$1000 + 3(2) - 3[10 + 0.5(y - 1000)]$$
$$y = \$990.40$$
$$\pi = 5.20\%$$

Period 2:

$$y = \$992.32$$
$$\pi = 1.36\%$$

Period 3:

$$y = \$997.70$$
$$\pi = 0.21\%$$

Period 4:

$$y = \$1001.23$$
$$\pi = 0.83\%$$

Period 5:

$$y = \$1001.90$$
$$\pi = 1.78\%$$

(b) See Fig. 10-28.

10.21 The equation for dynamic aggregate demand and dynamic aggregate supply are $y = y_{-1} + \beta(\dot{M} - \pi) + \alpha f$ and $\pi = \pi^e + \lambda(y - y_e)$, respectively. The inflation rate is 10%, full employment output is $1000, nominal money supply growth is 10%, $\beta = 3$, $\alpha = 2$, $f = 0$ and $\lambda = 0.5$. Concerned about the recessionary effect of slowing inflation, the central bank introduces a policy of "gradualism" where nominal money supply growth is reduced 2% during each of the next four periods. (Note: nominal money supply growth is reduced 8% as in Problem 10.20, but over four quarters rather than entirely in period 1.) (a) Find inflation and output for periods 1 through 5, which result from the decreased growth rate of the nominal money supply. (b) Plot the output and inflation rates found in part (a) in Fig. 10-29. (c) Compare the "cold turkey" (Problem 10.20) and "gradualism" (Problem 10.21) approaches to reducing the inflation rate.

(a) Period 1:

$$y = y_{-1} + \beta(\dot{M} - \pi) + \alpha f \qquad (DAD \text{ equation})$$
$$y = \$1000 + 3(8 - \pi) + 0$$
$$\pi = \pi^e + \lambda(y - y_e) \qquad (DAD \text{ equation})$$
$$\pi = 10 + 0.5(y - \$1000)$$

Substituting the DAS equation into the DAD equation, we have

$$y = \$1000 + 3(8) - 3[10 - 0.5(y - 1000)]$$
$$y = \$997.60$$
$$\pi = 8.80\%$$

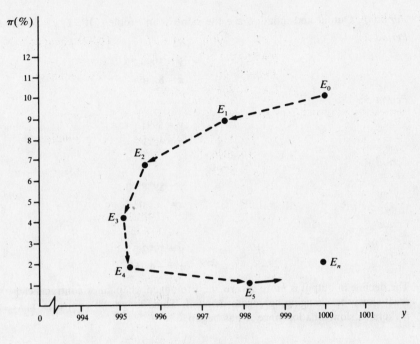

Fig. 10-29

Period 2: Substituting the *DAS* equation into the *DAD* equation, we have

$$y = \$997.60 + 3(6) - 3[8.80 + 0.5(y - 1000)]$$
$$y = \$995.68$$
$$\pi = 6.64\%$$

Period 3:

$$y = \$995.10$$
$$\pi = 4.19\%$$

Period 4:

$$y = \$995.41$$
$$\pi = 1.89\%$$

Period 5:

$$y = \$998.29$$
$$\pi = 1.04\%$$

(*b*) See Fig. 10-29.

(*c*) When nominal money growth is reduced 8% in one period (Problem 10.20), output and inflation experience a dramatic decline during the first two periods; by the third period output is rapidly approaching full employment output. The decline in output with the gradualism approach is less severe; however, output remains below full employment for more periods. The issue facing policy makers is to choose a sharp recession followed by rapid recovery or a mild but prolonged recession.

10.22 Suppose $\pi^e = f(\pi_{-2})$, inflationary expectations lag actual inflation by two periods because of labor contracts. (*a*) Use the parameters of Problem 10.21 but the specified, longer lag structure to find output and inflation for periods 1 through 5. (*b*) What effect does a longer lag structure have upon the adjustment path?

(a) *Period 1*: Output and inflation are the same as in Problem 10.21; $y = \$997.60$ and $\pi = 8.80\%$.

Period 2:

$$y = \$994.25$$
$$\pi = 8.56\%$$

Period 3:

$$y = \$991.94$$
$$\pi = 4.53\%$$

Period 4:

$$y = \$988.90$$
$$\pi = -1.02\%$$

Period 5:

$$y = \$992.52$$
$$\pi = -4.76\%$$

(b) The decline in output is more severe and prolonged when labor contracts cause aggregate supply to react slowly to changing aggregate demand. Thus, long-term contracts make it difficult for policy makers to slow inflation once it has begun.

Chapter 11

The Supply of and Demand for Money

This chapter investigates the factors which determine the supply of and demand for money ($M1$ definition). The $M1$ nominal money supply is determined by the Federal Reserve's creation of high-powered money, the reserve requirement on deposit balances and the private sector's preference for liquid assets. Those who hold money are assumed to be free of money illusion (money is held because of its purchasing power); their reasons for holding money balances include a transactions, a precautionary, and a portfolio demand for money.

11.1 THE FUNCTIONS OF MONEY

Money serves the following functions: medium of exchange, unit of account, standard of deferred payment, and store of value. As a medium of exchange, money facilitates the allocation of economic resources and the exchange of goods and services. For example, labor works for a money wage and then use money balances to purchase goods and services. The unit of account function provides a system of measurement; in the United States, units are measured in dollars and cents, which are specified as prices, revenues, costs and incomes. As a standard of deferred payment, wealth is loaned with repayment specified in dollars, the unit of account. Debt instruments are therefore dollar-denominated, i.e., the debt instrument specifies the dollar sum payable in the future. Money is a liquid store of value which allows its holder to postpone expenditures.

11.2 DEFINITIONS OF MONEY

In the United States, several financial instruments fulfill one or more of the functions of money. Currently, the Federal Reserve compiles and reports weekly $M1$, $M2$ and $M3$ measures of money. $M1$ is a transactions definition which includes currency outside banks, checking [demand deposits, negotiable orders of withdrawal (NOW), automatic transfer service (ATS), and credit union share draft (CUSD)] accounts, and travelers checks. $M2$ includes $M1$ and other accounts which are store of value substitutes for $M1$ balances but cannot be used for transactions. $M2$ adds to $M1$ small-denomination time deposits, money market deposit accounts, overnight repurchase agreements (RPs) at commercial banks, overnight Eurodollars held by U.S. residents, and noninstitution money market mutual fund balances. $M3$ includes store-of-value substitutes for $M1$ balances which are primarily owned by the business sector; $M3$ consists of $M2$ plus large-denomination time deposits, term RPs at deposit institutions, term Eurodollars held by U.S. residents and institution-only money market mutual funds.

EXAMPLE 1. Table 11-1 gives the components of the various money supply measures. The currency total excludes the amount of currency held by the Treasury, Federal Reserve Banks, and commercial banks. The demand deposit total does not include demand deposits held by the United States government and foreign banks and official institutions at commercial banks or interbank demand deposits. Other checkable deposits consist of ATS and NOW account balances, CUSD balances, and demand deposits at mutual savings banks. Small-denomination time deposits are time deposits which are less than $100,000.

11.3 CREATION AND CONTROL OF THE $M1$ MONEY SUPPLY

The $M1$ money supply is the product of the monetary base B (also called high-powered money) and an $m1$ money multiplier, or $M1 = m1B$. The monetary base consists of currency outside banks

Table 11-1　Money Stock Measures
August 1989
(In Billion Dollars)

M1		777.8
Currency	219.3	
Traveler's checks of nonbank issuers	8.1	
Demand deposits adjusted	276.8	
Other checkable deposits	273.6	
M2		3,137.5
M1	777.8	
Money market deposit accounts	465.4	
Savings deposits	405.0	
Small-denomination time deposits	1,128.8	
Overnight RPs and Eurodollars	74.9	
Noninstitution money market funds	285.5	
M3		4,011.2
M2	3,137.5	
Large-denomination time deposits	568.7	
Term RPs and Eurodollars	204.4	
Institution-only money market funds	100.6	

Source: *Federal Reserve Bulletin*, July 1986.

plus reserves (currency in vault plus deposits at Federal Reserve Banks) held by depository institutions. The Federal Reserve exerts control over the $M1$ money supply by changing the monetary base through open market operations. Federal Reserve purchases of government securities in the open market increase B, and sales decrease B, *ceteris paribus*. [It should be noted that other factors can affect B: B increases when the Fed purchases any asset; B decreases when Fed liabilities increase. (See Problem 11.9)] When additions to the monetary base are held by depository institutions, there is a multiple increase in transaction accounts, and the $M1$ money supply increases as these institutions expand loans and create check-writing deposits. (See Example 2.) When additions to the monetary base are held by households, expansion of the $M1$ money supply equals the increase in the monetary base (Example 3). The effect on $M1$ of an increase in the monetary base depends on the amount of the base held as reserves by depository institutions and as currency by the nonbank private sector. The relationship between B and $M1$ is presented by the formula $M1 = m1B$. $m1$ is the money multiplier and equals $[(1 + k)/(k + r_D + tr_T + e)]$; k is the currency ratio, the ratio of currency preferences C relative to checking deposits D; r_D is the reserve requirement on checking deposits; t is the ratio of large time deposits T to checking deposits D; r_T is the reserve requirement on large time deposits; and e is the excess reserve ratio, the quantity of excess reserves E held by depository institutions relative to checking deposits D.

EXAMPLE 2.　When Federal Reserve Banks purchase Treasury securities valued at $100,000 from the commercial banking system, the following changes occur on the balance sheets of these institutions:

Federal Reserve Banks

Δ Assets			Δ Liabilities
Treasury securities	+$100,000	Deposits of depository institutions	+$100,000

Commercial Banking System

Δ Assets			Δ Liabilities
Treasury securities	−$100,000		
Deposits at Fed	+$100,000		

The commercial banking system's reserves have increased $100,000 (it now holds excess reserves), since deposit liabilities have not changed, but its earning assets have decreased by an equal amount since the Fed pays no interest on deposits. The banking system can reduce excess reserves by lending and creating checking deposits. (We shall assume a 10% reserve requirement on checking deposits.) If the banking system lends until excess reserves equal zero, checking deposits D will expand by an amount equal to the banking system's holding of excess reserves E divided by the reserve requirement on checking deposits r_D, i.e., $\Delta D = \Delta E/r_D$, assuming no currency outflows and no change in other reserve requiring deposits. Loans and checking deposits thereby increase by $1 million: $\Delta D = \Delta E/r_D$; $1 million = $100,000/0.10. The Federal Reserve's purchase of $100,000 in Treasury securities from the commercial banking system expands the $M1$ money supply $1 million.

EXAMPLE 3. Suppose Federal Reserve Banks purchase Treasury securities valued at $100,000 in the open market; at the same time, households decrease their holding of Treasury securities by $100,000 and increase their currency holdings by $100,000. These transactions have the following net effect upon the balance sheets of households and Federal Reserve Banks:

Federal Reserve Banks

Δ Assets			Δ Liabilities
Treasury securities	+$100,000	Federal Reserve notes	+$100,000

Households

Δ Assets		Δ Liabilities
Treasury securities	−$100,000	
Currency (Federal Reserve notes)	+$100,000	

Because the expanded monetary base is held by households and not by the banking system, there is no check deposit expansion. The $M1$ money supply increases $100,000.

EXAMPLE 4. Suppose $r_D = 0.10$; $r_T = 0.05$; $B = \$200,000$; currency held outside banks is $100,000; reserves held by the banking system is $100,000. Checking deposits equal $500,000 when banks wish to hold excess reserves of $25,000 and large-denomination time deposits are $500,000. (Banks reserve holdings are allocated as follows: $50,000 to support checking deposits, $25,000 to support large-denomination time deposits and $25,000 held as excess reserves.) The $M1$ money supply is $600,000, the sum of currency outside banks ($100,000) plus checking deposits ($500,000). Should banks elect to hold no excess reserves, *ceteris paribus*, checking deposits would then total $750,000 and the $M1$ money supply would equal $850,000

EXAMPLE 5. Suppose the monetary base is $200,000, $r_D = 0.10$, $r_T = 0.05$, $k = 0.20$, $t = 1.0$, and $e = 0.05$. The $m1$ money multiplier is $(1 + k)/(k + r_D + tr_T + e)$; $(1 + 0.20)/(0.20 + 0.10 + 1(0.05) + 0.05 = 3$. The $M1$ money supply is $600,000: $M1 = m1B$; $600,000 = 3(\$200,000)$. An increase in k, t, r_D, r_T and/or e reduces $m1$. Thus, $M1$ depends on the quantity of B supplied by the Fed, and the demand for B, represented by the currency, time deposit and excess reserve preferences of the private sector and the checking deposit and time deposit requirement set by the Federal Reserve.

11.4 THE QUANTITY THEORY OF MONEY

Monetary theorists have used the equation of exchange $MV = py$ to theorize about the long-run determinants of the price level. In the pre-Keynesian (pre-1930s) period, y was believed to tend in the long run toward its full employment level; V was assumed to be relatively stable over periods of time, influenced by factors such as population density, physical means of transporting money, spending habits and the payments mechanism. With y at full employment and V stable, nominal money supply changes would have a direct proportional effect on the price level. (Recall this is the conclusion reached in Sections 6.3 and 9.3, when *LM* and aggregate supply are vertical.] The behavior of velocity became pivotal to the effect of changes in the nominal money supply. In the Cambridge *k* version of the equation of exchange, rewritten as $M/p = (1/V)y$ or $M/p = k(y)$, the focus is upon *k*, the proportion of real output held as a real money balance. Keynes postulated that *k* was variable determined by a transaction, precautionary and speculative demand for money.

EXAMPLE 6. Suppose the nominal money supply is $20 billion, the general price level is 2.00, real income is $100 billion, and the private sector wishes to hold 10% of its real income in cash balances. The private sector holds a $10 billion real balance [0.10($100 billion)] which equals the $10 billion real money supply [($20 billion)/2.00]. Suppose the nominal money supply is increased from $20 to $40 billion. Assuming no change in the price level, the private sector now holds real balances of $20 billion; actual *k* increases from the desired 0.10 level to 0.20. The private sector increases spending to reduce its real balances, but prices rise because the economy is at full employment. The general price level increases until it reaches 4.00. At this level *k* is once again 0.10, and the supply of money equals the demand for money.

11.5 THE TRANSACTION DEMAND FOR MONEY

Although money expenditures by households, businesses and government are more or less continuous, money receipts tend to be periodic. Hence, idle money balances are held to meet a relatively continuous flow of expenditures. The size of these holdings is influenced by the frequency of money receipts, expenditure patterns and the rate of interest, *ceteris paribus*. Transaction balances held is found from the formula $Mt = (1/2)(Y/365)\gamma$, where *Mt* is the average money balance held for transactions, *Y* is nominal disposable income and γ is the number of days in a pay period. Example 7 shows that the average transaction (*M1* money) balance held is positively related to the length of the pay period.

When there is an opportunity cost in holding transaction balances (liquid financial assets, such as money market deposit accounts, generally yield a higher net return than transaction balances), the formula for *M1* demand is $Mt = (1/2n)(Y/365)\gamma$, where *n* is the number of transfers from a substitute liquid asset account to an *M1* transaction balance. *Mt* varies inversely with the number of transfers. Example 8 shows that, for a $14,600 annual income and a 7-day pay period, *Mt* is $70 when there is one transfer per pay period ($140 is withdrawn weekly) and $10 when there are seven withdrawals during the 7-day pay period. The optimum number of transfers depends upon revenues and costs associated with transfers. In Fig. 11-1 we assume a fixed cost *a* per transfer; total transfer costs therefore equal *an*, depicted by curve *C*. Total revenue *R* in Fig. 11-1 is given by the formula $R = i[(n-1)/2n](Y/365)\gamma$, where *i* is the annualized return on substitute liquid assets. The optimum number of transfers is n_1 (see Fig. 11-1) where net revenue *N* is at its maximum. The optimum number of transfers increases when *i*, *Y* and/or γ rises and/or *a* falls; hence the *M1* balance held

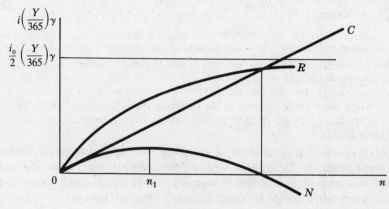

Fig. 11-1

decreases when i, Y and/or γ increases and/or a decreases. (See Example 9.) γ and a are unlikely to change in the short run; hence, the average $M1$ balance held is a function of the rate of interest and nominal income. In Fig. 11-2, the transaction demand for money appears as a family of schedules where Mt, Mt' and Mt'' represent the transaction demand for $M1$ balances at higher income levels.

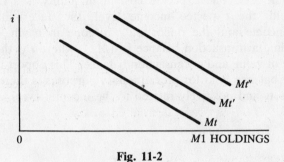

Fig. 11-2

EXAMPLE 7. Suppose a household's annual disposable income is $14,600 with income spent uniformly during the year. When the household is paid daily, the average $M1$ balance held is $20 [$Mt = (1/2)(Y/365)\gamma$; $20 = (1/2)(\$14,600/365)1$]. When paid weekly, the average $M1$ balance held is $140; when paid biweekly, it is $280.

EXAMPLE 8. Suppose a household's annual disposable income is $14,600; income is spent uniformly during the year, and the $280 weekly income is directly deposited to a savings account. When the household withdraws $280 in cash weekly from its savings account (number of transfers n is 1), the average $M1$ balance held is $140. [$Mt = (1/2n)(Y/365)\gamma$; $140 = (1/2)(\$14,600/365)7$.] However, should the household make daily cash withdrawals ($n = 7$) of $40, the average $M1$ balance held is $20. [$Mt = (1/2n)(Y/365)\gamma$; $20 = (1/14)(\$14,600/365)7$.]

EXAMPLE 9. The transaction demand for $M1$ balances is influenced by the fixed cost per transfer, the rate of interest, the level of income and the number of days in a pay period.

Situation I: When the fixed cost per transfer increases, *ceteris paribus*, the cost curve C in Fig. 11-1 pivots to the left, and there is a decrease in the optimum number of transfers. A decrease in the number of transfers results in larger transaction balances held. Hence, the transaction demand for $M1$ balances is positively related to the fixed cost per transfer.

Situation II: When the rate of interest increases, *ceteris paribus*, the revenue curve R in Fig. 11-1 shifts leftward, and there is an increase in the optimum number of transfers. A higher rate of interest reduces the quantity of transaction balances held. Thus, the transaction demand for money is negatively related to the rate of interest.

Situation III: When annual income increases, *ceteris paribus*, the revenue curve in Fig. 11-1 shifts leftward, and there is an increase in the optimum number of transfers. The effect that this has on the quantity of money demanded depends on the relative change in n and Y. From the formula for the optimum number of transfers, $n = \sqrt{(i/2a)(Y/365)}\gamma$, we find that the relative increase in n cannot exceed one-half the relative increase in income. When the relative increase in the optimum number of transfers is less than the relative increase in income, there is an increase in $M1$ balances held as income expands. The transactions demand for money is positively related to income.

Situation IV: When there is a decrease in the number of days in a pay period, *ceteris paribus*, the revenue curve in Fig. 11-1 shifts rightward, and there is a decrease in the optimum number of transfers. Since the relative change in n is always less than the relative change in γ, $M1$ balances held for transactions decrease as the number of days in a pay period falls. The transaction demand for money is positively related to the number of days in a pay period.

11.6   THE PRECAUTIONARY DEMAND FOR MONEY

A precautionary demand exists because there is uncertainty about the timing of receipt and expenditure of future income; for example, wage receipts might be delayed, sickness could require increased expenditures, and/or an unexpected profit opportunity might develop. The cost of illiquidity is greater the smaller the transaction balance held; this cost is depicted in Fig. 11-3 by negatively sloped schedule EC. The expected cost of illiquidity is a function of the quantity of transaction balances held, the expected income level, the uncertainty about the receipt and expenditure of future income and the opportunity forgone in having inadequate liquidity. The opportunity cost of holding a transaction balance is $i(M1)$, where i is the difference in the interest rate of a substitute store of value and a transaction balance. This opportunity cost is depicted in Fig. 11-3 as OC. The money balance held for precautionary purposes is thereby inversely related to the return on alternative assets and positively related to the income level, uncertainty and opportunity forgone in being illiquid.

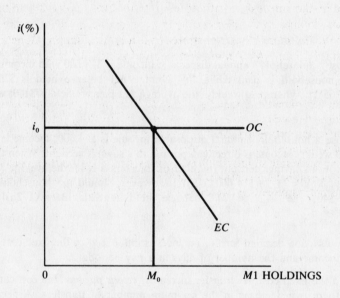

Fig. 11-3

EXAMPLE 10.   The expected cost of being illiquid and the opportunity cost of being liquid are depicted by schedules EC and OC in Fig. 11-3, where M_0 balances are held for precautionary needs. An increase in the return from substitute assets (e.g., money market deposit accounts) shifts OC upward, and the quantity of $M1$ balances held for precautionary needs decreases. An increase in expected income, uncertainty regarding the receipt and expenditure of income, and the opportunities forgone in being illiquid shift EC rightward, increasing the $M1$ money balance held for precautionary needs.

11.7   PORTFOLIO DEMAND FOR MONEY

Keynes conceived of a speculative demand for money when wealth holders have only two portfolio options: $M1$ balances and/or long-term bonds. Bonds are an imperfect store of value because there is a variable short-run return from holding a bond when there are fluctuations in the rate of interest. Money is thereby demanded to the extent that returns on a long-term bond are uncertain and investors are risk averters. Today, portfolio alternatives can be categorized as real assets, equities, long-term bonds, and liquid financial assets; $M1$ balances are a small subset of the liquid asset category. Investors' demand for liquid assets varies with the investors' aversion to risk and their perception of variability of return from nonliquid assets. However, the inclusion of $M1$ balances in a portfolio as a store of value is less likely, since substitute financial assets, included in the $M2$ and $M3$ definitions of money, are equally safe stores of value and generally provide a higher return than $M1$ balances. Hence, a portfolio demand for $M1$ balances is unlikely, and economists generally associate a portfolio demand for money with the $M1$ substitutes included in the $M2$ and $M3$ definitions of money.

11.8 MONEY SUPPLY OR INTEREST RATE MONETARY POLICY

The Federal Reserve's choice of an interest rate or money supply monetary policy depends on the stability of the IS and LM schedules. Changes in autonomous consumption, investment and net exports and changes in the interest sensitivity of private sector spending shift IS. LM shifts when there are autonomous changes in the demand for money and/or changes in the interest sensitivity of the demand for money. Example 11 demonstrates that a money supply monetary policy is called for when IS is more unstable than LM. An interest rate monetary policy is more effective in controlling the level of output when LM is less stable than IS.

EXAMPLE 11.   Equilibrium output is y_0 for schedules IS and LM in Fig. 11-4. When the LM schedule is stable, equilibrium output exists between y_2 and y_3 for shifts in commodity equilibrium between IS_1 and IS_2. Equilibrium output fluctuates between y_1 and y_4 when the Federal Reserve, in following an interest rate monetary policy, keeps the interest rate constant at i_0. In this static framework, then, a constant nominal money supply, with fluctuations in the rate of interest, has a greater stabilizing effect on equilibrium output than does one where the rate of interest is held constant. Nominal money supply targeting is called for when the goods market schedule IS is more unstable than the money market schedule LM.

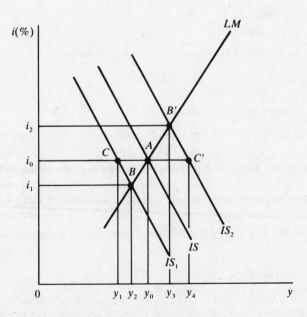

Fig. 11-4

Review Questions

1. The following functions of money are provided by a unique set of financial assets:

    (a) Medium of exchange, store of value and unit of account

    (b) Store of value, unit of account and standard of deferred value

    (c) Unit of account, standard of deferred value and medium of exchange

    (d) Standard of deferred value, medium of exchange and store of value

    Answer: (c)

2. The $M1$ definition of money is the sum of

    (a) Currency outside banks and checking deposits

    (b) Currency outside banks, checking deposits and travelers checks

    (c) Currency outstanding and checking deposits

    (d) Currency outstanding, checking deposits and money market deposit accounts

    Answer: (b)

3. The Federal Reserve controls

    (a) The monetary base through open market operations

    (b) The monetary base through reserve requirements on deposit accounts

    (c) The money multiplier through open market operations

    (d) The money multiplier through reserve requirements on deposit accounts

    Answer: (a)

4. When the reserve requirement on checking deposits is 0.10 and the Federal Reserve purchases government securities valued at $100,000, the $M1$ money supply

    (a) Is unchanged

    (b) Increases by $100,000

    (c) Increases by $1,000,000

    (d) Increases by an amount determined by the money multiplier

    Answer: (d)

5. According to the quantity theory of money,

    (a) An increase in the nominal money supply causes a proportional increase in the price level, *ceteris paribus*.

    (b) An increase in the nominal money supply causes a proportional increase in real GNP, *ceteris paribus*.

    (c) An increase in the real money supply causes a proportional increase in the price level, *ceteris paribus*.

    (d) An increase in the real money supply causes a proportional increase in real GNP, *ceteris paribus*.

    Answer: (a)

6. The average $M1$ balance held for transactions is

    (a) Negatively related to the length of the pay period and positively related to the income level

    (b) Positively related to both the length of the pay period and the income level (*c*)   Negatively related to both the length of the pay period and the income level

    (*d*)   Positively related to the length of the pay period and negatively related to the income level

Answer: (*b*)

7.   When there is an opportunity cost in holding $M1$ balances, the average $M1$ balance held is negatively related to the return on

    (*a*)   Currency, *ceteris paribus*

    (*b*)   Travelers checks, *ceteris paribus*

    (*c*)   Money market deposit accounts, *ceteris paribus*

    (*d*)   Demand deposits, *ceteris paribus*

Answer: (*c*)

8.   Which of the following statements is incorrect?

    (*a*)   The precautionary demand for money is unrelated to income.

    (*b*)   There is a precautionary demand for money because of uncertainty about the receipt of future income.

    (*c*)   The precautionary demand for money is affected by the opportunity cost of holding $M1$ balances.

    (*d*)   There is a precautionary demand for money because of unexpected expenditures.

Answer: (*a*)

9.   According to Keynes, there is a speculative demand for money because

    (*a*)   People like to speculate in the stock market.

    (*b*)   There is considerable risk in holding $M1$ balances.

    (*c*)   Money, at times, may be a better store of value than long-term bonds.

    (*d*)   Money always provides a certain, higher return than long-term bonds.

Answer: (*c*)

10.   The Federal Reserve should follow a money supply monetary policy when

    (*a*)   The *IS* schedule is negatively sloped.

    (*b*)   The *LM* schedule is largely insensitive to the rate of interest.

    (*c*)   The location of *IS* in space is more certain than that of *LM*.

    (*d*)   The location of *LM* in space is more certain than that of *IS*.

Answer: (*d*)

Solved Problems

THE FUNCTIONS OF MONEY

11.1   Explain the following functions of money: (*a*) unit of account, (*b*) medium of exchange, (*c*) standard of deferred payment.

    (*a*)   Money is a means of measuring economic phenomena. In hiring resources and exchanging goods and services, money facilitates economic decision making by serving as a common expression of value.

(b) Money allows employers to pay a money wage rather than physical goods to labor for its services. Workers use this money income to obtain goods and services of their choosing. Money's medium of exchange function results in the efficient allocation of resources; economic welfare is maximized by an efficient distribution of the resulting output.

(c) Money permits lending and borrowing with repayment specified in the unit of account. For example, a dollar-denominated debt instrument (repayment is to be made in dollars) is created when a saver lends dollars to a borrower, and the borrower promises to repay the lender a fixed sum of dollars at a future date.

11.2 (a) What is the *liquidity* of an asset? (b) What are *near monies*?

(a) The liquidity of an asset indicates the ease with which an asset can be converted to a medium of exchange without loss of nominal value. A savings account in a deposit institution is liquid since it is easily converted to a medium of exchange balance with no loss of nominal value. Although a long-term bond may be sold quickly, it is considered illiquid because the bond's market price (nominal value) depends on the market interest rate.

(b) Near monies are financial assets which cannot be used as a medium of exchange but are close substitutes for a transaction balance. The following near monies are transferable into a transaction balance with no loss of nominal value and are therefore liquid stores of value: savings deposits at deposit institutions, money market mutual funds balances, money market deposit accounts, time deposits and U.S. government savings bonds.

11.3 (a) Explain money's store-of-value function. (b) Is money the only asset which can serve as a store of value? (c) Are long-term bonds a store of value?

(a) Money allows the postponement of spending to later periods with no loss in its nominal value, i.e., money can be held for extended periods with no change in the nominal value of the sum held.

(b) Money is not a unique, liquid store of value. Other deposit accounts at deposit intermediaries also retain their nominal value over extended periods, since the deposit institution promises to repay the sum deposited.

(c) A long-term bond has a fixed nominal value like all debt contracts. However, its market value varies inversely with the current long-term rate of interest. Thus, a long-term bond is not a good store of value when funds are needed prior to the bond's maturity and the current interest rate is above the level which existed when the bond was purchased.

DEFINITIONS OF MONEY

11.4 Why is there more than one definition of money?

Money is an asset which serves as a unit of account, standard of deferred payment, medium of exchange and store of value. Focusing on the medium-of-exchange function, money consists of financial assets which can be used as a medium of exchange; $M1$ is a transactions definition of money which includes currency outside banks, checking accounts and travelers checks. Financial assets other than $M1$ balances can serve as a liquid store of value, i.e., provide the saver with liquidity. Thus, the existence of store-of-value substitutes for $M1$ balances has resulted in the Federal Reserve's publication of $M2$ and $M3$ measures of the money supply.

11.5 Federal Reserve definitions of the $M1$, $M2$ and $M3$ money supply are as follows: $M1$ is the sum of currency outside banks, checking deposits and travelers checks. $M2$ is the sum of $M1$ plus savings deposits, money market deposit accounts, small-denomination time deposits, overnight repurchase agreements and Eurodollars and noninstitution money market mutual funds. $M3$ is the sum of $M2$ plus large-denomination time deposits, term repurchase agreements and Eurodollars and institution-only money market mutual funds. From the data in Table 11-2, find $M1$, $M2$ and $M3$.

Table 11-2

(1)	Currency outside banks	$ 30
(2)	Checking accounts	262
(3)	Travelers checks	4
(4)	Savings and small-denomination time deposits	852
(5)	Overnight RPs and Eurodollars	38
(6)	Noninstitution money market mutual funds	175
(7)	Large-denomination time deposits	340
(8)	Institution-only money market mutual funds	35
(9)	Term RPs and Eurodollars	4

$$M1 = (1) + (2) + (3)$$
$$= \$30 + \$262 + \$4 = \$396$$
$$M2 = M1 + (4) + (5) + (6)$$
$$= \$396 + \$852 + \$38 + \$175 = \$1461$$
$$M3 = M2 + (7) + (8) + (9)$$
$$= M2 + \$340 + \$35 + 4 = \$1840$$

CREATION AND CONTROL OF THE $M1$ MONEY SUPPLY

11.6 Why is the banking system able to create money?

Check writing is both a convenient and safe means of payment. Transactions effected through check writing greatly exceed use of paper currency. Because of this more frequent use of check writing, a large proportion of currency is held as reserves by the banking system, and the banking system is able to create checking-writing deposits in excess of their currency holdings. The central bank limits the banking system's capacity to create checking accounts by imposing a reserve requirement on them and by controlling the quantity of reserves held by banks.

11.7 (a) What is the purpose of a reserve requirement? (b) Are all deposits subject to a reserve requirement?

(a) Reserve requirements were originally imposed to ensure convertibility of bank note liabilities (paper currency issued by banks) into gold and/or silver. Today, reserve requirements are used to control the quantity of check-writing deposits, i.e., a means of limiting the banking system's ability to create $M1$ money.

(b) The Federal Reserve imposes a reserve requirement on the following accounts: checking deposits; nonpersonal time deposits and Eurodollar liabilities of U.S. banks.

11.8 Why is the banking system willing to expand loans and create checking deposits when it has excess reserves?

A bank has excess reserves when reserve balances held exceed required reserves. Reserves are a nonearning asset. The banking system reduces excess reserves by making loans and creating reserve requiring checking deposits. When the banking system elects to hold no excess reserves, the change in the quantity of checking deposits is given by the formula $\Delta D = \Delta E/r_D$, where ΔD is the change in checking deposits, ΔE is the change in excess reserves, and r_D is the reserve requirement on checking accounts.

11.9 (a) What is the monetary base? (b) What happens to the monetary base when the Federal Reserve purchases Treasury securities in the open market, *ceteris paribus*? (c) Find the change in the $M1$ money supply when the Federal Reserve purchases $1000 in Treasury securities in the open market and the reserve requirement on checking deposits is 0.10. (*d*) Find the change in the $M1$ money supply when the Federal Reserve purchases Treasury securities valued at $1000 and households expand currency holdings by $1000?

(*a*) The monetary base consists of currency outside banks plus reserves held by the banking system (currency held by banks plus their deposits at the Fed). An alternative definition is currency in circulation plus deposits of the banking system at the Fed.

(*b*) The monetary base increases. The Fed purchases Treasury securities and pays for them by issuing currency and/or crediting the deposit account of banks at the Fed. Thus, the expanded monetary base is held as currency outside banks or as reserves by the banking system.

(*c*) As the T-account below shows, the banking system's reserves (deposits at the Fed) increase $1000. Since it now has $1000 in excess reserves, checking deposit liabilities and loans can increase $10,000. (Recall $\Delta D = \Delta E / r_D$.) The $M1$ money supply increases $10,000.

Banking System

Δ Assets			Δ Liabilities
Treasury securities	$-$1000		
Deposits at the Fed	$+$1000		
Loans	$+$10,000	Checking deposits	$+$10,000

Federal Reserve Banks

Δ Assets			Δ Liabilities
Treasury securities	$+$1000	Deposit of banks	$+$1000

(*d*) Currency outside banks has increased $1000; there is no check deposit expansion, since additions to the monetary base are held as currency outside the banking system. The $M1$ money supply increases $1000.

11.10 (*a*) What happens to the monetary base when the Federal Reserve acquires assets other than Treasury securities, *ceteris paribus*? (*b*) What happens to the monetary base when the Federal Reserve purchases gold, sells foreign exchange, lends (discounts) to banks?

(*a*) The Federal Reserve's purchase of any asset expands the monetary base, *ceteris paribus*. In the T-account below we see that purchases of Treasury securities, gold, foreign exchange, and/or other financial or real assets increase Federal Reserve note (currency) liabilities and/or deposits of banks, both components of the monetary base.

Federal Reserve Banks

Δ Assets			Δ Liabilities	
Treasury securities	$+$			
OR			Federal Reserve notes	$+$
Gold	$+$		OR	
OR			Deposits of Banks	$+$
Foreign exchange	$+$			
OR				
Other financial & real assets	$+$			

(*b*) The monetary base increases when the Federal Reserve purchases gold, decreases when it sells foreign exchange and increases when it lends at the discount window to deposit institutions.

11.11 The competing uses of the monetary base (the demand for the base) include currency held outside banks, excess reserves held by banks, reserves held by banks to meet the reserve requirement on checking deposits and reserves held by the banking system to meet the reserve requirement on nonpersonal time deposits. Derive a formula for the $M1$ money supply and the $m1$ money multiplier, given the following behavior for the demand for the monetary base:

1. The private sector's desire to hold currency C is a fraction k of checking deposits D, or $C = kD$.

2. Banks willingness to hold excess reserves E is a fraction e of checking deposits, or $E = eD$.

3. Nonpersonal time deposits T are a fixed multiple t of checking deposits or $T = tD$.

4. There is an r_D reserve requirement on checking deposits and r_T reserve requirement on nonpersonal time deposits.

The supply of the monetary base is B; from the behavior specified in items a through d, the demand for the monetary base includes currency held outside banks C, the bank's desire to hold excess reserves E, reserves required for nonpersonal time deposits R_T, and reserves required for checking deposits R_D. Thus,

$$B = C + E + R_T + R_D$$

Since $C = kD$, $E = eD$, $R_T = r_T T$, $T = tD$ and $R_D = r_D D$, the equation above can be presented as

$$B = kD + eD + r_T tD + r_D D$$

Solving for D, we have

$$D = B\left(\frac{1}{r_D + k + tr_T + e}\right)$$

which is a formula for the volume of checking deposits. By definition, $M1$ equals $C + D$. Substituting kD for C since $C = kD$, we have

$$M1 = kD + D$$
$$= D(1 + k)$$
$$= B\left(\frac{1 + k}{r_D + k + tr_T + e}\right)$$

Letting the sum in parenthesis ( ) be the $m1$ money multiplier, $m1 = (1 + k)/(r_D + k + tr_T + e)$. The $M1$ money supply is an $m1$ multiple of the monetary base. $M1 = m1B$.

11.12 (a) Find the $m1$ money multiplier and the $M1$ money supply when $B = \$200$, $t = 1.0$, $r_D = 0.10$, $r_T = 0.05$, $e = 0.05$ and $k = 0.20$. (b) Find the $m1$ money multiplier and the $M1$ money supply when $e = 0$ and $k = 0.15$.

(a)
$$m1 = \frac{1 + k}{r_D + k + tr_T + e}$$
$$= \frac{1 + 0.20}{0.10 + 0.20 + 0.05 + 0.05}$$
$$= 3$$

The $M1$ money supply is $600. $[M1 = m1B; \$600 = \$200(3)]$

(b) The $m1$ money multiplier increases to 3.83 when e declines to 0 and k is 0.15. The $M1$ money supply is then $766.

THE QUANTITY THEORY OF MONEY

11.13 (a) Explain the following variables used in the equation of exchange $MV = py$: nominal money supply M, velocity V, general price level p and real output y. (b) Why is the equation of exchange a tautology?

(a) The nominal money supply ($M1$ definition) consists of all financial assets used as media of exchange, specifically currency outside banks, checking deposits and travelers checks. Velocity is the average rate of turnover of the nominal money supply in effecting transactions. The general price level p measures the price level for final output relative to prices in a base year. Real output is the final market value of all goods and services measured in constant dollars.

(b) The equation of exchange is true by definition. MV represents the amount spent on final goods and services, and py is the nominal amount received from the sale of final output. Since, *ex post facto*, the amount spent equals the amount received, MV must always equal py.

11.14 Compare the equation of exchange with the Cambridge equation.

The Cambridge equation is $M = k(py)$, where k is the proportion of nominal income held as a cash balance. The equation of exchange and the Cambridge equation are alternative ways of expressing the relationship between the money supply and the nominal value of aggregate output. By rewriting the equation of exchange as $M = (1/V)py$, we derive the Cambridge equation with $1/V = k$. These equations differ in their focus on the use of money: "at what rate V does the private sector spend money balances?" in contrast to "what is the private sector's demand k for money balances?"

11.15 Suppose the nominal money supply is $400, the general price level is 1.00, real output is at its $2000 full employment level and k is 0.20. Why does the general price level increase to 2.00 when the nominal money supply increases to $800?

The $400 nominal money supply is willingly held (the demand for money equals the supply of money) when the nominal money supply is $400, k equals 0.20, the general price level is 1.00 and real output is $2,000. When the nominal money supply doubles to $800 and there is no change in either the price level or real output, households hold larger ($800 rather than $400) nominal balances, and k is increased to 0.40. Holding excess money balances, households increase their level of spending. Because output is at full employment, prices rise in response to the increased demand. Prices rise until the general price level is 2.00 and nominal income is $4000. At a $4000 level of nominal income, k is returned to the desired 0.20 level, and the supply of money equals the demand for money.

THE TRANSACTIONS DEMAND FOR MONEY

11.16 (a) Why is there a transaction demand for money? (b) From Table 11-3, find the average money balance held for situations (1), (2) and (3) when weekly income is $140.

(a) Money balances are held to budget expenditures over a pay period. The average money balance held depends on the timing of expenditures, the level of income and the length of the pay period γ.

(b) The average money balance held over a pay period is the sum of the average daily money balance held divided by the number of days in the pay period. Expenditures are uniform in (1), concentrated in the latter part of the week in (2) and concentrated in the earlier part of the week in (3). The average money balance held for the one-week period for situation (1) is $70, $80 for (2) and $40 for (3).

11.17 When spending is uniform over a pay period, the equation for the average $M1$ balance held during a pay period is $Mt = (1/2)(Y/365)\gamma$. (a) For the five situations in Table 11-4, find the income level for each pay period and the average money balance held during each pay period. (b) What is the relationship of Mt to Y and γ?

Table 11-3

	(1)	(2)	(3)
	Average Daily Money Balances Held		
Monday	$130	$140	$100
Tuesday	110	130	80
Wednesday	90	120	60
Thursday	70	110	30
Friday	50	40	10
Saturday	30	20	0
Sunday	10	0	0
Sum	$490	$560	$280

Table 11-4

Situation	Y ($)	γ (days)
A	10,950	7
B	10,950	14
C	10,950	28
D	16,425	7
E	21,900	7

(a) The income level for a pay period equals $(Y/365)\gamma$. The income level per pay period is as follows: A $210; B $420; C $840; D $315; and E $420.

(b) Mt is positively related to Y and γ; an increase in Y, *ceteris paribus*, raises the average money balance held during a pay period as does a lengthening of the pay period (an increase in γ).

11.18 Suppose a household is paid $140 weekly and spends this income uniformly over the pay period. Find the average $M1$ balance held during the pay period (*a*) when income is held as an $M1$ balance prior to expenditure or (*b*) one-half of the period's income is deposited in a money market deposit account at the beginning of the period with the balance transferred during mid-period to an $M1$ account. (*c*) When expenditures are continuous, show in Fig. 11-5 for the situations described in part (*a*) and (*b*) the $M1$ balance held at any time during the pay period.

(a) Table 11-5 presents the daily average money balance held when spendable income is held as an $M1$ balance. The average $M1$ balance held during the seven-day period is $70.

(b) Table 11-6 presents an alternative scenario where one-half of the income is placed in a money market deposit account for one-half the period and then transferred to a transactions balance. The average $M1$ balance held during the pay period is now $35.

(c) When only transaction balances are held, a $140 $M1$ balance is held at the beginning of the pay period and 0 at the end; line AEB in Fig. 11-5 measures the quantity of $M1$ held at any time during the pay period. When money market deposit balances are held for one-half of the period, line $CDEB$ measures the $M1$ balance held at any time during the pay period.

11.19 The average transaction balance held in an $M1$ substitute (Msub) and in $M1$ is found by the formulas

$$M\text{sub} = \frac{n-1}{2n}\left(\frac{Y}{365}\right)\gamma \qquad \text{and} \qquad M1 = \frac{1}{2n}\left(\frac{Y}{365}\right)\gamma$$

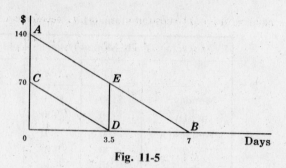

Fig. 11-5

Table 11-5

	M1 Balance Held (\$)		
	Start of Day	End of Day	Average
Monday	140	120	130
Tuesday	120	100	110
Wednesday	100	80	90
Thursday	80	60	70
Friday	60	40	50
Saturday	40	20	30
Sunday	20	0	10
Sum			490

Table 11-6

	M1 Balance Held (\$)		
	Start of Day	End of Day	Average
Monday	70	50	60
Tuesday	50	30	40
Wednesday	30	10	20
Thursday	10	60	35
Friday	60	40	50
Saturday	40	20	30
Sunday	20	0	10
Sum			245

where n is the number of transfers from an $M1$ substitute to an $M1$ account. (*a*) Find the average balance held in an $M1$ and an $M1$ substitute account when a household is paid weekly, receives \$14,600 annually and (1) one-half of the weekly income is invested in an $M1$ substitute for one-half of the period, (2) two-thirds of the weekly income is invested in an $M1$ substitute and one-half is transferred to an $M1$ balance after one-third of the period and the other one-half is transferred after two-thirds of the period, or (3) three-quarters of the weekly income is invested in an $M1$ substitute and one-third is transferred after one-quarter of the period, one-third after one-half of the period and the last one-third is transferred after three-quarters of the period. (*b*) What happens to the average $M1$ balance held when a household makes an increasing number of transfers between its $M1$ substitute and $M1$ account?

(a) The average balance in an $M1$ substitute and an $M1$ account are calculated below.

(1)
$$M\text{sub} = \frac{n-1}{2n}\left(\frac{Y}{365}\right)\gamma = \frac{1}{4}\left(\frac{\$14,600}{365}\right)7 = \$70$$

$$M1 = \frac{1}{2n}\left(\frac{Y}{365}\right)\gamma = \frac{1}{4}\left(\frac{\$14,600}{365}\right)7 = \$70$$

(2)
$$M\text{sub} = \frac{n-1}{2n}\left(\frac{Y}{365}\right)\gamma = \frac{2}{6}\left(\frac{\$14,600}{365}\right)7 = \$93.33$$

$$M1 = \frac{1}{2n}\left(\frac{Y}{365}\right)\gamma = \frac{1}{6}\left(\frac{\$14,600}{365}\right)7 = \$46.67$$

(3)
$$M\text{sub} = \frac{n-1}{2n}\left(\frac{Y}{365}\right)\gamma = \frac{3}{8}\left(\frac{\$14,600}{365}\right)7 = \$105$$

$$M1 = \frac{1}{2n}\left(\frac{Y}{365}\right)\gamma = \frac{1}{8}\left(\frac{\$14,600}{365}\right)7 = \$35$$

(b) The average $M1$ balance held over a pay period declines as a household makes a larger number of transfers from an $M1$ substitute account to an $M1$ account. Thus, holding Y and γ constant, the average $M1$ balance held is negatively related to the number of transfers made from an $M1$ substitute account.

11.20 (a) What determines the optimum number of transfers between $M1$ substitutes and $M1$ balances when there are costs associated with acquiring $M1$ substitutes and then transferring them to $M1$ balances? (b) What happens to the optimum number of transfers when there is (1) a decrease in the rate of interest, (2) an increase in annual income or (3) an increase in the fixed cost per transfer?

(a) For ease of analysis, we shall assume that $M1$ balances generate no revenue and incur no costs, whereas there are costs and revenues associated with $M1$ substitutes. Suppose there is a fixed cost per transfer between $M1$ and $M1$ substitute assets; cost schedule C in Fig. 11-6 represents the total costs associated with n transfers. Schedule R is the revenue associated with holding $M1$ substitutes, given a rate of interest, an income level, and a fixed pay period. The optimum number of transfers occurs when the net revenue $(N = R - C)$ from $M1$ substitutes is maximized; this occurs in Fig. 11-6 when there are n_1 transfers.

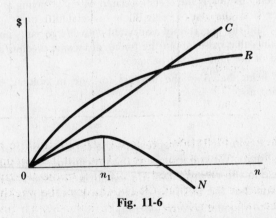

Fig. 11-6

(b) (1) Revenue curve R shifts downward, which causes the net revenue curve N to shift leftward. There is a reduction in the optimum number of transfers. (2) Revenue curve R shifts upward, causing a rightward movement of the net revenue curve. There is an increase in the optimum number of transfers. (3) Cost curve C pivots to the left, shifting the net revenue curve leftward. There is a decrease in the optimum number of transfers.

11.21 Suppose the total cost of transfers is $C = an$, and the revenue from holding $M1$ substitutes is $R = i[(n-1)/2n](Y/365)\gamma$. (a) Derive a formula for the optimum number of transfers. (b) What happens to the optimum number of transfers and the average $M1$ balance held when there is an increase in income?

(a) The optimum number of transfers occurs where $R - C = N$ is maximized:

$$N = i\left(\frac{n-1}{2n}\right)\left(\frac{Y}{365}\right)\gamma - an$$

Differentiating with respect to n,

$$\frac{dN}{dn} = \frac{i}{2n^2}\left(\frac{Y}{365}\right)\gamma - a$$

The maximum condition exists where dN/dn equals 0. Thus,

$$0 = \frac{i}{2n^2}\left(\frac{Y}{365}\right)\gamma - a$$

and solving for n,

$$n = \sqrt{\frac{i}{2a}\left(\frac{Y}{365}\right)\gamma}$$ Formula for the optimum number of bond transactions

(b) From the formula $n = \sqrt{(i/2a)(Y/365)\gamma}$ we see that $\Delta n = \sqrt{\Delta Y}$. Thus, if Y doubles, the increase in n equals $1.414n$. Since the relative change in n is less than the relative change in income, the quantity of money held for transactions is positively related to the level of income.

PRECAUTIONARY DEMAND FOR MONEY

11.22 (a) Why is there a precautionary demand for money? (b) What is the cost of being illiquid? (c) What is the cost of being liquid?

(a) Precautionary money balances are needed when income receipts and expenditures are uncertain. "Extra" money balances are needed should income not be received on time or unplanned spending develops.

(b) The cost of being illiquid is the cost associated with not having an adequate $M1$ balance to acquire goods and services. The cost of being illiquid is related to one's income (and therefore the level of expenditures) and the uncertainty associated with $M1$ receipts and disbursements. Obviously, the more uncertainty that exists about the timing of income receipts and expenditures, the greater the expected cost of not holding $M1$ balances.

(c) The cost of being liquid is the interest forgone in holding money rather than a substitute interest-bearing asset.

11.23 Suppose schedule EC in Fig. 11-7 represents the expected cost of being illiquid; OC represents the cost of being liquid. What happens to the precautionary demand for $M1$ balances when (a) there is a decrease in the return from $M1$ substitute assets, *ceteris paribus*; (b) the household sector is pessimistic that the business expansion will continue, *ceteris paribus*; (c) there is an increase in expected income, *ceteris paribus*.

(a) A decrease in the return from $M1$ substitutes causes the OC curve to shift downward; larger $M1$ balances are held.

(b) Less certainty about the future shifts EC rightward; larger $M1$ balances are held.

(c) An expected higher income level shifts EC rightward; larger $M1$ balances are held.

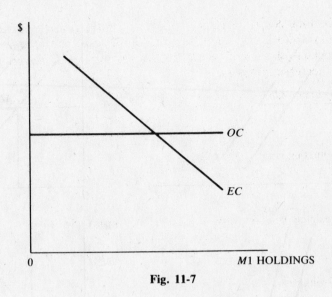

Fig. 11-7

PORTFOLIO DEMAND FOR MONEY

11.24 Relate the transaction and the portfolio demand for $M1$ balances to the medium of exchange and store of value functions of money.

The $M1$ money supply consists of transaction balances, which are the medium of exchange. $M1$ balances can also serve as a liquid store of value in that they retain their nominal value.

11.25 Explain Keynes's original presentation of a speculative demand for money.

Keynes assumed that investors had only two store-of-value alternatives: money and/or long-term bonds. Given these portfolio alternatives, a speculative demand for money existed at certain times because money would serve as a better store of value than long-term bonds. Bonds promise to pay the holder an interest return and capital repayment. When a bondholder sells a bond prior to maturity and the market rate of interest is higher than when the bond was purchased, the bond is sold at a price below its purchase price and there is a capital loss. Investors will hold money rather than bonds when they expect the capital loss to exceed the interest return. Thus, a speculative demand for money develops during a period of rising interest rates, when money is expected to be a better store of value than long-term bonds.

11.26 Is an investor more likely to have a portfolio demand for an $M1$, an $M2$ or an $M3$ money balance?

$M2$ and $M3$ definitions of money include financial assets that yield a higher return than $M1$ balances and have no real discernible difference from $M1$ with respect to loss of nominal value. $M2$ and $M3$ balances therefore are nearly perfect store-of-value substitutes for $M1$ balances. Hence, the portfolio demand for money is more likely a demand for $M2$ and $M3$ balances than a reason for holding $M1$ money balances.

MONEY SUPPLY OR INTEREST RATE MONETARY POLICY

11.27 What might cause uncertainty about the location of an IS or LM schedule?

In the absence of economic policy, IS or LM shifts when there is a change in investment, consumption or the demand for money. Increases in investment or consumption shift IS rightward,

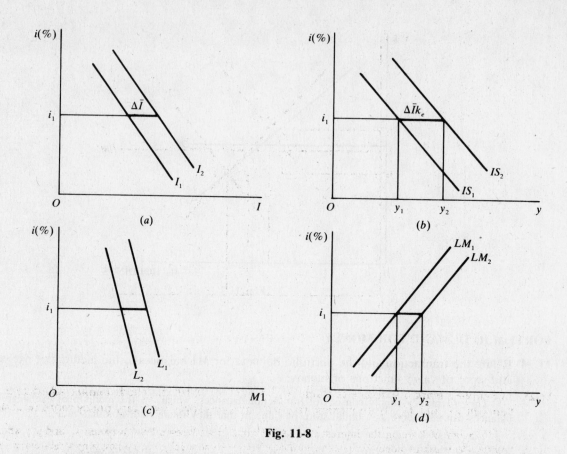

Fig. 11-8

whereas decreases in the demand for money shift LM rightward. Investment schedule I_1 in Fig. 11-8(a) is associated with IS_1 in Fig. 11-8(b). An increase in investment which shifts investment schedule I_1 to I_2 causes IS to shift rightward from IS_1 to IS_2. A decrease in the demand for money in Fig. 11-8(c) from L_1 to L_2 causes LM to shift from LM_1 to LM_2 in Fig. 11-8(d). When the investment, consumption or demand for money schedules are unstable, there is uncertainty about the location of IS or LM in space.

11.28 Suppose goods equilibrium schedule IS in Fig. 11-9 is stable; LM is located between LM_1 and LM_2 because of an unstable demand for money. (a) Suppose the Federal Reserve follows an interest rate monetary policy and maintains the interest rate at i_0. Find the possible income levels for this i_0 interest rate monetary policy. (b) Suppose the Federal Reserve keeps the nominal money supply constant; find the possible income levels when equilibrium in the money markets exists between LM_1 and LM_2 because of an unstable demand for money. (c) Is an interest rate or a money supply monetary policy more desirable when equilibrium in the goods market is stable and monetary equilibrium is unstable?

(a)   To maintain an i_0 interest rate, the Federal Reserve must expand or contract the money supply whenever the interest rate rises or falls below this level. Thus, the actual LM schedule is a horizontal line LM' at interest rate i_0. With the goods market schedule stable at IS, y_2 is the only equilibrium income level for an i_0 interest rate monetary policy.

(b)   Equilibrium income is y_1 when the money market schedule is LM_1 and y_3 when the money market schedule is LM_2. A money supply monetary policy produces a range of equilibria between y_1 and y_3.

(c)   In parts (a) and (b), an i_0 interest rate monetary policy produces only one equilibrium level of income, whereas equilibrium income exists between y_1 and y_3 for a money supply monetary policy. When the goods market schedule is stable and the money market schedule is unstable, an interest rate monetary policy is more desirable because it generates a more certain income level.

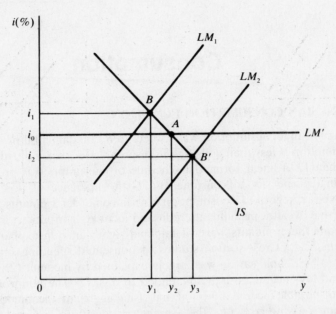

Fig. 11-9

11.29 The money market schedule is stable at *LM* in Fig. 11-10; the goods market schedule exists between IS_1 and IS_2. Is an interest rate or a money supply monetary policy more desirable?

A policy of keeping the interest rate at i_0 results in an income level between y_1 and y_2, whereas holding the nominal money supply constant results in income level y_1. A money supply monetary policy is more desirable because of its greater control of the income level.

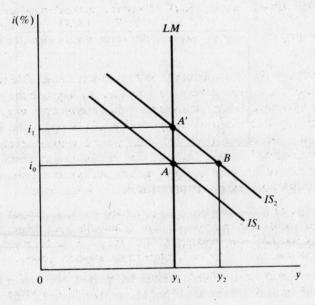

Fig. 11-10

Chapter 12

Consumption

12.1 THE KEYNESIAN CONSUMPTION FUNCTION

Keynes postulated that consumption was subject to a "fundamental psychological law" whereby a change in consumption is less than a change in disposable income, i.e., the marginal propensity to consume is less than 1. In linear form, the schedule of consumption is presented as $C = \bar{C} + cYd$, with c the marginal propensity to consume and $\bar{C}$ the influence of nonincome determinants on consumption. Keynes categorized consumption's nonincome determinants into subjective (psychological) and objective (wealth, installment credit and income distribution) factors, but he speculated that these nonincome determinants were of minimal significance in explaining short-run consumption. (See Problem 12.4.) Cross-section studies of household spending supported Keynes hypothesized behavior: (1) household saving was largely explained by income; (2) high-income households tended to save, and low-income households tended to dissave. The nonproportional relationship of consumption and disposable income indicated that rising aggregate income levels would be associated with a higher national saving rate, i.e., the average propensity to consume (APC) would decline as income rose (Example 1). Time-series data have shown, however, that over long periods the U.S. Economy's APC is constant (the relationship of consumption and disposable income is proportional). Milton Friedman's permanent income hypothesis and Franco Modigliani's life-cycle hypothesis are post–World War II consumption theories which reconcile the cross-section evidence of individual saving rates with time-series evidence of a constant APC. Both theories explain consumption by relating consumption spending to expected rather than current income.

EXAMPLE 1. Suppose the consumption equation is $C = \$40 + 0.80\,Yd$. The APC and MPC for a range of disposable incomes are given in Table 12-1. The relationship of consumption and disposable income is nonproportional since the APC declines as income increases.

Table 12-1

Yd (\$)	C (\$)	APC	MPC
200	200	1.00	$\cdots$
400	360	0.90	0.80
600	520	0.87	0.80
800	680	0.85	0.80
1000	840	0.84	0.80

12.2 THE PERMANENT INCOME HYPOTHESIS

Households are likely to smooth consumption over a business cycle in the same way that they smooth expenditures over a pay period. Hence, current consumption is a function not of current income but of expected income. According to the permanent income hypothesis, current income Y consists of permanent Y^p and transitory components Y^t, i.e., $Y = Y^p + Y^t$. Permanent income is that which households expect to receive over an extended period, whereas transitory income consists of any unexpected addition to or subtraction from permanent income. The permanent income hypothesis is consistent with cross-section and time-series data. Higher-income households are savers because their current income includes positive transitory components, whereas transitory income is most likely negative for dissaving, lower-income households. When we relate consumption to permanent income, a fixed, proportional relationship exists regardless of the distribution of permanent income. However, when we erroneously relate consumption to current income, we obtain a nonproportional relationship, since current income may include a positive or negative transitory component. Friedman used adaptive expectations to arrive at estimates of permanent income, with Y^p a weighted average of current and previous period permanent income. For example, applying a weight of j to current income and $(1-j)$ to previous period permanent income, we have $Y^p = j(Y) + (1-j)Y^p_{-1}$. The theory also maintained that, regardless of the permanent income level, each household consumes approximately the same proportion of its permanent income. Hence, regardless of the distribution of income, aggregate consumption can be presented as $C = c(Y^p)$, with c the aggregate marginal propensity to consume.

EXAMPLE 2.   Table 12-2 presents the fluctuation of a household's current income over a business cycle; years 1 and 5 are periods of recession, and years 2 through 4 and 6 through 8 are periods of economic expansion. Suppose this pattern is repetitive; the household's income averages \$12,000 over the business cycle, designated permanent income in the third column. Transitory income, presented in the fourth column, is the difference between the second and third columns. If the household's marginal propensity to consume permanent income is 0.90, \$10,800 (the fifth column) is consumed each year. $[C = c(Y^p); \$10,800 = 0.90(\$12,000).]$ The household's APC is constant at 0.90 in the sixth column when we relate current consumption to permanent income; however, it fluctuates over the business cycle in the last column when we relate consumption to current income.

Table 12-2

Period	$Y(\$)$	$Y^p(\$)$	$Y^t(\$)$	$C(\$)$	C/Y^p	C/Y
1	10,000	12,000	−2,000	10,800	0.90	1.08
2	11,000	12,000	−1,000	10,800	0.90	0.98
3	12,500	12,000	500	10,800	0.90	0.86
4	14,500	12,000	2,500	10,800	0.90	0.74
5	10,000	12,000	−2,000	10,000	0.90	1.08
6	11,000	12,000	−1,000	10,800	0.90	0.98
7	12,500	12,000	500	10,800	0.90	0.86
8	14,500	12,000	2,500	10,800	0.90	0.74

12.3   THE LIFE-CYCLE HYPOTHESIS

Modigliani's theory of consumption maintained that households stabilize consumption over time as they relate consumption to expected lifetime income. A household is thereby likely to save while employed to acquire a level of savings which would allow for a planned level of consumption during retirement. When people plan a constant level of consumption over their lifetime and annual earnings are constant during the employment years, a fixed percentage of annual income is saved for retirement and an individual's APC is constant during its years of employment (Example 3). However, when a household's annual income increases yearly and plateaus prior to retirement, less is saved during the initial working years and more in later years. A new entrant into the work force, whose income is expected to increase over time, is likely to have an APC greater than 1, whereas the APC for an individual near retirement is likely to be less than 1. This behavior is consistent with cross-section studies where lower-income households tend to dissave and higher-income households tend to save. The aggregate APC would be constant over time when the labor force consists of equal proportions of young, middle-age, and older workers, which is also consistent with time-series data. The following factors could change consumption behavior: the interest return on financial assets, inherited asset endowments, age at retirement and expected number of retirement years.

EXAMPLE 3. Suppose an individual enters the labor force at age 25; annual disposable income until retirement at age 65 is $30,000; and life expectancy is 75 years. If this person has no initial asset endowment, there is no interest return on financial assets, there is no private or public pension benefit program, and the individual plans to spend income uniformly during his or her lifetime, $6000 is saved annually during employment years and $24,000 is consumed annually. [Lifetime earnings of $1.2 million (40 years times $30,000 a year) spent uniformly over 50 years equals annual consumption of $24,000.] The individual's APC is 0.80 during the employment years ($24,000/$30,000 = 0.80). At retirement, savings equal $240,000, and annual consumption is $24,000 during the 10 years of retirement. (When interest is earned on the amount saved, individuals will save less during the employment years, and their APC is higher.) Fig. 12-1(a) presents an

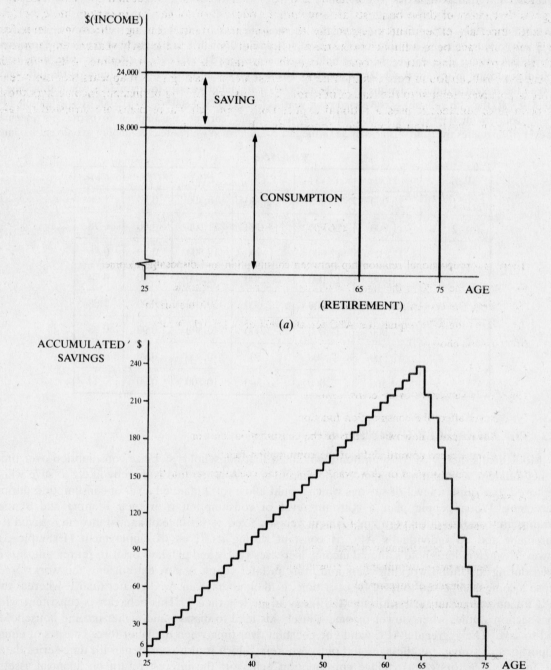

(a)

(b)

Fig. 12-1

individual's consumption of $24,000 throughout her or his lifetime and annual saving of $6000 during the employment years. Fig. 12-1(b) shows the accumulation of financial wealth during years of employment, which peaks at $240,000 on retirement; financial wealth is consumed during retirement.

12.4 OTHER FACTORS AFFECTING CONSUMPTION

Recent writings on consumption consider the effect that bequests, liquidity constraints, interest rates and formation of expectations have on consumption. A large proportion of the wealth accumulated by individuals is not consumed during retirement but bequested to heirs. Research suggests that many of these bequests are involuntary because of longer but uncertain life expectancies and uncertain expenditures (especially those for medical care) during retirement. Imperfect credit markets have been a financial constraint to individuals who, in the early years of employment, wish to borrow against future income to smooth consumption over their lifetime. Although little association has been found between the rate of interest and the saving rate, it appears that the rate of saving is positively related to the rate of inflation. The forward-looking permanent income hypothesis has been reformulated; it uses a rational expectations approach where plans are adjusted to take account of new information about the economy as it becomes available.

Review Questions

1. There is a proportional relationship between consumption and disposable income

    (a) When the APC is the same for all levels of disposable income

    (b) When the consumption function is a straight line through the origin

    (c) When the MPC equals the APC for all levels of disposable income

    (d) All the above

    Answer: (d)

2. Changes in subjective or objective factors

    (a) Never affect the consumption function

    (b) Always cause downward shifts of the consumption function

    (c) Always cause upward shifts of the consumption function

    (d) May cause upward or downward shifts of the consumption function

    Answer: (d)

3. Keynes considered subjective and objective factors

    (a) Important determinants of consumption

    (b) Unimportant determinants of consumption

    (c) Determinants of investment

    (d) Determinants of business' willingness to supply

    Answer: (b)

4. According to the permanent income hypothesis, all increases in

    (a) Permanent income are saved

    (b) Permanent income are consumed

(c)   Transitory income are saved

(d)   Transitory income are consumed

Answer: (c)

5.   When current income includes a negative transitory component, relating consumption with current income will produce

(a)   An average propensity to consume that is lower than the long-run average propensity to consume

(b)   An average propensity to consume that is higher than the long-run average propensity to consume

(c)   An average propensity to consume that equals the long-run average propensity to consume

(d)   None of the above

Answer: (b)

6.   The permanent income hypothesis is consistent with cross-section and time-series data because

(a)   Higher-income households are savers, since their current income includes positive transitory components.

(b)   Higher-income households are savers, since their current income includes negative transitory components.

(c)   Lower-income households are savers, since their current income includes negative transitory components.

(d)   Lower-income households are dissavers, since their current income includes positive transitory components.

Answer: (a)

7.   According to the life-cycle hypothesis, consumption is related to

(a)   Current income

(b)   Past peak income

(c)   Expected lifetime income

(d)   Price expectations over one's lifetime

Answer: (c)

8.   Suppose a 25-year-old individual expects to earn $25,000 annually until retirement at age 70. When income is spent uniformly during the individual's lifetime and life expectancy is 80, the

(a)   Individual consumes $22,000 a year during the employment years.

(b)   Individual's endowment at retirement is $204,545.

(c)   Individual saves $4000 a year during the employment years.

(d)   Individual's lifetime income is $1.3 million.

Answer: (b)

9.   Suppose an individual intends to spend income uniformly during her or his lifetime. During the employment years, the APC

(a)   Is constant when annual income is unchanged

(b)   Decreases with age when annual income increases during the individual's employment years

(c)   Increases with age when annual income decreases during the individual's employment years

(d)   All the above

Answer: (d)

10.   Which of the following best describes the reasons for involuntary bequests?

   (*a*)   Interest rates had increased in recent years.

   (*b*)   There was considerable uncertainty associated with expenditures during retirement.

   (*c*)   There were substantial gains in the stock market.

   (*d*)   Individuals wanted to leave an inheritance to their children.

   Answer: (*b*)

Solved Problems

THE KEYNESIAN CONSUMPTION FUNCTION

12.1   (*a*) Explain Keynes subjective factors affecting consumption. (*b*) What effect will the following events have on the consumption schedule? (1) An impending war is expected to result in a shortage of goods and adoption of a rationing system. (2) Substantial increases in the price of oil are expected to result in a higher consumer price index. (3) There is a consensus that the recession is over.

   (*a*)   Subjective factors are psychological factors which affect the willingness to buy goods. Buying attitudes are influenced by factors such as advertising, attractiveness of products, expectations about the price level, availability of goods and income.

   (*b*)   (1) Households are likely to "hoard" goods before an actual shortage develops; increased demand shifts the aggregate consumption schedule to the left. (2) Households are likely to increase their purchases of goods prior to an expected increase in the price level; the consumption function shifts to the left. (3) When consumers believe that economic recovery is near, they are more willing to purchase goods and services; the consumption function shifts to the left.

12.2   Explain the following objective factors identified by Keynes: (*a*) wealth, (*b*) consumer installment credit and (*c*) income distribution.

   (*a*)   A household's ability to consume is directly related to its possession of wealth. Households add to their wealth (stock of financial and real assets) by saving. By saving annually, *ceteris paribus*, household wealth increases consumption, and the consumption function shifts leftward. Rightward shifts of the consumption function are likely to occur when wealth is destroyed by a stock market "crash."

   (*b*)   The cost and availability of consumer installment credit affects the buying capacity of individuals. When credit is more readily available and/or costs less, individuals are more likely to borrow and, in the aggregate, save less. Increased consumer borrowing, *ceteris paribus*, shifts the consumption function leftward.

   (*c*)   A change in income distribution affects aggregate consumption when all income recipients do not have the same marginal propensity to consume. An income redistribution from wealthy to lower-income households, effected through increased taxes taken from higher-income households and returned to lower-income households through welfare payments, shifts aggregate consumption leftward.

12.3   (*a*) From Fig. 12-2, prove that consumption function C' is proportional and C'' is nonproportional. (*b*) What happens to the aggregate saving rate when income increases and the consumption function is proportional or nonproportional?

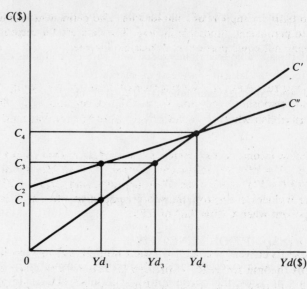

Fig. 12-2

(a) A consumption function is proportional when the APC is constant and nonproportional when it changes with the level of income. The MPC is constant along a straight-line consumption function; the APC does not change when the APC equals the MPC at more than one point along the consumption schedule. Schedule C' intersects the vertical axis at the origin. Consumption function C' is proportional because the APC always equals the MPC. (Note that the APC and MPC are equal when the change in income is $0Yd_1$ or $0Yd_3$ along schedule C'.) Schedule C'' intersects the consumption axis at consumption level C_2; the APC exceeds the MPC at income level $0Yd_1$, whereas the APC equals the MPC at income level $0Yd_4$. Consumption function C'' is therefore nonproportional.

(b) The APC is constant at each level of income when the consumption function is proportional; thus, the national saving rate (average propensity to save) is also constant for all income levels. The APC declines as income increases when the consumption function is nonproportional; the saving rate is greater for higher income levels.

12.4 Why was Keynes' consumption theory considered unsatisfactory?

Keynes presented consumption as principally a function of current disposable income. Subjective and objective factors which might affect the level of consumption over time were not incorporated into the theory in a systematic manner and were considered unimportant even in the long run. This theory proved unsatisfactory because it could not explain, other than by chance, the statistical long-run proportionality of consumption and disposable income.

THE PERMANENT INCOME HYPOTHESIS

12.5 Do the data in Table 12-3 support the permanent income hypothesis?

Table 12-3

Consumption ($)	360	390	420	450	480
Current income ($)	400	440	480	520	560

There is no basis for support or contradiction. The permanent income theory holds that consumption is related to permanent disposable income. The data are for current measured disposable income which may or may not equal permanent disposable income.

12.6   Suppose the long-run APC is 0.90 but one obtains the following APCs by relating consumption to current disposable income: 0.91, 0.89, 0.88 and 0.92. Use the permanent income hypothesis to establish whether current disposable income has a positive or negative transitory component.

The permanent income theory contends that current income consists of permanent and transitory components, i.e., $Y = Y^p + Y^t$. When the long run APC is 0.90, $C = 0.90(Y^p)$. Thus, Y^t is 0 when $C/Y = 0.90$. $C/(Y^p + Y^t) > 0.90$ when Y^t is negative, and $C/(Y^p + Y^t) < 0.90$ when Y^t is positive. Current income includes a negative transitory component when C/Y is 0.91 or 0.92 and a positive transitory component when C/Y is 0.89 or 0.88.

12.7   Table 12-4 presents current income for Household A. (*a*) Present in the third column of Table 12-4 permanent income for years 4 through 10 when Y^p is an unweighted average of income for the current and past three years. (*b*) Present in the fourth column consumption for years 4 through 10 when $C = 0.90Y^p$. (*c*) Present transitory income for years 4 through 10 in the last column of Table 12-4.

Table 12-4

Year	$Y(\$)$	$Y^p(\$)$	$C(\$)$	$Y^t(\$)$
1	10,000			
2	11,000			
3	12,000			
4	10,000	10,750	9,675	−750
5	13,000	11,500	10,350	+1150
6	14,000	12,250	11,025	+1750
7	15,000	13,000	11,700	+2000
8	11,000	13,250	11,925	−2250
9	16,000	14,000	12,600	+2000
10	17,000	14,750	13,275	+2250

12.8   Plot in Fig. 12-3, the following data from Table 12-4: consumption and current income; consumption and permanent income. Comment on the data plotted.

The plotting of consumption and permanent income is noted by *x*s in Fig. 12-3, and consumption and current income are noted by dots. Consumption and permanent income has a linear, proportional relationship. The relationship of consumption and current income is nonproportional and gives the appearance of actual points on an upward-shifting consumption function.

12.9   (*a*) According to the permanent income hypothesis, what is the likely behavior of transitory income and the rate of saving over the business cycle? (*b*) The permanent income and life-cycle hypotheses do not include purchases of consumer durables (e.g., cars) in the

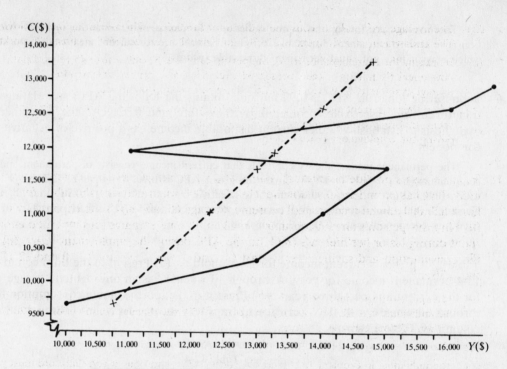

Fig. 12-3

definition of consumption. What would you expect to happen to the rate of saving when durable good purchases are included in the definition of consumption; and households "save" a large percent of transitory income through purchases of durable goods?

(a) Transitory income should be positive during an economic expansion and negative during an economic contraction. When the saving rate is calculated by comparing saving to permanent income, the rate of saving (APS) should be constant over the business cycle. However, when saving is related to current income, the rate of saving should increase during an expansion and decrease during a contraction.

(b) The saving rate should decrease during an expansion and increase during a contraction when durable good purchases are included in the definition of consumption and saving is compared to permanent and/or current income.

LIFE-CYCLE HYPOTHESIS

12.10 Suppose assets provide no interest return; and no public or private pension system exists. An individual enters the labor force at age 20, has a $20,000 annual income until retirement at age 65, has a life expectancy of 75 years, and has no initial endowment of assets at age 20. (a) Find annual consumption when this person spends income uniformly over his or her lifetime. (b) Find the APC during the individual's working years and the endowment at retirement. (c) What happens to the APC during the person's employment years when the retirement age is raised to 70, *ceteris paribus*? (d) Find the APC when the retirement age is 65 and life expectancy is 80.

(a) Lifetime earnings equal $900,000 [$20,000 (45 working years)]. Annual consumption is $16,363.64 when lifetime earnings of $900,000 are spent uniformly over the expected lifetime of 55 years.

(b)　The average propensity to consume is 0.818, or $16,363.64/$20,000 during the employment years. The endowment at retirement is $16,363.20 (annual saving of $3636.36 times 45 working years).

(c)　By raising the retirement age to 70, the person can work 50 rather than 45 years. Lifetime earnings now equal $1 million. When consumed over 55 years, annual consumption is $18,181.82. The average propensity to consume is 0.909 during the employment years.

(d)　When the retirement age is 65 but life expentancy increases to 80, lifetime earnings of $900,000 are spent uniformly over 60 rather than 55 years. Annual consumption is then $15,000, and the APC during the employment years is 0.75.

12.11　Suppose assets provide no interest return, and no public or private pension system exists. An individual has an inherited endowment of $200,000 when entering the labor force at age 20, has a $20,000 annual income until retirement at age 65, and has a life expentancy of 75 years. (a) Find this person's annual consumption when lifetime earnings plus inherited endowment is spent during his or her lifetime. (b) Find the APC during the employment years. (c) Compare the consumption and saving rates in part (a) and (b) of Problems 12.10 and 12.11. Why do they differ?

(a)　Lifetime earnings equal $900,000. When lifetime earnings are added to the inherited endowment, the individual has $1,100,000 to spend over a lifetime. Annual consumption is $20,000, or $1.1 million lifetime earnings/55 years.

(b)　The APC during his or her working years is 1.0.

(c)　The individual in Problem 12.10 part (b) has no initial endowment and therefore must save for the 10 years of retirement; $3,636.36 must be saved annually to provide for the planned level of consumption during retirement. The individual in Problem 12.11 (a) and (b) has a $200,000 inherited endowment which is sufficient for the retirement years; the individual therefore can consume his or her entire income each year during the employment years. Without an inherited endowment, the individual in Problem 12.10 has a higher saving rate throughout the employment years than does the person in Problem 12.11.

12.12　Suppose assets provide no interest return, there is no interest cost in borrowing, and no public or private pension system exists. An individual enters the labor force at age 25, has a life expectancy of 75 years, spends the entire income evenly over a lifetime and has no initial endowment of assets. (a) Find this individual's yearly consumption when $25,000 is earned each year during the first 10 years of employment, $35,000 is earned annually during the second 10 years, $45,000 during the third 10 years and $50,000 during the last 10 years. (b) Find this person's APC during the employment years and the endowment at retirement.

(a)　Lifetime income is $1,550,000. Consumption is $31,000 a year when total income is spent uniformly over a lifetime.

(b)　During the first 10 years of work, the individual's APC is 1.24 ($60,000 is owed by the end of the tenth year of employment). The APC during the second 10 years of employment is 0.886 ($20,000 is owed after 20 years of employment). For the third 10 years, the APC is 0.689 (accumulated savings is now $120,000). The APC for the last 10 years of work is 0.62; the endowment at retirement is $310,000.

12.13　Suppose an individual enters the labor force at age 25, has a $25,000 annual income until retirement at age 65, has a life expectancy of 75 years and has no initial endowment of assets at age 25; no public or private pension system exists. (a) Find this person's annual consumption when earnings are spent uniformly during a lifetime and there is no interest return on assets. Also find the APC during the employment years and the endowment at retirement. (b) The sum of $1 paid annually into an annuity for n years is $[(1 + r)^n - 1]/r$, where r is the annual rate of interest. What is this person's endowment at retirement when

$5000 is saved annually and the rate of interest is 2% or 5%? What most likely happens to the APC and therefore the amount saved annually when there is an interest return on savings?

(*a*) Lifetime income is $1 million, or $25,000 times 40 working years. Annual consumption is $20,000, and annual saving is $5000 when this income is spent uniformly over this person's life. During the employment years, the APC is 0.80; the endowment at retirement is $200,000.

(*b*) When the rate of interest is 2%, the sum of $1 paid annually into an annuity for 40 years is $60.402; thus, the sum of $5000 paid annually into an annuity is $302,010.00. When the rate of interest is 5%, the sum of $1 paid annually into an annuity for 40 years is $120.79; the sum of $5000 paid annually into an annuity is then $603,950. The APC during the employment years is likely to be higher when interest is earned on savings. The APC is most likely higher the greater the interest return on assets.

12.14 Holding other factors constant, explain the effect that the following variables might have on saving during the employment years: retirement age, life expectancy, age at entry into labor force, inherited asset endowment and interest earned on financial assets. Assume that consumption is based on lifetime income and is uniform throughout one's lifetime.

An individual's saving rate is most likely higher during employment years the earlier the age at planned retirement, the longer the person's life expectancy and/or the later the persons' entry into the labor force, *ceteris paribus*. When consumption is uniform over one's lifetime, there are fewer working years during which one can accumulate an endowment for retirement when one retires early and/or is a late entrant into the labor force. A person's saving rate during the employment years must also be greater when there is a longer life expectancy because of the need to accumulate a larger endowment during the employment years to provide support during more years of retirement. Inheriting an endowment reduces an individual's need to accumulate a personal endowment; hence, the larger the endowment inherited, the lower the saving rate during the employed years. The saving rate during the employment years is negatively related to the rate of interest, since wealth accumulation for retirement is greater the higher the interest earned on savings.

OTHER FACTORS AFFECTING CONSUMPTION

12.15 Why might an individual bequest accumulated wealth to heirs and not consume it in its entirety during the retirement years?

Bequests may be voluntary and/or involuntary. A voluntary bequest occurs when it is planned whereas a bequest is involuntary when the individual dies before spending the endowment allocated to the retirement years. Parental concern for the economic welfare of children and/or grandchildren may induce parents to set aside a portion of their endowment for heirs upon death. In doing so, heirs can have a higher standard of living during their lifetime, since consumption over their lifetime is not solely dependent on income from their own employment. Consumption during retirement and age at death are uncertain. Spending during retirement depends upon an individual's need for health care. Because these needs and costs are unknown, individuals must set aside a portion of their retirement endowment for this purpose. Obviously, if the retiree has continuous good health, the allocated sum is not spent and is therefore left to heirs. Similarly, age at death is unknown. Hence, the endowment must be adequate to support an unexpected long life; bequests occur when life is equal to or shorter than one's expectancy.

12.16 How can liquidity constraints restrict consumption?

Individuals who expect income to increase throughout the employment years borrow during the initial working years to smooth out consumption over their lifetime. The ability to borrow, however, depends not on the individual's but on the bank's perception of future earnings. When the bank's expectation is below that of the individual, consumption during early employment years is constrained, and consumption will be at a lower level than what the individual had planned. When this occurs, consumption is more closely tied to current disposable income than expected income over one's lifetime.

Chapter 13

Theories of Investment

13.1 THE ACCELERATOR THEORY OF INVESTMENT

The accelerator theory of investment explains net investment in terms of expected growth in aggregate output. In the *rigid version* of the accelerator theory, firms maintain a stable relationship between the stock of capital and aggregate output. This relationship is presented as $K = vY^e$, where K is the stock of capital, v is the capital-output ratio (the ratio of the desired stock of capital to expected aggregate output), and Y^e is expected output. Additions to the economy's capital stock, i.e. net investment In, take place when output is expected to increase. Hence, $In = v\Delta Y$. Because v is greater than one, net investment fluctuates when growth of expected output is not continuous over time (Example 1). There is also replacement investment, since a portion of an economy's capital stock "wears out" (depreciates) in the course of producing current output. Thus, gross investment may change because of the need to replace some of the existing capital stock and/or the need to add to the economy's stock of capital (Example 2).

EXAMPLE 1. When $v = 2$, net investment is twice the change in expected output ($In = 2\Delta Y$). Suppose the capital stock and actual output is $1200 and $600 in period 0 and expected output in successive periods is $610, $625, $635, $640 and $640. Table 13-1 presents the net investment (capital additions) which is necessary in successive periods to keep the capital output ratio at 2. Net investment is $20 during period 1 because output is expected to increase $10 during that period; net investment is $30 during period 2 when output is expected to increase $15; net investment is $20, $10 and 0 in periods 3, 4 and 5.

Table 13-1

Period	Expected Output	Net Investment
0	$600	0
1	610	$20
2	625	30
3	635	20
4	640	10
5	640	0

EXAMPLE 2. Suppose the capital-output ratio is 2. A $2000 capital stock was accumulated uniformly over 10 periods and has a uniform, useful life of 10 periods. Beginning in period 11, firms must replace worn out capital; thus, replacement investment is $200 per period for periods 11 to 20 (Table 13-2). Gross investment consists of net investment and replacement investment. Gross investment increases from $200 during period 11 to a peak of $400 during period 14 due to uneven increases in expected output between period 11 and 16. The variability of gross investment would have been greater had the initial capital stock not worn out evenly during periods 11 to 20.

13.2 THE DESIRED STOCK OF CAPITAL

The business sector's desired stock of capital K^* depends on expected output Y^e, the user cost of capital u, and the real wage paid labor w, i.e., $K^* = f(Y^e, u, w)$. In determining the business sector's desired stock of capital, it is customary to hold labor's compensation constant. When real output is not held constant, the desired stock of capital is a function of the user cost of capital and the

Table 13-2

Period	Expected Output	ΔY	Net Investment	Replacement Investment	Gross Investment
11	$1000	$0	$0	$200	$200
12	1050	50	100	200	300
13	1125	75	150	200	350
14	1215	100	200	200	400
15	1300	85	170	200	370
16	1325	25	50	200	250
17	1325	0	0	200	200

marginal productivity of capital. (See Problem 13.10.) When we hold real output constant, the desired stock of capital depends on the user cost of capital and the cost saving associated with using fewer labor inputs and more capital inputs to produce a specific level of output. Thus, the demand for capital can be presented as a schedule of the marginal productivity of capital or as a schedule of the marginal cost benefit from capital. The marginal cost benefit schedule is used in this section. (See Problems 13.9 and 13.10 for marginal productivity of capital analysis.)

The user cost of capital (stated as a percentage) is the real cost of using capital for a specified period of time. The user cost of capital consists of the real rate of interest (the real financial cost associated with acquiring real capital) and the rate of depreciation (real capital used in producing output). User cost can be specified as $u = r + d$ or as $u = i - \pi^e + d$, where r is the real rate of interest, d is the rate of depreciation of the capital stock, i is the nominal rate of interest and π^e is the expected rate of inflation. The user cost of capital is reduced by increasing the real money supply and/or by a fiscal action such as an investment tax credit or an acceleration of the rate at which a machine is depreciated for tax purposes. (See Problem 13.7.)

EXAMPLE 3. Suppose a machine's purchase price is $100,000, the firm's cost of securing funds to purchase the machine is 8% or $8000 a year, and the machine depreciates (wears out evenly) over 10 years for an annual rate of 10%. The machine's user cost per annum (cost of using the machine for one year) is thereby 18%, or $u = r + d$ and $18\% = 8\% + 10\%$. The user cost of capital is below 18% when the monetary authority reduces the real rate of interest by increasing the nominal money supply. Fiscal actions also affect the user cost of capital. Because depreciation is a precorporate income tax expense, depreciation of a machine at an accelerated rate for tax purposes reduces the cost of using the machine over its lifetime. An investment tax credit, which reduces the net purchase price of a machine, also lowers user cost.

An increase in the capital stock, *ceteris paribus*, reduces the need for labor inputs. For example, an increase in the capital stock from K_0 to K_1 in Fig. 13-1 decreases the need for labor inputs from N_0 to N_1 when real output is $500. Decreased use of labor inputs results in a cost saving, which is measured as a dollar cost benefit or as a marginal cost benefit when the dollar cost saving is related to the dollar cost of the capital addition (Example 4). A marginal cost benefit schedule is presented and labeled MBK in Fig. 13-2. Because capital and labor are imperfect substitutes in producing a constant level of output, continuous capital additions result in declining cost benefits. Hence, in Fig. 13-2, the marginal cost benefit schedule MBK is downward sloping. The marginal cost benefit schedule in Fig. 13-2 shifts rightward from MBK to MBK' when there is a higher level of real output.

EXAMPLE 4. Suppose reduction of labor inputs and expansion of the capital stock from $500,000 to $600,000 reduces the annual cost of labor from $750,000 to $730,000. There is a 20% marginal cost benefit in expanding capital from $500,000 to $600,000 when the capital addition has a 10-year useful life ($20,000 labor saving/ $100,000 capital expansion = 20%).

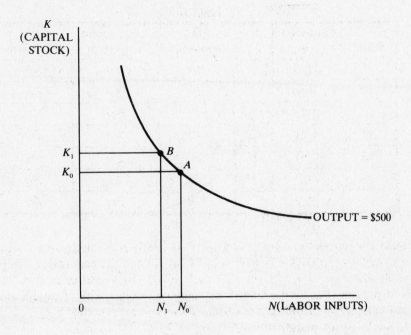

Fig. 13-1

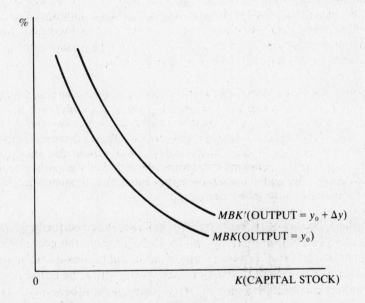

Fig. 13-2

The desired stock of capital exists where the user cost of capital (the cost associated with capital additions) equals the marginal cost benefit from using less labor to produce a fixed level of output. The desired stock of capital is $1000 in Fig. 13-3 when expected real output is $500 and user cost is u_0. At user cost u_1, *ceteris paribus*, the desired stock of capital is $1100. The decrease in the user cost of capital from u_0 to u_1, *ceteris paribus*, makes the production process more capital intensive and increases v, the capital-output ratio.

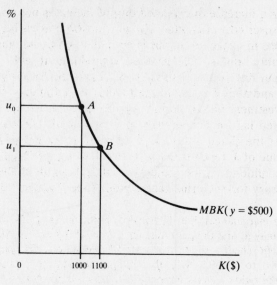

Fig. 13-3

EXAMPLE 5. The desired stock of capital is $2000 in Fig. 13-4(a) when user cost is u_0 and expected output is $1000. When user cost is lowered to u_1, *ceteris paribus*, the desired stock of capital increases to $2100. The u_0 to u_1 decrease in user cost increases the capital-output ratio from 2.0 to 2.1. In Fig. 13-4(b), the desired stock of capital is initially $2000 for schedule *MBK* when user cost is u_0 and expected output is $1000. A $50 increase in expected output shifts the marginal cost benefit schedule from *MBK* to *MBK'*. When user cost is constant at u_0, the desired stock of capital increases to $2100; the capital-output ratio remains at 2.0.

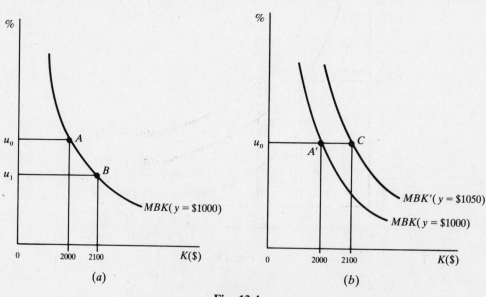

Fig. 13-4

13.3 THE FLEXIBLE ACCELERATOR

The flexible accelerator theory of investment amends the rigid accelerator model: the desired stock of capital is affected by the user cost of capital; additions to the desired stock of capital may occur over time. First, we consider the effect of changes in expected output and user cost on the desired stock of capital. An increase in expected output increases net investment by $In = v\Delta Y$ when there is no change in the user cost of capital. The production process becomes less capital intensive, however, when an increase in expected output is accompanied by a higher user cost and there is no change in the cost of labor inputs. The lowered capital-output ratio reduces the effect that an expected increase in output has on the desired stock of capital (Example 6). Production constraints and/or firms' willingness and ability to add to their stock of capital may be distributed over a number of periods. Thus, net investment in any period may be only a fraction of the change in the desired capital stock. A distributed lag for net investment is presented by the equation $In = \lambda(K^* - K_{-1})$, where λ is the fraction of the change in the desired stock of capital which takes place each period (see Example 7). The value of λ depends on factors such as the productive capabilities of the capital goods industries, firms' confidence in the projections of higher output and firms' ability to obtain the financial resources necessary for acquiring real capital. (See Problem 13.13.)

EXAMPLE 6.   Suppose the marginal cost benefit schedule MBK in Fig. 13-5 is associated with a $1000 level of real output; user cost is initially u_0 and the desired stock of capital is $2000. A $100 increase in expected output shifts the marginal cost benefit schedule rightward to MBK'. When user cost remains at u_0, the desired stock of capital increases from $2000 to $2200. [Note that v, the capital-output ratio, remains constant, and net investment is explained by the rigid accelerator model: $In = v\Delta Y$: $200 = 2($100).] However, when the user cost of capital increases, as output expands from $1000 to $1100, *ceteris paribus*, the desired stock of capital increases from $2000 to $2150. Net investment is $150 instead of $200; there is a decline in the capital-output ratio from 2.00 to 1.95, and the production process becomes less capital intensive. [Note that this analysis assumes no change in the real wage. The production process would become more capital intensive (v would increase) had a relative increase in the real wage exceeded the relative increase in user cost.]

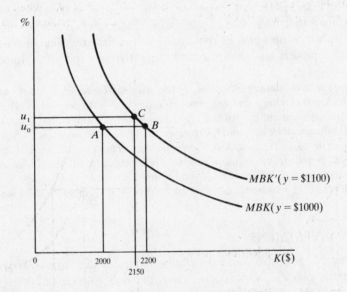

Fig. 13-5

EXAMPLE 7.   The desired capital stock expands in Example 6 from $2000 to $2150 when expected output increases $100 and user cost rises to u_1. Suppose net investment in any period is 50% ($\lambda = 0.50$) of the difference between the actual and desired capital stock, i.e., $In = \lambda(K^* - K_{-1})$. Net investment in the initial period is $75, or 0.50($2150 - $2000). When λ is unchanged at 0.50, net investment is $75, $37.50, $18.75 and $9.375 in successive periods, and the desired stock of capital is reached over time. Net investment during successive periods is presented in Fig. 13-6(*a*); the eventual $150 expansion in the stock of capital is presented in Fig. 13-6(*b*).

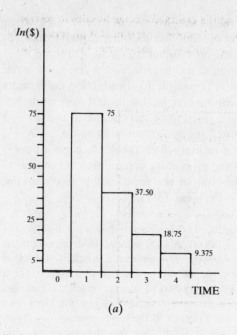

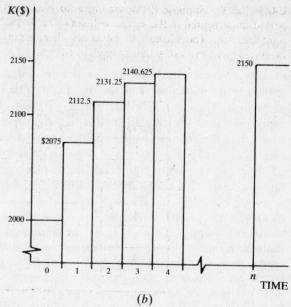

Fig. 13-6

13.4 TOBIN'S q-THEORY

James Tobin advanced a dynamic theory of business investment by relating net investment to a q ratio—the ratio of the market value of corporate financial assets to the replacement cost of corporate real assets. He reasoned that firms add to their capital stock when $q > 1$, since firms enhance their profitability when the acquisition cost of real assets is less than the financial cost of acquiring them, i.e., the user cost of capital is less than the cost benefit from capital additions (see Example 8).

EXAMPLE 8. Suppose a firm finances all assets by the issuance of common stock. Currently there are 1000 shares of common stock outstanding, and the market value is $40.00 per share. The firm's market value is therefore $40,000. If the replacement cost of the firm's real assets is $40,000, the q ratio is 1.00, and there is no benefit in adding to the firm's stock of capital. However, suppose a decrease in the real rate of interest causes the market value per share to increase to $50, *ceteris paribus*. The q ratio is now 1.25, since the user cost of capital is below the cost benefit from capital additions. The firm could purchase additional capital at a price of $10,000, financing the acquisition by issuing 200 additional shares of stock at $50 a share. A 25% (that is, $40,000 to $50,000) increase in real assets is financed by only a 20% increase ($50,000 to $60,000) in equity.

13.5 INVENTORY INVESTMENT

The practicalities of production and distribution require that firms carry an inventory of raw materials, goods in the process of production and finished goods. Variables that affect inventory levels include expected sales, the cost of holding inventory, possible delivery delays of raw materials and uncertainty about the economy. Inventory investment can be presented as a stable function of expected sales when variables other than expected sales are unchanged. In doing so, the rigid accelerator theory is used to model the change in inventory investment over time, e.g., $\Delta Inv = n\Delta R$, where ΔInv is the change in inventory investment, n is the inventory-sales ratio, and ΔR is the change in expected sales (Example 9). The model has limitations, as does the rigid accelerator theory, because variables are assumed constant which could change n, the inventory-sales ratio. For example, n would most likely decrease when there is increased uncertainty about future sales, there are increased costs in holding inventory, and/or there is greater availability and therefore more rapid delivery of raw materials. (See Problem 13.19)

EXAMPLE 9.   Suppose the desired inventory-sales ratio is 0.25, and the expected change in sales in successive periods is presented in the second column of Table 13-3. The change in inventory investment is presented in the right column. The change in inventory investment is greater or smaller to the extent that the desired inventory-sales ratio of 0.25 changes over time.

Table 13-3

Period	Expected Change in Sales ($)	Change in Inventory Investment ($)
1	+200	+50
2	+300	+75
3	+100	+25
4	0	0
5	−100	−25
6	−200	+50
7	+300	+75

Review Questions

1. In the rigid version of the accelerator theory of investment, net investment in successive periods is as follows when the capital-output ratio is 2 and the expected increase in output is $15, $20, $20 and $15.

    (a) $30 each period
    (b) $15, $20, $20 and $15 in successive periods
    (c) $30, $40, $40 and $30 in successive periods
    (d) $7.50, $10, $10 and $7.50 in successive periods

    Answer: (c)

2. Which of the following statements is true?

    (a)   Gross investment is more stable than net investment when replacement investment is constant over time.
    (b)   Net investment is more stable than gross investment when replacement is constant over time.
    (c)   Replacement investment equals $v\Delta Y$.
    (d)   Net investment is greater than $v\Delta Y$ when the capital-output ratio decreases.

    Answer: (a)

3. The user cost of capital is

    (a)   The real rate of interest
    (b)   The nominal rate of interest
    (c)   The real rate of interest plus the rate of depreciation
    (d)   The nominal rate of interest plus the rate of depreciation

    Answer: (c)

4.   Which of the following economic policies will *not* lower the user cost of capital?

(*a*)   A 5% increase in the nominal money supply, which causes a 5% increase in the expected rate of inflation

(*b*)   The introduction of an investment tax credit

(*c*)   An increase in the rate at which firms are allowed to depreciate machinery for tax purposes

(*d*)   A reduction in the corporate income tax rate

Answer: (*a*)

5.   The marginal cost benefit from capital is the

(*a*)   Incremental output associated with an addition to the stock of capital

(*b*)   Cost saving associated with employing less labor inputs and additional capital inputs to produce a fixed level of output

(*c*)   Incremental cost of capital associated with the addition of a unit of capital

(*d*)   Incremental profit associated with the addition of a unit of capital

Answer: (*b*)

6.   A decrease in the user cost of capital will result in the production process becoming

(*a*)   More capital intensive and the capital-output ratio decreasing

(*b*)   More capital intensive and the capital-output ratio increasing

(*c*)   Less capital intensive and the capital-output ratio decreasing

(*d*)   Less capital intensive and the capital-output ratio increasing

Answer: (*b*)

7.   A distributed lag for net investment may be due to

(*a*)   A decrease in the capital-output ratio

(*b*)   An increase in the capital-output ratio

(*c*)   Limited, short-run production capabilities in the capital-goods industry

(*d*)   A decrease in the expected level of output

Answer: (*c*)

8.   Tobin's *q*-theory of investment indicates that firms add to their stock of capital when

(*a*)   The replacement value of their real assets exceeds the market value of their financial assets.

(*b*)   The market value of their financial assets exceeds the replacement value of their real assets.

(*c*)   The market value of their real assets exceeds the book value of their financial assets.

(*d*)   The market value of their financial assets exceeds the book value of their real assets.

Answer: (*b*)

9.   When the inventory-sales ratio is 0.25, a

(*a*)   25% increase in expected sales results in a 100% increase in inventory.

(*b*) $25 increase in expected sales results in a $100 increase in inventory.

(*c*)   100% increase in expected sales results in a 25% increase in inventory.

(*d*) $100 increase in expected sales results in a $25 increase in inventory.

Answer: (*d*)

10. Which of the following results in an increase in the inventory-sales ratio?

(a) A decrease in the cost of holding inventory, *ceteris paribus*

(b) An increase in the probability of delivery delays for materials, *ceteris paribus*

(c) An increase in expected sales, *ceteris paribus*

(d) An increase in the uncertainty of expected sales, *ceteris paribus*

Answer: (b)

Solved Problems

THE ACCELERATOR THEORY OF INVESTMENT

13.1 (a) What is a capital-output ratio? (b) Is the capital-output ratio constant over time?

(a) A capital-output ratio is the amount of capital resources needed to produce output; it is found by dividing the economy's stock of capital by the level of output.

(b) The economy's capital-output ratio may change over time for any of the following reasons: a change in the cost of producing real capital, a change in the cost of financial capital, a change in the cost of human and natural resources, a change in the taxation of financial and real capital and a change in technology.

13.2 (a) Find net investment for periods 1 through 5 when the capital-output ratio is 3; output is initially $100, and increases in successive periods are as follows: period 1, $120; period 2, $140; period 3, $155; period 4, $165; and period 5, $170. (b) What happens to net investment when absolute output increases by decreasing amounts each period?

(a) $In = v\Delta Y$; thus, net investment is $60 in period 1 $[In = 3(\$20)]$. Net investment in successive periods is presented in the right column of Table 13-4.

Table 13-4

Period	Change in Output ($)	Net Investment ($)
1	+20	+60
2	+20	+60
3	+15	+45
4	+10	+30
5	+ 5	+15

(b) Incremental output increases by smaller amounts in successive periods, which results in a decrease in net investment. Net investment thereby falls when the absolute increase in output declines in future periods.

13.3 What objections are there to the rigid version of the accelerator theory of investment?

A number of objections may be made with respect to the rigid version of the accelerator theory of investment: (1) The capital stock is unlikely to respond immediately to changes in expected output. Willingness to add capital depends on business confidence about expected output. Firms are unlikely to add plant capacity if there is a high probability that expected output will be temporary and/or not materialize. In addition, there may be lags in capital additions because capital takes time to build and/or order backlogs exist in capital-producing industries. (2) Technology may alter the use of capital in producing output and therefore the capital-output ratio. Technological change, which makes capital more productive, results in the substitution of capital for labor and increases the capital-output ratio. (3) The cost of capital and/or other economic resources may change. For example, an investment tax credit lowers the cost of capital, whereas an increase in the cost of labor encourages the substitution of capital for labor. Either of these events makes the production process more capital intensive and increases the capital-output ratio.

THE DESIRED STOCK OF CAPITAL

13.4 (a) What is meant by the desired stock of capital? (b) How is the desired stock of capital influenced by expected output, the user cost of capital and labor compensation?

(a) The desired stock of capital is the optimum quantity of capital demanded by businesses to produce a specific level at output.

(b) Holding user cost of capital and labor's real compensation constant, the desired stock of capital is positively related to expected output. Recall that the desired stock of capital is a fixed multiple of expected output, *ceteris paribus*, in the rigid version of the accelerator theory of investment. Holding real output and labor's compensation constant, the desired stock of capital is inversely related to the user cost of capital. Profit-maximizing firms substitute capital for labor when the user cost of capital decreases, *ceteris paribus*, i.e., firms substitute less costly capital for labor whose cost has not changed. The desired stock of capital is positively related to labor's real compensation. With no change in user cost and real output, an increase in the real wage raises the relative cost of employing labor inputs in the production process. Hence, capital is substituted for the relatively more expensive labor inputs, increasing the business sector's desired stock of capital.

13.5 (a) What is the user cost of capital? (b) Can capital maintenance affect the user cost of capital? (c) How does monetary policy affect the user cost of capital?

(a) The user cost of capital is the cost of using (renting) real capital over time. It consists of the depreciation cost of using real capital plus the financial cost of raising the necessary financial capital (debt plus equity funds) to purchase real capital.

(b) Properly maintained capital has a longer, more productive life than capital with no preventive maintenance. Since depreciation cost is less when capital is maintained, poor capital maintenance increases the user cost of capital.

(c) When inflationary expectations are unrelated to changes in the nominal money supply, an increase in the nominal money supply reduces the real rate of interest, the firm's cost of financial capital and therefore the user cost of capital.

13.6 Suppose a machine's rate of depreciation is 10% and the cost of financial capital is 13%. (a) Find the user cost of capital. (b) Is the user cost of capital the same for each firm?

(a) The user cost of capital is the sum of depreciation and the cost of financial capital; the user cost of capital is 23%.

(b) The user cost of capital may differ because real assets do not depreciate at the same rate, and perceived riskiness of the firm's profits from operations affects its cost of financial capital. For example, suppose a longer-lived machine has a depreciation rate of 8% rather than 10%, and the cost of issuing financial capital is 10% rather than 13%. The user cost of capital is then 18% rather than 23%.

13.7 Explain how a fiscal measure, such as an investment tax credit or acceleration of the rate of depreciation for tax purposes, affects the user cost of capital.

An investment tax credit or an accelerated rate of depreciation for tax purposes lowers the user cost of capital. An investment tax credit permits business to reduce its tax liability by $X\%$ of the purchase price of new equipment in the year purchased. For example, a 5% investment tax credit allows a firm to reduce its tax liability $5000 when it purchases new equipment that costs $100,000. Through an investment tax credit, the government subsidizes (reduces the price of) new equipment, which lowers the user cost of the machine over its lifetime. Allowing business to accelerate the rate at which it can depreciate equipment also reduces the firm's tax liability and subsidizes newly purchased equipment. Although equipment may have an annual 10% rate of depreciation over a 10-year period, government could allow business to depreciate newly purchased equipment in 5 years. In doing so, the firm's taxable income is reduced during the first 5 years, and the firm has larger cash flows from the investment during the earlier years.

13.8   Production functions Y_1, Y_2 and Y_3 in Fig. 13-7 present the combinations of capital and labor used to produce three levels of output. Output Y_3 is greater than Y_2, which is greater than Y_1. For user cost u_1 and real wage w_1, N_1 labor inputs and K_1 capital inputs are employed to produce output Y_1. (*a*) Holding real wage w_1 and real output Y_1 constant, what happens to the employment of labor inputs and capital inputs when the user cost of capital falls from u_1 to u_2, *ceteris paribus*? (*b*) Holding real wage w_1 and labor inputs employed constant at N_1, what happens to the employment of capital inputs and real output when the user cost of capital falls from u_1 to u_2, *ceteris paribus*?

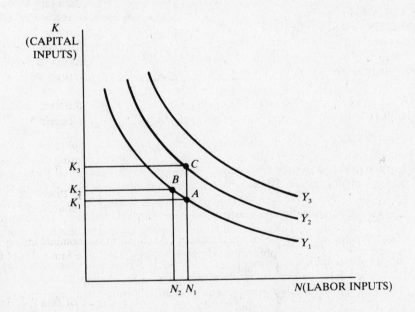

Fig. 13-7

(*a*)   The u_1 to u_2 decrease in the user cost of capital alters the least-cost combination of labor and capital inputs in producing output Y_1. Capital inputs are substituted for labor inputs in producing output Y_1, with output Y_1 produced by employing N_2 labor and K_2 capital inputs in Fig. 13-7. The production process becomes more capital intensive.

(*b*)   With no change in the employment of labor inputs and a decrease in the user cost of capital, output increases to Y_2 in Fig. 13-7, and K_3 capital inputs are employed.

13.9   (*a*) What is a marginal productivity of capital schedule? (*b*) What is a marginal cost benefit from capital schedule? (*c*) Explain the difference between a marginal productivity of capital schedule and a marginal cost benefit from capital schedule.

(a) The marginal productivity of capital is the incremental output associated with an additional unit of capital input, holding constant the employment of other factor inputs. Due to the law of diminishing returns, each additional unit of capital input is associated with a lower level of incremental output. Thus, the marginal productivity of capital declines as capital inputs are increased. The marginal productivity of capital is measured as a rate of return by relating the dollar value of incremental output to the cost of a capital addition. A marginal productivity of capital schedule (MPK) is presented in Fig. 13-8.

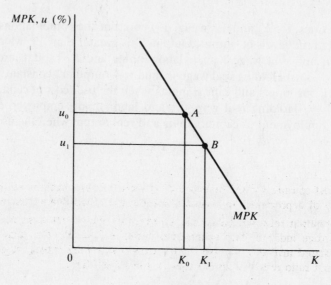

Fig. 13-8

(b) The marginal cost benefit from capital is the cost saving associated with using less labor inputs, holding output constant. Because capital and labor inputs are imperfect substitutes in producing a fixed output, continuous capital additions result in declining cost benefits. The marginal cost benefit from capital is measured as a relative cost benefit by relating the cost saving from reduced use of labor inputs to the cost of capital additions. A marginal cost benefit from capital schedule (MBK) is presented in Fig. 13-9.

(c) The MPK and MBK schedules in Figs. 13-8 and 13-9 represent demand for capital schedules. The MBK schedule holds real output constant, allowing for changes in the employment of labor; the MPK schedule holds labor employment constant, allowing for changes in real output.

13.10 The desired stock of capital is K_0 along schedule MPK in Fig. 13-8 when the user cost of capital is u_0. (a) Suppose the nominal money supply increases, there is no change in inflationary expectations and the user cost of capital decreases to u_1. Explain what happens to the desired stock of capital. (b) What is net investment as a result of the decrease in the user cost of capital? (c) What fiscal measures would also lower user cost? (d) What has happened to the capital-output ratio?

(a) At user cost u_0, the desired stock of capital is K_0 where the marginal productivity of capital equals the user cost of capital. When user cost falls to u_1 in Fig. 13-8, the marginal productivity of capital is greater than user cost u_1 for capital stock K_0. Capital inputs are added until the return from capital additions equals the cost of these additions, i.e., until the desired stock of capital increases from K_0 to K_1.

(b) Net investment equals the change in the desired stock of capital; thus, net investment equals $(K_1 - K_0)$.

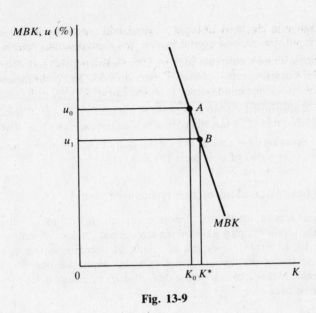

Fig. 13-9

(c)   The user cost of capital could be lowered by fiscal measures such as an investment tax credit, an acceleration of depreciation rates and/or a reduction in corporate income tax rates.

(d)   The capital-output ratio has increased. A downward movement along a marginal productivity of capital schedule indicates that incremental output is less than the additional product of capital inputs, or stated inversely, the percentage change in capital exceeds that of output. Hence, the capital-output ratio must rise as the user cost of capital falls.

13.11 The desired stock of capital is K_0 along schedule MBK in Fig. 13-9 for user cost u_0. (a) Suppose economic policy lowers user cost from u_0 to u_1. What happens to the desired stock of capital? Why? (b) What is net investment as a result of this decrease in user cost? (c) What happens to the capital-output ratio?

(a)   The desired stock of capital increases from K_0 to K^* in Fig. 13-9 as user cost declines from u_0 to u_1. Because the cost of capital relative to that of labor has decreased, firms substitute capital for labor to produce output.

(b)   Net investment is $(K^* - K_0)$, the difference between the desired stock of capital at user cost u_1 and u_0.

(c)   The production process becomes more capital intensive as capital is substituted for labor in producing a fixed level of output. The capital-output ratio increases.

THE FLEXIBLE ACCELERATOR

13.12 Suppose there are constant returns to scale and a 5% increase in output. (a) What happens to the employment of labor and capital inputs and the capital-output ratio when there is no change in the cost of factor inputs? (b) What happens to the employment of labor and capital inputs and the capital-output ratio when there is a decrease in the user cost of capital and no change in the real wage? (c) What happens to the employment of labor and capital inputs and the capital-output ratio when there is an increase in the real wage and no change in the user cost of capital? (d) What happens to v in the equation $In = v\Delta Y$ for the situations described in parts (a) through (c).

(a)   Constant returns to scale exist when a proportional increase in factor inputs results in an output which increases in the same proportion. Since there is no change in the cost of factor inputs, there is no change in the least-cost mix of labor and capital inputs. Output increases 5% as does the employment of labor and capital inputs. The capital-output ratio is unchanged.

(b)   A decrease in user cost indicates that the least-cost method of producing is now more capital intensive. Capital inputs increase by more than 5% and labor inputs by less than 5% when output increases 5%. The capital-output ratio increases.

(c)   Capital is substituted for labor because of a higher real wage. Capital inputs increase by more than 5% and labor inputs by less than 5% when output increases 5%. The capital-output ratio increases.

(d) v in the equation $In = v\Delta Y$ is the capital-output ratio. There is no change in v in part (a) and an increase in the value of v in parts (b) and (c).

13.13 What is the flexible accelerator theory of investment?

The flexible accelerator theory of investment retains the link of net investment to expected output but qualifies the relationship by also linking the desired stock of capital to the user cost of capital and by introducing a lag structure for capital additions. A decrease in the user cost of capital increases the capital intensiveness of production; hence, a higher capital-output ratio increases the desired stock of capital. It is unlikely that a change in the desired stock of capital is fully realized in one period; it is more likely distributed over time.

13.14 (a) Suppose the user cost of capital and the real wage is constant. An increase in expected output raises the desired stock of capital from K_{-1} to K^*. Why might capital additions of $(K^* - K_{-1})$ occur over time? (b) The lagged effect of capital additions can be presented by $In = \lambda(K^* - K_{-1})$. What determines the value of λ?

(a)   Capital additions may be distributed over time because of capacity constraints in the capital-goods industries, business uncertainty about increases in expected output, financial constraints to expansion, and expectations about monetary and fiscal policy. Capital additions are not instantaneous. Capital expansions must be planned. Orders must be placed. Backlog orders may exist in the capital goods industries. And in some industries, it may take a year or longer for capital to be built. Capital expansions may be deferred because of uncertainty about expected sales. No firm wants to overexpand; therefore, a firm will not immediately expand productive capacity unless relatively certain that higher output levels will be sustained. Financial constraints may also limit the rate at which capital is added. Firms do not have unlimited financial resources; hence, the availability of funds acts as a constraint to capital expansion. And firms may accelerate or slow capital additions depending on expectations about monetary policy (current and expected cost of funds) and fiscal policy (availability of investment tax credits and accelerated depreciation).

(b) λ is the fraction of the change in the desired stock of capital which occurs each period. Its value depends on the variables discussed in part (a). The faster the delivery of new capital, the larger the value of λ. Similarly, λ is larger when the firm has cash flows available to undertake capital additions and is certain about continuance of higher output levels, and monetary and fiscal policy are supportive of capital additions.

13.15 Suppose the capital stock is initially $1000, output is $500, and the capital-output ratio v is 2. (a) Find the desired stock of capital when there is no change in expected output but v increases to 2.1 due to a decrease in the user cost of capital. (b) Find the desired stock of capital when there is no change in the user cost of capital (v remains at 2) and expected output increases 10%. (c) Find net investment for four successive periods for parts (a) and (b) when $In = \lambda(K^* - K_{-1})$ and $\lambda = 0.50$. (d) Recalculate net investment for part (c) when $\lambda = 0.60$.

(a)   The desired stock of capital is a multiple of expected output, i.e., $K = vY$. With output remaining at $500 and v increasing to 2.1, the desired stock of capital increases from $1000 to $1050.

(b)   A 10% increase in expected output raises Y from $500 to $550. With no change in v, the desired stock of capital increases from $1000 to $1100.

(c)   When the desired stock of capital increases $50 in part (a), net investment during four successive periods is $25—$In = \lambda(K^* - K_{-1})$, $In = 0.5($50)$, $In = 25—$12.50, $6.25 and $3.125. When $\lambda = 0.5$, a $100 increase in the desired stock of capital from part (b) results in net investment during four successive periods of $50, $25, $12.50 and $6.25.

(d)   When the desired stock of capital increases $50 [part (a)], net investment during four successive periods is $30, $12, $4.80 and $1.92 when $\lambda = 0.60$. Net investment during four successive periods is $60, $24, $9.60 and $3.84 when the desired capital stock increases $100 [part (b)] and λ is 0.60.

TOBIN'S q-THEORY

13.16 (a) What is Tobin's q-theory? (b) Relate Tobin's q-theory to changes in the user cost of capital.

(a)   Tobin's q-theory explains net investment by relating the market value of financial assets (the market value of the firm's equity and debt) to the replacement cost of the firm's real assets. The firm adds to its capital stock when the market value of its financial assets exceeds the replacement cost of its real assets ($q > 1$) because the incremental return from capital additions exceeds the cost of these additions.

(b)   The market value of a firm's securities is directly linked to the real rate of interest. The market value of the firm's equity is the capitalized value of the earnings generated by real assets, i.e., $MV = E/k_r$ where MV is the equity's market value, E the earnings generated by real assets and k_r the market-determined rate of return for earnings of a given level of risk. Holding E constant, MV varies inversely with k_r. Hence, a decrease in the real rate of interest reduces user cost and increases the market value of the firm's financial assets because of a lower value for k_r. If $q > 1$ after the decrease in the real rate of interest, the reduction in user cost is associated with capital additions, since the market value of the firm's financial assets exceeds the replacement cost of its current capital stock.

13.17 Suppose a firm is totally financed by equity; it is earning $2.50 per share; its capitalization rate k_r is 20%; there are 10,000 shares outstanding, and the replacement cost of the firm's real assets is $125,000. (a) Find the firm's market value and the q ratio. (b) Find the firm's market value and its q ratio when the capitalization rate falls to 18% due to a decline in the real rate of interest. (c) What has happened to the relationship of the user cost of capital to the marginal cost benefit from capital? (d) Why does a decline in the real rate of interest increase the firm's desired stock of capital?

(a)   The market value of the firm is equal to the earnings per share divided by the capitalization rate, with the sum multiplied by the number of shares outstanding. The market value MV is (E/K_r)10,000 or ($2.50/0.20$)10,000 = $125,000. The q ratio is 1, the ratio of the market value of the firm's financial assets to the replacement cost of its real assets.

(b)   The market value increases to $138,888.89 or ($2.50/0.18$)10,000. The q ratio increases from 1 to 1.11.

(c)   The user cost of capital is below the marginal cost benefit from capital assuming that the user cost of capital initially was equal to the marginal cost benefit from capital.

(d)   The firm's cost of funding real asset acquisitions exceeds the return from real assets; there is an increase in the firm's desired stock of capital.

INVENTORY INVESTMENT

13.18 Suppose the desired inventory-sales ratio is 0.20; the change in inventory investment is presented as $\Delta Inv = 0.20(\Delta R)$, where ΔR is the change in sales. Find the change in inventory investment when sales are currently $1900 and are expected to reach the following levels in successive quarters: Q1.1, $2000; Q1.2, $2100; Q1.3, $2100; Q1.4, $2400; Q2.1, $2200; Q2.2, $2350.

Table 13-5

Quarter	Change in Sales ($)	Change in Inventory Investment ($)
Q1.1	+100	+20
Q1.2	+100	+20
Q1.3	0	0
Q1.4	+300	+60
Q2.1	−200	−40
Q2.2	+150	+30

The change in inventory investment is $20 during Q1.1: $\Delta Inv = 0.20(\Delta R)$; $\Delta Inv = 0.20(\$100)$. The change in inventory investment for successive quarters is presented in the right column of Table 13-5.

13.19 (a) A firm holds inventories (materials, semifinished goods and finished goods) to ensure no disruption to the production and sale of output. Explain how the following variables might affect a firm's inventory-sales ratio: cost (interest and storage) of holding inventory, uncertainty about projected sales and availability of material supplies. (b) Suppose a firm's inventory-sales ratio is 0.20 and current sales are $2000. Find the change in inventory investment when there is no change in expected sales but the firm increases the inventory-sales ratio to 0.25 because of possible delays in receiving materials from suppliers.

(a) An increase in the cost of holding inventory should decrease the inventory-sales ratio; higher financing and/or storage costs, *ceteris paribus*, have a negative effect on profits. Firms therefore attempt to produce and sell output with lower inventories. Uncertainty about sales, *ceteris paribus*, should lower the inventory-sales ratio. Firms will keep inventory levels as small as possible when there is a high likelihood that sales will not occur. Scarcity of materials, *ceteris paribus*, encourages firms to keep larger inventories to maintain production and sales levels; the inventory-sales ratio would increase.

(b) Concern about delays in receiving materials will increase inventory holdings. The increase in the inventory-sales ratio from 0.20 to 0.25, with no change in expected sales, raise a firm's inventory investment $100. [Inventory investment is increased to 0.25($2000) from 0.20($2000).]

Index

The letter *p* following a page number refers to a solved problem.